UNFRIENDLY TO LIBERTY

UNFRIENDLY TO LIBERTY

LOYALIST NETWORKS AND THE COMING OF THE AMERICAN REVOLUTION IN NEW YORK CITY

CHRISTOPHER F. MINTY

CORNELL UNIVERSITY PRESS

Ithaca and London

First published 2023 by Cornell University Press

Library of Congress Cataloging-in-Publication Data

Names: Minty, Christopher F., 1988– author.
Title: Unfriendly to liberty : loyalist networks and the coming of the American Revolution in New York City / Christopher F. Minty.
Description: Ithaca [New York] : Cornell University Press, 2023. | Includes bibliographical references and index.
Identifiers: LCCN 2022025628 (print) | LCCN 2022025629 (ebook) | ISBN 9781501769108 (hardcover) | ISBN 9781501769115 (pdf) | ISBN 9781501769122 (epub)
Subjects: LCSH: American loyalists—New York (State)—New York. | New York (State)—Politics and government—To 1775. | New York (N.Y.)—History—Colonial period, ca. 1600–1775. | New York (N.Y.)—History—Revolution, 1775–1783. | United States—History—Revolution, 1775–1783.
Classification: LCC E277 .M65 2023 (print) | LCC E277 (ebook) | DDC 974.7/102—dc23/eng/20220930
LC record available at https://lccn.loc.gov/2022025628
LC ebook record available at https://lccn.loc.gov/2022025629

For Heather

What say you to an American Parliament *Only to meddle with Supplies*[?] . . . We had the Royal licence to Emigrate, and there is a merit besides in Extending the Trade and Dominion and encreasing the number of your Subjects—so your Kings thought: Else why all these little Parliaments begot & forbid the Crown—This numerous Partition of Provinces seems now to render the Machine of Empire too Complex—Whose Fault is that? But it is a fault—agreed—Provide then a new Model Correspondent to this new State—If the ancient Constitution did not prevent this wide dispersion of its subjects, nor consequently made an equal and suitable Provision for their Government let it be confessed on both sides that so it is, and a proper one be continued, in which the millions abroad that are Collecting Money for the House at Home, and those who never came out for it may both be safe. Don't Startle at a Parliament in America . . . Your Colonies will exhaust you.

    —James DeLancey to the Marquess of Rockingham,
    November 8, 1765

Contents

Acknowledgments

Many people, organizations, and institutions have helped me complete this book. My sincere thanks go to Colin Nicolson and Emma Macleod at the University of Stirling. Their support, advice, and encouragement over the years has been extraordinarily helpful, and this book would not have been completed without them. I also owe many thanks to Frank Cogliano and Ben Marsh for their insight, mentorship, and encouragement. I am grateful for the support and advice of Elaine Abelson, Peter-Christian Aigner, Noelle Baker, David Bebbington, Carol Berkin, Michael Blaakman, Mark Boonshoft, Rebecca Brannon, Christina Carrick, Michael Crowder, Tom Cutterham, Fiona Duncan, Matthew P. Dziennik, Andrew J. B. Fagal, Federico Finchelstein, Jim Folts, Joanne B. Freeman, Robb K. Haberman, Ellen Hickman, Brian Lander, Katy Lasdow, Miriam Liebman, Elizabeth Mancke, Sally Mason, Simon Middleton, Aaron Noble, Danny Noorlander, Richard Oram, Ken Owen, Benjamin E. Park, Dora Petherbridge, Joshua Piker, Jessica Chopin Roney, Helena Yoo Roth, Stuart Salmon, Emily St. Denny, LC Santangelo, Nora Slonimsky, Chris Taylor, Kathryn Tomasek, Fredrika J. Teute, Shaun Wallace, Peter Walker, and Karin Wulf. I am also particularly grateful to Benjamin L. Carp, John Dixon, and Michael D. Hattem, who generously read portions or all of this book prior to publication, sometimes more than once.

I revised most of this book as an editor at the Adams Papers Editorial Project at the Massachusetts Historical Society. My thanks to my colleagues R. M. Barlow, Gwen Fries, Sara Georgini, Sara Martin, Amanda M. Norton, Neal Millikan, Jim Taylor, and Hobson Woodward for their support and good cheer. My thanks also extend to my Historical Society colleagues Catherine Allgor, Peter Drummey, and Conrad Edick Wright, along with everyone in the library. I finished this book as an editor at the Center for Digital Editing at the University of Virginia (UVA). My thanks to Katie Blizzard, Erica Cavanaugh, Katy Gehred, and Jennifer Stertzer. My thanks also extend to other editors in the UVA community, especially Bill Ferraro and David Hoth.

For support and help during my research, I thank staff at the American Philosophical Society; the British Library; the William L. Clements Library, University of Michigan; Columbia University; Eugene Lang College, The New School; Fraunces Tavern; Harvard University; the Huntington Library; the Library Company of Philadelphia; the Library of Congress; the Museum of the City of New York; the National Archives of the United Kingdom; the National Archives of the United States; the National Library of Scotland; the New York State Archives; the New York State Library; the Nova Scotia Archives; the Provincial Archives of New Brunswick; the University of Edinburgh; the University of Glasgow; the University of New Brunswick; the University of Stirling; the University of Virginia; and Yale University. The archivists and librarians at the New-York Historical Society and the New York Public Library merit additional thanks. At New-York Historical, where I spent 2014–15 as a Bernard and Irene Schwartz fellow, my thanks to Joseph Ditta; Alex Krueger; Nick Mancini; Maureen Maryanski, who is now at the Lilly Library at Indiana University; Louise Mirrer; Ted O'Reilly; Valerie Paley; and Michael Ryan. At the New York Public Library, my thanks to Tal Nadan and Thomas Lannon, who is now at Lafayette College Libraries. Michael McGandy and his colleagues at Cornell University Press, especially Clare Jones, have been supportive, patient, and considerate as I worked on this book. I have greatly enjoyed and appreciated working with them.

Financial support for this project was provided by the Canada-UK Foundation; the Eccles Centre at the British Library; the David Library of the American Revolution (now part of the American Philosophical Society); the Houghton Library, Harvard University; the Huntington Library; the New-York Historical Society; the New York State Archives; the New York State Library; the John D. Rockefeller Jr. Library at Colonial Williamsburg; the United Empire Loyalists' Association of Canada; and the University of Stirling.

My friends and teammates at various football clubs have also provided support and welcome distraction. My thanks to Kendall Wanderers F.C. players Jason Besse, Jon Cartwright, Paul Casement, Mark Devlin, Tyler Flack, Barry McShea, Dylan McSparren, John O'Toole, and the rest of the lads. At Flushing Futbol Club, my thanks to Nikolas Kaloudis, Mike Nicolosi, Cris Prada, and Ryan Wiedman. At New York International F.C., my thanks to Anthony Carrabotta, Corentin Claisse, Simon Czaplinski, Ian Goodall, Charlie Lopez, Gary Philpott, and Nick Platt, along with the rest of the team.

I thank my family members who have championed this project in various ways. My parents, Alister and Jacqueline, and my brother, Ross, have been extraordinarily supportive. My wife, Heather Lonks Minty, encouraged me to finish, and it is to her that I dedicate this book. Our daughter, Isla, was born shortly before I submitted the final manuscript, and I'm certain it will quickly become one of her favorite before-bedtime books.

A Note on Editorial Method

Language in eighteenth-century New York City and indeed throughout the entire world was messy. Spelling, capitalization, and punctuation varied. Many people did not know how to read or write. Others adjusted their spelling on a weekly or even daily basis. In this book, I have attempted to present the words as they were originally composed. I have not corrected punctuation or spelling, except for starting a new sentence. If a letter was lowercase in the original manuscript, I have silently capitalized it. I have also rendered underlined text in italics and have retained all shorthand marks, ampersands, and contractions. All other editorial interpolations, in accordance with the standards of the Association for Documentary Editing, are indicated with square brackets.

UNFRIENDLY TO LIBERTY

Prologue
Popular Politics and Mobilizations

As he traveled through New England toward Philadelphia for the meeting of the First Continental Congress, John Adams, a candid and opinionated lawyer from Braintree with bulging blue eyes, thought long and hard about New York City. A week after his August 10 departure, he confided in his diary, "We are told here that New York are now well united and very firm." Writing from New Haven, Adams was a few days away from Manhattan. But he was curious about the urban center and its people. He was hopeful—confident, even—that New Yorkers would join him and his colleagues from Massachusetts and across many of the North American colonies to protest recent evolutions in British imperial governance, something Adams believed had become increasingly oppressive.[1] The Braintree lawyer arrived in the city on August 20, and his curiosity only increased. Again, confiding in his diary, which he maintained sporadically not only on this trip but throughout much of his life, Adams noted, "This City will be a Subject of much Speculation to me." And so it was.[2]

Adams's fascination with Manhattan did not abate after he departed for Philadelphia. Instead, he focused his attentions on the city as the American Revolutionary War developed and allegiances were determined. "What is the Reason, that New York is still asleep or dead, in Politicks and War?" Adams raged to his former law clerk William Tudor in late June 1776. Independence was not yet declared, and the forty-one-year-old Adams was worried. New

Yorkers, Adams believed, should fall in line. "Must it always be So?" "Cannot the whole Congregation of Patriots and Heroes," he continued, "inspire it, with one generous Sentiment? Have they no sense, no Feeling? No sentiment? No Passions?" Adams thought New Yorkers' "Motions . . . rather retrograde." They were not mobilizing behind the war effort, or at least to a sufficient level to satisfy Adams. But for all his political acumen and education, he could not work out why New Yorkers' politics did not match those from other colonies, especially his own. What confused Adams further was New Yorkers' history of opposing Parliament from the 1760s and to the mid-1770s. Perhaps that op-position, which was arguably stronger than anywhere else in colonial North America, was what originally piqued his interest in 1774. Had something changed? Adams thought so. He wondered if there had been an atmospheric change that accounted for their behavior. He wondered if there was "any Thing in the Air, or Soil" that was "unfriendly to the Spirit of Liberty." He wondered whether New Yorkers were "destitute of Reason, or of Virtue?" "What is the Cause?" he asked. For a city ardent in its opposition to Parliament's imperial reforms of the 1760s and early 1770s, its ostensible U-turn was concerning.[3] When Tudor replied in early July, Adams could not possibly have been aware of how severe the situation was in the so-called city of speculation. It was worse than Adams imagined, Tudor explained. "Hundreds in this Colony are active against Us and such is the Weakness of the Government, (if it can de-serve the Name) that the Tories openly profess their Sentiments in Favour of the Enemy, and live unpunished." "Indeed the great part of the colony," Tudor continued, "are fitted for Slavery."[4]

John Adams's provocative comments about New Yorkers' political resolve were compounded by his belief that the potential mobilization of loyalists—that is, those who acted against the revolutionaries' and his cause—was particularly strong in Manhattan. Adams was not alone, either. His comments to Tudor cap-tured the ideas and thoughts of other revolutionaries, or "rebels" and "patriots," as they are more commonly known. For instance, George Washington, of Virginia, was among the worried. In early 1776 he feared that "the Tories" would take the city. Such an event, he predicted, "might prove fatal to our Interests." With or without Manhattan, revolutionaries and loyalists alike appreciated the importance of the city in almost every respect.[5]

A few months later, British officers inspired loyalism throughout Manhat-tan. Their military might, their naval supremacy, their absolute conviction that the British Empire would not, and could not, be challenged brought thousands of people to their projected cause of reconciliation. Taking Manhattan was among the most important military moments of the Revolutionary War, and although Adams and others believed it was the British Army and Royal Navy's

"Ne Plus Ultra"—that is, their high point—the occupation of the city proved decisive.[6]

Indeed, four years later, John Adams appreciated the significance of holding New York City. Then based in France, he told Charles Gravier, Comte de Vergennes, French foreign secretary, that any American pretensions to retaking the city were pointless. "I have no hopes of their Success," Adams wrote, adding, "New York will never be taken. It is so situated, it is so fortified, it is garrisoned with Troops so accustomed to War, and so imbittered and inflamed by cruel passions carefully nursed up in their Breasts by their King and their generals." New York City was British. It stayed that way until November 25, 1783.[7]

Beginning with the Revolutionary generation, scholarship on the American Revolution has often been compartmentalized into groups. Various schools have come and gone, putting forward similar or contrasting views, but almost all adhere to a general framework: there were loyalists, or "Tories," and there were "patriots," and often their respective paths to the American Revolution were fundamentally different and they were determined long before shots were fired in 1775. What's more, whether you're reading Mercy Otis Warren, George Bancroft, or more recent works, most write from the perspectives of those who became revolutionaries—looking at what inspired and motivated them to question their identities as Britons and produce something new. Others focus almost exclusively on those who became loyalists.[8]

Most have interpreted its origins and causation from the standpoint of those who became patriots, or revolutionaries. After all, who would be interested to find out how and why people became Tories? Many were viewed as traitors then and throughout much of US history. Did they merit further study now? The proliferation of documentary editions in the mid-twentieth century and beyond undoubtedly encouraged this interpretation. In the mid-twentieth century, standalone editions of prominent Americans' papers were collected and published to promote a greater understanding of American history among the populace. "Dear Mr. President," wrote Edmund F. Mansure, "I have the honor to transmit to you the report of the National Historical Publications Commission (NHPC), *A National Program for the Publication of Historical Documents*." Writing to President Dwight D. Eisenhower, Mansure, administrator of the General Services Administration, added, "The Commission has prepared the report in accordance with its responsibility . . . for planning and encouraging the publication of 'the papers of outstanding citizens of the United States' and 'documents . . . important for an understanding and appreciation of the history of the United States.'"[9] The NHPC offered several recommendations, including, most notably, "the comprehensive publication of the papers" of various Founding Fathers and "documentary histories of (a) the ratification of the Constitution and the Bill of Rights, and (b) the work of the First Federal Congress." In total, the report recommended "the names of 361 persons . . . for possible inclusion in a publication program." None of these people became loyalists in the American Revolution.[10]

Through the publication of historical documents, the NHPC hoped US citizens would better "understand the history of their country and its relation to the rest of the world." "The better they understand the historical background of our present-day institutions," the report went on, "and the ideals, hopes, accomplishments, and even the failures of the men and women who have made the United States, the safer will be our democracy and the more secure our rights as free men." These materials—materials that documented the history of the United States—had to be published. And the materials selected were the patriots' materials. Their history was equated with US history, and loyalists were left out.[11]

These papers remain available and invaluable. Some have been federated in online resources such as Founders Online and Rotunda, the University of Virginia Press's digital imprint, increasing accessibility beyond the letterpress editions. Through the publication and long-term preservation of these sources, however, a one-sided interpretation of the American Revolution (and early American history, more broadly) has emerged. Those who became loyalists no doubt feature in these editions, but the context in which they appear is often negative. As George Washington put it, loyalists were "very Dangerous Characters."[12]

These kinds of labels stick, and they are difficult to remove. When loyalists have been studied, they have often been grouped together into a monolithic bloc or treated as biographical subjects. In some cases, historians write toward loyalism, as if it were predestined or assumed, and study "The Loyalists," without further investigating loyalism's complicated origins or how colonists or, later, loyalists understood and interacted with the British imperial state. Most often, scholarship has focused on individual loyalists or their behavior during the Revolution. More recently, some work has appeared that has focused on their reintegration into US society. Most, however, do not examine their lives before 1775 or 1776.[13]

Just as many patriots' papers have been collected and published, the reality that they were preserved in the first instance is something many loyalists did, and could, not do. Their papers are often scattered across multiple collections and repositories. Large collections are few in number, and those that do exist—such as the Loyalist Claims Commission Records, kept in over 150 volumes at the UK National Archives—should not be used in isolation.[14]

This is especially the case for New York. As Patricia U. Bonomi wrote in 2001, "the story of early New York politics and government rests on a foundation that tilts sharply toward the 'patriot' side."[15] The DeLancey family and faction, for example, as many historians have argued, sought nothing but to advance themselves and their interests, and they used New Yorkers to achieve their goals.[16] As one historian put it, "New Yorkers never did fully develop the kind of persisting group consciousness and symbols of political identity essential to the practice of 'party politics.'" The same historian adds, "there was no development of effective party organizations."[17]

These interpretations often take us to the American Revolution and beyond. Along the way, a familiar cast of characters occupy central or leading roles. But nobody in colonial British America was predestined to become a loyalist or a revolutionary. Nothing was inevitable, or automatic. It did not matter if they lived in New York City or New Bern, North Carolina, or Athens, Georgia, or Worcester, Massachusetts. Colonists' respective journeys to the American Revolution, wherever they were, were influenced by a variety of factors—social, political, economic, historical, cultural. Some paths were similar. Others overlapped. Friends and family no doubt discussed the imperial relationship and, perhaps, what it meant to them. There can be no doubt, however, that the coming of the American Revolution inside New York City and out divided friends and family.[18] It also brought others closer together. To a remarkable degree, colonists mobilized in the years before the Battles of Lexington and Concord of April 19, 1775. Their choices, political or otherwise, affected not only whom they spent their time with but also how they were perceived by others—by people in their communities, their colonies, and their continent.

Inside New York City and out, various crises—political, institutional, religious, economic, social—affected how colonists lived their lives, and local circumstances made it possible. This book offers a fresh interpretation of these political mobilizations in the decade or so before 1776, examining not only the origins of loyalism but the origins of the American Revolution in one urban center. By focusing on arguably the most important city in the British Empire except London, this book questions the traditional narrative of the Revolutionary War. It reorients historians' understandings of its origins and causation through its examination of ideas and interests to show how colonists' behavior was heavily influenced by their private and public ideas as well as their self-interests.[19] It reveals how the interplay between political culture and organizations shaped and, in some cases, determined allegiances during the Revolutionary War. Indeed, even if imperial politics were important to New Yorkers' daily lives, local politics—factions, institutions, behaviors, and more—were arguably more significant in shaping how they responded to a worsening imperial relationship throughout the 1760s and 1770s.[20]

Equally important, though, this book also shows how people who became loyalists contributed to the origins of American political practice. They pushed to involve more people in the political process, used innovative and engaging methods to mobilize people, and created institutions that are still in existence today. Associations, too, occupy a central role in this book. A great deal of scholarship has examined Americans' social and political practices during the Revolution, but they have done so in relation to the Early Republic. Instead of being a product of the American Revolution and a key arbiter of political behavior in the Early Republic, *Unfriendly to Liberty* shows how associations shaped the course of the Revolution.[21] Indeed, loyalists were not backward-looking or disorganized. Rather, in many cases, elite and non-elite loyalists, working together, were more organized and inclusive than their revolutionary opponents. On various occasions, it was people who became loyalists who laid the groundwork for the establishment of an expansive and more inclusive political republic in the 1780s and beyond. To a degree that has not been fully appreciated, future loyalists came together prior to the Revolutionary War to form a tightly knit political association with a shared group consciousness that used symbols to advance their beliefs. At the center of their associationism was a firm interpretation of what Manhattan's political economy should be and how New York should fit into the British Empire. Defined as "the study of the relationship between political institutions and the economic system," as three scholars have recently put it, New Yorkers throughout the 1760s and 1770s contested how to respond to imperial crises and what policies and approaches to adopt and pursue. How they understood New York City's place within the empire evolved and developed, and some New Yorkers came to hold competing interpretations about the purpose of the empire and whom it served.[22]

Unfriendly to Liberty spans the period from roughly winter of 1768 until the spring of 1777. Chapter 1, "Outwrote as well as Outvoted," examines the 1768 election in New York City and County for the colony's General Assembly. It begins by offering an introduction of the DeLanceyites' candidates before moving onto the faction's campaign strategies. It focuses on their innovative use of print and the city's tavern culture to mobilize broad-based support from the city's considerable voting population. Next, chapter 2, "Too Much Power over Our Common People," looks at how the DeLanceys legislated when they were in power. It shows how they implemented their political beliefs and followed through on much of what they campaigned on. Chapter 2 examines how the DeLanceys gained a majority of seats following the dissolution of the assembly in early 1769. By examining how their main political opponents, the

Livingstons, tried to mobilize support, this chapter shows how politically astute the DeLanceys were in their election materials and in how they interacted and engaged with New Yorkers.

Chapter 3, "The Minions of Tyranny and Despotism," looks at how the DeLanceys governed in the assembly after the 1769 elections. It examines how they tried to maintain support considering fresh opposition and politically naïve governing as New Yorkers increasingly believed that Parliament was exerting undue control over their lives. Chapter 4, "All the Sons of Liberty," follows on from chapter 3 to examine how Alexander McDougall, a Scottish immigrant, mobilized support in opposition to the DeLanceys and successfully created a political association that offered an alternative vision for Manhattan's future.

Chapter 5, "Liberty and No Importation," begins by exploring the citywide debates over the Townshend Acts and nonimportation. It shows how the DeLanceys and McDougall held competing political economies and interpretations of how New York City fitted into the British Empire. The chapter then explores the practical consequences of political mobilization, using three DeLanceyites' networks to show how their associationism dramatically influenced whom they interacted with and how often. Ultimately, this chapter shows how the DeLanceys coalesced into an inward-looking association that was composed of politically like-minded individuals.

Chapter 6, "The Mob Begin to Think and Reason," examines the Tea Act of 1773 and its impact on popular politics in Manhattan. It shows how the legislation brought Alexander McDougall and his supporters back into the popular political sphere, leading to chapters 7 and 8, "Unite or Die" and "The Din of War," which examine popular and institutional politics in Manhattan between 1774 and 1775. These chapters show how McDougall capitalized on the DeLanceys' inaction to mobilize support not only in New York but across the Eastern Seaboard. Moreover, these chapters show how political and wartime circumstances affected colonists' behavior, examining how revolutionaries like McDougall dictated how New Yorkers behaved and were able to push some of their opponents out of the political sphere—and sometimes out of the city. Chapter 8, however, also shows how the British military influenced events, prompting a large-scale outburst of loyalism in Manhattan and beyond.

At the heart of this study, then, are a broad range of individuals and groups drawn from the population of New York, all of whom participated in the mobilization of support. Foremost among these was a political set known as the DeLanceys. Their de facto leaders were James DeLancey, a former British soldier who was educated at the University of Cambridge, served as Lt. Gen. James Abercromby's aide-de-camp during the French and Indian War, and was arguably the wealthiest man in New York; John Cruger, the forty-first mayor of New York City, uncle of British member of Parliament Henry Cruger, and instigator of the Stamp Act Congress of 1765; James Jauncey, a Presbyterian merchant; and Jacob Walton, son of the inimitable William Walton and husband of John Cruger's niece, Mary. Together with the support of James DeLancey's brutish uncle, Oliver DeLancey, a correspondent of James Otis Jr. and John Hancock, who by the mid-1760s lived in an extravagant and opulent home with his widowed sister, and with a host of other individuals, including Frederick Rhinelander, Joseph Allicocke, Charles McEvers, and Isaac Heron, among others, the DeLanceys formed an organized and ideologically inspired political group.[23]

At key moments between 1768 and 1775, the DeLanceys and their supporters mobilized broad-based support to achieve their political goals. To do this, they used print and in-person meetings to bring New Yorkers into their orbit, and they consolidated their connections by meeting in stores and coffeehouses and through shared investments. By March 1770, the DeLanceys' supporters had matured into an informal voluntary association whose members often referred to themselves as *"the Club."* In July 1770, they broadened their support-base to include both voters and nonvoters as they advocated the resumption of trade after a two-year nonimportation agreement against Great Britain. During these campaigns of mobilization, their political discourse centered on eighteenth-century idioms related to republicanism. They promised that they would protect the public welfare—that they would enhance New Yorkers' economic self-sufficiency and that they would promote virtue and masculinity within society. As James DeLancey urged in the early 1770s, their goal was "the Erection of a Republic in this Colony."[24]

As the imperial crisis with Britain worsened, politically like-minded individuals came together to show their opposition to Parliamentary measures. Doing so brought people together, and more importantly, it kept them together. Among the social consequence of their mobilization was that they developed relationships with one another that transcended their political origins. As people came together and spent more time with one another, in various settings, including taverns, coffeehouses, shops, and people's private lives, they soon looked beyond religion or ethnicity—they were not defining factors in determining their relationships. Elites and non-elites of different ranks, religions, and nationalities discarded their differences and worked toward a common goal. And in doing so, they became friends and, in some cases, family members.

But these people could not escape the world in which they lived. Parliamentary measures fractured relationships and dislocated colonists' beliefs in the strength and holistic value of the British Empire. People questioned if it was right for them, and in New York City, the imperial crisis led to the emergence and evolution of two oppositional groups. Though the colonists initially worked together in their opposition to the British government, by late 1769, colonists' political sentiments had polarized. This initial polarization, fired by the in-house debates of the New York Assembly, developed between early and mid-1770 to such an extent that between July 1770 and the start of the American Revolution, two opposing groups of politically like-minded men dominated New York City's political public sphere.

Both groups thought the other was working against New Yorkers' needs and interests, working against the common good, working against liberty. By focusing on one of these groups—those who became loyalists—we can understand how pre-wartime mobilization developed shared ideological and political mentalities that shaped how future loyalists lived their lives. Indeed, these New Yorkers became a distinct political and ideologically inspired group that opposed those who became revolutionaries. They did so not because they opposed the Revolution or supported the British government and its imperial measures but because they had a history of opposing them. They held a competing vision of how New York should operate within the British Empire. Ultimately, these people felt that the city could move forward by maintaining their connections to Parliament. By 1775 those who became revolutionaries adopted a different viewpoint, one that was governed by a competing ideological and political interpretation of Manhattan's and the colony's place within Britain's imperial framework. Taken together, these New Yorkers disagreed with their opponents' ideas as well as their interests. Their allegiance during the American Revolution became a statement of their existing and ideologically inspired partisanship.[25]

Their stories, moreover, do not present a declension narrative. New Yorkers' or, indeed, Americans' loyalism was not backward, and their attitudes toward Manhattan or colonial British America and the liberties they shared did not deteriorate or weaken. On the contrary, these people viewed their actions as measured toward protecting their liberties, protecting their city, protecting their country. Through their political mobilization and voluntarism, they created new identities within their public and private lives. To them, it was the people who are commonly labeled as "Patriots" who had deteriorated into an unnatural state of rebelliousness. The rebels, one loyalist wrote, were seized by "Military madness." "Nothing but blood & slaughter pleases," they continued, adding, "they seem delighted with their ability to do hurt." Another loyalist neatly captured what they and his like-minded associates thought of the so-called patriots; it was they who were the "American demagogues," not Manhattan's, New York's, or indeed colonial British America's loyalists.[26]

CHAPTER 1

Outwrote as well as Outvoted
The Assembly Election of 1768

On February 21, 1768, Robert Livingston, the founder of the Livingston family's Clermont estate, wrote to his nephew and the third lord of Livingston Manor, Robert Livingston Jr. The topic was a familiar one for the family: political power in the colony of New York. Livingston of Clermont, an old man at this point, was writing about the upcoming General Assembly election in New York. Gov. Sir Henry Moore, the highest-ranking official and the king's representative in the colony, had dissolved the General Assembly on February 6. On the 10th, he issued writs for new elections, and returns were due on March 22. It was the first assembly election in seven years, the longest period that the Septennial Act of 1743 allowed in the colony, and although Livingston of Clermont had not sat in the popularly elected assembly since the 1720s, he was interested in the result—and hoped it would go in his and family's favor. After all, Livingston's family's political set were then the most powerful group in the assembly and perhaps even the entire colony, and the elder Livingston, born in 1688, had helped shape and secure his family's place.

Writing from his estate over one hundred miles north of New York City, he thanked his nephew for all his efforts to promote the election of two pro-Livingston candidates in Dutchess County. "I am much obliged to you," he wrote, "for what you have done & obliged to do in my Favour." Although Livingston was confident, he sought to make the election result certain. He asked his nephew to send Walter Livingston, the son of Peter Van Brugh Livingston, the younger Robert's brother, to stabilize voting on election day by making sure the people who were meant to vote for the family's candidates did so. Walter Livingston was known to invest considerable energy in securing his family's status, and his methods were effective. This method had served the Livingstons well for generations. Many of their tenants on the manor and elsewhere voted for Livingston because they felt or knew that they had to. Livingston of Clermont was confident, writing, "I think my Interest very strong."[1]

By the time Livingston of Clermont wrote to his nephew, Manhattan, where the assembly was based, was the nucleus of the colony. It was a walkable urban center that was roughly a mile long. In the decade up to the Revolutionary War, the city was filled with coffeehouses, taverns, marketplaces, shops, and churches, and the edges of its harbor were dotted with wharves that were often labeled with families' names and populated by sailors, merchants, and ships' captains. Together, they linked Manhattan—and the colony—to the British and French Atlantic and beyond. The city itself was divided into seven wards, and it was filled with narrow streets, producing daily interactions few were averse to. As William Smith Jr. wrote in his noted history of the colony, "New-York is one of the most social places on the continent."[2]

New York City was also the most diverse urban center in British North America. More than twenty church steeples punctured the city skyline; there were Anglicans, French Huguenots, Catholics, Presbyterians, Lutherans, Dutch Reformists, and more. Just as important, Europeans flooded the city throughout the 1760s, increasing its population from about eighteen thousand to about twenty-two thousand—a roughly 20 percent increase. The number of houses in the city also increased, from 1,140 in 1743 to about 2,600 in 1760. People came from various countries in Europe—especially the British Isles—and a considerable number of enslaved Africans also entered the city. Their population increased by nearly 40 percent between 1756 and 1771. With what seemed like an ever-growing population, networks formed throughout the city that were based on shared ancestries, experiences, histories, interests, and more (see figure 1.1).[3]

Networks were important across colonial British America, but in Manhattan, an urban, political, and commercial center, they were especially important. And in no realm were the city's networks more influential than its politics. Indeed, the interdependence of those within the city was of note because of its unusually large electorate, which was broader than almost all colonial America's other urban centers. To vote, a white, male New Yorker had to be a freeholder or a freeman. Freeholders were those who owned estates that were worth at least £40; freemen were merchants or artisans who had been extended the right to vote or who had purchased freemanship. New Yorkers were sometimes both.

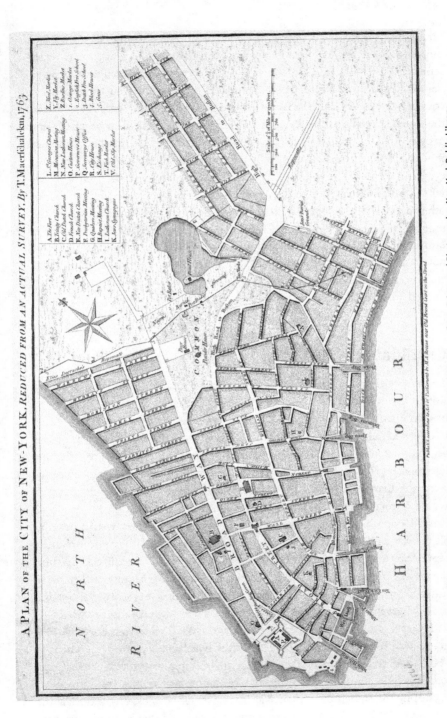

FIGURE 1.1. *A Plan of the City of New-York*, 1763, Miriam and Ira D. Wallach Division of Art, Prints and Photographs, New York Public Library

Voting was done in open-air public spaces, without any degree of privacy, and those who were eligible placed up to four votes. These New York voters represented the overall diversity of the city—they were of varied religious denominations, spoke in different languages and dialects, and hailed from different countries. Above all, their votes carried weight; anyone who sought election to the assembly required their support. Deference played a role, to be sure: some people voted for candidates because they felt they had to, perhaps because they lived in a home or on land owned by the candidate. By the 1768 election, however, candidates in New York City could not possibly be connected to every voter—professionally, personally, or otherwise. Deference, though significant in other parts of the colony, was not enough in Manhattan. Instead, successful, progressive candidates formed personal bonds with voters, and those who were unmindful of New Yorkers' interests or were resentful toward the electorate did not stand a chance. The DeLanceys, more than anyone else, understood this, and through the democratization of the city's political spaces and practices, they formed an inclusive, accessible political association with their supporters.[4]

Candidates

The 1768 General Assembly in New York City tested the electoral strength of Robert Livingston of Clermont and his family's interests. It was always going to be a competitive election for the city's four seats—the only place in the colony to offer such a legislative reward. But the city's broad and diverse electorate was going to the polls for the first time since the Stamp Act crisis of 1765, and new networks had formed which had nearly three years to mature. The Livingstons were not unaware of this. They put forward a slate of candidates who they felt would attract voters. The candidates—Philip Livingston, John Morin Scott, Amos Dodge, and William Bayard—ran individually, but they were a ticket in all but name. The ticket was designed with hopes that if they put forward a representative sample of the city's population, they would mobilize a large portion of the city's electorate. Thus, the slate boasted two prominent merchants (Livingston and Bayard), a carpenter (Dodge), and a lawyer (Scott). With them, the Livingstons hoped to capture the votes of elites as well as non-elites.

It was a strong group of candidates, too. Philip Livingston, born in 1716, graduated from Yale College in 1737, after which he became a merchant in Manhattan. A deacon in the Dutch Reformed Church with round cheeks and a long nose, Livingston made a considerable amount of money from privateering during the French and Indian War, setting up his business on the dock at the bottom of Wall Street, and he also made and sold rum that he produced in his own distillery in Brooklyn. He was a municipal alderman between 1754 and 1762, and three years later he served in the Stamp Act Congress of 1765. John Morin Scott also graduated from Yale. He received his bachelor of arts degree in 1746 and a master of arts degree three years later. In 1752, he was admitted to the bar, and between 1756 and 1761 he was a municipal alderman. William Bayard was born in 1729 and became a prominent merchant. His family had deep roots within the colony. His father, Stephen, served on the Royal Council and was New York City's mayor from 1744 to 1747. Like Livingston, William Bayard served in the Stamp Act Congress, and he lived on a lavish estate north of the city. Amos Dodge was the least educated person on the ticket, and almost certainly the least prominent. Some people, it seems, did not think his candidacy was genuine.[5]

With a ticket that was made up of two members of the Stamp Act Congress, the Livingstons felt their candidates were strong. But Scott's inclusion proved to be especially problematic because he was a lawyer. The 1768 election was the culmination of over a decade of nascent antipathy toward the colony's lawyers, many of whom New Yorkers believed were elitist, self-interested, and corrupt. They saw lawyers as part of a homogeneous, monopolizing, and enclosed small interest group. In a way, they were right. There were no colonial law schools. Nor was there a standard legal literature. Lawyers, who represented 0.1 percent of the population by 1770, mastered their craft through an apprenticeship system, in which students studied under established lawyers whose private libraries held the requisite texts. This system encouraged the professionalization of the bar, but it came at a high literal and figurative cost to clients: people complained that the fees they paid were unjustifiably high.[6]

Some insisted that lawyers sought only to fill their pockets. During the Stamp Act crisis, one New Yorker wrote, "the Lawyers have come to a Resolution not to do any business . . . (Unless their Clyents will Indemnify them.)" Because of the lawyers' behavior, they alleged, New Yorkers were "in the Greatest Confusion imaginable," adding that unless Parliament repealed the act, New York City and its inhabitants "must Inevitably be ruined." Consequently, they went on, New Yorkers were in a state of "helplessness." The following year, this same New Yorker attributed the city's "deplorable situation" to lawyers' fees. This one New Yorker was not alone, either. Another classified lawyers as "Robbers" and added that they and any who came into contact with them were "Vermin." In another letter, they described lawyers as the kind of people who sought to involve their clients in "the hatefull Labyrinths of the Law" for their own gain. Despite New Yorkers' resentment, lawyers were one of the most powerful groups within the province. They had deep pockets and robust political connections. The Yale-educated John Morin Scott was among the first generation of lawyers that were trained in colonial British America. The Livingstons' main opponents, the DeLanceys, used New Yorkers' disdain to their advantage, putting forward a ticket that was neither associated with nor connected to the city's lawyers. Their ticket was made up of three merchants— James DeLancey, Jacob Walton, and James Jauncey—who revived the long-standing Livingston-DeLancey rivalry.[7]

Indeed, these groups had clashed for a generation. Whereas the Livingstons' wealth came from estates, the DeLanceys' originated from commerce and trade. As such, their interests, though related, often clashed within the colony's political institutions. Indeed, in an unpublished history of the colony, Abraham Yates Jr., an Albany County official, wrote, "This Colony of New York at least as far back as memory will carry on, has been Devided into violent Parties." But they were "not known by the epithets of Whig and Tory[,] Republican or aristocrat." Instead, Yates went on, interests dominated their behavior—what each felt was the best vision for the colony. William Smith Jr., the noted historian of the colony, offered something like Yates's assessment, writing, "The Province of New York is divided into two great Parties." For Smith, it was "the Livingstons" and "the DeLanceys." In 1768, their competing visions for the city's and the colony's future were on display. Gone was the so-called shallow factionalism of the 1740s and 1750s as New Yorkers firmly embraced party for the first time since the 1730s.[8]

Likely born in a Broad Street home that later became famous as Fraunces Tavern, now situated at 54 Pearl Street, James DeLancey was the de facto leader of this competing political group. By the late 1760s DeLancey's hair was already turning gray. He had a round nose and face with dark blue eyes. A highly educated colonial American, DeLancey attended Eton College and Corpus Christi College at the University of Cambridge, after which he studied law at the Honourable Society of Lincoln's Inn, one of London's four Inns of Court, where he likely established connections and took advantage of the city's vibrant social life. The extent of DeLancey's education was astounding. He was one of the most learned men not only in the colony of New York but across the British Empire—and he was able to pursue such an education because of his family and connections.

His family was among the wealthiest in colonial British America. Their colonial founder, Étienne de Lancy, was born in Caen, France, in 1663 and immigrated to New York in 1686 after French King Louis XIV had revoked the Edict of Nantes in 1685. De Lancy, who soon converted to Anglicanism, anglicized his names, becoming Stephen DeLancey. He rose quickly within New York's political and social ranks. He served in the assembly and married into a historic, well-connected Dutch family, the Van Cortlandts, whose patriarch,

Stephanus Van Cortlandt, was the first native mayor of New York City and the patroon of Cortlandt Manor near Croton-on-Hudson. DeLancey, shifting away from his origins, became a true New Yorker.

His son and heir was named James, and James and his siblings consolidated and built upon their father's legacy. They consolidated their political and social connections through marriage and occupational alliances, and James DeLancey Sr., as the family patriarch, enhanced the family's financial status. First, he married Anne Heathcote, the daughter of Caleb Heathcote, New York's mayor in the early 1710s. Second, James Sr.'s sister Susannah married Peter Warren on July 20, 1731. Then a captain in the Royal Navy, Warren was later knighted and made an admiral, largely due to his actions during King George's War (1744–1748), in which he reputedly made over £127,000 in prize money. Warren spread his vast wealth through his family. He paid James DeLancey Jr.'s tuition fees at Cambridge and Lincoln's Inn, costing Warren nearly £1,300. It was an exceptional education for an exceptionally privileged individual (see figure 1.2).

The younger DeLancey returned to the colonies after Lincoln's Inn, but he did not practice as a lawyer. For him, his legal education was akin to a liberal arts education. It allowed him to become a well-rounded, educated individual. Instead, he enlisted in the British Army, serving in the French and Indian War (1754–1763) (and avoiding the accompanying criticism that a legal career brought). After James DeLancey Sr. died in 1760, the younger DeLancey became the family patriarch. He inherited the DeLancey estates and returned to New York City, becoming possibly the wealthiest man in Manhattan, if not the entire colony or Eastern Seaboard. He invested in property, adding to an already-impressive number of properties on what is now the Lower East Side, the most valuable part of the city. DeLancey, who lived on a 343-acre estate on Bowery Lane that was valued at upward of £70,000, also owned a thirty-five-acre farm at Bloomingdale as well as land in New Jersey and Pennsylvania. Altogether, DeLancey brought in over £1,200 from the rents of his estates alone each year. One New Yorker noted of DeLancey's estate, "It was always esteemed."9

Also on the ticket, Jacob Walton was not on DeLancey's level—socially, politically, economically, ancestrally—but he was not far from it. Walton, whose grandfather was acting governor of New York for over two months in 1710, was the same age as DeLancey, and they were related through his brother's marriage to DeLancey's sister, Maria. He hailed from a prominent mercantile family whose wealth was based on regular trade with St. Augustine and the West Indies, a trade bolstered through Britain's imperial clashes with Spain in King George's War and France in the French and Indian War. Indeed, vessels owned and operated within the city rose from 150 to 450, and between 1740

FIGURE 1.2. Portrait of James DeLancey, ca. 1785, by Gilbert Stuart, Metropolitan Museum of Art

and 1760, imports from Britain rose from £135,487 to £480,106. The Walton family benefited greatly from these developments, establishing what might be considered a monopoly over the West Indies trade. In Manhattan, they did well, too. The family was based in Franklin Square. They occupied and held receptions and other social events in a stately residence that some compared to a palace. Like the DeLanceys, they were among the most prominent and visible merchants in the city, and sometime between September 18, 1770, and August 18, 1774, Jacob Walton built a lavish riverside property that was known as Belview. The 6¾-acre estate, located at what is now East Eighty-Eighth Street and East End Avenue, overlooked the East River, and it was a welcome escape and place of relaxation away from the bustle of lower Manhattan. (The site was likely destroyed by the British Army during the Revolutionary War. It is now occupied by the Archibald Gracie Mansion, the official residence of New York City's mayor.)[10]

James Jauncey, the third candidate on the ticket, was born on Bermuda in 1723. By the 1740s, he was the master of a vessel trading between New York City and Jamaica. His older brother, John, was also the master of a merchant vessel, trading to and from New York. He settled in Manhattan in 1737, and six years later he was joined by his brother, James, who, on July 28, 1743, married Maria Smith. Smith was two years his junior and the daughter of a sea captain. Soon after, Jauncey, with his wife, separated themselves from life on the sea and settled in Manhattan, where James Jauncey became a prominent merchant. During the French and Indian War, he was a successful privateer, owning at least six vessels, and, on June 10, 1758, he was appointed one of the wardens to New York's port, a prominent role in which he inspected goods coming in and out of the city. The role made him one of the most recognizable people on the waterfront and among the most well-known merchants in the city. Jauncey was someone who knew firsthand how commerce could benefit Manhattan, and although he was quiet, he was also incredibly generous. He often supported the city's impoverished residents by handing out money by the doors of his Presbyterian church. Jauncey lived in an old three-story house on Queen Street, but he was easily one of the Manhattan's most successful and prominent merchants.[11]

Strategies

With this group of closely connected, successful, elite merchants, the DeLanceys designed a political campaign that linked themselves with positive qualities associated with merchants and lawyers with their opponents. To put it differently, they sought to identify themselves with the city's voting population, elite and non-elite. They realized that the city's voters were aware of the city's political issues; as voters, they took a collective interest in the city's well-being and appreciated that its politicians could improve their everyday life.[12]

To mobilize support, they used the city's well-developed print trade, something that elite and non-elite New Yorkers could access easily. Three newspapers were published throughout the week: John Holt's *New-York Journal*; Hugh Gaine's *New-York Gazette; and the Weekly Mercury*; and James Parker's *New-York Gazette; or, the Weekly Post-Boy*. Gaine's and Parker's papers were published on Mondays, and Holt published on Thursdays to differentiate himself and capture as many readers as possible. Printed materials—newspapers, broadsides, pamphlets, cards—were often available in New York's various coffeehouses and taverns, making these venues where people could learn in an informal atmosphere. House visits required appointments and introductions; accessing coffeehouses and taverns was easy—so easy that people could visit multiple establishments on the same day. The circulation of news, real and fake, also depended on word of mouth and the physical distribution of newspapers. People who subscribed to newspapers customarily picked them up directly from the printers' offices, but some employed news carriers to deliver papers, including Gaine, to drop them off in coffeehouses, taverns, and elsewhere.[13]

In New York City, taverns were particularly hard to avoid. There were roughly twice as many in Manhattan than in other urban centers. By 1770 there was a tavern for every thirteen white adult men, and almost all the city's proprietors were men. (There were a small number of women proprietors and workers, but there were fewer in Manhattan than in other urban centers.) The city's tavern culture was largely homosocial and -racial, too—venues where women and other minorities were often excluded—helping to mold a collective identity for those who participated. That sense of shared identity might have been brief or temporary, but it was powerful. People enjoyed going to taverns. They were places where alcohol flowed, and food was consumed in an almost always hospitable environment. The DeLanceys recognized the potential for mobilization—and they took full advantage of the networks taverns created and nurtured. Indeed, in taverns and coffeehouses colonists discussed the news: what they had read, what someone else had read, or what they had not managed to read. Conversations covered wide-ranging topics, including the price of meat, the weather, and the constitutional history of the British Empire. Colonists also discussed contemporary politics, developing their political beliefs and identities alongside their associates in the process.[14]

As taverns and coffeehouses mediated social differences between elite and non-elite colonists, printed materials mediated geographic differences. News or gossip could spread quickly throughout a densely populated urban center like New York. In Britain, one late eighteenth-century newspaper estimated that its readership was between seven and seventy times larger than its nominal circulation. The same was true for colonial British America. Hugh Gaine, an Irishman who immigrated to Manhattan in 1745, believed his *New-York Mercury* was read "in every Town and Country Village" in Connecticut, Rhode Island, and New Jersey, as well as in Georgia, Nova Scotia, the West Indies, Great Britain, and the Netherlands. He believed his words had a global reach and given that copies of Manhattan newspapers are in archives across the world, he might have been right. Gaine also appreciated the importance of newspapers to his readers' lives, and he catered to their needs. "News-Papers are Meat, Drink and Cloaths, to both Soul and Body," reported one New Yorker.[15]

Manhattan's print culture was spurred on by its status as a rising commercial power, too. In various mercantile trades, literacy was almost a necessity to secure employment. Firms relied on meticulous record-keeping—they had to know who ordered what, when, and for how much. Merchants and their workers filled ledger after ledger, order-book after order-book, and account book after account book. Between 1751 and 1775, the literacy rate among men who left wills was 83.2 percent. Of those, 96 percent of merchants were literate. So, too, were 87 percent of shopkeepers, 79 percent of artisans, and 50 percent of laborers. Women's literacy rates were also high: between 1664 and 1775, over 68 percent of those who left wills were literate.[16]

The DeLanceys' use of print offers insight into the nature of New York City's population. It suggests that distinctions of rank neither inhibited nor shaped residents' ability to engage in political affairs in the public sphere. The universality of the city's print culture, in turn, enabled the DeLanceys to diffuse the potential for class antagonism throughout the city during the elections.

Almost as soon as the election was announced, their print campaign began with personalized advertisements to announce their candidacies and outline their motives for seeking election. And for each of them, the motive was simple: they were responding to New Yorkers' requests that they do so; it was not so much their choice as it was their civic duty. The DeLanceys' advertisements appeared in each of the city's newspapers throughout February and early March 1768, ensuring that their candidacies were known throughout the city. They primarily used two newspapers to mobilize support during their campaign: Holt's *New-York Journal* and Gaine's *New-York Gazette*. Occasionally, they worked with James Parker to ensure their political messages overcame the white noise of politics. By monopolizing the city's printers, they dominated weekly news cycles, attracting support, creating associational bonds, and showing that they were the people who would advance New Yorkers' interests. The Livingstons, on the other hand, did not advertise their candidacies. Instead, they relied on traditional modes of political mobilization—deference, word of mouth, or hand-written scraps of information—to publicize their names and ideas. They expected it would be enough.[17]

In eighteenth-century republican thought, candidates for public office were expected to emerge without constraint from the community in which they lived and with this claim that they were sacrificing their individual interests for the public good. The DeLanceys were signaling to New Yorkers that they adhered to the republican civic humanist ideal. On behalf of New Yorkers, they were sacrificing their individual interests to promote the public good. To be sure, the DeLanceys sought election to the assembly not only for ideological reasons—after all, they were aspiring politicians who wanted to be elected. But through their advertisements, which were published throughout the campaign, they presented themselves as Whigs, people who were virtuous, disinterested, and committed to the community.[18]

Their advertisements were only the first step of their multifaceted political campaign. They also exploited commonplace views of the legal profession in their printed materials, particularly the Livingstons'—and specifically John Morin Scott's—well-known association with William Smith Jr. and William Livingston in a legal alliance known as the "Triumvirate." In contrast, the DeLanceys depicted themselves as moral individuals who would protect New Yorkers' welfare and advance their interests. They published many pseudonymous pieces in the press that appealed to New Yorkers of all statuses, intelligences, or reading abilities. They also commissioned the printing of a pamphlet, a range of broadsides, and a series of short, focused cards, all of which were in English. (Tellingly, despite a small but vibrant Dutch print culture, the DeLanceys did not print anything in Dutch that remains extant.) Their pamphlet and lengthier broadsides were probably left on coffeehouse- or tavern-tables and in parlors. People could pass them around as easy conversation-starters. Shorter broadsides and cards were designed to be read quickly. They were likely placed in windows and on posts, trees, and walls, easy to read by passers-by. The brevity of broadsides and cards also suited the culture of eighteenth-century coffeehouse and tavern life. Some people preferred not to read as they drank or socialized. They might not have had the time or the patience to do so, especially if their working days began at 6 a.m. or earlier or if they worked throughout the night. Consequently, broadsides and cards were often left on tables for people to glance at, any time, day or night. Some cards also served a dual purpose. Not only were they political advertisements, but they were also traditional playing cards, items that could be taken home and used in other social settings.[19]

Through their wide-ranging propaganda arsenal, the DeLanceys quickly labeled the Livingstons as unsuited for political office in almost every respect. The Livingstons' record as assemblymen was poor, their morals were neither virtuous nor honorable, and they were part of an exclusive cabal that worked against New Yorkers' needs and interests. In A CARD, which was supposedly sent from an offshore ship, the author offered voters two guiding principles for the election. The intended audience was those involved in New York's laboring and mercantile trades, specifically, cartmen and those on the waterfront, who had neither the time nor the space to read longer pieces. The card discussed what type of person was best fitted to represent all New Yorkers in the assembly by using the eighteenth-century conception of masculinity that held that an individual in debt or dependent on another person could not act independently. Drawing on the city's status as a commercial entrepôt, the writer argued that the Livingstons impinged on New Yorkers' masculinity and economic independence. The DeLanceys, on the other hand, would work to protect New Yorkers' earnings—and this would enable them to achieve and maintain economic self-sufficiency. These were well-known republican idioms in the colonies during the eighteenth century. The DeLanceys added an economic vision: a mercantile, specialized world that prioritized and celebrated the autonomy of men. (Such a view echoed James Harrington's *Commonwealth of Oceana*, which linked property ownership and economic independence. A 1700 edition of Harrington's book had been purchased by James DeLancey Sr. in the early 1730s.) The DeLanceys argued that economic independence would advance the public good and improve the political economy of New York City. If the Livingstons, as lawyers, were elected, however, they would only advance themselves and their associates. "The good People of this City," the card declared, "are supported by Trade and Merchants." "Lawyers," on the other hand, "are supported by the People." To put it differently, the DeLanceys argued that they would support the public. The Livingstons, as lawyers, would not.[20]

Other pieces of propaganda were printed for New York's laboring, mercantile, and non-elite populations. They outlined ideas like those expressed in *A CARD*. First, the fate of the city's laboring and mercantile populations were intertwined. Second, lawyers could not represent their interests. In *A CARD*, published from *"Tradesman's-Hall"* on February 29, 1768, "Mr. Axe and Mr. Hammer" offered a unique paradigm for understanding whom the DeLanceys hoped to mobilize. In the card, Axe and Hammer offered "hearty Thanks" to "Mr. Hatchway and Mr. Bowline." Both "hatchway" and "bowline" relate to workers on the waterfront; a "hatchway" is an opening leading onto the deck of a ship, and a "bowline" is an oft-used knot used on board a ship or hoist. *A CARD* also suggested that New York's *"Leather-Aprons"*—*"a very respectable body"* that included shoemakers, blacksmiths, and tinmen, among others, as well as apprentices and servants—were "clearly of their Opinion, That it is TRADE, and not LAW supports our Families." Finally, Axe and Hammer argued, "honest *Jolt* the Cartman" alleged "he never got Six-Pence for riding Law-Books, tho' he gets many Pounds from the Merchants." Thus, a direct financial connection was made between New York's artisanal population and its cartmen and the city's merchants. The term *"Leather-Aprons"* was a semantic tool used by the DeLanceys, one earlier taken up by a sixteen-year-old Benjamin Franklin in a series of newspaper essays written in the voice of a middle-aged widow, "Silence Dogood." Early eighteenth-century meanings of the term "leather-apron men" was a class-based insult on labor. Franklin, however, used it as a classless, honorific title—something that was open not only to skilled artisans but also to apprentices, servants, and slaves. The DeLanceys were attempting to mobilize support in a similar way. The card concluded with a simple message: "No Lawyer in the Assembly" (see figure 1.3).[21]

Their cards were hard to avoid, and their message was persistent. In *A Word of Advice*, they used poetic verse to attack lawyers' political abilities and their potential objectives for office. Through careful language, they attacked the Livingstons' only candidate who was a lawyer, John Morin Scott. By targeting Scott, the DeLanceys conflated all of his alleged flaws with the Livingstons' morals as potential assemblymen, arguing that lawyers "will rob, under the Sanction of Law" and "sell [New Yorkers' rights] . . . for Gold." Warning voters to "Beware . . . the Wolf's griping Paw," the DeLanceyite author posited that if Scott and the Livingstons were elected, it would be "too late to repent." New Yorkers would become political slaves because the Livingstons encroached on colonists' rights and liberties. To counter this threat to liberty, the DeLanceys called for New Yorkers to mobilize in opposition. In another card, also titled *A WORD OF ADVICE*, Scott was labeled a "Wretch" who would enslave New Yorkers. His sole aim, the card declared, was to "banish Freedom, and to fix our Chains." Scott, the card added, was "the Barrator"—someone who took people into costly lawsuits to ruin them financially. The only way New York-

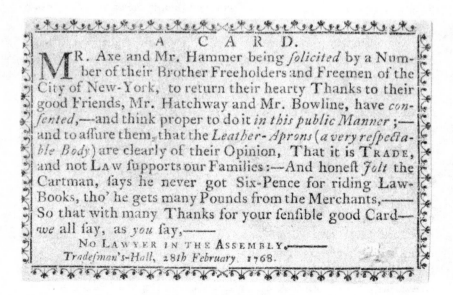

Figure 1.3. *A Card* (New York, 1768), courtesy Library Company of Philadelphia

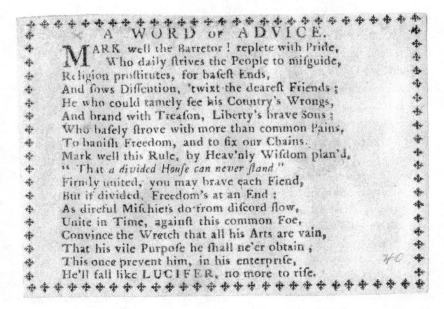

FIGURE 1.4. *A WORD of ADVICE* (New York, 1768), courtesy Library Company of Philadelphia

ers could escape the corrupting hand of the law was to "Unite in Time, against this common Foe." And if they did so, the DeLanceyite argued, "He'll fall like LUCIFER, no more to rise." The message was stark and simple: voting for the DeLanceys was not so much a choice as it was a necessity (see figure 1.4).[22]

Their cards and broadsides were everywhere, and they overwhelmed the Livingstons. Because of their brevity and focus, they became an effective outlet for non-elites to become involved in the political sphere and the electoral process. It was a particularly advantageous moment for this propaganda, too. New York City was amid an economic downturn after the end of the French and Indian War. The Atlantic economy had slumped in Manhattan, as well as in other urban centers, forcing people out of work. At the war's high point, over three thousand men worked aboard New York's privateers, and wages had risen accordingly. Now, years after the war's end and with few positive options on the horizon, wages fell and more and more people were out of work and groups of hundreds of people—men, women, children—traveled north of Manhattan in a desperate search for food. Others sought assistance from churches, which offered food and firewood whenever possible. The economic depression, which began in earnest in 1759, affected the city's laboring population more than any other group. To make ends meet, non-elite colonists had to work as often and for as long as they could. These were the realities of life. It was frantic, and people were busy, but they often wanted something better, a more embracing view of Manhattan's future and their place within it.[23]

New York City's marketplaces and workspaces were among the busiest of them all, and they provided the DeLanceys with their target audiences—people who would embrace a commercial vision for the city's future. New Yorkers assigned the economic depression to outdated banking and credit practices, as well as poor judgment and selfishness. The DeLanceys, however, assigned blame to the assembly, arguing that the Livingstons did not promote New Yorkers' interests—and as merchants, they would. The DeLanceys thus took their overall election message to the city's market—and workplaces. By 1768 there were six markets, more than in either Boston or Philadelphia, and more than 250 warehouses, distilleries, and sugar refineries, all manned by the men of the laboring classes. Indeed, Oliver DeLancey, James DeLancey's uncle and a royal councilor, managed two such properties on Broadway, almost exactly opposite the always-bustling Oswego Market. He was also instrumental in the development and construction of Warrens Wharf at the foot of Cortlandt Street that eased congestion on the wharves and became the main quay for the British Army and Royal Navy. Neither marketgoers nor workers had much time to stop and read lengthy treatises on municipal politics, but the DeLanceys' propaganda could be read in minutes.[24]

Elites had never courted non-elites' support with such frequency, and electoral materials had never been published with such regularity. To be sure, courting support was not a new development in New York City. During the 1730s, supporters of Lewis Morris Sr. appealed to New Yorkers for their support, marking a turning point in the city's social and political history. David Clarkson, Cornelius Van Horne, Henry Cruger, and Paul Richards did the same in the assembly election of 1748. During an election in the 1750s, one Livingstonite reported, a "Paper war is declared, on the Topick of Elections." But the DeLanceys' campaign was the next step in the development of the city's political practice. Indeed, the almost continuous publication and large-scale dissemination of materials represented a shift toward a more popular kind of politics, one in which grassroots support was integral.[25]

The Livingstons, however, produced few materials throughout the election, and those they did release were unconvincing. They were defensive, not proactive. They responded to the DeLanceys' materials instead of creating their own. Many tried to present the Livingstons in a positive light or defended or countered the attacks on John Morin Scott. "Lawyers," one Livingston piece contended, for instance, "were as honest and competent as any merchant." Another piece contended that the DeLanceys supported the establishment of an Anglican bishopric in colonial British America. The writer alleged that James DeLancey's recent journey to Britain, which occurred during the election campaign, was primarily so he could plead his case to prominent Anglicans and British members of Parliament. In the same piece, the Livingstons criticized DeLancey's love of horse racing, which was probably why he was in Britain. The writer also mocked any connections between John Morin Scott and the devil and, somewhat ironically, suggested that British and Dutch dissenters should not serve in the assembly.

The DeLanceys responded swiftly to the criticisms, issuing a broadside that rebuffed the notion that their leader was not committed to New Yorkers' interests. "I believe," the DeLanceyite author stated, "that some People Sow the Seeds of Contention," adding, "some People would make the religious Rights of their Neighbours, the Bone of Dissention, while they themselves are stealing the Flesh." The idea, it continued, that DeLancey would spend time in Britain and not promote the interests of New York was "only fit for the flames." To maximize their reach the DeLanceys also had their pamphlet published as a supplement to the *New-York Journal* of March 4, 1768. And, as an added precaution, they took out an advertisement disassociating James DeLancey from anything related to an American bishop. Here, not only did the DeLanceys rebut the Livingstons' allegations, but they also politicized the Livingstons' campaign, depicting them as unvirtuous, career-driven politicians. They turned the Livingston broadside on its head.[26]

But non-elites' support could not guarantee the DeLanceys' election. Despite the broad-based electorate, not every laborer or every cartman could vote. To garner as much support as possible, they had to ensure that voters from other classes were mobilized. Thus they targeted the city's well-read population, commissioning the publication of longer, more complex pieces of propaganda, including a six-page pamphlet that was "PRINTED" in 1768 "BUT NEVER PUBLISHED," *A Few Observations on the Conduct of the General Assembly*, which attacked the Livingstons' historical performances as assemblymen. *A Few Observations* argued that the Livingstons had worked against the public welfare throughout their seven-year tenure as the assembly's leading political group. The DeLancey author, who wrote under the Greek pseudonym Philanthropos, which roughly translates to loving mankind, argued that the Livingstons were not civic-minded individuals. They sought only to advance their own interests. In particular, the DeLancey author targeted the 1766 land riots as a case study that showed the ways in which the Livingstons were "the greatest tyrants that can possibly be conceived," people who were "guilty of so much baseness and ingratitude." The Livingstons, Philanthropos argued, could not be reelected; they were ungrateful, corrupt, and selfish; they had wantonly "disposed" of New Yorkers' property and, by extension, their economic independence. Philanthropos accused landlords like the Livingstons of driving "the tenants to the disagreeable necessity of seeking redress through violent means" during the land riots that rocked Albany, Dutchess, and Westchester Counties in 1766. The resulting violence and the mobilization of the British Army against the rioters was, Philanthropos alleged, a result of the Livingstons' close relationship to the bar. The rioters were "absolutely barred against" legal action because the rioting occurred on the Livingstons' property. The DeLanceyite author also made it clear that the Livingstons supported the harsh punishments that followed. This allegation was particularly hard for the Livingstons to counter: John Morin Scott sat on the bench at the trial of William Prendergast, who was one of the leaders of the rioters in Dutchess County and was convicted of high treason and sentenced to death. Prendergast was ultimately pardoned, but Scott's participation in the affair became a black mark on the Livingstons' ticket. This was a particularly partisan issue, one that showed the political acumen of the DeLanceys as well as the Livingstons' shortcomings. Various DeLanceyites also participated in the trial—John Watts, William Walton, Oliver DeLancey—but they were not criticized, either by Philanthropos or in any Livingstonite piece. Indeed, Philanthropos argued that the Livingstons' role in the land riots proved they were "repugnant to the general interest" and no longer deserved to be "the guardians of [the people's] sacred rights and liberties." Under a Livingston assembly, New Yorkers would become "some of the most abject slaves under Heaven." If they were reelected, Philanthropos wrote, they would pursue "a separate interest from the rest of the community," adding that a vote for the Livingstons would be a vote for "those of such a nature as may put it in their power to act inconsistent with, and repugnant to, the general interest of the community."[27]

The pseudonym Philanthropos would be used again when John Holt printed it as a newspaper supplement and reproduced it as a broadside. "As a Maritime City," Philanthropos argued, "our chief Dependence is upon Trade." It was "Merchants . . . [who were the] properest Persons to represent us . . . not Lawyers." Philanthropos also alleged that lawyers had not supported the broadbased mobilization against the Stamp Act in the winter of 1765. On the contrary, he argued, "so far were they from supporting the Cause" that "the very Man, who now offers himself as a Candidate, for this City," he was opposed not only to New Yorkers' protests but to those across British America.[28]

Their other materials continued the narrative of depicting themselves as deserving of voters' support. *The OCCASIONALIST* proposed that "*it must be held dangerous . . . to choose from the* Profession of the Laws" when electing assemblymen. Indeed, in the four-page broadside, which was likely designed for coffeehouse and tavern tables, the DeLanceyite author claimed that there were "more betrayers" of the public welfare within the law "than in any other profession." In *A PORTRAIT*, the author again labeled John Morin Scott—and, by extension, the Livingstons—"The Barrator." The DeLanceyite also alleged that Scott did not have the moral compass to perform the necessary duties of office. Scott, the DeLancey supporter declared, was a "philistine" who believed that "all men besides himself are fools, / And fit for nothing but to be his tools." All Scott cared about was "His self-importance and his self applause." This broadside was notable for being double-sided, which was rare during the 1768 election, but its inclusion is not surprising. Designed to be placed on windows, *A PORTRAIT*'s double-sided layout enlarged its potential audience—those inside a tavern or coffeehouse as well as those outside could consume its contents. In this instance, the reverse side's arguments were even more fierce, depicting Scott as engaging in a fictional, election-related conversation with the devil. Discussing how he would use New Yorkers to advance his own interest— which, by implication, suggested he was a devil-dealer—Scott declared that lawyers would impose "Excessive fees" to "trick the ninnies." In response, the devil cried, "Oh! Hoh! . . . Your office and my own, beyond a doubt, / Are both alike . . . / I gull them of their souls, you of their guineas."[29]

The Voter's New Catechism also criticized Scott's morals. Like *A PORTRAIT*, this broadside was a fictional conversation. In this instance, it was between two colonists. It served as a fictionalized representation of the discussions New Yorkers were having across the city, and to increase its audience the broadside was also printed in John Holt's *New-York Journal*. Its chosen theme was a familiar one: the city's lawyers and how they had corrupted and defiled the political arena. Like so many of the DeLanceys' broadsides, this one attempted to show how lawyers worked against the public welfare and associated them with social instability and political factionalism. *The Voter's New Catechism* used recent and not-so-recent events to depict the DeLanceys as the Livingstons' moral and political opposite. It argued that lawyers had worked against the public welfare for generations. The DeLanceys' use of history in *The Voter's New Catechism* dated back to the reigns of English kings Edward III (1327–77) and Charles I (1625–49). When the fictional New Yorker asked, "Who advised King Charles the First that it was lawful for him to do those Things that lost him the Hearts of his Subjects, and afterwards brought him to the Block?" the answer he received was, "The Lawyers.—" Then, when the DeLanceyite was asked, "Are there any Instances of such ill judging pernicious Lawyers in our Days?" his educated colleague responded, "Innumerable Instances." The New Yorkers' conversation then moved from fourteenth- and seventeenth-century England to eighteenth-century New York, and it centered on the Stamp Act crisis and Scott. Like other materials, it alleged that he did not support New Yorkers' protests.[30]

The Voter's New Catechism was a well-written and thoughtful piece of propaganda. The English history it employed might not have been widely known in New York City, though elites might have had some knowledge of it. The DeLanceys overcame this potential problem by using accessible language that made the events intelligible and their rhetoric more inclusive. Lawyers, they argued over and over and over, could not be a "proper Person to be chosen a Representative."[31]

They also realized that their politicking might not translate into political mobilization at the polls. Ideas or arguments might be misunderstood. Printed materials might be passed over. Not everyone went to a tavern or coffeehouse to read; others went to drink and eat. James DeLancey wanted to ensure that he presented himself in such a way that he articulated who he was and what he represented. During the eighteenth century, clothing and fashion were weaved into politics. Through fashion, people could express what they thought about a body of people, a society, a nation. Their fashion was symbolic. It told people which community they belonged to, and it was a part of their identity. New York City was a perfect venue in which its inhabitants could articulate their identities, whether they were in its coffeehouses, stores, or taverns, on its city wharves, or on its streets. Manhattan was a see-and-be-seen city with a burgeoning face-to-face culture. James DeLancey was fully aware of this. Shortly before the polls opened, presumably when he was in Britain, he purchased clothing from Matthew Walker & Johnson. He made several purchases, including a "dark [colored] cloth french frock suit," with "all meteralls" that came with it, and six "fine striped linen [Waistcoats]." His suit was likely single- or double-breasted, cutting off by his knees.[32]

By purchasing a French frock suit, DeLancey reaffirmed his commitment to and belief in the British Empire. He appreciated the progress that his Huguenot family had made since they emigrated from France to the colonies in the seventeenth century, recognizing that the opportunities they were presented with partly came their way because they lived in New York City and the British Empire. (Their conversion to Anglicanism also helped.)

Picture a scene. DeLancey, walking down a New York street, meets a friend or colleague, who asks him where he purchased his suit. To be sure, DeLancey would almost certainly note that he purchased it in Britain, reaffirming his Britishness, but depending on whom he met, and whether they were also French Huguenot descendants, he might have also noted its French connections. In such a diverse city as New York, this scenario was very likely. After the Edict of

Nantes was revoked, some two hundred thousand Huguenots fled France, a considerable proportion of whom settled in Manhattan. DeLancey was a skilled, innovative politician. He knew other Huguenots lived in New York City, and he sought their support in the election as well as the support of those seeking to articulate their Britishness. If called for he would not forget he was the descendent of a Huguenot. After all, DeLancey was not only a Briton but a New Yorker. And if elected he would represent everyone, British, French, or otherwise. For him, as for his colleagues, they were New Yorkers—and he wanted their vote.[33]

The city's taverns also offered an opportunity. This time, however, they did not produce items that were to be left on tables. They used the taverns for their other, perhaps more important, purpose: sociability. The DeLanceys used their city's tavern culture of sociability to mobilize support, holding regular meetings in George Burns's and Benjamin Stout's taverns at the corner of Broad and Dock (now Pearl) Streets, opposite the Bowling Green, and at the entrance of Bowery Lane. These primary taverns catered for one of the DeLanceys' audiences. They also placed frequent advertisements in the press to ensure that their supporters were aware of and attended their events. They did not specify any requirements; any white male could attend, and when they got there, they were greeted with long tables covered with a wide array of expensive alcoholic beverages and food. As each man sat down, huddled up to one another, drinks and conversation flowed. When the event was over, the attendees departed without having to pay for their meal. Why? They paid for everything.[34]

These events were loud. They were a spectacle. A gentleman walking through the city one evening in February 1768 strolled past a tavern, and he noticed that the DeLanceys and their patrons were inside. When he opened the door, he "discovered a number of people collected," who were making "a great noise." As soon as he saw what was going on, he disapproved. "A dramshop was opened," one New Yorker told him, adding "that every Freeholder and Freemen, who was willing to part with his vote, might there meet with a purchaser." In this instance, those "purchaser[s]" were the DeLanceys. It was a well-attended event. The tavern was filled with voters "greatly heated with passion, and intoxicated with liquor." And because it was a DeLancey event, discussions likely centered on or at least related to the elections. Indeed, the patrons touched on a typical DeLancey theme: lawyers and their suitability for office. They were debating "Whether a Lawyer could possibly be an honest Man?" They decided that a lawyer could not. Together, amid fumes and drunken furor, the patrons sang out: *"No Lawyer in the Assembly! No Lawyer in the Assembly!"*[35]

Events like this were popular in the election campaign. Hundreds of potential voters took advantage of the DeLanceys' offers. In one bill from Benjamin

Stout, James DeLancey was charged for 248 "meals of victuals," 134 bottles of wine, 106½ "Double Bowls of punch," 117 "mugs of Beer & Seyder," and an assortment of other beverages for events that ran from Monday to Friday in the run-up to the election. The DeLanceys were determined to mobilize as many voters as possible, offering as many events as they could, with the hope that those who could not make the event on a Monday, Tuesday, or Wednesday could possibly attend Thursday's or Friday's proceedings. The self-interest of their direct appeals to New Yorkers was clear, but their meetings were not without meaning or significance. They were also political moments in which free food and drink mediated points of division between attendees and established bonds and trust that transcended issues of religion, ethnicity, or rank. In Stout's tavern, the DeLanceys invented and reaffirmed New Yorkers' political sentiments, bringing diverse peoples together.[36]

Even the choice of Stout's tavern was a conscious one. It was positioned at the tip of Bowery Lane, close to the popular Chatham Street water pump, where the city's cartmen received regular business. Not only did the pump provide the city with the best water for tea, but it also acted as the city's main waterworks until well after the Revolutionary War. The pump was popular. Almost every house in the city took at least some of its water from it. It was a bustling place. And so, too, was Stout's tavern. The noise bouncing off its walls and bursting through windows would have piqued people's interest, and the DeLanceys were not able to turn people away. On the contrary, using Stout's tavern reaffirmed their commitment to bringing New Yorkers together. In fact, the DeLanceys' hopes to create a political association reached out further than the patrons. Their tavern-going also established an economic system of reward with the tavern-keeper. Along with paying for the food and drink, they rented the tavern-keepers' private rooms. Thanks to the DeLanceys' generosity and their political goals, men like Stout received considerable incomes and were well positioned to publicly endorse their sponsors to their customers and suppliers.[37]

Whether they realized it, hundreds of potential voters were making political statements by drinking and eating in a tavern alongside prominent political actors. This not only made Stout's and Burns's taverns partisan political venues, but it also made the Chatham Street water pump a political venue—all well before anything had happened. Though the event itself took place within the private sphere—that is, tavern-goers' activities were hidden from public view—the fact that New Yorkers were aware of the DeLanceys' meeting days beforehand meant the meetings were public events as much as private ones.

Results

The DeLanceys' political tactics redefined the political culture of the city, making it more accessible, at least for white males, and the Livingstons did not like it. But the evolving relationship between the electors and the candidates was clear in the election's results. The polls opened on March 7, 1768, for five days, and the viva voce–style of voting brought political canvassing into voters' faces. Not to let an opportunity go by the wayside, the DeLanceys also used this to their advantage. During the voting, two of the leaders of New York's Sons of Liberty, John Lamb and Isaac Sears, secured votes for the DeLanceys from across the lower orders of society. Oliver DeLancey, meanwhile, canvassed voters on Broadway near his home and in Oswego Market, and other DeLancey partisans picketed at City Hall or stationed themselves around Trinity Church. Tavern keeper David Grim was paid £5 and David Fareley £6 after the election for "Election Services" and "Collecting" votes during the election. All of this was designed to aid the DeLanceys. By walking and talking alongside other DeLancey partisans, these men were creating a political network that was based on shared beliefs and attitudes. In this instance, the 1768 election was the time when the DeLanceys, the "SINCERE FRIENDS to the TRADE and PROSPERITY of the City," would have their supporters "join HEART and HAND to hinder a Lawyer being chosen to represent" New York, their "Commercial City." "Let all *true Friends to Trade* declare their minds freely," the DeLanceyite continued, "and they may depend on being protected from any Oppression, that any Lawyer shall dare to attempt." "We will remember your good Offices with warm Gratitude," the DeLanceys assured their voters.[38]

Between 1,924 and 1,960 New Yorkers voted in the assembly election for New York City and County, and the results indicated a stunning political realignment:

"Philip Livingston, Esq.	1320
James DeLancey, Esq.	1204
Jacob Walton, Esq.	1175
James Jauncey, Esq.	1052
John Morin Scott, Esq.	870
[William Bayard, Esq.	584]
Mr. Emos [*sic*] Dodge	257"

All the DeLancey candidates were elected, securing three of the four New York City and County seats. Still, Philip Livingston, a prominent, fifty-two-year-old merchant, received the most votes. The DeLanceys had tried to bring Livingston on board their ticket, partly because it would have enabled them to promote an all-merchant slate. More important, they knew he was a popular figure because of his long career of public service. He had served as an alderman between 1754 and 1762, had been an assemblyman since 1759, and had engaged in civic-minded acts throughout his life, including endowing a professorship at Yale in 1746 and cofounding the New York Society Library in 1754 and the St. Andrew's Society in 1756. At the time of the election, he served as the assembly's speaker; he was an individual known to promote and protect the public good. He secured 68 percent of the popular vote and 66 percent of non-elite votes.[39]

But the significance of their collective performance outweighs Philip Livingston's election. From an analysis of the election's poll list, it is clear that the DeLanceys expanded and diversified their support base. In the 1761 election, the DeLanceys received 1,769 votes. The Livingstons received 3,271. Seven years later, with the added qualifier that some Livingston voters could have died and other DeLancey voters came of age, the DeLanceys increased their votes by 96 percent, to 3,431, and the Livingstons' votes decreased by 25 percent, to 2,447. In 1768, the DeLanceys obtained a large proportion of their votes from New York's non-elite population. Of 1,039 non-elite voters, 60 percent voted for James DeLancey, 58 percent voted for Jacob Walton, and James Jauncey received about 53 percent of their votes. DeLancey and Walton received over 60 percent of the popular vote, and Jauncey received around 55 percent. The DeLanceys' direct appeals to the city's cartmen was also effective: nearly 70 percent of the city's 65 voting cartmen voted for Jauncey, and DeLancey and Walton each received over 50 votes. The social composition of John Morin Scott's voters suggests that his appeal was neither as wide nor as diverse as the DeLanceys'. Fewer than half of New Yorkers voted for him, and he received only 45 percent of non-elites' votes as well as only 40 cartmen's votes. In the opinion of New York City's voters, who was elected mattered. But it was not only who they were within the city's social pyramid that mattered but also what they stood for. They had to have a commitment to advancing the public good and protecting the city's moral economy. This sentiment was felt throughout society as voters came together to evaluate their politicians. As one newspaper essayist argued, New Yorkers looked for "good common-Wealths-men" to represent them. They looked for politicians who would "cheer the distressed" and "contribute to public spirited Measures so essential to our well being." New Yorkers voted for the DeLanceys and Philip Livingston because they thought they would represent their interests and advance the public good.[40]

Among the DeLanceys' voters were people like Grove Bend, George Brewerton, and William Ustick. Bend, a freeholder, was a merchant who lived on

Smith Street, and Brewerton was a municipal alderman for the city's North Ward who became a freeman on November 24, 1741. Ustick, both a freeholder and a freeman, was thirty-four years old at the time of the election. He was an iron merchant who was based near the water between Burling's and Beekman's slips, and he occasionally sold slaves. Together, they voted for all the DeLancey candidates. They also had Dutch, Irish, and French voters, among others. Their appeal was widespread.[41]

Their campaign was not conservative; the Livingstons were not moderate. Far from it. The DeLanceys' campaign democratized the city's political spaces and practices like never before. Indeed, the 1768 election initiated a process in which partisan allegiances formed in New York City. These allegiances shaped colonists' behavior in the years to come, as the election enabled them to develop political networks. For some, the election signified their commitment to the DeLanceys and their ideological foundations. Voting for them reinforced New Yorkers' commitment to and belief in the DeLanceys' political economy, namely, their promotion of both republican and commercial interests. Like-minded white males correlated and understood their political beliefs in relation to one another, and they understood who shared their ideas.[42]

But it was more than partisanship. The 1768 election began a process in which colonists who became loyalists associated with the DeLanceys, and one another. More future loyalists voted for the DeLanceys than for the Livingstons in 1768. The number of future loyalists' votes the DeLanceys received in 1768 had also increased from 1761, too. In 1761, the DeLanceys received at least 360 votes from future loyalists, while the Livingstons received 657 votes. But in 1768, with more voting New Yorkers, voting patterns changed. The DeLanceys increased the number of votes they received from future loyalists by at least 136 percent, to 850. This was a much larger increase than the Livingstons received, whose proportion of future loyalist votes increased by at least 4 percent to 682. Their political economy and their promotion of open political debate were a more attractive prospect than anything the Livingstons offered.[43]

But it must be remembered that everyone in New York, as well as in the rest of colonial British America, was far from decided on whether they were a loyalist or a revolutionary, as we understand the terms today. These people were New Yorkers and loyal subjects of George III. In a sense, all New Yorkers, as well as all other colonial Americans, were "loyalists" in that they almost certainly did not imagine life outside the British Empire. In this instance, their mobilization occurred along a spectrum. New Yorkers were given an option of two relatively similar political groups: both were grounded in eighteenth-century Whiggism. There were no liberals or conservatives—terms that were used and gained traction in the nineteenth century—and people were not on the "left" or "right." Modern political categories seldom apply to eighteenth-century New York City or, indeed, anywhere. They were republicans, and both successfully brought many New Yorkers into their orbit from across society.[44]

The 1768 election kick-started a process through which New Yorkers became increasingly involved in public political affairs, ones that took place on the streets and waterfronts and in taverns, coffeehouses, and people's homes. More importantly, though, the election results had a demonstrable impact upon colonists' views of the DeLancey-Livingston rivalry. John Wetherhead, a New York merchant, told the superintendent of Indian affairs for the northern department, Sir William Johnson, 1st Baronet, that the Livingstons had been "egregiously outwitted." They were unable to comprehend the popular "Opposition & Spirit" that were directed against them by "the people in generale." Another DeLancey supporter and future loyalist, Rev. Charles Inglis, boasted that the election result "was the greatest Overthrow the Faction [i.e., the Livingstons] ever received here." "They were outwrote as well as outvoted." "This has enraged them to a Degree of Phrenzy," he added. The dramatic shift in voters' sentiments was due, in part, to the two groups' strategies. Whereas the DeLanceys' involvement of non-elites in the political process worked in their favor, the Livingstons' reliance on deference worked against them. As pro-Livingston New Yorker Robert Morris wrote after the election, their campaign had been based around "presuming too much upon the favor of the Town."[45]

The DeLanceys' techniques were effective not only in Manhattan but across the colony. Thirteen new assemblymen were elected, most of whom did not support the Livingstons. Only nine out of twenty-seven members were reliable Livingston supporters. Nor was Robert Livingston Jr. of Clermont right in his prediction that his family's interest would secure them victory in Dutchess County. His son, who was widely known as Judge Robert R. Livingston to distinguish him from the other Robert Livingstons in the family, was defeated. So, too, was Henry Livingston, Robert of Clermont's nephew. The Livingstons were replaced by Leonard Van Kleeck and Dirck Brinckerhoff, the latter of whom was largely a supporter of the DeLanceys. Of the election, Lt. Gov. Cadwallader Colden reported that although Judge Livingston's "family interest" had returned him and his family for more than a generation, "he had so far lost the esteem of the Freeholders." "The general cry of the People both in Town and Country was *No Lawyer in the Assembly.*"[46]

The political tide had shifted toward the DeLanceys, whose inclusive campaign had enabled them to communicate their ideas, organize support, and encourage partisan behavior. As the people's representatives, they reclaimed New York's government. Despite their comparative electoral success, the Livingstons held a tiny majority in the assembly, at least on paper, and with the merchant Philip Livingston's seat secured, it took another election and another bout of DeLancey politicking to reinforce their position.[47]

CHAPTER 2

Too Much Power over
Our Common People
The Assembly Election of 1769

The elected assemblymen, returning and new, had to wait until October 27, 1768, to assume their positions. In his opening address to the assembly of October 28, Gov. Sir Henry Moore cited the summer weather as a reason for not convening them earlier and noted that there was nothing of "immediate Service" they could do. Shortly after, the assembly formed a committee to respond to Moore's message, and on November 2, James DeLancey presented a draft for colleagues' consideration. "*We shall endeavour to proceed*," the assemblymen stated, "*to concur with your Excellency, in any Measures that may be proposed for his Majesty's Service, and the Welfare of the Colony.*" The response was approved the next day, and Philip Livingston, who had been reelected as speaker, signed it, after which two Livingston partisans were dispatched to deliver the message to Moore in his council chamber in Fort George. Moore approved of the address, citing the assembly's "Assurances" that they would work with him to promote "his Majesty's Service, and the Welfare of the Province." Such an approach would be of "the greatest Advantages to your Country."[1]

By then, Moore was about three years into his gubernatorial tenure, and he was hopeful for a quiet, peaceful session. But tranquility was not on the agenda. On February 11, 1768, the Massachusetts House of Representatives passed a circular letter calling for intercolonial opposition to Parliament's Townshend Acts of 1767, which levied import duties on products such as glass, lead, china, paper, and East India Company tea. The revenue that would be generated from the new taxes was to be used to defray the salaries of colonial officials, a consequence of which would emancipate colonial governors from their respective legislatures that had previously permitted governors' salaries. The circular letter was written by Samuel Adams and James Otis Jr. Together, they alleged that the duties were "Infringements of their natural Constitutional Rights" because colonists did not have representation within Parliament. It was a power-grab—an attempt to limit the power of colonial legislatures, classify colonists as unequal to native-born Britons, and reassert Parliament's absolute authority over the colonies.[2]

Adams and Otis sought to mobilize intercolonial support for their cause. They submitted the letter to legislatures throughout colonial British America. But because Moore did not convene the assembly, New York's assemblymen were unable to respond to it until after Hillsborough delivered his own response, stipulating that if colonial legislatures responded to or even discussed the circular letter, the colony's governor was to dissolve the legislature. Moore, however, was confident that New Yorkers would not support their fellow colonists. He believed a strong response would quash colonists' aspirations, whether it was for representation within Parliament or the repeal of the Townshend Acts. But New Yorkers, including the DeLanceyite assemblymen, held other ideas. In April 1768, the city's merchants declared a nonimportation agreement after November 1 and the city's artisans agreed to boycott anyone who imported British goods.[3]

On October 31, moreover, Philip Livingston presented a circular letter to the assembly from Peyton Randolph, the speaker of Virginia's House of Burgesses. It also opposed the Townshend Acts. The letter made many of the same points as the Massachusetts circular letter, and on November 8 the assemblymen formed a committee to draft petitions to the Parliament and George III. The assembly was challenging the constitutionality of the Townshend Acts, as well as Parliament's authority over it, without addressing the Massachusetts circular letter. Outside of the assembly, DeLanceyites met to determine the best course of action. Many believed the most effective means to show their opposition to the Townshend Acts was the same way they protested the Stamp Act: a riot in which they symbolically attacked the person or people who they believed were the driving force behind the legislation. In this case, it was Gov. Francis Bernard of Massachusetts and Stephen Greenleaf, the sheriff of Suffolk County. Between 8 p.m. and 9 p.m. on November 14, then, effigies of Bernard and Greenleaf "hanging on a Gallows" appeared on the streets. Hundreds of people poured out of their homes and the city's coffeehouses and taverns to see what was happening. Many cheered as the effigies went past and when they were burned outside of a coffeehouse near Queen Street (now Pearl Street).[4]

New York's assemblymen condemned the riot in their official proceedings, but the DeLanceys' constitutional opposition to the Townshend Acts came out in other areas. In John Holt's *New-York Journal* of November 17, a writer questioned why their representatives had not yet officially addressed the Massachusetts circular letter. The DeLanceys were aware that they were elected to protect and advance the public good and New Yorkers' economic independence. The Townshend Acts, they believed, were a threat to both. And so, in Holt's *New-York Journal* of December 1 they announced a public meeting. New Yorkers' engagement with their newly elected officials during the 1768 election campaign had set a standard. The circular letter was close to a year old at this point, and the assembly had been in session a few weeks. New Yorkers believed it was the time for their assemblymen to act. If they chose not to, one person wrote, they would be working toward "a quite different or opposite Interest." The writer alleged, moreover, if the new assemblymen did not respond they would be considered "Instruments of Oppression," something the DeLanceys were keen to avoid.[5]

The DeLanceys mobilized popular support for the circular letter, going around the city canvassing signatures to a petition that opposed the Townshend Acts. In so doing they continued the process of building a network of like-minded New Yorkers. Signing a petition, regardless of its motivation, was not something to be done on a whim. Signatures were often divided into vertical columns, where those signing—and those thinking about it—could see whose signatures would precede their own, giving them a moment to evaluate whether they wanted their names to be associated with the other signatories. Signing, then, required careful thought. It was a declaration on many levels—ideological, social, cultural, and economic—and for some it could have been among the first political documents they had ever signed. Equally important, as people signed their names, they rearticulated their own commitment to protecting the public good and economic independence—the platform the DeLanceys had ran on earlier in the year. Signing thus became a collective pronunciation of not only their political association with the DeLanceys but also their separation from the Livingstons, who were still ill-prepared to handle the DeLanceys' on-the-street tactics. When Philip Livingston was asked to sign the petition, he refused, noting, "Let them that would choose Tools to Instruct them."[6]

By December, James DeLancey was on the cusp of introducing a motion to discuss the Massachusetts circular letter. At this stage, many New Yorkers recognized him to be, as Smith put it, "the Oracle of the Sons of Liberty." He was their public spokesperson—the elected official who represented and advanced their views within the assembly. People recognized his role, and the Livingstons used Philip Schuyler, one of their partisans, to try to stop him. Instead of

DeLancey presenting a motion to discuss the circular letter, Schuyler did it instead. DeLancey, not wanting the dissolution of the assembly, opposed Schuyler's motion, and it was dropped until the end of the month, after all legislative affairs had been taken care of. On December 31, the assemblymen discussed the Massachusetts circular letter, expressing their opposition to the Townshend Acts as well as their support for their peers in Massachusetts. Moore was left with no choice. If he wanted to retain his position as governor of New York, he had to dissolve the assembly, which he did on January 2, 1769. But the DeLanceys were not afraid of holding another election. Far from it. It provided them with an opportunity to consolidate their position by building upon the tactics they had successfully implemented in 1768.[7]

As leaders among the Sons of Liberty, the DeLanceys recognized that the Townshend Acts threatened New Yorkers' economic self-sufficiency. Equally important, they recognized an imperial evolution within the British imperial state, whereby Parliament was becoming increasingly authoritarian and asserting its supremacy. With the city's non-elites, they hoped to work together to advance the public good to lift the city out of its economic downturn and into a new era of sustained economic growth, one in which New York's relative independence could be maintained.[8] Indeed, the DeLanceys had not responded to the Massachusetts circular letter solely out of political self-interest. Nor did they enjoy New Yorkers' popular support solely because of their association with the Sons of Liberty. Their responses to the Townshend Acts and their affiliation with the Liberty Boys were largely determined by their political economy—something that they had articulated throughout their albeit brief tenure in the assembly. The Townshend Acts dominated much of the DeLancey assemblymen's discourse outside of the assembly, but during the session they were also leading proponents of various pieces of legislation that advanced their political economy. Using the advantages they had earned in the 1768 election, they sought to shape the colony's laws to define its identity. On October 28, 1768, for instance, Jacob Walton and James Jauncey were part of a DeLancey-led committee to review expiring laws to determine whether they should be renewed. On November 21, Walton presented a bill to increase the number of the city's firemen. Firemen were considered important members of the urban community. They were men who sacrificed their needs for the public good through their service, protecting their neighbors' property. Women also participated in colonial firefighting, maintaining equipment and assisting during fires. Voluntary fire companies like New York's were an equalizing force within the city. Aside from the so-called Engenier and his two assistants, firemen were largely governed through consensus, as elites and non-elites worked together to protect the city. Firefighting also came with a social life, as fire companies often met in a tavern or coffeehouse, thus bringing the volunteers closer together. Walton's advocacy for more firemen was effective: between 1768 and 1769 the number of firemen in New York City increased by nearly 63 percent.[9]

The Livingstons were not unaware of the DeLanceys' behavior. Far from it. Not long after the assembly convened, the defeated Livingston candidate John Morin Scott questioned the legitimacy of James Jauncey's election. Meanwhile, Lewis Morris, another Livingston partisan, challenged John DeLancey's election in the Borough of Westchester. The Livingstons' legislative protests against the DeLanceys' election was serious. The implication of their challenges was that the DeLanceys were corrupt. As with the discussion of the Townshend Acts, spirits ran high. In this instance, debates were too heated to be resolved by a subcommittee. The whole assembly discussed Jauncey's and DeLancey's election. Witnesses were called and testimonies were heard. Jauncey was accused of purchasing votes, which he denied, claiming that he had refused such an offer from upward of forty people. More, with the support of James Duane, his lawyer, Jauncey presented evidence showing that Scott had engaged in the exact type of fraudulent behavior that he was alleging Jauncey had participated in. Scott was also accused of further underhand conduct, including threatening to sue someone if that person did not vote for him and bribing carpenters. Morris alleged that some of DeLancey's voters were illegitimate because the voters did not have the right to vote in Westchester. Both Scott's and Morris's charges were eventually dropped, but not before James DeLancey attempted to have the assembly denounce Scott's charges as "frivolous, vexatious, and litigious" in its official proceedings. DeLancey's motion was unsuccessful—it received the support of only two other members, John DeLancey and Jacob Walton—but his language was indicative of the partisanship that permeated the assembly. The factionalism is not altogether surprising, either. The 1768 election had altered the factional makeup of the chamber in favor of the DeLanceys, which, in turn, had affected how the assembly determined New York's laws. Between 1761 and 1768 the Livingstons won roughly 40 percent of the legislative decisions in the assembly. In the DeLanceys' short-lived assembly, they won 56 percent of the votes. In the election of 1769, the second election in a year, the DeLanceys' and Livingstons' disdain for one another came to a head.[10]

Livingstons

With imperial issues looming, the local issue that dominated the 1769 election was religious in nature, namely, the possible establishment of an Anglican episcopate in colonial British America. This issue was not new, either, but it did not overtly affect the 1768 election. Indeed, Anglicans had a hostile relationship with the colony's Dissenters for a long time. Throughout the seventeenth and eighteenth centuries, they clashed over what role the Church of England had or could have in New York, if any. In particular, New York's Dissenters worried about the advancement and subsequent establishment of the Church of England in the colony. They believed that if there was a colonial British American bishop, they might jeopardize not only New Yorkers' religious freedoms but the freedoms of all Dissenters in colonial America. In other words, they were concerned that Anglicanism would become a state religion.

Dissenters were right to be concerned. Anglicanism was, after all, a minority faith in New York, making up 10 percent of the colony's population. In 1750 only 12 percent of the colony's churches were Anglican. By 1776 this number had decreased to under 11 percent. Though inferior numerically, the church's status was buoyed by constant support from the Society for the Propagation of the Gospel (SPG) and the colonial governor. Throughout the eighteenth century, the SPG invested over 40 percent of its funds for the Middle Colonies in New York to strengthen Anglicanism among its diverse population. The SPG also dispatched missionaries to the colony, including Samuel Seabury and Charles Inglis, and encouraged local inhabitants to establish Anglican ministries on newly cultivated lands.[11]

The tension between Anglicans and Dissenters worsened from midcentury. Prominent clergymen clashed with Dissenters with greater frequency throughout the 1750s because Anglicans' perception of the role the church could—or, as they argued, should—play in the colonies evolved. Under the leadership of Thomas Secker, archbishop of Canterbury, British and colonial support for the establishment of a North American Episcopate became more vocal and insistent from as early as 1741. Secker's advocacy was complemented by the campaigning of leading clerics, including Samuel Johnson and Thomas Bradbury Chandler. In the 1760s, they were joined by Seabury, Inglis, and Myles Cooper. Together, these men evinced what has been referred to as "imperial Anglicanism."[12]

Imperial Anglicans viewed the role of the church as essential to the success of Britain's empire. They felt that the religious diversity of colonial America impeded the ability of the church and Britain to strengthen their presence across the Atlantic. To undermine the perceived threat of Dissenters and assert Britain's religious control over the colonies, they championed the establishment of an Anglican Episcopate. As Samuel Johnson reasoned, ministers faced "a very great obstruction to the propagation of religion" without a secure and consistent Anglican presence. Johnson was a seminal figure within imperial Anglicanism and a frequent correspondent of Thomas Secker. When he moved to New York City from Connecticut in 1754, his new home became, and remained, the center of Episcopal debates.[13]

Discussions of an Anglican episcopate reemerged in the late 1760s. Anglicans convened in Shrewsbury, New Jersey, to draw up a program that would eventually result in the establishment of a colonial American bishop. In March and May of 1767, meetings were held in New York City to further discuss the topic. Later that year, Thomas Bradbury Chandler, who was one of the fiercest advocates for a bishop, published *An Appeal to the Public, in Behalf of the Church of England in America* to articulate part of the Anglicans' argument that, they believed, might influence Parliament and the Church of England; namely, their church was hamstrung by high expenses and the dangers of Atlantic travel. Chandler, for one, wanted his pamphlet to be distributed "throughout this County," hoping "the Affair might be carried without *open* Opposition."[14]

William Livingston, however, assemblyman Philip Livingston's brother, had other ideas. "I think it is a Shame to us all that D^r. Chandler's pamphlet has so long remained unanswered," he told Rev. Noah Welles. "'Tis Noise and Clamour that is at present our best Policy." Livingston considered authoring a pamphlet as his rebuttal, but decided a weekly newspaper would be more effective, noting it "would be more generally read & constantly reprinted." Livingston hoped that his literary efforts would show high-ranking members of the Church of England in Britain that "the Apprehension of a Bishop's being sent, has raised a Flame" in New York City. In secret, Livingston went to work.[15]

The first issue of "The American Whig," as it was titled, was published in James Parker's *New-York Gazette; or, Weekly Post Boy* on March 14, 1768—the same issue in which the DeLanceys' election to the assembly was announced. Despite planning the series in secret, word of Livingston's plan leaked. He enlisted the literary talents of Welles, William Smith Jr., John Morin Scott, Charles Chauncy of Boston, and Francis Alison of Philadelphia. With many people in the know, it was not long until the news made its way to Chandler, who knew Livingston was the literary architect. "I am threatened with a weekly Paper," he told Sir William Johnson ten days before the first essay was published, adding, "I am not in the least terrified with these Threatenings." "I think I can deal with all their Reasonings and Arguments." News of Livingston's plans mobilized his Anglican opponents, and they designed a response that, they felt, would rebut his arguments. Chandler was determined not to be outdone, telling Johnson, "Not a single Argument shall escape me." In early March, he enlisted his Anglican colleagues Charles Inglis, Myles Cooper, and Samuel Seabury in his cause. Inglis also enlisted his friend Isaac Heron, an Irish watchmaker, to help—and by mid-March they were ready to respond. "We are this Week," Inglis wrote, "to fix on a plan of Operations." "I hope we shall be able to check the overgrown, intolerable Insolence of these Factors in Dissention."[16]

Published first in Hugh Gaine's *Mercury* and written under the pseudonym Timothy Tickle, "A Whip for the American Whig" responded to Livingston's work with the same level of literary temerity. In the first response, written by Inglis and published on April 4, Livingston was labeled "a hackneyed journeyman," someone who was making his religion "a political engine to accomplish" his designs. Another essay series soon appeared alongside Livingston's in New York, while in Philadelphia, "The Centinel" joined the debate, arguing against the idea of an Anglican bishopric with comparable hostility. Livingston's choice of Parker as his printer was successful, as the protégé of Benjamin Franklin increased his circulation, selling "200 more than usual" in the series' inaugural week. As a result of Livingston's work, Parker welcomed more than one hundred new subscribers. John Holt also took advantage of the paper war, distributing copies of the essays for his subscribers and selling individual essays for paying customers. (The demand for information was so high that Holt later published a two-volume collection of all the articles and essays associated with the dispute.) As one Boston minister commented, "the Episcopalian controversy at present engrosses the attention of the public." "So much the better."[17]

It was unlikely that a colonial American Episcopate was ever seriously considered, but it did not matter for those involved. The paper war started almost immediately after the 1768 election and continued throughout the 1769 election campaign. Even if people did not read every essay, New Yorkers were at least aware of the weekly influx of religious materials into their news cycle, as well as the disturbing news surrounding the Townshend Acts. In total, Livingston orchestrated the publication of sixty-four essays. They appeared every week until July 24, 1769. Chandler and his colleagues matched Livingston, almost word for word, publishing until July 10, 1769, a consequence of which was a direct impact on the assembly elections of 1769.[18]

By writing "chiefly upon Politicks," William Livingston wrote, he wanted "to open the Eyes of this Province" to the threat of Anglican domination. In short, he was attempting to mobilize Dissenters. William Livingston's attempts to do this reflected his desire to regulate New York City's political arena in his image by tempering the impact of the DeLanceys' methods—in particular, their inclusive and populist behavior. Livingston believed in a meritocratic society and advocated for it since the 1740s. In 1748 Livingston founded the Society for the Promotion of Useful Knowledge to advance New Yorkers' education in politics. The society's membership was made up of "the *Litterati* of all *Ranks, Dignities, Offices, Denominations, Characters* and *Callings*, in, and about this City."

As the membership of the society suggested, Livingston felt that prior to non-elites' political engagement, they must have a firm grasp of politics. Only with their political education could New York City move forward and distance itself from aristocratic, or arbitrary, rule. New Yorkers needed to "improve the[ir] Taste, and *Knowledge*, to *Reform*, and *Correct*, the[ir] manners," Livingston wrote in 1749. "It was Learning that . . . now distinguishes the true Gentleman," not the "vanity of Birth and Titles." Nine years later, the importance of education had not withered in Livingston's mind; far from it. It was essential to "making a figure in Life." And, he believed, enlightened workers meant enlightened voters, attuned to Livingston's ideological meritocracy and disdainful of the pretensions of the DeLanceys.[19]

Livingston also opposed the DeLanceys' tavern-going. He believed it exploited non-elites' political naivety, portraying them in a negative light because it impinged on their ability to make an informed decision if they voted. Livingston also argued that the DeLanceys' promotion of masculine civic virtue through sociability and tavern-going encouraged effeminacy. In taverns, Livingston wrote, "Conversation turns upon the most trifling Subjects" and patrons did not engage in polite political discussion. Instead, "a set of noisy Fops Bluster away the Evening in a Storm, others Smoke their Pipes with a senseless Stupidity, some, impertinently chat away whole Hours, with effeminate Observation[s]." This, in turn, inhibited the cultural development of New York City, opening "a Door . . . to all Social Misery: Slavery, Torture, Rapine, Violence, and all manner of Injustice." Livingston believed that alcohol-infused events would push New York City "into Licentiousness," where New Yorkers would be "lost, in a total Ignorance, of every thing Genteel and Manly." By 1769, his views had not changed. In Livingston's mind, through their cocktail of politics and alcohol, the DeLanceys' "forc'd civilities" "cajole[d] the freeholders and freemen, into a declaration in their favour [that was] contrary to their more deliberate sentiments." As such, they were "election-Jobbers," "Boasters," "supple Temporizers," and "flatterers." The DeLanceys were, Livingston believed, "proof of our degenerating from the virtues of our ancestors."[20]

When Governor Moore dissolved the assembly, then, the election gave the Livingstons an opportunity to rearticulate their belief in the importance of a deferential and meritocratic political society. They wanted to move the city away from the DeLanceys' opportunistic radicalism and toward their principled republicanism. After failing at the polls a year earlier, partly because of their opponents' use of print, they would not let their opponents control the news cycles this time, either. Through "The American Whig" and a range of other newspaper essays and broadsides, they adopted DeLanceyite techniques, disseminating printed propaganda and engaging in popular politics. Foremost in their rhetoric was religion. It was their "political Engine." William Livingston led his family's election campaign as he tried to show New Yorkers that the DeLanceys were pro-Anglican demagogues. They wanted to "erect an Episcopal Tyranny" and "force from the Dissenters the Tithes of their Estates."[21]

Other pro-Livingston essayists put forward similar arguments during the election campaign. Sir Isaac Foot, the author of a complementary series to Livingston's titled "A Kick for the Whipper," declared, "THE CHURCH shou'd *sink* and *drown,*" lest it "*immortalize[d]*" itself through the appointment of an American bishop. In another issue of "The American Whig," Livingston argued that Anglicans viewed Dissenters as a "horrible monster," "*a great red dragon having seven heads and ten horns,*" "*who have no natural right to any degree of civil or military power.*" It was thus Anglicans' goal to remove Dissenters within the colonies. In their place, they would establish "extensive bishoprics and metropolitan sees of the church." "All other denominations" would become "proselytes to the church of England."[22]

The Livingstons' essays also evaluated the DeLanceys' political integrity, arguing that their opponents were opportunists who had preyed upon New Yorkers during the 1768 campaign. They were "pretenders" who could never have "the character of sons of liberty." Instead, they used the Liberty Boys to encourage "the ruin and destruction of their country." They would "clamour against the laws destructive to civil liberty" and, if reelected, "gain a credit and power to rob us of what is infinitely dearer to us," religious liberties. Livingston criticized their tavern-going, too. Through their "tumultuous shoutings, displayings of colors, and other artifices," they "inspire[d] terror," cultivating fear in "every part of the town." In the end, Livingston wanted New York's Dissenters to believe that the DeLanceys would make them "*tributaries to the church.*"[23]

But Livingston's most potent piece during the election campaign was *REASONS For the present glorious combination of the dissenters in this city.* Published in a newspaper and as a broadside, *REASONS* was written in simple language that ordinary people would understand. Its focus was the history of New York. In eighteenth-century British America, history was a constant feature of colonists' lives. Taverns, coffeehouses, and courtrooms often had portraits of royal figures on their walls. Noteworthy dates were celebrated each year. When toasts were made, alongside the customary ones to members of the royal family, colonists often drank to other significant historical individuals, artefacts, or events. These historical images, celebrating colonists' liberties and shared heritage, became a perennial feature of their political cultures and often served as the primary means through which people understood their place within the British Empire—and the world.[24]

In *REASONS*, Livingston argued that New York's history from the late seventeenth century until the 1769 election defined by religious conflict between Anglicans and Dissenters, showing that Anglicans had attempted to proscribe Dissenters' religious liberties since the seventeenth century. By reference to the pro-Anglican governorship of Edward Hyde, third Earl of Clarendon, known widely as Lord Cornbury, Livingston articulated a viewpoint that if Anglicans were elected, they would behave as Cornbury had done, whereby all other religions would fall foul to Anglicanism and its adherents and supporters. Tantamount to political slavery, Livingstone encouraged New Yorkers to look toward the Livingstons. As he explained, "the episcopalians in this city, are preparing the way for the better reception of an American bishop, by filling our house of representatives with members of that denomination."[25]

It was an unrelenting attack on the place of Anglicanism within the province's religious framework. Livingston accused Anglicans of wanting to "more effectually rivet our chains" by appointing an American bishop. "With all his spiritual courts and tremendous powers," Livingston continued, they "aimed at securing the whole" of New York society under their control. They were willing to sacrifice other religious denominations to do so. Livingston used the past as a guide for the present to mobilize support, arguing that if the DeLanceys were elected, New Yorkers' liberties were under threat. Voters had to appreciate "the politics of the church" and realize that, because of their strong Anglican ties, the DeLanceys would work against the public good because they were associated with the church. There was no alternative, Livingston argued: "it is the politics of the church,—its domineering spirit,—its perpetual strides toward universal dominion,—its pride,—its power and its thirst of domination, a thirst not to be satiated but by our absolute destruction." New York City's Dissenters had to vote to defend their religious freedom. "Up therefore and be doing," Livingston wrote. "Your only strength consists in your union," adding that if the DeLanceys were elected, Anglicans would control "the three branches of our legislature," after which there was only one outcome: New Yorkers would become "tributaries to the church."[26]

Livingston's assaults on Anglicanism were well timed. The Presbyterian Church of New York City had attempted to obtain a charter of incorporation on four occasions between the 1720s and 1760s. Each attempt was rejected, partly because of Anglicans' opposition and subsequent interference. In Livingston's estimation, then, Anglicans had shown not only that they would never afford Dissenters the same legal rights as Anglicans but also that they would remove Dissenters as and when they saw fit.[27]

The Livingstons, however, were not solely reliant on the efforts of The American Whig. To complement their printed materials, they added "Election

Jobing" to their arsenal of political mobilization, engaging in popular politics to extend their electoral reach with hopes that it might bring more voters into their orbit. Thirty-two-year-old Princeton graduate Peter R. Livingston fought hard to secure his family's electoral success, telling a friend that he was "so immersed" in electioneering that he was campaigning "with all my might." They also used oratory to galvanize support. John Morin Scott was a gifted public speaker, and he often took to the streets to rally New Yorkers to the Livingstons' cause. In one "3 hour Harangue," as one DeLanceyite described, "he told the Mob, that the Church of England had fixed on a Design to extirpate all other Denominations of Christians & that unless they would all rise up like One Man & Stick close to him, they woud Soon have their Steeples puled down & their pulpitts & Pews burnt [in] the Streets." Unlike the DeLanceys' private gatherings, those the Livingstons held were open-air events, somewhat resembling a modern-day rally, during which they encouraged supporters to display their political sentiments. On the eve of the 1769 election, the Livingstons were "in high Spirits."

Alongside their open-air caucuses, they also proposed that political gatherings in taverns be banned. On January 19, three members of the Livingstons' ticket—John Morin Scott, Theodorus Van Wyck, and Peter Van Brugh Livingston—sent the DeLanceys six proposals to reconfigure the electoral campaign, the first of which spoke to the DeLanceys' use of taverns: "1. That no treating or open Houses shall be directly or indirectly made Use of by either Party, or their Friends or Agents, from this Time to the Closing of the Poll." They also wanted to prohibit party colors, slanderous propaganda, and political ballads and limit the number of associates who could be near the polling stations. They also proposed that railings should be used on election days, arguing that they facilitated "more easy Access of the Electors." To put it differently, the Livingstons were attempting to inhibit the DeLanceys' style of popular politics and their ability to mobilize support, even though they were using some DeLanceyite tactics themselves.[28]

DeLanceys

On the other side of the political fence, however, the DeLanceys were aware of what was going on, and they understood the potential negative impact the Livingstons' rhetoric could have on New Yorkers' political sentiments. After somewhat predictably rejecting the Livingstons' proposals for regulating political conduct, they launched a broad-based counter-campaign to show New Yorkers that they were principled reformers, not self-interested radicals. On

January 5, three days after the election was announced, they made it clear that they sought reelection with Philip Livingston, arguing that they merited New Yorkers' votes because they had shown their civic virtue, as assemblymen, over the preceding year. To gauge Livingston's interest, they dispatched his nephew, James Duane, to find out what he thought of the alliance. The DeLanceys felt it was almost crucial that their ticket include all the current assemblymen for New York City and County, including Livingston. Because they "made such an honourable Exit" when calling for intercolonial opposition to the Townshend Acts, one DeLancey broadside declared, the election gave New Yorkers "an Opportunity . . . *once more* . . . to elect none but Men of *approved* Integrity and Fortitude." The elected assemblymen, he continued, had "distinguished themselves" throughout the year because they had "zealously pursued the Instructions" New Yorkers gave them, following them "with Pleasure," and had firmly illustrated "their Atachment to the Interest of their Country." The New Yorker added, "They have done Credit to your Choice" in the 1768 election. Reelecting them, then, was the sensible, correct choice.[29]

Other New Yorkers made similar statements using similar language, and many were confident that those elected in 1768 would be returned. One boasted they "will again be unanimously elected." A newspaper reported that the populace indicated their approval with "three Huzza's." In another, a freeman delivered a vivid account of the assemblymen, noting that the assembly was dissolved due to their "true Noble and PATRIOTIC Spirit." "Every Member of the Community," he continued, "should applaud their Conduct, and give his Assent to their spirited Resolves, by voting for the Old Members." If they were not reelected, it would be "absurd and unseasonable." The DeLanceys and Philip Livingston had "distinguished themselves on this glorious Occasion, in an exemplary Manner." "Their Conduct," wrote another voter, "in every Instance has been unexceptionable." "You cannot fail to reelect them."[30]

But Philip Livingston made it clear that he did not want to be reelected in the current political climate. He believed New York City politics too partisan, telling New Yorkers he would only stand "if there was a Probability of a peaceable Election." Livingston likely realized this was almost impossible. He probably recognized that through his public withdrawal he was all but ensuring an even more partisan election. Livingston's behavior caught the DeLanceys by surprise. When they heard Livingston's statement, they "did every Thing in their Power" to persuade him to reconsider. The DeLanceys viewed Livingston's candidacy as an effective means to ensure their reelection. Together, they had the widespread support of New Yorkers. They argued that their joint candidacies would maintain "the Peace of the City," not least because it was "the general Voice of the Inhabitants" to reelect them. They were rebuffed.[31]

Livingston's reluctance to stand could have stifled the DeLanceys' election, but they adapted. They realized that his municipal experience was crucial in his election in 1768. Thus, they replaced him on their ticket with someone who was equally experienced and almost certainly as well regarded and well respected, John Cruger. A popular Dutch merchant with a receding hairline and a pointed nose, Cruger had held multiple civic positions during the 1750s and 1760s. As New York City's mayor during the French and Indian War, he clashed with the commander-in-chief of British forces in North America, John Campbell, fourth Earl of Loudoun, over the billeting of British troops in New York City, vigorously defending New Yorkers' rights. Cruger, who never married, was the city's mayor for a decade. He served in the Stamp Act Congress, in which he contributed to its Declaration of Rights and Grievances.[32]

Cruger's public service, as well as his focus on the public good, fitted well within the DeLanceys' political remit in 1769. Like them, he articulated a public image as a repository of virtue, a man who wanted to promote New Yorkers' "Union and Harmony." Cruger's reach also extended to the city's cartmen. During his tenure as mayor, he licensed over two hundred cartmen, giving them their livelihood. As the DeLanceys sought to secure the cartmen vote in 1768, they wanted to reaffirm it a year later. Coupled alongside this self-interest was Cruger's belief that he would "promote the Welfare and Interest" of New Yorkers. And his selection enabled the DeLanceys to circumvent any detrimental effects of Philip Livingston's decision not to stand, thereby becoming another public demonstration of their commitment to the public welfare and understanding of New York's political ecosystem.[33]

To their surprise, however, Philip Livingston's name soon appeared on election materials alongside those of John Morin Scott, Peter Van Brugh Livingston, and Theodorus Van Wyck. Van Brugh Livingston was one of Philip Livingston's three older brothers, and their lives closely mirrored one another's as they grew up. Both graduated from Yale—Peter in 1731 and Philip in 1737—after which they each became well-recognized and well-established merchants in New York City, both of whom were active in the fur and slave trades. Philip was among New York's leading slave traders, investing in at least fifteen slaving voyages throughout his career. Peter was based in Hanover Square and Philip on Duke Street (now Stone Street). In 1755 Van Brugh Livingston's firm, which he co-owned with his brother-in-law, William Alexander, Lord Stirling, was given a contract to supply provisions for British military expeditions to Crown Point and Niagara. In fulfilling the contract, Van Brugh Livingston had some assistance from his family, but he was largely charged with finding most of the goods to supply. The contract was short-lived, however, primarily due to the DeLanceys: James DeLancey Sr. replaced Van Brugh Livingston's firm with his brother's, prompting widespread dismay from the Livingston family, at least internally, as Van Brugh Livingston had to content himself with trading to the West Indies, North Carolina, and the frontier.[34]

Born in 1718 and a member of the Dutch Reformed Church on Nassau Street, Theodorus Van Wyck also had a history of public service. In the mid-1750s, he was assistant alderman, and a decade later he had graduated to become an alderman. In both positions he served in the ward in which he lived, the Dock Ward, which was one of the two most expensive wards within the city. And it was in the Dock Ward where he helped his sister, Magretta Van Wyck Schuyler, raise her three children following the death of her husband in the 1750s. In 1768 three of Van Wyck's relatives presented him with a twelve-inch silver salver to commemorate his "exemplary justice" as well as his "kindness."[35]

With Van Brugh Livingston and Van Wyck, as well as William Livingston's literary efforts, the Livingstons believed they had a good chance at capturing New Yorkers' votes, especially with Philip Livingston's name on the ticket (see figure 2.1). The DeLanceys, however, were furious at Livingston's behavior. They responded quickly with pointed newspaper essays and a broadside criticizing his behavior, in all of which they argued that Livingston had declared that he would not stand. In one essay, DeLancey supporters Isaac Sears and Isaac Corsa, an importer who co-owned a shop off Peck's Slip, alleged that they heard that a long-standing supporter of Philip Livingston had deserted him. In doing so they depicted him as a corrupt politician, one who turned his back on the public to stand with a faction. Sears and Corsa claimed a Livingston supporter believed he

FIGURE 2.1.   List of Livingston New York Assembly Election Candidates, 1769, Library of Congress

had behaved like "a snake in the grass." Livingston was deceitful, and his actions showed that he held traits that rendered him "very unfit for a Representative of this City." Other New Yorkers echoed these sentiments. John Jay wrote that Livingston had "played a Double Game," adding, "Appearances are ag^t. him." James Duane also commented on the affair, noting that Livingston's public move toward "the prespeterian party" damaged his popularity as he became complicit with the relentless religiosity of his faction's campaign.[36]

Not to be outdone, the DeLanceys also built upon the methods they used in the 1768 campaign. They published materials that advanced and trumpeted their political economy and criticized the Livingstons' track records. For instance, they attacked John Morin Scott as "The Man . . . who declared the Virginia Resolves to be little less than *Treason.*" In one essay, they argued that Scott's behavior during the Stamp Act crisis had attempted "to stifle the rising Flame of Patriotism," leaving New Yorkers "obnoxious to Beggary and Servitude." The Livingstons were not the "proper Persons" to be "Guardian[s] of our Rights and Liberties."[37]

The DeLanceys also continued their criticism of the city's lawyers, again arguing that they were not suited for civic service. According to *The Examiner*, the interests between lawyers and New Yorkers were "diametrically opposite." "Employment for the Lawyer," *The Examiner* wrote, "clogs and embarrasses Trade." It was a familiar theme for them and their readers. Lawyers would not advance the public good; merchants would. Unlike their opponents at the bar, they worked for "the Emolument of the Community." In another broadside, *The Querist* hit the same notes. Because New York was a trading city, its assemblymen should be trading men. Thus, it was not "right in a trading City to prefer a Man of Law to a Merchant." Furthermore, as they did in 1768, they printed essays in newspapers and issued them as broadsides. They also distributed materials that were the size of a playing card that used familiar names, one of which drew upon memorable characters from the literary works of Tobias Smollett who were familiar with the nautical world, "Jack Hatchway," from *The Adventures of Peregrine Pickle* (1751), and "Tom Bowling," from *The Adventures of Roderick Random* (1748). Both "Hatchway" and "Bowling" were referenced in 1768. A year later, as they did with almost all their election materials, the DeLanceys added nuance and intellectual sophistication to their arguments. They, like the New York voters they courted, were moving forward—and they were doing so together.[38]

A Contrast was the most virulent and sexual broadside the DeLanceys published. It was a piece of yellow journalism that was corrosive and hostile in tone. Defamation permeated its lines, as the DeLanceys hoped to spread gossip about the Livingstons throughout society. The scandalmongering broadside compared the characteristics of James Jauncey and John Morin Scott, depicting them as representing alternative political futures. The narrative in *A Contrast* was specific and sensationalist. They hoped it would make it impossible for the eighteenth-century man of virtue to elect Scott—and, by extension, the Livingstons—guaranteeing the DeLanceys' election. The broadside depicted Jauncey as a philanthropic man of virtue. He was someone who gave back to the community as much as he could and, by extension, so, too, did DeLancey, Walton, and Cruger. In contrast, Scott was depicted as effeminate, corrupt, and self-interested. So, too, were the Livingstons. Whereas Jauncey was "Modest, diffident, and inoffensive," Scott was "Impudent, assuming, and abusive." Scott, the DeLanceyite author wrote, "lives upon the Spoils of the Public," sought to "impoverish all those, by or *against* whom he has the Happiness to be employed." The DeLanceys also emphasized their masculine qualities in contrast to Scott's effeminacy, who, the author alleged, prostituted himself and participated in unnatural acts that were inhuman. Scott "puts MONEY into THE BOX . . . and dances with, and *kisses (filthy Beast!)* those of his own Sex." This gendered narrative effeminized Scott, suggesting he was possibly a homosexual and that his election would destabilize New Yorkers' virtuous principles. It would, the author argued, "ruin the Peace of the Community." James Jauncey, however, was "Of strong natural Parts," his behavior was "fostered and improved by Temperance and Sobriety," and his "CHARITIES have been more extensive than those . . . of any other Individual upon the Continent." Voters could not, the DeLanceyite urged, vote for an effeminate, "utterly bigoted" individual. To legitimize the importance of masculinity and virtue and to protect the public welfare, New Yorkers had to vote for them. If they did not, they would be sacrificing their economic self-sufficiency and undermining their manhood.[39]

They also used the broadside to distance themselves from factional disputes. In the vocabulary of republicanism, factionalism was unvirtuous. It was a threat to the health of the republic. Individuals who fell victim to party politics became a "slave to party." Denigrating an individual as factious was an astute means to criticize their republicanism and undermine their virtue. In the DeLanceys' case, by using masculine language that correlated them with nonpartisanship and promoted their roles as civic-minded individuals who would advance the public good, it reinforced their argument that they were the only ones who were fit to represent New Yorkers' interests. This rhetorical technique also enabled the DeLanceys to justify their own political position—that is, their partisanship—by arguing that their election would abolish factionalism in New York City. Jauncey was thus a man "Who is attached to no Party," but Scott had "nothing but Party Spirit to recommend him."[40]

The DeLanceys also countered the Livingstons' religious attacks. PHILO PATRÆ, which loosely translates from Latin as loving one's country, responded to the Livingstons' religiosity, addressing their allegation that the DeLanceys were servants of the Anglican Church. PHILO PATRÆ clarified that the DeLanceys were not all Anglicans and to suggest they were controlled was ridiculous. They were "Candidates of different Persuasions" and independent people who sought to represent New Yorkers. PHILO PATRÆ was correct—the DeLanceys' ticket was made up of two Anglicans (DeLancey and Walton), a Presbyterian (Jauncey), and a member of the Dutch Reformed Church (Cruger). More importantly, though, the broadside promoted the ecumenism of the DeLanceys' cause. The DeLancey candidates dissociated themselves from it, writing, "We can assure the publick, that it was done without our consent, knowledge, or approbation." The overtly religious nature of the broadside did not fit well within their political remit. They were aware that religion was divisive, and it could potentially inhibit their ability to mobilize support from across society—exactly what William Livingston was trying to do. The DeLanceys thus distanced themselves from religious topics, arguing that they had "no dislike to any person for his religious tenets," adding, they "entirely disapprove of such reflections on any denomination whatsoever." Pseudonymity protected the DeLanceys from any claims that they were behind the broadside. To be sure, they probably were; its contents adhered to their political message. PHILO PATRÆ's essay, though factual and useful for some of their base, might have fragmented their support. By disassociating themselves from it but not challenging its content, the DeLanceys showed themselves to be virtuous, nonpartisan assemblymen who, unlike their opponents, would cater for all New Yorkers, irrespective of their religion.[41]

PHILO PATRÆ's essay was not the only one that countered the Livingstons' propaganda, either. THE FREEHOLDER declared that it was irrelevant, arguing that the Livingstons were attempting to "revive old Occasions of Differences, and recal from Oblivion, unhappy Disputes, and long neglected Prejudices." According to THE FREEHOLDER, the Livingstons' tactics demonstrated that they were self-interested politicians. With their "groundless Jealousies," the Livingstons' election would "disturb the Quiet and Repose of" New York City. As another broadside argued, the Livingstons were attempting "divide & impera—Divide and rule." Instead of the DeLanceys, it was the Livingstons who were "Friends to arbitrary power."[42]

The secular and inclusive nature of the DeLanceys' propaganda became an important aspect of their campaign. Following their initial responses, other printed materials reinforced the argument that they were not running on potentially divisive principles. Take nationality, for example. The DeLanceys were aware that the selection of Cruger might appeal to the city's Germans and Dutch, and DeLancey's, Jauncey's, and Walton's candidacies might appeal to the city's Britons and colonial Americans. But they realized that the city was made up of more than Dutchmen, Britons, and colonial Americans. And the DeLanceys wanted their support. They released two German-language broadsides, which like their English-language materials, showed how their opponents did not, and could not, represent voters' needs. One warned New Yorkers of *"der Herr John Morin Scot"* (the Lord John Morin Scot) and *"Scots Partie."* The DeLancey authors, *"Zwey Hoch Teutsche"* (two High Germans), called for all Germans to discard religious discord and vote for the DeLanceys, asking them to give *"ihre Stimmen und Interesse bey der bevorstehenden Wahl, an die Herren James DeLancey, Jacob Walton, James Jauncey, und John Cruger"* (their vote and to give interest in the upcoming election, to Messrs. James DeLancey, Jacob Walton, James Jauncey, and John Cruger). Moreover, as a parting slight to John Morin Scott, who also released a German broadside that was badly spelled and poorly written, the DeLanceys alleged that Scott's illiterate laundryman must have written it. The second broadside directly endorsed Cruger's election.[43]

They also printed broadside ballads to mobilize support. In sixteenth- and seventeenth-century England, ballads were the cheapest form of printed literature. They were often set to well-known tunes to broaden their appeal. Distributed in marketplaces, taverns, and coffeehouses and stuck on windows, ballads were sung indoors and outdoors. They augmented the development of an aural culture that allowed citizens to come together and develop an inclusive, reciprocal culture that transcended social and ethnic distinctions, enabling people to invent and revise new social and political identities.[44]

In New York City, the DeLanceys understood the role ballads could play in the city's election, an urban center that was famous for its narrow streets. In 1744, Dr. Alexander Hamilton wrote, "the streets in general are but narrow, and not Regularly disposed." Given that the city had, to use Hamilton's phrase, "more of an urban appearance than Philadelphia," the compactness of its streets facilitated close interaction between its inhabitants. The DeLanceys used this along with their ballads to broadcast their message. In *A SONG, To the Tune of Hearts of Oak*, the DeLanceys encouraged New Yorkers to "join Heart and Hand" and vote for them. "Heart of Oak" was written by David Garrick about British successes in the French and Indian War, and it was no doubt known by New Yorkers. Using the song did not require any further effort by the DeLanceys; New Yorkers knew the tune, associating former victories with the DeLanceys. By avoiding the *"unblushing Chieftan—perverter of Laws,"* John Morin Scott, they were to turn to the DeLanceys: *"good* CRUGER," Jauncey, who *"gave to the Poor," "brave* DELANCEY," and Jacob Walton, whose

"Prudence attracts." These men, the author alleged, were "the *Patriots!* whose Virtue is *tri'd*" and, if they were elected, "With *Heads* ever *clear*, and with *Hearts* ever *true!*" they would pursue and protect "*Liberty's Welfare.*" The DeLanceys also printed a broadside ballad in German that hit many of the same notes: "Wachet auf ihr Teutsche Brueder" (awake their German brothers) and "Last uas fuer die Herren stimmen; / Die uns hier beschrieben seyn; / Meister *Cruger, DeLancey*: / Meister *Walton* und *Jaunsey*" (Let us agree for the Gentleman; / Their Being described to us here / Master Cruger, DeLancey: / Champion Walton and Jauncey).[45]

They tailored their discourse to New York's diverse population. It did not matter who they were; what did matter was what they were. Voting for the DeLanceys became a means to legitimate New Yorkers' belief in virtue and advancing the public welfare, which, in turn, would allow New York City to become an independent, stable society. New Yorkers thus had to vote for the DeLanceys. As an independent OLD BURGHER argued, there needed to be "a general Union of us all in seconding and supporting the Defenders of our Rights and Privileges." If voters looked elsewhere, they would lose "the only Means we have left to prevent the Collar of Slavery being thrown over our Heads." Voters must, the author declared, look to "THE THREE PATRIOTS, who have heretofore done Honour to your Choice, and the Man who has not been Ashamed NOR AFRAID to join the Sons of Freedom."[46]

With all the politicking, the 1769 election was "the Strongest Election ever known" in New York City. Polling stations were open between 23 and 27 January. When the voting ended, the results were much more favorable to the DeLanceys than they were a year earlier. James DeLancey received 936 votes; Jacob Walton, 931; John Cruger, 882; and James Jauncey received 877. The Livingstons were defeated. Philip Livingston received 666 votes; Scott, 646; Van Brugh Livingston, 515; and Van Wyck received 518. The Livingstons' campaign had failed. Their "offensive" publications, wrote John Watts, were too hostile and divisive. They were put aside by "the more substantial people." Other statements followed. According to one commentator, the Livingstons' attempts to "put the Contest on a broader Basis" hurt them at the polls, while the DeLanceys' behavior and rhetoric delineated sources of division, cultivating a sense of community between the like-minded white male voters. As Peter R. Livingston lamented, the DeLanceys had "too much power over our Common people."[47]

The entire ticket was elected, and the Livingstons lost support across all levels of society. Though the number of voters decreased from between 1,924 and 1,960 to 1,515, the DeLanceys increased their proportion of New Yorkers' votes by 6 percent, from 3,431 votes in 1768 to 3,625 in 1769. The Livingstons' proportion of the vote, on the other hand, decreased by 4 percent, from 2,447 to 2,361 votes. The shift was caused by non-elites moving toward the DeLanceys, or by not voting for the Livingstons. There were also at least 738 non-elite voters, more than 60 percent of whom voted for the DeLanceys. James DeLancey and Jacob Walton both received 63 percent of their votes; John Cruger, 62 percent; and James Jauncey, 61 percent. All the DeLancey candidates who stood in 1768 increased their proportion of the non-elite vote in 1769, with Jauncey increasing his by about 9 percent (52.6 to 61 percent). In contrast, Philip Livingston's support from non-elite voters decreased from 66 to 46 percent. The most popular candidate in 1768, he was the fifth-placed candidate a year later, likely because of his initial reluctance to stand. Furthermore, although John Morin Scott endured fierce criticism, his non-elite vote increased, albeit by an insignificant amount (1 percent). The other two Livingston candidates, Peter Van Brugh Livingston and Theodorus Van Wyck, received 38 and 37 percent of non-elite votes, respectively. The DeLanceys also captured some of the cartmen's vote. James DeLancey received 51 percent of the cartmen's vote. Cruger, Walton, and Jauncey received 37 percent, the same proportion as Livingston and Scott.[48]

The DeLanceys had expanded the ways in which non-elites could take part in their city's political culture, inundating public spaces with eighteenth-century conceptions of manliness and civic virtue, to create an informal civic-minded political association with broad-based support. They also rearticulated their commitment to be the people's representatives within the assembly. On January 21, 1769, Moore wrote to Hillsborough, explaining that James DeLancey had refused a place on the Royal Council. Shocked, Moore told Hillsborough that DeLancey "could not accept the appointment," adding that DeLancey did not give a reason for rejecting it. Moore was embarrassed. A position on the council was by royal appointment only, and being offered a place on it was usually considered fait accompli. But being an assemblyman, particularly in New York, offered more legislative power than in the Royal Council as well as a greater ability to interact with and represent ordinary New Yorkers. Councilors did not have to build connections with people or control their political future, but assemblymen did, and in the process of being elected, the DeLanceys created an informal political association that contained a large proportion of future loyalists. They increased their future loyalist votes in 1769 by 44 percent: 850 future loyalist votes were cast for them in 1768, and 1,220 were cast in 1769. The Livingstons' future loyalist votes fell, too, by 29 percent. The DeLanceys' rhetoric about securing economic independence spoke to the interests that mattered to these men. It was not religious discord that dominated their lives in

1769. Amid nonimportation and economic stagnation, it was maintaining their stability and their autonomy, and their electoral message offered them a means to achieve it.[49]

To correlate these individuals' voting behavior with their future loyalism underplays their life experiences between 1769 and 1775. Just because the DeLanceys became loyalists did not mean they or their voters were automatically destined for that path. Voting in 1769 (and 1768) occurred within different contexts. It was not inevitable. The colonies were not at war with Britain. But New Yorkers were, in one sense, fighting with and for one another. Many future loyalists associated with the DeLanceys, and through their association, they cultivated a group consciousness that encouraged partisanship within New York. For many of the DeLanceys' supporters, their association was their political coming-of-age. Before the elections, they had neither been involved in the city's political arena nor engaged with its elites, but their association, whether it was in a tavern or coffeehouse or on the streets, cultivated a sense of camaraderie that gave them a shared place within the city's urban political framework. They were a tightly knit unit, ready to support each other.

At no time was the DeLanceys and their supporters' political coming-of-age clearer than when the election results were announced. The streets were lined with thousands of onlookers. According to one report, it was the largest crowd ever assembled in the city's history. Music was played and political colors were worn. As the elected candidates moved down Broadway, they were greeted with *"loud Huzzas, and every other Demonstration of Joy, that could be shewn."* It was *"one of the finest and most agreeable Sights ever seen in this City."* The procession was a visual affirmation of the DeLanceys in almost every sense, legitimizing their rhetoric, ideas, and behavior. They were the dominant group within the assembly, commanding support from assemblymen from the counties of Dutchess, Kings, Orange, Queens, Richmond, Suffolk, and Westchester. The Livingstons, left with support in Ulster and Albany Counties, Cortlandt, Livingston, and Rensselaerswyck Manors, and the Township of Schenectady, were a much-depleted political voice. As one DeLancey partisan wrote, it was "a complete victory." They added that the election was "a lasting monument to the power of the mercantile interest," that is, their political economy.[50]

CHAPTER 3

The Minions of Tyranny and Despotism

The DeLanceys' Assembly

New Yorkers hoped that the DeLanceys' election would bring stability to the province. The public, citywide celebrations that occurred after the results were announced indicated as much. It was a patriotic, collective display of civic unity, one that also displayed their local identity and commitment to the DeLanceys' ideas and interests. One New Yorker stated that the DeLanceys had "remarkably distinguished themselves" by "supporting the Rights and Liberties of their Country." The DeLanceys, the writer continued, deserved universal support. But in a city as partisan as New York, they likely recognized that was impossible. For one, Gov. Sir Henry Moore did not share their supporters' sentiment. He was loosely aligned with the Livingstons, and even employed a member of their family as his private secretary— Philip Peter Livingston, Peter Van Brugh's twenty-nine-year-old son.[1]

Moore had witnessed their rise, and he tried to keep himself somewhat separated from their methods and politics. No longer. Moore could not afford to ignore or distance himself from them. For the first time in his tenure, the assembly convened with a DeLancey majority on April 4, 1769. A few months earlier, Moore had celebrated his fifty-sixth birthday. Born on Jamaica, he was educated at Eton College and Universiteit Leiden (Leiden University), the oldest university in the Netherlands, and he had a long history of colonial service. During the 1750s and 1760s, he served in various offices in Jamaica, including its governorship, during which time he successfully managed a difficult legislature, imposed martial law, and put down a slave rebellion. In that rebellion, known as Tacky's Revolt, enslaved people attempted to establish an African kingdom in Jamaica. It was a bloody affair. Over one hundred slaves were executed, and five hundred were transported to Central America for the murder of at least sixty whites. One slave was burned to death over a slow fire. Others were gibbeted for up to three days, after which they were burned alive. The revolt shocked the British imperial system. It shocked Moore, too. He was almost killed on three separate occasions. But he oversaw it all, ensuring white Jamaicans were united in their efforts to quell the revolt. For his service, he was made a baronet in January 1764, and the following year he was appointed governor of New York. Moore recognized the difficulties New York presented, particularly about its legislature, but he did not think it beyond his talents—Livingston, DeLancey, or whoever, he could handle them. Moore's greatest skill, however, lay in his ability to recognize the sense of the city. His perception of what New Yorkers wanted, and needed, played an important role during his tenure. But he never lost sight of his role as the king's representative in one of Britain's colonies.[2]

Nine days after the assembly convened, Moore wrote to Wills Hill, first Earl of Hillsborough, conveying his disappointment in the recent election results. Moore told him that he felt the DeLanceys were becoming too powerful—in the assembly, Royal Council, and Common Council—and stated that he would use "every means in my power to break through" their rise. He thought they were "courting popularity." The DeLanceys, Moore believed, were "tenacious" and were imposing their "turbulent spirits" to influence the other assemblymen. After James DeLancey refused a place on the Royal Council, Moore's thoughts about and reaction to his "extraordinary" behavior pushed him further toward the Livingstons. Henry White, a Welsh merchant who supported the DeLanceys and lived in a stately residence between the Fly Market and coffeehouse, was appointed in DeLancey's place. The governor's "point of acquaintance and private friendship" with the Livingstons sharpened his view of the DeLanceys. He soon believed they were a threat to his authority. Moore might have been right, too. Many New Yorkers viewed the assembly as the most powerful political organ in the province—more powerful than the Royal Council or even the governor. As Colden wrote, "men of the Best Capacity & greatest Interest of the Country choose to be of the assembly where they perceive they can make a better figure & advance their own Interest more effectually."[3]

They put Colden's description into action when the assembly convened. Throughout the spring and summer, they advanced their political economy, upsetting Moore and challenging the remnants of the legislative and political power of the Livingston faction. With major Livingston figures out of office, the DeLanceys believed they would be able to fulfill their earned political advantage for their constituents.

But the Livingstons were not going to sit back and let them legislate. Nor would they permit the DeLanceys to have a peaceful session. First, they worked the institutional system to ensure that they would not be without their most powerful political voice. Peter R. Livingston was elected to represent the family manor, but he let his uncle, Philip Livingston, take his seat. The elder Livingston still carried enough political clout that his family believed he could influence how other assemblymen voted.[4]

The Livingstons' move did not go unnoticed. The DeLanceys recognized Philip Livingston's continued popular appeal, even though he was handily defeated in the 1769 election. More importantly, though, the DeLanceys recognized that Livingston was not the chosen candidate for Livingston Manor. Nor could he be. He lived in New York City. Livingston Manor was not his home, which, in the DeLanceys' mind, he would represent people he seldom encountered, if ever. The Livingstons also used a similar tactic with Lewis Morris, who was elected to represent the Borough of Westchester. But he, too, did not live there. Morris's election mobilized his opponents, who recognized the problem of his election. Written by the borough's voting and nonvoting population, they called for John DeLancey to be returned, who loudly complained of Morris's "undue Election." How could Westchester's inhabitants be represented by someone who did not live among them? How could he know and advance their interests? Some of Morris's supporters petitioned to counter any legislative action, but he was ousted on April 20.

A couple of weeks earlier, John Thomas, a twenty-seven-year veteran assemblyman for Westchester County, applied the same principle to Livingston's seat and called for his removal. After Thomas's resolution, the assemblymen debated whether they should move forward to discuss Livingston's eligibility. In a partisan vote, the DeLanceys voted to consider it; the Livingstons voted in favor of dismissing it. Then, George Clinton, an assemblyman for Ulster County, unsuccessfully motioned that Thomas should pay for everything involved with testing Livingston's eligibility. The faction that bore Philip Livingston's family name had not earned the right to set the agenda, but they would not let their leader be expelled without a fight. On May 12, a petition from five prominent Livingston partisans and twenty-two Livingston Manor freeholders was presented to the assembly. In the petition of April 21, the Livingston supporters cited "party Spirit" as the cause of the dispute, alleging that the DeLanceys were inspired by factionalism instead of advancing the colony's political structure. The Livingstons' petition was not enough, though, and they could not muster enough support to keep their man in the assembly. In a vote that, like all the others, went along factional lines, Livingston, like Morris, was ousted. What likely annoyed the Livingstons more was that prior to Livingston's expulsion, it was determined on April 26 that nonresident freeholders could vote in elections, meaning that voters did not have to live where they cast their votes. Gov. Sir Henry Moore reluctantly signed a bill into law ensuring that assemblymen had to live in the area they were elected to represent, and on May 13, he issued new election writs for Livingston Manor. The following month, Moore credited the DeLanceys' actions to their close association with the people and the Sons of Liberty.[5]

The Livingstons were no doubt frustrated at proceedings, but the DeLanceys' behavior was not surprising. By bringing in a residency qualification, they were advocating for New Yorkers' interests and democratizing the assembly. In this instance, they alleged neither Livingston nor Morris could represent their constituents because they did not interact with or know them. The Livingstons remained committed to the deferential style of politics that had defined their political economy for more than a generation. The DeLanceys, however, reinforced their inclusivity, particularly when it is considered that they were hoping to improve representation on their opponent's landed stronghold.

They were not finished democratizing the political system, either. They believed that royally appointed supreme court judges should not be able to concurrently serve as assemblymen, something that Robert Livingston, the judge, had done as a Dutchess County assemblyman for seven years. The DeLanceys advocated for a separation of powers between the colony's judicial and legislative branches, whereby neither an assemblyman nor a judge could, or should, influence the other's conduct. On May 17, without much debate, serving on the supreme court and in the assembly was prohibited, bringing the colony in line with Britain as well as advancing political and judicial practice in the colony. So, when the judge was elected assemblyman for Livingston Manor as Philip Livingston's replacement, the assembly disqualified his election and removed him. (The judge was elected again and again; he was turned away again and again, until he eventually gave up in 1774, and he died in 1775.)[6]

The DeLanceys' actions during the 1769 assembly sessions were not purely inspired by political idealism. Although they believed they were advancing the colony's political and legislative structures, most of the people who fell victim to their legislation were their opponents—and they no doubt realized what they were doing and recognized how it would help them politically. The DeLanceys were no doubt influenced and guided by their political economy, but since they had the right to legislate, they did not shy away from advancing their partisan interests, either.[7]

The Lieutenant Governor

The assembly disbanded for its customary summer break in May. In September, less than one year into the DeLanceys' tenure as assemblymen, Gov. Sir Henry Moore died after a sixteen-day illness. According to one report, his death caught many by surprise, throwing the city "into the deepest Distress." Philip Peter Livingston, his secretary, noted "general grief diffused thro' all ranks of Men," and newspapers printed eulogies that celebrated Moore's governorship, depicting him as a model of republican virtue. One stated that the province "never had a Gov. whose death was more *deeply* and *deservedly* lamented," the colony never had someone as devoted to "gratifying *public Wish*[es], and advancing the *common Weal.*"[8]

Moore was a popular governor. One person later reflected that Moore was among "the first characters on the continent." For the most part, New Yorkers liked him, too. Their views of Moore were partly influenced by his behavior during the Stamp Act crisis. When he arrived in New York City, on November 13, 1765, he dismantled Fort George's defenses and quickly acquiesced to New Yorkers' demands, the most notable of which was allowing stamped papers to be stored in City Hall. Moreover, between late 1765 and early 1766, when opposition to the act was high and prior to its repeal, Moore embraced homespun goods, a symbol of colonists' resistance to the legislation, and indirectly supported their opposition. Moore, Colden decried, "Put on a Homespun Coat, the Badge of the Faction & suffered the Mob to insult the officers of Government without interposing." Other people offered similar comments. David Clarkson, a merchant who lived near Fort George, wrote that when Moore arrived in the city, he brought "Universal Joy" to the city's inhabitants. Shortly after, Moore had secured "peace & Quietness, & a Happy Unanimity."[9]

Moore's passing was, then, felt throughout New York. He was possibly the most popular governor the colony ever had. Anne Grant, a Scottish immigrant, remarked that Moore had turned Fort George into "the seat of a little court," one that was largely populated by members of the Livingston faction. His funeral thus attracted many of the city's leading figures—political, financial, religious, military. "All of the Clergy in Town of every Denomination" led the procession, followed by four of the city's doctors, after which came Moore's casket. Among the ten pallbearers were Oliver DeLancey, William Smith Jr., Henry White, and John Cruger. A lengthy train of people followed: Gen. Thomas Gage, commander-in-chief of the British Army in North America; various ship's captains; land commissioners; judges of New York's supreme court; a judge of the admiralty; and the city's treasurer, who walked beside the DeLanceyite assemblymen for the city: James DeLancey, James Jauncey, and Jacob Walton. They held a prominent spot within the procession, enabling thousands of New Yorkers to see them pay their respects. After them followed an array of city officials—the mayor, aldermen, the sheriff, the coroner, and so forth—after which came customs' officers and the surveyor general. The last group were the governor's "intimate acquaintances & such principal Gentlemen in Town." As such, it included many Livingstons, family and faction: Peter Van Brugh Livingston, Philip Livingston, William Livingston, Peter R. Livingston, Philip Peter Livingston, and John Morin Scott, among others. Philip Livingston, the most prominent in the city, had been marked to walk behind William Alexander, Lord Stirling, but his name was struck through, indicating that even though he was given the opportunity to walk with Stirling, he likely chose to walk with his partisans. Together, they wanted to commemorate their ally instead of walking near or being seen with the DeLanceys. As the Livingstons looked forward, and as the DeLanceys looked backward, both groups likely realized that Moore's death created a power vacuum within the city's political structure, one that would be temporarily filled by his predecessor.[10]

In New York, upon the in-office death of a governor, the position temporarily fell to the most senior politician in the colony until a new person was appointed by the monarch. In this instance, the most senior politician was Cadwallader Colden, who had served the colony since the early 1720s. On the long, difficult journey from his estate in Spring Hill in Flushing, Long Island (now Mount Hebron Cemetery), the elderly Scotsman likely reflected on what lay ahead. Colden, who had a long, large nose and translucent white hair, had lived at Spring Hill since at least the summer of 1762. He probably enjoyed his separation from the city. It was his children who encouraged him to move away from Manhattan. Spring Hill, a mansion on a 120-acre estate with high ceilings and open, spacious rooms, was a place where he could focus on science and philosophy, two lifelong interests that brought him some international recognition. But as is well known, Colden returned to Manhattan in 1765 to assume the governorship temporarily, during which time he became possibly the most disliked colonial official in the history of New York. A few years later, Colden was not oblivious to his public perception. The Stamp Act riots of 1765 were never far from his memory, or his pen, either, and he recognized how difficult it was to oversee the colony's government. Other people also thought New York was particularly difficult to govern. Francis Bernard, governor of Massachusetts, who openly sought a gubernatorial appointment to New York, noted that New York's governor was routinely opposed by "Men of Rank and Ability." "It appears to me," Bernard added in a comparison of the governments of Massachusetts and New York, "the Administration of N York is more difficult than that of" Massachusetts. Colden, if he read this letter, would agree. This time, however, when he returned as acting governor, he was well motivated to ensure that the events of 1765 did not happen again.[11]

Colden settled into his temporary role quickly. He was an ambitious politician, forever hoping to serve George III as best and for as long as he could. But he knew he could not aspire to hold the governorship permanently if New Yorkers publicly and consistently opposed him. And so, not long after he arrived in the city, Colden touched upon an issue that he felt would show his goodwill toward New Yorkers: the repeal of the Townshend Acts. He recognized that its repeal would almost certainly elicit positive responses from both New York's politicians and its people.

Since November 1, 1768, the city enforced an effective nonimportation agreement. After it was introduced, it was reported in the press that the value of imports into the colony fell from £482,000 to £74,000 in a year, a drop of nearly 85 percent, most of which was felt in New York City, the colony's commercial center. New York's losses were unmatched across colonial British America. Pennsylvania's imports fell by 54 percent; New England's fell by 51 percent. Colonies that implemented a nonimportation agreement experienced considerable losses, but none were as severe as New York's.[12]

Indeed, without British imports the city and its inhabitants struggled to make ends meet. When Colden received news from Hillsborough that Parliament was going to propose that the Townshend Acts be repealed, he trusted the news would offer New Yorkers a glimmer of hope. Colden would help New Yorkers secure economic independence; he would help them return to their daily lives. "There is now the greatest Probability," Colden noted November 21, 1769, "that the late Duties imposed by the Authority of Parliament . . . will be taken off in the ensuing Session." The assembly welcomed the news. John Cruger, who was unanimously elected as its speaker, reported, "The Information your Honour has given us of the great Probability that the late Duties . . . will be taken off [in] the ensuing Session, affords us the most sincere Pleasure." Colden knew that the repeal would be well supported. He perhaps even dared to believe that his governorship would be uneventful. It might be successful; perhaps it would lead to a permanent appointment. The repeal of the Townshend Acts would help, but so, too, would a positive relationship with his assemblymen, prior to which Colden had to show them that his interests matched theirs. The elderly Scotsman was no doubt aware of what he had to do: he had to show New York's assemblymen, as well as its inhabitants, that he wanted to protect and indeed advance the public good. These tasks, he alleged, were "The great Desire" of his temporary governorship. He told the assembly that he sought to "to promote, by every Means . . . the Welfare and Happiness of the People of this Province." He also tried to disassociate himself from the assembly's infighting. To show that he was independent of the assembly's factionalism, he relieved Philip Peter Livingston of his secretarial duties and replaced him with his son, David. Colden's attempts to distance himself from the assembly's factionalism was not going to be easy, though. His relationship with the DeLanceys was poor, and it had been for decades.[13]

During the 1740s, Colden served as Gov. George Clinton's chief advisor, and Colden and James DeLancey Sr., then the colony's chief justice, clashed frequently. The former believed that DeLancey was forever mobilizing his partisans not only against him but against the governor, as well. Clinton was a largely incompetent colonial official, inexperienced and unable to fully grapple with the colony's politics. But with Colden as his chief adviser, Clinton, at least in official correspondence, appeared more suited than he was. He regularly offered advice and drafted most of Clinton's letters, giving him a considerable amount of editorial influence. In one such letter to British prime minister Henry Pelham in 1746, Clinton described how DeLancey's faction had fashioned "a design to take the powers of the Government," adding, "This Assembly in all their proceedings treated the person of the Governor with such contempt of his authority & such disrespect to the noble family where he had his birth that must be of most pernicious example." In a report on the state of the colony upon his departure, Clinton reported that despite his and Colden's best efforts, DeLancey was more powerful than he was.[14]

In 1769 Colden felt he had to repair his relationship with the DeLancey faction. He thus approached the assembly session with an open mind and reconciliatory attitude. To improve the environment, he also appointed DeLanceyite New Yorkers to other offices, including George Duncan Ludlow to the colony's supreme court, James DeLancey (James DeLancey Jr.'s cousin) as sheriff of Westchester County, and Thomas Jones as recorder of New York City. Colden also removed people from other positions. He removed Albany County's sheriff, Harmanus Schuyler, for publicly supporting nonimportation. For their part, the DeLanceys also sought a reconciliation. They appreciated that if they were on good or even amenable terms with Colden, he was less likely to dissolve the assembly. Colden's approach, as well as his appointments, had the necessary effect. When Cruger responded to Colden's address, he stated that his cooperation would be "highly Satisfactory to the Representatives of the People." Colden also received support from the DeLancey-led Royal Council. John Watts, the council's speaker, stated that Colden's "great Desire . . . to promote the Welfare of the People of this Province cannot but be accepted." With Colden's support, the colony's politicians would do everything to make him "conformable to the general inclination of the people."[15]

From William Smith Jr.'s as well as the Livingstons' perspectives, however, the Colden–DeLancey reconciliation was not a positive development. Not only did it threaten the Livingstons' dwindling political clout, but it also gave the DeLanceys another opportunity to assert themselves as the most powerful group both inside and outside the assembly. With Moore gone, they filled the political vacuum. Smith viewed the reconciliation as nothing but a "Contract," something that neither of them might enjoy but that they would both fulfill to pursue their respective objectives. It "was advantageous to both Parties," Smith wrote. The DeLanceys, Smith continued, sought to gain favor with the British crown, even if they had to associate with "a most unpopular" colonial official. Smith also commented on Colden replacing Philip Peter Livingston as his secretary: he was "incompatible" because of his surname and Colden's newfound association with the DeLanceys.[16]

Smith's partisanship clouded his judgment. Writing in his "Historical Memoirs," Smith was grieving over Moore's death and venting about what he viewed were unfortunate political developments. He did not support the DeLanceys' or Colden's politics. He did not like their personalities, either. What likely made matters worse for Smith was that the DeLanceys were still gaining ground. Their popularity was higher than ever. Reconciling with Colden was in their self-interest, too. They did not want Colden to call an election. By repairing their relationship, they sought to reinforce their place within the assembly. It is unlikely that they sought a royal appointment, particularly when James DeLancey Jr. rejected Moore's offer earlier in the year. Instead, their association with Colden was another illustration of their commitment to advancing the public good as well as their political economy when their popular support was, arguably, at its highest point. Indeed, Smith wrote, the DeLanceys "possessed as uncontroulab[l]e an Influence over the People as a Scotch Lord over his Clan." They were inspiring loyalism to their political cause, which was based on securing New York City's commercial stability and growth, and some New Yorkers believed the developments would result in a positive outcome. David Clarkson wrote, "americans in Generall are Boying themselves up wth Hopes that y[e] promises made by Lord Hillsborough"—namely, the repeal of the Townshend Acts.[17]

The Assembly

There was, perhaps, another reason for Colden's reconciliatory attitude toward the DeLanceys. Prior to his death, Moore had been discussing the colony's finances, something that Colden knew he could neither avoid nor postpone.

Since 1763, New York City's economy had been stagnating, with more and more New Yorkers falling into poverty. What's more, during George Grenville's two-year premiership he sought to address what he viewed as a financial and political crisis, one that was largely caused by Britain's imperial ventures, particularly the French and Indian War. Grenville and his like-minded ministers implemented an extractive form of British imperialism that reoriented the empire. Most of their changes affected colonists' economic freedom. As well as the American Revenue Act, which made it harder to import molasses from the Caribbean, Parliament passed the Currency Act of 1764, making paper money a rare commodity. It also made it almost impossible to borrow money, a consequence of which was merchants' increasing inability to pay their debts. As government contracts were fulfilled without renewal, specie went back to Britain and per capita imports fell. With Grenvillean austerity, New Yorkers, as well as those across the colonies, found it harder to pay their debts. People were forced to sell their property, and more paupers appeared on the narrow streets. As one New Yorker noted, "Everything is tumbling down."[18]

Their message of economic liberty was, then, an effective way to mobilize support. Their ideas about stabilizing and developing the city's economy presented New Yorkers with a political economy they could support. To be sure, the 1768 nonimportation agreement worsened the city's economic status. But prior to Moore's death, he had been working with the assembly to relieve New Yorkers' economic worries by securing the issuance of £120,000 in paper currency. Doing so, Moore and the DeLanceys hoped, would not only ease the shortage of paper money and remove citizens from their "present impoverished State," but, more important for the DeLanceys, it offered them a means to advance the public welfare by ensuring that the city's economy had an adequate circulating medium of exchange. This, in turn, advanced their political economy, which was based on growing the economy. The paper money bill would, they alleged, raise New Yorkers from "an *aggrieved* and *distressed*" position, lifting them from "the wretched state" they endured in their daily lives. James DeLancey was appointed to a committee to draft the bill, giving him a clear opportunity to articulate his political economy. Despite his personal feelings toward DeLancey, Moore agreed with the committee's bill. Soon thereafter, he sent it across the Atlantic, telling the Hillsborough and the Board of Trade it would placate numerous "Clamours raised in the Country." Moore also asked for New York's exemption from the Currency Act. In response, the Board of Trade stipulated that New York could issue the money if it included a suspending clause in the bill that subjected it to the approval of George III. Unfortunately, however, Moore died two days after he submitted the proposed bill. The issue thus fell upon Colden's shoulders. Like his predecessor, Colden supported the bill, anticipating that it would ensure that New Yorkers would remain "in good Humour." As he told Hillsborough, he hoped it might make his administration "easy." As we have seen, however, this was not the case.[19]

After the assembly convened on November 21, the monetary issue dominated much of the assemblymen's discussions. But it was not the only issue they tackled. The DeLanceys continued to advance their political economy and democratize the political process in New York. Specifically, they sought to increase non-elites' participation. On December 6, they moved that the assembly pass two resolutions, the first of which concerned the opening of a public viewing gallery above the assembly chamber. The assemblymen agreed to the measure. The resolution blended institutional politics with its popular iteration. Those who were "out of doors" were "indoors." With the viewing gallery, New Yorkers could watch as their assemblymen pursued—or did not pursue—their interests, helping to mediate differences between the politicians and the people they represented. At least for a moment, those in the gallery could feel a sense of parity with their representatives as they each walked into City Hall before moving into their respective spaces. The DeLanceys, however, appreciated the potential difficulties a viewing gallery could present. To overcome any issues that could cause disorder, they also regulated how spectators had to behave. For instance, if someone wanted to watch assembly proceedings, they were to "behave orderly and decently, and make no noise or talk together as to disturb the House." They were also prohibited from talking to assemblymen during debates or when the speaker was sitting. Nor were they allowed to cover their faces or heads when entering the gallery. Finally, it was stipulated, "No spectator shall be admitted within the Doors until the Speaker has taken the Chair." The viewing gallery was both a measure to open the assembly to non-elites—and thereby increase New Yorkers' political participation—and a partisan tool to reinforce associationism. As their supporters watched on, spectators would, in theory, grow closer to their representatives.[20]

The second bill the DeLanceys proposed was a means to reinforce how the spectators perceived their assemblymen. It concerned how assemblymen behaved and engaged with one another while in the chamber, not to expedite their work but to preserve decorum before the gallery. Equally important, it was a means through which the assembly, as an institution, could control its members, something that was a well-established practice in the House of Commons. In this instance, as when they determined the speaker's position vis-à-vis the viewing gallery, the DeLanceyite assemblymen were regulating procedure. When an assemblyman was about to propose a motion or make a speech, they were to "stand up in his Place uncovered" and address the assembly through the speaker. If two individuals rose at the same time, the speaker was to determine who rose first. The new regulations sought to remove the problems of character politics in the political process, at least officially. The DeLanceys also introduced one further resolution, prohibiting assemblymen from "mention[ing] the Name of any other Member" when they had the floor. Finally, when an assemblyman proposed a question, the other assemblymen were given one opportunity to respond. All this placed greater demand on assemblymen's rhetorical skills. In the process, it also reinvigorated the performative aspect of New York City politics and brought the assembly closer to the House of Commons, its parallel institution in Britain.[21]

At no time in New York City history was the art of public speaking more important. Political voices could appear, be heard, and be understood across society. The language of public political debate had changed, too. Words dictated how politicians were perceived and the role(s) they held within society. Political rhetoric was constructed with great care to ensure it appealed across the political and social spectrums of New York society, accounting for diversity as well as interest. If an assemblyman moved too far, he risked losing valuable support, even his seat. *"An Episcopalian"* summarized politicians' position by offering New Yorkers advice on how to engage with them. They argued that if assemblymen were perceived as not advancing the public good, the people had "an undoubted Right" to voice their concerns. "Every Man whose *all* depends upon the public Welfare, is as much interested in it, as the first Nobleman," they went on, "all have an equal Right to declare their Sentiments and to have them regarded." Politicians had to be aware of not only what they were saying but also how they were performing.[22]

The assembly's gallery was indicative of how New York City's political arena was becoming occupied by non-elites, not only elites. Assemblymen not only had to deliver more powerful and relevant content in their speeches, but now, because New Yorkers were above watching, they also had to consider the way their rhetoric was delivered. New Yorkers could—and indeed would—monitor their assemblymen. As one New Yorker explained, the assembly chamber was "on the first Floor of the City hall." When assemblymen entered and took their seats, they "occupi[ed] . . . about two thirds of the Room." There was not much space. It was intimate. It was tight. Assemblymen were almost on top of each other, which could be good or bad, depending on their performance.[23]

With support from assemblymen across the colony, the DeLanceys' regulation of politicians' conduct was not without self-interest. Even with their legislative majority, changing how their opponents could behave removed any possibility that they could be harassed, mocked, insulted. Political debates could not descend into shouting matches, either—something that the DeLanceys were concerned about after the Livingstons' comprehensive defeat in the 1769 election. They were right to be concerned. Peter R. Livingston was almost certain that if the Livingstons launched animated attacks on the DeLanceys, it would mobilize enough support to secure "another Dissolution," and another round of elections. But this was no longer possible, at least in the chamber. Not only had the DeLanceys removed Philip Livingston and Lewis Morris from the assembly and stopped Robert R. Livingston from serving, but they had also codified how assemblymen could behave and ensured that their partisans could watch them articulate their political economy, as well as their masculine sense of honor, almost unchallenged.[24]

One of the assembly's first debates with an open viewing gallery touched upon a sensitive political issue. Its members had to discuss New York's requirements for provisioning and settling British soldiers under the terms of the Quartering Act of 1765, which stipulated that colonies had to provide shelter British troops and provide them with day-to-day goods. It became a piece of legislation that colonists were particularly averse to, even if they had, at times, appreciated the need for a military presence prior to 1763. After the end of the French and Indian War, however, stationing troops became a constant issue for the assembly, in large part because the city was the headquarters of the British Army in North America. Manhattan was the nucleus of British military operations. This intensified soldier-citizen relations, especially after the passage of the Quartering Act. In 1766 one New Yorker wrote that inhabitants were "very uneasy" with the presence of British troops. There was not "any visible Occasion for them," the New Yorker added, noting that the city sometimes looked like "a Military or conquer'd Town." Others felt the same. In their eyes, soldiers were not needed. Some New Yorkers were also resentful toward British soldiers who deserted or were discharged and chose to remain in the city. Many took low-paying jobs that would ordinarily be held by New Yorkers, depriving them of much-needed and sought-after jobs.[25]

New Yorkers had other interactions with the British Army. Due to the considerable military presence in the colonies, the British Army restructured its supply and payment structure. Prior to 1767 the commander-in-chief, then Maj. Gen. Thomas Gage, handled such issues by drawing bills of exchange upon the paymaster general. This approach was slow and tedious. Equally important, it hurt the exchange rate. Thus in 1767 the commissioners of the British Treasury entered a contract with John Drummond, a banker, and the deputy governor of the Bank of England, Sir Samuel Fludyer. Acting as Messrs. Fludyer & Drummond, they delivered monies from the Treasury for remittance in the colonies, which were then converted into Spanish and Portuguese coin and paid over to the deputy paymasters. The Crown received all interest and profits, and paid charges. Due to the large amounts of interaction, Messrs. Fludyer & Drummond appointed agents to help manage and coordinate work-flow and to ensure on-the-ground updates and requests. As a central outpost of the British Empire, New York was a base.

By the end of 1768, the agents in Manhattan for Messrs. Fludyer & Drummond were DeLanceyites John Watts and Charles McEvers. (Henry White, another DeLanceyite, offered his services, too, upon the death of Watts's and McEvers's predecessor, James McEvers, Charles's brother.) Previously, Oliver DeLancey had served as an agent, working with his brother-in-law Moses Franks. A few years later, Watts and McEvers were responsible for New York and Nova Scotia, including Louisburg, and they maintained regular commu-nications with the bank. The positions involved considerable sums of money, with one estimate that the agents were collectively remitted above £200,000 from the British Treasury. Fludyer died in January 1768, but he was succeeded by Thomas Harley, son of the third Earl of Oxford and Mortimer, who worked closed with Henry Drummond after John Drummond's health worsened.[26]

The Drummonds' and their associates' contract for army remittances re-mained in place until the Revolutionary War. McEvers and Watts were each paid a fee to provide a weekly ration to those British troops stationed in Man-hattan and beyond. Much of the produce they ordered came from Ireland, but true to their DeLanceyite nature, Messrs. Watts and McEvers, as they were known, afforded many of their associates the benefits linked to providing the British Army with supplies. On January 27, 1769, for instance, they drew a bill on Messrs. Fludyer and Drummond for £100 on behalf of Peter Goelet. Goe-let, a DeLancey voter in 1769, was a Dutch merchant with business in Europe. He sold clothes, hats, and various kinds of metal, as well as "a great variety of other articles," including musical instruments and accessories, in a Hanover Square store. It is perhaps unsurprising that he provided items for the British Army given the diversity of his supplies, but what is, perhaps, curious is that Watts and McEvers drew the bill on January 27—the day the polls closed in the assembly election. Equally important, in an April 25, 1770, letter, Watts and McEvers told their superiors in Britain that Goelet would not accept pay-ment "untill the American Revenue Acts are Repeal'd." A true DeLanceyite, Goelet prioritized consumption and the advancement of a developmental economy in Manhattan.[27]

Other like-minded New Yorkers profited, too, including merchant Uriah Hendricks and Elias Desbrosses, whom Watts and McEvers drew bills for £50 and £300, respectively, on March 21. More DeLanceyites had bills drawn throughout 1769, including Abraham Brinckerhoff, Walter and Thomas Buchanan, John Wetherhead, Hugh and Alexander Wallace, James Jauncey, Evert Bancker Jr., Robert Cheeseman, Thomas Pearsall, Isaac Sears, and Joseph Allicocke. Overall, the total for DeLanceyites who had bills drawn on their behalf was comfortably over £8,000 in 1769 alone. DeLanceyite opponents also got in on the action: Philip Schuyler had a bill drawn on his behalf for £600 in late 1768 and Philip Livingston had a £375 bill drawn in the summer of 1769. But DeLanceyites far outnumbered their opponents, primarily because it reinforced their political economic vision for Manhattan, and the colony.[28]

For these New Yorkers, maintaining a military presence was a boon the economy. Manhattan was the military headquarters for the British Army in North America, and they understood that, in a way, they lived in a military society, and British soldiers were their consumers. New Yorkers were able to furnish the soldiers with supplies, catering to their needs, and with the money they earned, they could reinvest it into the city's local marketplace, as well as the economy of the Atlantic world. The year 1769 was a difficult one for all New Yorkers, and some thought the short- and long-term stability the British Army offered would help lift the city, and the colony, upward. The Quartering Act, though far from popular, would ensure soldiers' wages would be spent in New York's coffeehouses, taverns, and shops while the city's artisans and tradesmen provided for the army. This political economic vision of New York's place within the empire prioritized the city's development through the creation of colonial consumers and, with extra cash at hand, opened other marketplaces that would, in the long run, reduce debt and promote growth within the British Empire. Equally important, though, these DeLanceyites effectively wove themselves into the fabric of the British imperial infrastructure, creating a commercial network of like-minded New Yorkers that was based on a shared political economic vision for the city and, by extension, the colony. But not all New Yorkers shared the DeLanceys' developmental vision.[29]

Assembly debates on the Quartering Act were scheduled to take place on December 15, 1769. It would have been a debate that many New Yorkers would have been keen to observe from the viewing gallery. That debate, perhaps more than any other, might have provided them with real insight into their politicians' motivations and behavior. But when they came to the assembly chamber in City Hall, they were not allowed in. No spectators were. The doors were locked. As the crowd gathered, people no doubt realized something was amiss. Speaker John Cruger was absent, and due to the DeLanceys' recently incorporated procedural rules, no spectators were permitted inside the viewing gallery. As everyone stood outside, the assemblymen privately began their discussions of the Quartering Act. "Several hours" later, Cruger appeared, after which the doors were unlocked. Everyone was allowed in. Not long after they took their seats, eager to catch up with what they had missed, the proceedings were read. "Debates ran high," one newspaper later reported.[30]

The DeLanceys, with their political economy in mind, associated the quartering of British troops with an opportunity to secure the issuance of £120,000 in paper currency. They moved that both bills—one to quarter the troops, another to issue the money—should be passed concurrently. In their view, securing a fresh injection of paper money superseded possible complaints. John Cruger reported to Gov. Sir Henry Moore on May 20, 1769, the bill was "so evidently calculated to promote the Interest and increase the Trade of *Great-Britain*, and relieve the Distresses of the Inhabitants of the Colony." Cruger presented the double-bill as an effective way to secure the economic independence of New Yorkers as well as the colonial government, something that it had struggled with over recent months. For instance, the British Army's provisions suppliers, Evert Bancker and Gerard Bancker, were owed nearly £700 in the fall of 1769. A few months later they were owed over £1,000 and were only getting by thanks to their politically like-minded creditors, among them Oliver DeLancey and David Johnson. New Yorkers, including the Banckers, were on the cusp of further economic issues. The DeLanceys wanted to alleviate their issues with the paper currency bill, whereby they insisted that New Yorkers' economic liberty was reliant on the city embracing and advocating for a political economy that was based on growth. They believed that if more money were invested into the city's economy, it would encourage increased rates of production and consumption. With more people working, more money would be in their pockets, after which New Yorkers would reinvest into the city economy, acquiring property, which, in turn, would promote the city's economic independence and security. As "PHILANDER" argued a year earlier, "For a man without care without employment must become a burden to himself." "Industry & attention to business really sweeten life," "PHILANDER" continued, adding that working New Yorkers would be "more necessary and beneficial both to themselves and to society." "By a well regulated industry, they become sober and temperate in their enjoyments; steady in their pursuit, and thoughtful and active in life." "To *society*," they went on, "because the same spirit of industry multiplies the comforts of life; promotes the mutual conveniences of mankind; and makes us happy in a reciprocal interchange of useful offices."[31]

But the assemblymen were divided, at least on paper. The Livingstons stifled the DeLanceys' plans. Colden noted that the Livingstons' opposition developed out of their feelings toward the DeLanceys; they opposed them because they did not want their opponents to "gain to[o] much Credit." That is, they were concerned that the DeLanceys would mobilize further support and thereby diminish their own. Although the Livingstons probably supported the funding of British troops—most of the assemblymen did—because "they have not the Lead," they opposed the DeLanceys' measures. Hence, when DeLanceyite John DeNoyelles moved that £2,000 be granted to the troops out of the £120,000 of paper bills, twelve Livingstonite members voted against it. Eleven DeLancey votes were for the measure, and they were defeated. Then, William Nicoll, another DeLancey associate, moved that 50 percent of the funds be taken from the public treasury to billet troops. The remaining £1,000, Nicoll proposed, would come from the interest on paper currency after the bill was put into law. It was clear that the DeLanceys would not release funds for billeting troops without the issue of paper currency. It was central to their political econ-omy. When Nicoll's compromise proposal was voted on, the division was re-versed on equally partisan lines: twelve for, eleven against. The assembly's divisions were not based on ideological differences. They were based on parti-sanship. But for the men sitting in the viewing gallery, only one difference mat-tered: the DeLanceys supported the Quartering Act.[32]

Before he died, Moore noted that the "great objection" of New York City's inhabitants to the Quartering Act was "having any Troops at all." New Yorkers' views had not changed by 1769, but it appeared as if their popularly elected of-ficials' views had. From New Yorkers' perspectives, the DeLanceys voluntarily proposed that British troops should be issued funds, making their central elec-tion claim—that they represented and would protect the public welfare—seem disingenuous, if not entirely false. To make matters more severe, the under-handed methods they used made them appear corrupt and self-serving, the antithesis of civic-minded politicians. It appeared as if their political economy was dictated by their interests instead of New Yorkers' interests. As one colo-nist alleged, the DeLanceys moved "as private Interest dictated," adding that they were galvanized by "The Sweets of Dominion & the Gratification of pri-vate Pique." They were "intoxicated with the present State of their Interest."[33]

Opposition to the DeLanceys mobilized quickly. This was a reaction, in part, to their election campaigns, during which they had invested considerable financial and moral capital in developing and cultivating popular support that was predicated upon the belief that they were civic-minded politicians who would advance the public welfare. But their behavior over the Quartering Act seemed to contradict this, indicating their apparent abandonment of popular politics. By locking New Yorkers out of the assembly and funding the pres-ence of British troops, it appeared as if they were not civic minded after all. By sanctioning an act that was "ever dangerous to a free state," they appeared to be self-interested, corrupt politicians who were using the legislature to advance their place within the British Empire. Keeping New Yorkers out of the viewing gallery challenged their political right to participate in the colony's legislative process. The DeLanceys' motives for supporting the Quartering Act did not matter to them; it was the legislative and political consequences of merely supporting the act that did. For the DeLanceys, they failed to recognize that ideas and interests do not always complement one another. Their actions had gone against the identity they had carefully constructed, violating the political culture they had shaped over the past two years. According to one analysis, the DeLanceys had become "Enemies to the Public, in their open Attempts."[34]

News spread quickly of the DeLanceys' actions. Printed in the London *Middlesex Journal* in early 1770, a letter writer from New York alleged to a British correspondent that the DeLanceys' "infamous behaviour" had "forfeited the confidence of their constituents." It was, they added, *"Butenean policy"* at its best, and they went on to allege that the DeLanceys' actions were motivated almost entirely by their Anglo-American interests.[35]

But the DeLanceys neither betrayed New Yorkers by addressing the issues the Quartering Act presented nor showed that they were self-interested, imperialist politicians who did not care what the popular will was at that moment in time. In advancing their political economy, they believed they were adhering to the people's wishes. A little over a month before, Isaac Sears and other DeLanceyites, including Miles Sherbrooke, John Harris Cruger, Theophylact Bache, Isaac Low, Edward Laight, and Jacob Walton, among others, signed a "Private Association" of November 12, 1769, advocating for their "common Rights." At this time, the Sons of Liberty remained united with the DeLanceys. In fact, Sears and the other DeLancey supporters agreed to form a secret "Society" to protect Manhattan's and New York's interests and enforce the nonimportation agreement.[36]

Soon thereafter, John Cruger and James Jauncey consulted with Isaac Sears about the Quartering Act issue. Sears told them that New Yorkers would support the assembly's addressing of the Quartering Act if it came with "a Money-Bill." Otherwise, they could not support it. The DeLanceys followed this course of action, but it was a colossal miscalculation. In merely a few hours, their focus on financial stability presented them as holding imperial ambitions, not local ones. Their commitment to advancing the public good had not abated, but in this instance their actions showed that they had not accurately captured the sense of the city's non-elites. The reality of political power in New York in the late 1760s, as it had been for generations, likely indicated to them that they could simply hold steady and non-elites' criticisms and concerns would fissure, lessen, and eventually disappear. The compromise Sears proposed—attaching one piece of hated legislation to a much-needed one—

would, they thought, appeal to the utilitarianism of the city. For many, their identities were, as one historian as written, "provincial and metropolitan." They were both New Yorkers and Britons. Partly because James DeLancey was educated in Britain and served in the British Army, he maintained comparatively strong connections to people in Britain. For DeLancey, as for many of his supporters, their loyalty to New York and Britain went together. They lived in an Anglo-American world, and they believed the relationship could and ultimately should work.

But their political rise in 1760s Manhattan was driven by and dependent on their inclusion of non-elites in the political economic process, and their focus on financial stability was a form of economic reductionism. Their mistake challenged their political ascendancy, as some New Yorkers saw them as somewhat Manichean. One person confronted them head on, Alexander McDougall.[37]

The Scotsman

Alexander McDougall went to the assembly "almost daily" between November 22 and December 15. Clearly, he appreciated the assembly's viewing gallery. McDougall was born in 1731 in the Parish of Kildalton on the island of Islay, Scotland. McDougall's family immigrated to New York when he was nine years old. By the 1760s he was a successful merchant, having earned an estimated £7,000 as a privateer during the French and Indian War. His family left the Scottish Inner Hebrides for a better life, one that provided better economic opportunities beyond arable farming and small rural villages like Lagavulin and Kilarow, as well as parishes like Kildalton. McDougall had broad shoulders, a high forehead, a small mouth, and a pointed nose. Given his roots, he spoke with a thick Scottish accent. He was also a committed Presbyterian. Earlier in 1769, he was a founding member of the Society of Dissenters, where he worked and socialized with the likes of Peter Van Brugh Livingston, William Livingston, and John Morin Scott, three of the most prominent and outspoken anti-DeLanceyites in the city.[38]

When McDougall visited the assembly, he wanted to see what his assemblymen did, how they behaved, how they represented and advanced his interests. After all, he was invested in its economic success. On December 15, McDougall was among the people who were locked out of the assembly, and when he learned of the DeLanceys' actions, he emerged as their fiercest critic. A day later, after the assembly granted £2,000 to British troops, James Parker printed a broadside by McDougall, who wrote under the penname "A Son of Liberty" and sought to bring the assembly's proceedings into the public eye.

The pseudonymous broadside was entitled *To the Betrayed Inhabitants of New-York*, and it was a critical attack on the DeLanceys and an outright attempt to mobilize New Yorkers against them. The thirty-seven-year-old McDougall argued that if New Yorkers did not move against the DeLanceys, they would be made "minions to tyranny and despotism." While Britain's MPs were "minions of tyranny and despotism," the DeLanceys had "trampled on the liberties of the people." By "taking money out of our pockets without our consent" and consenting to the Quartering Act, McDougall went on, the DeLanceys were also consenting to the Townshend Acts. Instead of promoting New Yorkers' economic independence, with Colden they were working against New Yorkers' constitutional liberties. The DeLanceys were using the troops as a means of self-protection. McDougall also argued that the "coalition" between Colden and the DeLanceys indicated why the DeLanceys had sanctioned the quartering of British troops. They were not there "to protect" New Yorkers, McDougall argued. Instead, they were there to "enslave" them, "to secure to them the sovereign lordship" of New York. They had betrayed "the common cause of liberty," and by joining with Colden the DeLanceys had "left no stone unturned to prevent a dissolution." In other words, the DeLanceys had seized power and they sought to keep it. Instead of working for the good of the people, the DeLanceys sought to maintain their positions. McDougall argued that it was of the highest priority to them—and so he asked, "Is this a state to be rested in, when our all is at a stake?" "No, my countrymen, rouse!"[39]

To the Betrayed Inhabitants, written by a politically insignificant Scotsman who was once a milkman, was among the most important and influential documents that was written during the American Revolutionary era. It contributed to the redefinition of Manhattan's political culture and reoriented its political landscape, largely because it was accessible and well circulated. Indeed, *To the Betrayed Inhabitants*, like other documents written later, was written in accessible language, ensuring that McDougall's ideas and his arguments could be understood by elites and non-elites, rich and poor. Equally important, though, it was "distributed thro' the Town." James Parker employed teenage boys to post it around Manhattan in each of its wards. To offer an extra layer of anonymity, Parker also gave his post-boys detailed instructions about posting the broadside across the city. Parker was aware of the broadside's contents. He did not want to be identified as its printer. He instructed the boys, who carried the broadsides in a wooden box, to lean against a wall and pause for a moment, relaxed. Then, they were to place the box on the ground, after which they were to open it, take out a broadside, and paste it onto a wall or tree. Once *To the Betrayed Inhabitants* was securely pasted, they were instructed to begin the process over again at a new spot. It was a slow process, one that required an awareness of who was around them. But given that Parker's printing office was on Beaver Street, Mc-Dougall's broadside could easily have been taken to at least three nearby taverns, four marketplaces, and various coffeehouses and religious institutions.[40]

However long it took to circulate all the broadsides, Parker's employees did their job. *To the Betrayed Inhabitants* sharpened non-elites' partisanship into distinct pro- and anti-DeLancey groups. Those against the DeLanceys alleged that they were not protecting the public welfare, that they were instead supplanting New Yorkers' liberties to advance their own personal interest. It did not take long for New Yorkers to respond, either.

On December 18, two days after the publication of *To the Betrayed Inhabitants*, some fourteen hundred people assembled at the city commons in an area known as the Fields. Located at the northern edge of the city, the Fields were located near the popular Chatham Street water pump, where Broadway split into roads that went to Greenwich Village and the Bowery. With its wide, open spaces, the Fields was a popular spot for open-air meetings, militia musters, and celebrations, historic and political. There, New Yorkers gathered to show their opposition to their assembly's recognition of the Quartering Act. The crowd, echoing McDougall's ideas, argued that the DeLanceys had acted against "the common Cause of Liberty." It was at this moment that the DeLanceys' long-standing supporters, the Sons of Liberty and its leaders, Isaac Sears and John Lamb, deserted them. Despite what Sears had earlier told the DeLanceys, they could not support the assembly's proceedings. Now they were actively campaigning against them. Indeed, during the meeting Lamb's skills as a political mobilizer emerged as he asked the crowd, "Whether they approved of the Vote of the House of Assembly, for granting the Money to support the Troops." According to one report, of the fourteen hundred in attendance, only five or six approved, after which Lamb asked if New Yorkers were against funding troops at all. Several people indicated that they were against such a measure, but it was not unanimous. Most New Yorkers were against the way the assembly had discussed the Quartering Act, but they were not all against the DeLanceys' motives for addressing it. For McDougall, Lamb, Sears, and their supporters, however, this was not an option—funding a military presence was against the public welfare, and it all but ensured New York's de facto acceptance of the Townshend Acts. They were pursuing "the glorious Cause of Liberty," Sears later said, adding that he was convinced that McDougall's actions were for the public good. Having associated with the DeLanceys throughout 1768 and most of 1769, Sears admitted that, at one time, he thought McDougall was "a rotten-hearted fellow." By the end of the year, he was firmly with McDougall.[41]

Equally important, though, McDougall did not just mobilize ordinary New Yorkers. He also mobilized some members of the Livingstons, linking the elite group to people whom the DeLanceys had courted in 1768 and 1769. Most notably, William Livingston and John Morin Scott aligned themselves with Mc-Dougall. But it was the Scotsman, rather than the elite lawyers, who was leading. Philip Livingston's eventual unification with his family's political association severely weakened their ability to mobilize support. And given that he was arguably the group's most significant public official, his stumbling political display hurt the Livingstons dearly. McDougall offered them a lifeline, a means to regain support, and they were with him.[42]

And they had to be. The Livingstons' behavior in 1768 and 1769, and before, pushed people away from them. On various occasions between the fall of 1765 and winter of 1769, they adopted and defended positions that many believe ran against the public good. After the DeLanceys routed them in the 1769 election, moreover, some members distanced themselves from political life. Philip Livingston, for instance, considered relocating to Dutchess County. (William Livingston departed New York for New Jersey in 1772.) By supporting Alexander McDougall, they retained some relevance in Manhattan's popular political sphere.[43]

McDougall's opposition to the DeLanceys presented New Yorkers with a competing political economy. A radical Whig, he believed they supported the Townshend Acts and the Quartering Act, which, in turn, indicated their support of an extractive British Empire—one designed so they could reinforce—or possibly even build upon—their already-powerful position within the city's and the colony's political framework. Like many other radicals, he vehemently opposed Parliament's reorientation of the British imperial state. McDougall, like many others in different colonies, believed government should be continuously monitored and checked to make sure it was not working against people's or society's freedoms or liberties. The British constitution was thus designed to protect its citizens from arbitrary government, monarchical or parliamentary, and when government or its representatives worked against the people, they should act. Equally important, McDougall believed the colonies contributed a suitable financial amount to Britain. They were paying their way, stimulating economic growth in Britain that, in turn, stimulated economic growth in the colonies. As such, McDougall rejected the Grenvellian approach to reorient the British imperial framework. These beliefs, which McDougall and his like-minded associates shared, were fundamental to his social and political understanding of and engagement with his world. And these beliefs influenced whom he interacted with and where he went.[44]

There were profound ideological differences between McDougall and the DeLanceys. Both were Whigs and supported republicanism, but they held competing interpretations of New York's place within the British Empire. The

DeLanceys, as we have seen, embraced the economic advantages the empire presented. It reinforced their political economy and their ideological belief in commercial republicanism. McDougall's interpretation of the DeLanceys' actions, however, was based largely their supposed threats to New Yorkers' political liberty. To McDougall, the DeLanceys and Colden were abusing the authority New Yorkers had vested in them. But it was not a zero-sum game for McDougall, either. He understood and no doubt appreciated New Yorkers' economic aspirations. After all, he was a merchant. In another broadside, released shortly after *To the Betrayed Inhabitants*, "A Son of Liberty" alleged that because of the DeLanceys' double-dealing with Colden about the Quartering Act, New Yorkers would disproportionately contribute to the costs of keeping the British Army in colonial America. The DeLanceys' argument about the paper currency bill, then, was disingenuous, since New Yorkers would forever have to fund a military presence they did not want. The author of this broadside was almost certainly McDougall.[45]

On December 19, three days after the broadside's publication and a day after the meeting at the Fields, the assembly moved against the author of *To the Betrayed Inhabitants* and, by extension, its supporters. John DeLancey moved that it be classified "an infamous and scandalous Libel." A majority in the assembly agreed, and it was resolved that the broadside was "calculated to inflame the Minds of the good People of this Colony, against their Representatives in General Assembly." The DeLanceys interpreted McDougall's broadside as a threat to the stability of the assembly and their legitimacy in it. They also recognized that the broadside threatened their popularity within the city. Indeed, because the broadside questioned the DeLanceys' civic-mindedness, McDougall had created opportunities for new political groups to emerge in New York City in opposition to the DeLanceys. The assembly moved to identify and imprison the author of *To the Betrayed Inhabitants* for denigrating its DeLanceyite members and the royal governor. To widen efforts to catch "A Son of Liberty" and involve ordinary New Yorkers in the process, Colden offered £100 for information pertaining to the broadside's authorship. A manhunt began for McDougall.[46]

But during the assembly's search, the issues presented by the British Army intensified. The behavior of British soldiers billeted in the city exacerbated tensions between them and the inhabitants, partly because the soldiers were often drunk. On January 13, 1770, a few weeks into the assembly's search, forty soldiers from the Sixteenth Regiment of Foot decided that they wanted to make a political statement by destroying or at least damaging the city's liberty pole. New York's liberty pole was first erected in May 1766 after the repeal of the Stamp Act. The first of its kind in the colonies, atop its mast was an inscription that read "George 3rd, Pitt—and Liberty." A flag with the cross of St. George was added later, as well as a gilded weathervane that was inscribed "LIBERTY" and a cap representing liberty, an important symbol of freedom from slavery in early America and among the first of its kind in the colonies. British troops who were stationed in New York City opposed the symbolism of the pole, thinking it was a beacon of disloyalty and sedition. On August 10, 1766, the newly stationed the Twenty-Eighth Regiment of Foot cut down the liberty pole. Enraged, New Yorkers erected a new one the following day, sparking clashes with British troops during which two civilians were wounded. One month later, the same regiment cut down the new liberty pole, only for another replacement to be erected soon thereafter. This process— troops cutting down the pole and inhabitants erecting a new one—kept happening until March 19, 1767, when New Yorkers erected a pole with a base encased in a sturdy foundation of iron, stone, and earth. This was the pole that the Sixteenth Regiment of Foot crept toward in 1770.[47]

The soldiers recognized that they were both the cause and the target of New Yorkers' angst. But whereas New Yorkers viewed the soldiers as the problem, the soldiers thought people like McDougall were. Such reciprocal hostility bred resentment, and some of the soldiers wanted some measure of retribution. They also wanted to reclaim the city's public spaces. They sought to reassert their control over the Fields, which was not only where the liberty pole stood but also where the soldiers were billeted in a large barracks. The upper barracks, as they were known, was the second largest structure in the city, and it was filled with young, highly trained, and disgruntled British soldiers who believed that the New Yorkers who erected and defended the liberty poles were articulating a kind of social and cultural separation—or independence—from Britain by defining the city's spaces as their own.[48]

On the evening of the 13th, a group of soldiers who had been billeted in an empty house nearby crept up to the pole and tried to pull it down. Together, they pushed. Together, they pulled. But it would not move. This iteration of the pole, they soon realized, was reinforced. It could not be pulled down. To overcome its foundation, then, the tired British soldiers covered the base with gunpowder. This was noisy business, to be sure. The soldiers, who were probably drunk, were loud, and they caught the attention of one New Yorker who was walking down Broadway to Abraham Montayne's tavern. He saw and almost certainly heard what the soldiers were doing—and as soon as he entered the tavern, raised the alarm. Well-lubricated tavern-goers spilled out of the tavern, calling "Fire" to attract more attention and mobilize bystanders to their cause. As they ran toward the pole, the soldiers saw them coming, prompting a confrontation. As tempers flared and harsh words were no doubt exchanged, the soldiers moved first. They stormed Montayne's tavern, barging through its doors with their swords and bayonets drawn. They "destroy[ed] every thing they could," assaulted a waiter, and destroyed "Eighty-four Panes of Glass, two Lamps and two Bowls." Montayne, almost an innocent bystander, was left a hefty bill. More importantly, though, the liberty pole remained standing. The soldiers had failed, but they soon determined to return the next night, and this time, they were better prepared. They hid near the pole and posted guards on street corners to make sure they would not get caught. This time, after sawing the pole's supports and its base and planting gunpowder, they succeeded in blowing up the liberty pole, after which they dumped fifty-eight one-foot pieces in front of Montayne's tavern.[49]

The behavior of the soldiers at Montayne's tavern on January 13 intensified citywide concerns about their presence. "The Town has been greatly disturbed," wrote William Smith Jr. The soldiers' behavior also moved people away from the DeLanceys, who were criticized through their association with the soldiers and likely lost support. Montayne's tavern was a popular drinking spot for the city's cartmen, who often hitched their wagons and carts outside. As they saw the soldiers' destruction, the connection to the DeLanceys was obvious. In the aftermath of the destruction of the liberty pole, there were several published essays that criticized the troops' presence, indirectly criticizing the DeLanceys in the process. For instance, on January 17, 1770, "the Inhabitants of the City" announced that the soldiers' behavior offered "incontestable Proof that they are not only Enemies to the Peace and good order of the City but that they manifest a Temper devoted to destroy the least Monument raised to shew the Laudible Spirit of Liberty." "We are all in confusion," wrote another inhabitant, because the soldiers "cut and blowed up the Liberty pole." "What will be the end of this?" the inhabitant soliloquized. "God only knows." At another meeting, seventy-nine New Yorkers passed a series of resolutions about the presence of British troops. They argued that the soldiers were in New York "to enslave us." Another New Yorker echoed these sentiments, declaring that the troops were New Yorkers' "Enemies Mortal Enemies." They threatened the public good. Consequently, they resolved not to use troops for any form of labor. They also stipulated that troops were not allowed to walk the streets at night with arms unless they were on sentry duty. Another essay compared the soldiers' wives and children to "Whores and Bastards." John Lamb also took advantage of local concerns, writing in a broadside that called for New Yorkers to employ "his Neighbor" instead of off-duty soldiers.[50]

Time did not ease the situation, either. The troops fought back with their own broadside, in which they described the Sons of Liberty as the "real enemies to society." The troops argued that colonists were "ungrateful" for the protection they brought, adding that New Yorkers' attachment to the liberty pole was unnatural. It was "a piece of wood." Three soldiers who were tasked with posting the broadsides were caught by Isaac Sears and other Sons of Liberty. After a brief scuffle, in which Sears defended himself with a ram's horn, the Sons of Liberty marched the soldiers to Mayor Whitehead Hicks, whose home at the corner of Queen and Wall Streets had been littered with the soldiers' broadside earlier in the day. The soldiers were held briefly, but twenty soldiers from the lower barracks intervened, armed with cutlasses and bayonets, and demanded their release. Hicks backed down, ordering the soldiers to return to their barracks. As they went toward Golden Hill, a former wheat field at the top of John Street, they were joined with a reinforcement of British regulars. The date was January 19, 1770.

The Battle of Golden Hill was the first clash between British troops and colonists, and it preceded the Boston Massacre by six weeks. Led by Isaac Sears, New Yorkers armed with "clubs and sticks" confronted more than a dozen soldiers. It was a violent, chaotic affair. Francis Field, a Quaker who was standing in his doorway watching the altercation, severely injured his cheek. Three other New Yorkers were wounded, one of whom was stabbed with a bayonet. Worse, a seaman was killed, prompting a comment that if British officers had not intervened, the soldiers would have "drove them over the docks." It was, as Colden described, "a very dangerous affair." A similar confrontation happened the following night. On Nassau Street, a large group of seamen clashed with soldiers in another riot. This time, Hicks and city aldermen intervened.[51]

In February 1770, the Sixteenth Regiment, which had been based in New York since 1767, was shipped to Pensacola in West Florida. British officials hoped their removal would placate tensions in the city. Gage also tightly controlled those regiments that remained in the city, isolating them from the city's public places to improve relations. Despite one regiment moving south, their symbolic destruction of the liberty pole, the continued presence of other regiments, and the tensions that they brought remained. Moreover, the assembly's decision to fund billeted troops had not been reversed, crystallizing popular opposition to the DeLanceys. As Rev. Charles Inglis told Sir William Johnson, "Party Spirit ranges still with great Violence." "Our good Friends, the Whigs will neither be quiet themselves, nor suffer others to live in Peace."[52]

Alexander McDougall and his supporters used the destruction of the liberty pole to reinforce their newfound political association. Public symbols were important arbiters of sentiment in colonial America. They reinforced shared feelings by validating connections between like-minded individuals, giving them a place within the political framework and a visual representation of their political ideas. On January 30, 1770, five Liberty Boys, including McDougall and Sears, petitioned Mayor Whitehead Hicks for a new liberty pole. A few days later, Hicks conveyed the letter to the city's Common Council. The five Liberty Boys argued that the pole was "sacred" and a symbol of "Triumph of Constitutional Liberty over the Attempts of arbitrary Power." It was a "monument of freedom." They proposed it should be erected in "the most publick place," a place where it would become a beacon of community solidarity and a symbol of their political ideas. If that were not possible, they would find space "on private Ground," noting that the new pole, clearly already in construction, was almost ready to be erected. The Liberty Boys were attempting to establish a new permanent reference-point for their supporters. Most important, because New Yorkers knew British troops destroyed the previous pole and that the DeLanceys had funded their presence, a new one would show that it was the Liberty Boys, and not the DeLanceys, who advocated the protection of the public welfare.[53]

Like the assembly, most of the members of the Common Council in New York City were DeLanceyites. And they were aware of the symbolism a new liberty pole would mean for the DeLanceys' popular support. As such, they rejected the Liberty Boys' request. Among those who rejected the request were aldermen Andrew Gautier and Elias Desbrosses; recorder Thomas Jones; and assistant alderman Jacob Brewerton and Benjamin Huggett, all of whom were DeLancey voters in 1768 and 1769 and prominent adherents to and promoters of their political economy. Thomas Jones, meanwhile, was James DeLancey's brother-in-law. More than partisanship, however, the Common Council did not want McDougall and his supporters to compound the worsening relationship between the British Army and the people. Nor did they want to legitimize their efforts. Indeed, they recognized the political motivations that ran alongside McDougall's and his colleagues' ideological motivations. If the Common Council authorized the erection of a new liberty pole and further hostilities occurred between troops in the British Army and New Yorkers, then, by extension, any attack on the liberty pole could be construed as an attack not only on New Yorkers' rights as Britons but on the city government itself. McDougall and his colleagues, the DeLanceyites thought, were trying to sow discord. More importantly, though, the Common Council noted that McDougall and his colleagues did not need their "allowance," that is, their permission, on this occasion because they had already granted it when they authorized the erection of March 19, 1767, liberty pole. Their refusal to reauthorize the erection of a liberty pole was, in their eyes, a neat way to sidestep the issues the British Army had created.[54]

But the coalition of McDougall, Sears, and Lamb sought permission to make a statement, and even though they did not get it, they were not disheartened.

Instead, they erected their new liberty pole regardless of the Common Council's decision. On February 3, 1770, Sears acquired private land in the Fields through a quitclaim deed. The plot of land faced the east side of Broadway. On February 5, the minutes of the council meeting were printed in the press, prompting "great uneasiness to a numerous Body," another newspaper reported. A day later, accompanied by flag-bearers and a marching band, six horses carried an eighty-foot pine mast up the Fields to a spot of recently purchased private land at what is now 252 Broadway, between Warren and Murray Streets. As they lifted the new pole into the sky, its foundation sank twelve feet into the ground. The new liberty pole, which stood there for the next six years, was topped with a gilded weathervane that was inscribed "LIBERTY" and a large flag, which was also inscribed "LIBERTY." It was among the tallest and most stable structures in the city. Its base was armored with iron bars, nails, and metal hoops.[55]

The liberty pole became a partisan symbol that New Yorkers could mobilize around. A day after the new liberty pole punctured the skyline, however, James Parker, McDougall's printer, was pressured by the Royal Council into naming the Scotsman as the author of *To the Betrayed Inhabitants*. On February 7, McDougall was arrested and imprisoned for seditious libel. His rise within New York City's political world was rapid, but it looked as if his fall would occur just as quickly. He was about to face the institutional wrath of New York's government. Lt. Gov. Cadwallader Colden, ready to defend his honor and his executive position as acting governor, was not going to hold back. As he reported to Wills Hill, first Earl of Hillsborough, McDougall "highly deserves punishment." But McDougall and his supporters recognized the opportunity. One wrote, "Capt. McDougal is indeed in Jail, & I hope if he is brought to tryal, he will come off with flying colours." McDougall's arrest gave his supporters an opportunity to mobilize around him as he became the de facto leader of the Sons of Liberty—and he took full advantage.[56]

CHAPTER 4

All the Sons of Liberty
The Rise of Alexander McDougall

As the winter worsened and the cold air was trapped within the city streets, Alexander McDougall sat in a prison cell on the second or third floor of the New Gaol. He was cold, underfed, alone. The city prison was located at the northeastern corner of the Fields, by the High Road to Boston. The New Gaol was three stories high and was the first built to be exclusively used as a jail. From his window, McDougall might have been able to see the British soldier's barracks, forever reminded of how he ended up in a cell. His ascent, and ostensible descent, within New York City's popular political sphere occurred within a matter of weeks. He had gone from being an engaged, voting New Yorker to being an outspoken, if albeit anonymous, critic of the DeLanceys and Lt. Gov. Cadwallader Colden. A Livingston voter in 1768 and 1769, McDougall had opposed the DeLanceys since at least the 1768 elections. But nearly two years later, he was their most vehement critic, and he maintained his opposition until the Revolutionary War.[1]

McDougall's activism in 1769 was his first foray into the city's political sphere. No substantive evidence has been found to show that he participated in, or led, the Stamp Act riots of 1765, and he was certainly not a leader of the Sons of Liberty. His leadership is often assumed because of his importance within the city's political framework in later years. McDougall almost certainly opposed the Stamp Act, but given that it was widely despised across society, his opposition is unsurprising. What was surprising was the impact of his entry into the city's political arena.[2]

On February 8, 1770, city sheriff John Roberts confronted McDougall. Roberts, an imposing man, marched him to the colony's chief justice, seventy-eight-year-old Daniel Horsmanden. A formidable figure within the city's political framework and its highest judicial officeholder, Horsmanden had issued a warrant for McDougall's arrest a day earlier, and he was determined to secure a confession. Horsmanden was born in England, was educated at the Middle Temple and Inner Temple, and immigrated to New York in the early 1730s. He quickly established himself as one of the leading legal minds in the colony. In 1741 he was one of the judges who presided over the Slave Conspiracy Trials. Over twenty years later Horsmanden was chief justice. He was also a devout Anglican, committed supporter of King's College, and unreservedly loyal to George III, Parliament, and British control over its colonies. Throughout his career, Horsmanden had tried to increase Britishness in New York. For instance, he insisted on British legal formalities and decorum in his courtroom.[3]

In McDougall, Horsmanden saw an opportunity to flex his legal muscle and set an example. He was a man who was driven by ambition and civic duty. "You have brought yourself into a pretty Scrape," he told McDougall, when Sheriff Roberts escorted the prisoner into the chief justice's chambers. "May it please your Honour," McDougall replied, "that [I] must be judged of by my Peers." "Old Horsey," as Horsmanden was known, was a large man with a long nose and piercing eyes. McDougall's glib response did not worry him. Old Horsey responded quickly. He proudly reported to McDougall that "there was fully Proof" that they had identified him as the writer of *To the Betrayed Inhabitants of New-York*, a work that the chief justice described as "*a false, vile, and scandalous Libel.*" Unnerved, McDougall responded coolly, "This must also be tried by my Peers." Horsmanden's nerve was being tested. He gave McDougall two options: go to prison or give bail. "Sir," McDougall answered, "I will give no Bail." Horsmanden was no doubt pleased to send him to prison. As the sheriff escorted McDougall out, Horsmanden formally charged him as the author of *To the Betrayed Inhabitants of New-York*.[4]

A day later, McDougall wrote down his recollections of his interaction with Old Horsey with one thing in mind: he wanted to publicize his arrest and imprisonment to mobilize supporters. It was an astute move, an indication of his organizational skills and political acumen. On February 15, writing *"From the New Gaol,"* McDougall published his address *"to the* FREEHOLDERS, FREE-MEN, *and* INHABITANTS *of the Colony of New-York; and to all the Friends of* LIBERTY *in* North-America" in John Holt's *New-York Journal*. And in doing so, he not only publicized his message but also successfully depicted himself as a martyr for New Yorkers' liberties, as well as the liberties of everyone in colonial British America. Horsmanden, it seems, had met a worthy opponent. Prosecuting McDougall would not be easy.[5]

Alexander McDougall was committed to securing and advancing New Yorkers' constitutional rights. His active, public opposition to the DeLanceys' legislating in the winter of 1769 to 1770, and his subsequent incarceration, showed the city's inhabitants all they needed to know. His arrest, as well as the events that followed, mobilized people who were against the DeLanceys, or apathetic toward them. McDougall might also have captured the support of disillusioned Livingston supporters, politically active individuals whose leaders were no longer challenging the DeLanceys, inside or outside of the assembly. But McDougall's supporters recognized the effectiveness of the DeLanceyite methods of political mobilization, and they adopted similar approaches to mobilize support. As one pro-DeLancey author complained, McDougall's supporters distributed "printed Cards, & doggerel Verse" to encourage support for the incarcerated Scotsman. His imprisonment made "the greatest [no]ise," one New Yorker told Sir William Johnson, adding, "Fine times indeed a son of liberty sent to jail." The same correspondent also noted that McDougall's supporters were still criticizing the DeLancey-led Common Council because they "refused them [gro]und to put up the liberty pole."[6]

With Alexander McDougall in jail at the New Gaol, Isaac Sears and John Lamb had moved quickly to mobilize support for their new associate. Like McDougall, they were now, and would remain, against the DeLanceys. To counter their actions, the three men decided on a scheme that emphasized the Britishness of colonial New York's political culture, using recent, relevant political characters and events to advance their cause.

"The Wilkes of America"

Six days after the Scotsman's arrest, on the forty-fifth day of the year, forty-five men visited McDougall at the New Gaol. They headed to share a feast and celebrate their opposition to the DeLanceys and Parliament's measures. They ate forty-five pounds of beef, "cut from a Bullock of forty-five Months," and had forty-five bottles of wine at their disposal, gifted by Peter R. Livingston. These people also articulated their continued constitutional opposition to the DeLanceys, describing themselves as "real Enemies to internal Taxation." The DeLanceys, they surmised, were working with Parliament. Together, these new Yorkers celebrated "the great Cause of American Liberty." Later, forty-five forty-five-year-old virgins visited McDougall and sang the forty-fifth Psalm. At the same time, McDougall refused to link himself with *To the Betrayed Inhabitants*—as its author, as a contributor, or as someone who knew anything about it. He also continued to refuse posting bail. He was determined to remain in his cell and mark himself as a martyr for colonists' rights and liberties. Some thought he was grandstanding. Lt. Gov. Cadwallader Colden was unsurprisingly among this group, writing to Wills Hill, first Earl of Hillsborough, that he thought McDougall was at the head of "a violent party" that was "working on the passions of the populace, and exciting riots." McDougall, Colden believed, was trying to mobilize support to challenge both his and the DeLanceys' political legitimacy. He also pointed out that McDougall was "a person of some fortune . . . he choose to go to Jail," adding that he was "imitating Mr Wilkes in every thing he can."[7]

Colden was referring to English radical John Wilkes and McDougall's and his supporters' appropriation of British political culture. Wilkes was arrested for seditious libel following his criticism of John Stuart, third Earl of Bute, and George III in the forty-fifth issue of *The North Briton*. Published in April 1763, Wilkes's essay referred to the Jacobite Rebellion of 1745, during which the Scots declared the so-called Old Pretender, James Francis Edward Stuart, as king of Scotland. Led by James's son, Charles Edward Stuart, known widely as "Bonnie Prince Charlie," the Scots advanced as far south as Derby before they were defeated at the Battle of Culloden, which effectively ruled out the possibility of a Stuart Restoration.

Wilkes's essay, which linked George III and Parliament to Jacobitism and an illegitimate government, was infamous in Britain and its North American colonies. In New York, it was reprinted in all three of the city's newspapers. More importantly, though, Wilkes's arrest mobilized support for his cause, whereby he became a symbol for liberty and Britons' rights. Further, toward the end of the 1760s, Wilkes was repeatedly denied a seat in Parliament even though he was repeatedly returned for Middlesex County, something that stirred up his supporters' animosity toward Parliament and Wilkes's opponents. New Yorkers thus appropriated the political symbolism surrounding Wilkes and used it to mobilize support for Alexander McDougall and his situation. Whereas "No. 45, Wilkes and Liberty" was a symbol for anti-administration feelings as well as Scotophobia in Britain, McDougall, a Scot, became the "Wilkes of America." He was someone who would fight for New Yorkers' rights and defend the city, and the colony, against perceived DeLancey absolutism and oppression. And because Wilkes's radicalism was well known in the colonies, McDougall's appropriation of his cause helped the Scotsman mobilize intercolonial support for his cause. For instance, the *Boston Gazette* noted that McDougall's "Case is similar to that of Mr. Wilkes, in Instances more important than the No. 45."[8]

Alexander McDougall's plight captured the support of prominent New Yorkers, including William Livingston and prominent members of his family's faction. They would not let him fight the DeLanceys alone. The day McDougall was arrested, William Livingston issued the first in a five-part series titled "The Watchman" that ran between February 8 and April 21. In installments of the series, which were published as broadsides and inserted in newspapers, Livingston defended McDougall and the freedom of the press. He also attacked the DeLanceys and their so-called alliance with Colden, likening them to the Stuart monarchs of England and Scotland. The close relation of the Stuarts to the '45 and McDougall's appropriation of it does not seem to have bothered New Yorkers. In the second essay Livingston described the DeLanceys and by extension their supporters as "domineering, designing, artful and venal." For Livingston, as for McDougall, the DeLancey-led assembly's recent actions had "violate[d] the rights of their constituents." Their actions were, Livingston explained, "dangerous unconstitutional innovations and infringements." They lacked "public virtue." They did not deserve "to be the guardians . . . of the liberty of their constituents." Instead, their "insatiable thirst for domination" had taken over.[9]

Naturally, the DeLanceys responded to Livingston's series with one of their own. Entitled "The Dougliad," James Duane criticized the Livingstons and Alexander McDougall's newfound association with Isaac Sears in twelve essays that were published between April 9 and June 25, 1770. In each of the series, the authors described their respective factions in similar terms. Duane, for one, identified himself "as a TRUE son of liberty" in his opening essay, in which he further castigated *To the Betrayed Inhabitants* as "an essay, better calculated, to blind and seduce, to distract and disunite, to foment discontent, tumults and sedition; and in short to trample down all legal authority, and shake the government to the foundation." Duane, like the DeLanceys had done before him, recommended modeling the colony's political institutions to replicate Britain's, whereby there would be a permanent upper house. In writing his series, Duane likely had at least some assistance from Lt. Gov. Cadwallader Colden, who advocated that truth should not be a defense to the charge of seditious libel against McDougall—as it was in Britain.[10]

These essays went back and forth throughout the spring and into the summer of 1770 as McDougall remained in prison, awaiting trial for seditious libel. Despite his predicament, he rallied more supporters to his cause, writing essays from his cell that were published in the press. In one, he continued to argue that "The [Quartering] Act . . . was designed to support a Standing Army." By extension, because the DeLanceys had supported it when they funded British troops, they, too, supported a standing army. It was a careful, well-thought-out rhetorical attack, using New Yorkers' long-existing fears, and directed them toward the DeLanceys. McDougall continued to turn the DeLanceys' arguments upside down, depicting the DeLanceys as corrupt politicians without virtue. Instead of accepting his fate, McDougall saw his imprisonment as a source of inspiration to do more. He declared he would "devote a considerable Part of my Time to do Justice to the Public, in the Cause for which I am imprisoned," in an attempt to promote New Yorkers' "common Principle[s]." He added that he "had the Honour of an Imprisonment for the Cause of *American* Liberty." As such, given that he was permitted to see visitors in his cell, so many wanted to see him that he had to set visiting hours. He was converting "Chains into Laurels" and was determined to turn "a Gaol into a Paradise."[11]

The DeLanceys' and Colden's move against McDougall set a precedent that if anyone criticized them, they would be imprisoned, or worse, polarizing New Yorkers and precipitating the development of two political associations in New York City. Since the mid-1760s and especially after the DeLanceys' election, New Yorkers appropriated virtue and freedom from corruption as essential components of their political framework. At each level of politics, from the governor to the Common Council, those undertaking civic service were expected to act as virtuous, independent citizens who advanced the public welfare. The political framework of the city was not supported by those in office alone. New Yorkers expected to have a consistent and active voice in its operations. And if politicians were perceived to move against their liberties, New Yorkers felt they had a right to show their opposition. As one newspaper essay put it, they were to "speak *freely* and *honestly*" about anything considered "repugnant to *American Liberty*."[12]

By early 1770, two popular political associations had formed in New York. On one side, the DeLanceys, though deflated, remained a formidable force, upheld by considerable institutional and popular support. On the other, McDougall had allied with Isaac Sears and John Lamb, leaders of the Sons of Liberty, as well as prominent members of the Livingston faction, who provided him with limited institutional support. McDougall, however, relied on popular support. It was his style of politics.

During this period of colonial history, the commemoration of the repeal of the Stamp Act was among the most celebrated date on the calendar. On March 18 across the thirteen colonies, people came together. Every year since the Stamp Act's repeal in 1766, the March anniversary was celebrated with extravagant dinners, during which colonists celebrated the people who, they believed, helped secure the act's repeal—Charles Watson-Wentworth, second Marquis of Rockingham, William Pitt the Elder, Isaac Barré—and the constitutional liberties and rights they believed that were restored. But in March 1770, New York's commemorations showed how fractured the city's politics had become.[13]

The mobilization of two groups on March 19, 1770, put the city's politics on display. The DeLanceys dined at the tavern of Abraham Montayne, a Dutch New Yorker whose tavern was the venue that British soldiers had attacked earlier in the year. The commemoration at Montayne's was an event where, inside and outside, the DeLanceys articulated their political economy and firm belief that republicanism and commerce were not in conflict with one another. For them, working toward, maintaining, and promoting civic virtue and the common good, key tenets of republicanism, did not run contrary to the promotion of commerce stability or growth. Republicanism was not static. Nor was it restrictive, socially, linguistically, or economically. It was dynamic. New Yorkers of all ranks sought to adhere to and achieve certain moral values while also securing themselves financially. The rhetoric of republicanism did not go against everyday life, and ideas did not go against behavior. Instead, they worked together and were intertwined.[14]

At Montayne's tavern, 233 diners erected a flagstaff where "Liberty Colours (inscrib'd with G. R. III. Liberty and Trade)" were visible for all passing New Yorkers to see. With the flag flying high in the city sky, the DeLanceys were putting their politics for all New Yorkers to see; as people walked by or near Montayne's, the DeLanceys wanted them to look over and see the people who were dining together. They also wanted to see a flag that represented their political economy. In this instance, the diners associated their individual freedom and virtue with their city's ability to engage in open, unrestricted trade.[15]

Rebuilding New York City's economic framework was of the utmost importance to them. In February 1769, James DeLancey urged the Marquis of Rockingham to "befriend the Colonies, by Promoting the Repeal" of the Townshend Acts and by "taking off the unnecessary Restrictions on the American Trades." DeLancey was echoing sentiments he had expressed to Rockingham in 1765, in which he told the marquis that his guiding principle was the pursuit of "Life Liberty & Commerce." In that same letter, DeLancey also proposed the establishment on an American parliament *Only to meddle with Supplies*, that is, trade. "Don't Startle at a Parliament in America," he told Rockingham. "You have got two in Europe—have made above twenty abroad." The main objective for DeLancey's American parliament was to enable the continued economic development of the colonies, from which colonists would "support the Government with all the Trappings & Splendour." For DeLancey and his associates, their political economy was intertwined with their ideological commitment to republicanism as well as their allegiance to Britain. In 1770, at Montayne's tavern, 233 men identified themselves as supporters of and adherents to DeLancey's political economy. Together, they were the "Friends of Liberty and Trade."[16]

The March 1770 event was the culmination of years of developing a political economy for New York City that was based on sustaining and building its economy. Between their election in 1768 and the celebration two years later, these "Friends of Liberty and Trade" were instrumental in the establishment and incorporation of two institutions that were invaluable in broadcasting their message not only to New Yorkers but to the world: the Chamber of Commerce and the Marine Society.

Founded in April 1768, the Chamber of Commerce was the first society of its kind in the colonies. It encapsulated the DeLanceys' political economy, largely because many of its founding members were DeLanceyites. These men included all the DeLancey assemblymen for New York City and County, as well as the likes of Elias Desbrosses, Hugh Wallace, William Walton, Isaac Low, and Theophylact Bache, all of whom were prominent supporters. John Cruger served as the chamber's first president, and it was under his leadership that the chamber focused its attention on advancing the public good through securing the city's economic independence and self-sufficiency, which would help the city and the colony better extract the wealth of the Americas and Europe. By extension, as the city thrived so, too, would its inhabitants, even the poor. The chamber proposed it would do this by introducing "laws and regulations as may be found necessary for the benefit of trade in general," and its founding members argued that its establishment enhanced the public welfare and protected New Yorkers' liberties. Its members advanced their political economy in several ways. They legislated for "the more effectual Inspection" of various everyday goods, set fixed currency rates, and were used to settle merchants' disputes.[17]

The founding of the chamber occurred during a golden period in New York City's history. Following the DeLanceys' electoral surge, the chamber's inaugural meeting took place in Fraunces Tavern, then known as "Bolton and Siegel's," the likely site of James DeLancey's birth, forever tying the chamber to the family and its interests. Indeed, the Chamber of Commerce tried to mobilize support to their political economy, noting how they were advancing the public good. For instance, on numerous occasions they declared in newspaper advertisements that "The Chamber do everything in its power for the interest of the community." The chamber's focus on New York City's development was rewarded by Lt. Gov. Cadwallader Colden during his temporary

FIGURE 4.1. Cadwallader Colden, ca. 1772, by Matthew Pratt, courtesy New York State Museum

governorship. Perhaps in another attempt to improve his relationship with the DeLanceys, he recommended the chamber's incorporation to George III. "I think it a good institution," wrote Colden, "and will always be glad to promote the Commercial Interests of this City." It brought "a peculiar happiness to a Society," Colden reasoned, because it was "so beneficial to the *general good* of the province." On March 13, 1770, amid the furor caused by Alexander Mc-Dougall's imprisonment, the New York Chamber of Commerce became the first of its kind to be incorporated. The DeLanceys viewed its incorporation as an opportunity to move above partisanship, to articulate their political economy, and to introduce people to their economic vision for the city. Colden, who had a portrait commissioned in recognition of his efforts, perhaps viewed incorporation as a means through which to reward the DeLancey merchants for their cooperation during his temporary governorship and, by the same token, a means through which to slight not only McDougall but the Livingston faction (see figure 4.1).[18]

The incorporation of the Chamber of Commerce afforded it and its members a hitherto unknown degree of protection and security. It bestowed security and prestige and quelled any doubts about members' financial concerns. But incorporation was also a partisan measure: it hurt some members in society. Incorporation was, as one New Yorker reported, "a vast hurt to the Lawyers." Put simply, given that the chamber settled disputes between merchants, lawyers were no longer required to adjudicate, a consequence of which was that they lost business. As such, he stated that many lawyers were "going to live in the [Country] for want of business." This same New Yorker also wrote that through incorporation the chamber's members "Established themselves" as economically independent actors within New York society. The DeLanceys' political economy had been institutionally legitimized.[19]

The chamber's members also used incorporation to articulate their political economy which, they hoped, would mobilize support. Every document related to the chamber's business required a legal seal. It was akin to a personal signature. Seals were often made of bronze or silver. They were durable and valuable. Their primary function was to authenticate official documents for an undefined period, months, years, decades. Seal designers thus carried out their work with great care and thought. But seals were more than a lump of metal; they were a material articulation display of an incorporated institution's cultural, economic, and political significance—an identity.[20]

The Chamber of Commerce's seal offered its members an opportunity to visually display who they were and what their goals were—a chance to explain their place within and goals for New York City's political economy. Members wanted to ensure that New Yorkers, as well as anyone else who handled the chamber's documents, recognized its public-minded objectives. They drew upon classical iconography and New York history to design a seal that complemented their goals, settling on Mercury, the Roman god of commerce, merchants, and profit. The symbolism would have been easily recognizable to eighteenth-century New Yorkers. Against a backdrop of a rising sun and a three-masted schooner that represented the colony's commercial promise,

FIGURE 4.2.   Seal of the Chamber of Commerce of New York, by Thomas Waterman Wood, 1877, courtesy New York State Museum

Mercury is surrounded by the natural resources that New York was known for: At his feet was a beaver, an anchor, two cannons pointing upward, barrels of flaxseed, goods ready for shipment, and the cornucopia, a symbol of abundance and the bounty that the land could produce. The cornucopia was a well-known and well-used iconographic tool, used in seals for the Lord Proprietors for Carolina and the Company of Scotland. It was also used in New York. In 1746, the artist William Burgis created a panorama of New York City that prominently featured cornucopias as well as classical iconography, beavers, and flaxseed. The chamber was intricately woven into the colony's history. In the center of the seal was Mercury, with shoulder-length blond hair, youthful rosy cheeks, and innocent blue eyes, gazing into the distance, the future. Its motto was also important. Invoking Cicero, the chamber's motto was "NON NOBIS SO-LUM NATI SUMUS," which translates to "We are not born for ourselves alone," articulating its identity as well as its objectives (see figure 4.2).[21]

It is likely that the Chamber of Commerce drew inspiration for its seal from Joseph Spence's *Polymetis*, which was first published in London in 1747. *Polymetis* contained detailed descriptions and engravings of Roman gods and goddesses. Mercury, "the god of shopkeepers and tradesmen," was described as wearing "his Pestatsus," a "winged . . . cap . . . [with] two little wings attached to it . . . tho' in some of the very oldest works, you see him sometimes only with two feathers stuck in it." He also had "wings [attached] to his feet; and his wand with the two serpents about it, which they call his Caduceus." Together, Mercury's caduceus and cornucopia symbolized peace and plenty, "which," Spence wrote, "are two of the principal ingredients of happiness." The use of a rising sun was also symbolic. An allegorical reference to the dawn, it represented a new beginning, the hope and potential of the Chamber of Commerce and what it could bring to New York society. The match was perfect.[22]

There was another association in New York City. It, too, was mandated to promote the economic welfare of the city. Founded in November 1769, the Marine Society's goals were also based on the DeLanceys' political economy. Its chief objectives were to improve merchants' knowledge and to care for "unfortunate Commanders of Vessels" and the orphans or widows they left in the city. On March 7, 1770, the Marine Society was incorporated, giving it the same legal protection as the Chamber of Commerce. This was of importance to the society because its funds were raised through charitable contributions. The Marine Society's membership was larger than that of the Chamber of Commerce. Alongside merchants, mariners and ship's captains could also join. Some of its DeLanceyite members were also in the Chamber of Commerce. Most were enterprising merchants, including William Walton, John Harris Cruger, James Jauncey, Theophylact Bache, Miles Sherbrooke, Henry White, and Elias Desbrosses.[23]

Equally important, when members of the Marine Society designed its seal it, too, ensured that the public understood its charitable and public-minded goals. Drawing on classical iconography, the seal depicts Ceres, Roman goddess of agriculture, handing a widow and three orphans a pot, depicting her as a mother-type figure, a life-giver and source of nourishment. Spence noted that Ceres was a distinct figure, writing, "her robes . . . fall down to her feet." Spence also noted that Ceres had an ample bosom, symbolizing innocence, nourishment, and protection, all the ideas the Marine Society articulated and sought to represent. Moreover, the symbol's English motto displayed the society's objectives: "Add to Charity Knowledge" (see figure 4.3).[24]

FIGURE 4.3. Seal of the Marine Society of New York, taken from 128th Anniversary Dinner of the Marine Society of New York, Buttolph Collection of Menus, Rare Book Division, New York Public Library

The Chamber of Commerce and the Marine Society were both well supported. They each promoted a citywide perception that the DeLanceys' political economy furthered the public good, augmented progress, and broke down social and cultural barriers.

Members of the chamber and of the society also regularly advertised their meetings in newspapers, publicizing their civic-minded goals to attract support. Their newspaper advertisements, as well as their meetings, gave them a consistent presence in the public sphere, showing New Yorkers that they were working toward the development of the city. Nonmercantile New Yorkers were not permitted in their meetings, but their regular advertisements gave New Yorkers a way to engage with them, even if they were not privy to their meetings. Their advertisements also ensured that they were under constant public supervision. Both were well received. For instance, one New Yorker claimed that the Marine Society was a "splendid Monument of national Benevolence," adding that it was of "infinite Service" to the public because its organization was based upon such "generous" principles. By the same token, another New Yorker noted that the Chamber of Commerce was "instituted on Principles of general Utility." The organizations were so successful that in a Marine Society address, its members declared that they "hope[d] to see others form Associations for Purposes equally useful and humane." The institutions' political economy wove them into the civic life of the city and its growth, promoting their ideas as well as their interests.[25]

For this reason, both the Chamber of Commerce and the Marine Society were also politicized institutions within New York. This was due, in part, to their ideological and political connections to the DeLanceys, whose supporters were closely connected to both. At the time of the March 1770 commemorations, the Chamber of Commerce counted seventy-three members. Thirty-two of these merchants voted in the 1769 election, of whom twenty-seven, or 84 percent, voted for all the DeLancey candidates. (Its inaugural president, John Cruger, was one of the elected DeLancey candidates.) Two members, Anthony Van Dam and Peter Remsen, divided their votes between the groups or did not vote for one DeLancey candidate. Only four of the voting members did not support a DeLancey candidate: Richard Sharpe, Jacobus Van Zandt, Alexander McDonald, and Henry C. Bogart.[26]

Nevertheless, to maintain at least a public display of nonpartisanship, members of the Chamber of Commerce dissociated themselves from displays of and associations with partisanship and factionalism. To be associated with political activity would discredit their republicanism—and, by extension, their political economy. As one DeLanceyite author wrote in the *New-York Journal* on April 12, "No Man has a Right to lug the Chamber of Commerce into any political Controversy." To be sure, the chamber was a partisan institution, founded to promote and institutionalize the DeLanceys' political economy. Indeed, the ties between the Chamber of Commerce and those who dined in Montayne's tavern were equally robust. Twenty-three members, around one-third of the total membership, dined on March 19. Moreover, sixteen of these men had voted for the DeLanceys in 1769.[27] Equally important, because members of the chamber were well connected with the DeLanceys, they were, by extension, also against Alexander McDougall. As one pro-DeLancey author argued in April 1770, McDougall had been "strenuously opposed by *most* of them [in the chamber] in all *his* political Manoeuvres." "It would be difficult," the DeLanceyite continued, "to find above 14 or 15 at most of the 73 Members, who do not regard Mr. M^c—l in the contemptible Light."[28]

Members of the Marine Society were also connected to the DeLanceys. Of its sixty-seven inaugural members, twenty-six voted in the 1769 election, 73 percent of whom voted for all the available DeLancey candidates. Of the remaining seven voters, two, Anthony Rutgers and William Heyer, voted for DeLancey and Livingston candidates, and one voter, Robert Sharpe, supported a single candidate, John Morin Scott. Only three voting members of the Marine Society voted for the Livingstons in 1769. The rest were DeLancey supporters.[29]

The ties between the Marine Society and the diners at Montayne's tavern in March 1770 were also strong. Of the sixty-seven inaugural members of the society, twelve spent a long afternoon and evening in Montayne's tavern, all of whom, except Capt. John Finglass and storekeeper Miles Sherbrooke, voted in 1769. Only one, Anthony Rutgers, voted against the DeLancey ticket, dividing his votes between the two groups. The DeLancey supporters included Theophylact Bache, John Harris Cruger, James Jauncey, Isaac Low, Anthony Rutgers, Miles Sherbrooke, Daniel Stiles, Willet Taylor, Jacob Walton, and William Walton. Rutgers voted for James DeLancey, Philip Livingston, John Morin Scott, and Theodorus Van Wyck. Of those who were members of both associations, all except Philip Livingston dined with the DeLanceys.[30] Of the 233 diners at Montayne's tavern, 110 voted for at least two members of the DeLancey ticket in 1769. Of these 110 voters, only three—Elias De Grusha, Anthony Rutgers, and Dirck Schuyler—did not vote for all the DeLancey candidates, voting for at least one Livingston candidate. Given that about 50 percent of white New York males could vote, it would appear that the DeLanceys' meeting was representative of the city's white male population and that their support-base included both voters and nonvoters. Several the diners' names were distinguished by social honors and titles. Fourteen men were lawyers; two were doctors; two were "Mr."; and four were distinguished either through their service in the city militia or, more likely, as ship's captains. Most of the diners—211—did not have titles that conferred social or professional distinction, possibly indicating middling to lower rank. Through their common interests and shared political economy, they associated with elites and were bound together. The diners were also culturally diverse. There were Dutch, English, Scottish, French, and Irish surnames present. Moreover, multiple family members attended. There were, for example, Brewertons, Lispenards, Beekmans, Van Cortlandts, Waltons, Brownjohns, Ludlows, Van Alstynes, Laights, and Nicolls. Alongside these men were prominent members of the Sons of Liberty Joseph Allicocke, Charles Nicoll, and Edward Laight, DeLancey tavern-keepers Edward Bardin (who used to own the tavern they were in), David Grim, and Benjamin Stout, and Marine Society president Leonard Lispenard. Montayne's diners thus constituted a blend of tightly knit elite and non-elite colonists who represented not only the city's diversity but its interconnectivity. Merchants were alongside shopkeepers, lawyers, public officials, and artisans. By dining together to commemorate a significant political event in a male-dominated arena, the diners reinforced not only their commitment to the DeLanceys, but their commitment to their associationism, partisanship, and political economy. For these people, economic progress advanced and served the public good. They were committed to establishing a new commercial society in New York City, one that would usher in a market-orientated commercial system based on consumption. This pursuit of consumer culture, the DeLanceys believed, would establish financial security throughout the city and the colony—anyone who participated in the commercial marketplace that they sought.[31]

Their political economy was predicated on New York City being a provincial city within the British Atlantic, and it was popular. Through the DeLanceys' inclusive focus on economic self-sufficiency and the consistent rhetoric of the Chamber of Commerce and the Marine Society, these men coalesced into a distinct political association. Its members were not distinguished by gradations of ethnicity, rank, or status. Rank was not a distinguishing factor. The sustained interaction of elites and non-elites in New York was distinct in comparison to other urban centers like Boston and Philadelphia, where sustained popular mobilization was largely controlled by elites.[32]

For those who dined in Montayne's tavern, its inclusive atmosphere provided them with a face-to-face setting to maintain their political engagement outside of electoral politics, giving marginalized New Yorkers a voice in the political arena and binding them together as a result. As the DeLanceys' social events did in the late 1760s, the mobilization of Montayne's silverware in March 1770 encouraged his diners to develop and strengthen the relationships they held with one another. Together, these men were united by ideas and interests. They sought to promote New York City's economic independence and growth—and, by extension, their own. These men were the "Friends to Liberty and Trade," the "Friends *to true Commerce*," and, as one newspaper article put it, those who wanted to be involved in the "Commerce of Life."[33]

The meeting of the "Friends to Liberty and Trade" was also a statement of partisanship. By meeting in Montayne's tavern, even though their meeting occurred behind closed doors, it was a public event. People knew what was happening before, during, and after the event had taken place. They had known about it for well over a month. This meeting was advertised in the press from February 5, 1770, well over a month prior to the event taking place. The DeLanceys were willing to spend extra money to inform their supporters, and their opponents, when and where they would be celebrating. In doing so they maximized their ability to mobilize their broad base of support. It also reminded their opponents that, despite McDougall's ascent, their support base remained. "The sons of Liberty, are desired to meet at the house of Mr. *De La Montayne's*," they announced in the press. But as word of their meeting inevitably reached New Yorkers' ears, Montayne made explicit whom he would and would not cater for. Only those associated to the DeLanceys would be allowed to attend. It was to be a DeLancey meeting. "I shall not," wrote Montayne in another advertisement, "entertain any other company than those gentlemen and their connections who engaged my house for that day."[34]

When the DeLanceys were in Montayne's tavern, they made the most of it. Food was aplenty. Drink was flowing. It was an enjoyable occasion. But the diners did not forget why they were there, and as the evening progressed their thoughts turned toward commemorating the moment, the anniversary, and their associationism through a series of toasts. Toasting was a common feature of men's visits to taverns. Aside from the food and drink, it was a highlight of such events, and they were often used to make a political statement. Every word of every toast was chosen with great care. The diners in Montayne's tavern used toasts to reinforce and develop their political sentiments. Their toasts offered another way for them to coalesce, as an inspired political toast and the ensuing glass-clinking reinforced their partisanship, developed their group identity, and confirmed their political economy.[35]

Toasts were also often printed and reprinted in newspapers and as broadsides. John Holt and Huge Gaine printed the thirty-four toasts from Montayne's tavern "without the least Deviation or Alteration," transforming them into proactive, public political statements that demonstrated the toasters' place within and view of the city's political framework. Printing toasts performed another important function. Seats in Montayne's tavern were limited. Not all the DeLanceys' supporters could attend, but printing their toasts circumvented this issue. Reading the list of toasts may not have the same effect as being there in person but engaging with them through print put the diners' partisan ideas into the public sphere, linking the "Friends to Liberty and Trade" with their nonattending supporters and bringing them together.[36]

The diners' toasts also offered the "Friends to Liberty and Trade" a perfect moment to define, and upon publication articulate, their political economy. Several of the thirty-four toasts offered in Montayne's tavern that day emphasized the importance of economic security and independence. They drank to "Trade and Navigation, and a speedy Removal of their Embarrassments"; "The Corporation of the Chamber of Commerce"; and the "Marine Society." Other toasts highlighted the British monarchy and events and individuals in the history of New York, as was custom at the time, but their final toast was most significant. It illustrated that New York City's political arena had splintered into two competing groups. After thirty-three earlier toasts, they toasted to "Loyalty, Unanimity, and Perseverance to the *true* Sons of Liberty in America." The DeLanceys, defining themselves as "Friends to Liberty and Trade," were declaring that they were the guardians of the public welfare. Their ideas, and not McDougall's, would advance it.[37]

New York City's inhabitants mobilized around the DeLanceys during the elections. Their support had not faltered by early 1770. They articulated a distinct political persona that brought them and their supporters closer together.

As a supporter argued in April 1770, their long-standing ties had resulted in their continued voluntary activism in what he called *"the Club."* Furthermore, as they coalesced their negative views about and attitudes toward McDougall and his supporters were reinforced. As James Duane wrote, McDougall's supporters were "PUBLIC ROBBERS AND TRAITORS." Another DeLancey writer argued that McDougall was "VAIN, IDLE, FORWARD, MALEVOLENT, CONTENTIOUS, MEDDLING, IMPERTINENT, TURBULENT, FACTIOUS, SEDITIOUS." The elected DeLancey assemblymen, on the other hand, were New Yorkers' *"Guardians"*—men who acted for "the public Welfare," "the *real and independent Sons of Liberty.*" In contrast, McDougall was "NOT a Son of Liberty." On the contrary, McDougall and his supporters had taken advantage of New Yorkers' fears of political corruption and had "riggled themselves into popular Esteem."[38]

The Chamber of Commerce, the Marine Society, and the DeLanceys were effectively an interconnected political association that remained faithful through the Revolutionary War. Indeed, a large proportion of the diners in Montayne's tavern and the members of the Chamber of Commerce and the Marine Society became loyalists during the American Revolution. Of the seventy-three members of the Chamber of Commerce at this time, forty-four became loyalists (60.2%). Thirty-eight out of the seventy-one (53.5%) inaugural members of the Marine Society became loyalists, and out of the 233 men who dined in Montayne's tavern, 125 became loyalists (53.6%). These numbers might not seem overwhelming, but it must also be noted that some members were neutral and revolutionaries and other members' allegiances are unknown.[39]

Nevertheless, these individuals' allegiance here and at any point during the Revolutionary War was not preordained. To correlate their loyalism with their partisanship here would be teleological and simplistic. Not all DeLancey voters became loyalists. Nor did all the members of the Chamber of Commerce, the Marine Society, or the diners in Montayne's tavern. Some became revolutionaries, or "patriots." Among the chamber's future members who became revolutionaries were Philip Livingston, who signed the Declaration of Independence, and Isaac Sears. Livingston was also a member of the Marine Society. Of those at Montayne's, James Beekman, Joseph Bull, and Daniel Dunscomb became revolutionaries. Some also identified themselves as neutrals; most notably, John Cruger. While a significant proportion decided which *side* they would be on in the Revolution, allegiances could not be determined for others, including a majority of the members of the Marine Society.[40]

Despite this qualifier, the high number of future loyalists within *"the Club"* is suggestive, indicating that the development of pre-wartime opposition to men like McDougall played an important role in arbitrating a large proportion of their conduct during the Revolutionary War. What this suggests, in turn, is that their loyalism should not be understood only as a statement related to their relationship to New York's place within the British Empire. It was not only an explicit illustration of their continued allegiance to George III or Parliament but a reaffirmation of their political economy and their partisanship.

Hampden Hall

Alexander McDougall did not have the chance to celebrate the repeal of the Stamp Act in 1770. He was still in jail on March 19. But his imprisonment did not stop his supporters celebrating any less vigorously than their opponents in Montayne's tavern. They, too, used the moment to articulate their partisanship and associationism. Their event also emboldened the political zeal of their opponents. Indeed, having indicated that they initially sought to dine in Montayne's, upon reading that attendance was circumscribed and they were not invited, they offered their supporters—who were also addressed as "the Sons of Liberty"—another option. In February, not long after Alexander McDougall's arrest, John Lamb, Isaac Sears, McDougall, and ninety-seven others paid £6 to use a new venue. They named it Hampden Hall, and their landlord was a former hatter named Henry Bicker. It was a tavern of their own, located near the liberty pole at the southwest corner of Broadway and Warren Street, toward the lower end of the Fields. As McDougall's supporters had done with John Wilkes, they again appropriated McDougall's situation with British political culture: Hampden Hall was named in commemoration of John Hampden, an Englishman who opposed King Charles I and contributed to the start of the English Civil War (1642–51).[41]

McDougall's supporters also published advertisements in the press throughout February and March in Holt's *New-York Journal*. Montayne's tavern, the advertisement read, "was engaged for a certain set of Gentlemen." Hampden Hall, located at what is now the Western Electric Building at 222 Broadway, was a necessary purchase, and their advertisements announced that they would accept and dine with "all the Sons of Liberty, without Discrimination, who choose to commemorate" the repeal of the Stamp Act. Hampden Hall was for future occasions, too—any that would enable them to advance "the Promotion of the Common Cause."[42]

On March 19, these New Yorkers replicated the celebratory political event taking place at Montayne's tavern. "About 300 Gentlemen, Freeholders and Freemen of the City," "real Friends to Liberty," mobilized Hampden Hall's silverware for a feast after dispatching ten men to provide McDougall with his meal. Their choice of venue made an important political statement, as did their self-description. Instead of dining in a local tavern, these men invested in an exclusive location, a place where discussions and events were free from unwanted interruptions and uninvited guests. Hampden Hall afforded them a degree of privacy, and it became the center of their political world, reinforcing their partisanship and moving their views further away from their opponents. During the daylong celebration they drank forty-five toasts, among which were toasts highlighting the colonies' connections to Britain, William of Orange, John Wilkes, the freedom of the press, King Robert I of Scotland, who some believed was related to McDougall, and the continuance of the nonimportation agreement of 1768. The DeLanceys, however, were opposed to the nonimportation agreement's continuation, having themselves toasted to "Trade and Navigation, and a speedy Removal of their Embarrassments." Here was a firm indication of a key difference between their political economies. As Whigs, they held competing understandings of the relationship between republicanism and commerce, between ideas and interests. On other toasts that McDougall's supporters delivered, they made it obvious that they were in clear opposition to the DeLanceys' political economy, arguing that those at Montayne's were designing and ambitious men who would not advance the public good. McDougall's supporters thus drank to "*More* public Virtue and Integrity, and *less* Venality." And of the Chamber of Commerce, McDougall described its members as "insiginificant" and "self-conceited." Their toasts were printed in all the city's newspapers and a broadside to ensure that their political ideas were well known.[43]

Publication of the toasts sharpened competing interpretations of New York's political economy. Those at Montayne's believed that for New Yorkers to obtain virtue, they needed to be independent, something that was more attainable if the city was free from economic restraints. But for those at Hampden Hall, virtue was synonymous with freedom of speech, freedom of the press, an absence of corruption, careerism, and an absolute sovereign legislature. To men like McDougall, the DeLanceyite assemblymen were firm illustrations that the city's political framework was corrupt. They believed that they sought unfettered authority and would sacrifice New Yorkers' needs to advance their own interests. McDougall and his supporters probably accepted Parliament's sovereignty in some respects. More important to them, though, was that Parliament's authority was and should remain limited.

The changes that Parliament implemented had upset the imperial relationship. Radicals like McDougall believed that it had acted unconstitutionally, almost as if it had unlimited power, as seventeenth-century monarchs had done. For McDougall and his supporters, the DeLanceys were legitimizing Parliament's absolute power and hoped that they, too, could wield such influence. The republic was in danger, and New Yorkers' role in the city's and indeed the colony's political processes was being usurped. To overcome this, McDougall and his supporters articulated a kind of republicanism in which the health of the republic—in this case, New York City—depended on the virtue of its members. Their civic identity and virtue, in turn, were maintained by their active resistance to forces of corruption, which, in this case, were their opponents across town. For the DeLanceys in Montayne's tavern, their toasts indicated their belief that the city's impoverished citizens and its stagnating commercial professionalization were impeding its inhabitants' ability to become virtuous citizens. Embracing eighteenth-century Scottish Enlightenment theorists such as Adam Ferguson and Adam Smith, they were promoting the notion that common economic interests were the surest means to achieve success in a sophisticated republican society.[44]

The sun was coming down as the events at Hampden Hall ended, but McDougall's partisans were not finished. They wanted to pay further tribute to McDougall at the New Gaol. After their meals, they marched toward him, singing songs with their "Colours flying." Once they arrived at McDougall's cell, they saluted him with three cheers, after which the imprisoned Scotsman delivered a short address through the bars. It must have been an impressive site. All told, John Holt reported, "The Day was celebrated with great Joy and Decency." On March 24, the forty-fifth day of McDougall's incarceration, he was visited again. This time, it was the "real Friends to American Liberty" who enjoyed the experience of dining with McDougall. One of the diners later reported a thirty-minute spell he spent alone by McDougall, writing that the Scotsman was "as well read in History as any Person" he had ever met. The visitor added that despite McDougall's situation, he spoke with clarity and conviction. He did not waver in his commitment to his "Ideas." The diner further noted McDougall's "Language composed of as well Chosen Words as you would expect from an accomplished Speaker." During this short meeting, the report on which was written later that day, McDougall's visitor recognized that he was a figure that could mobilize support not only inside New York City but across British North America, writing, "His Cause gathers Partizans Daily from one End of the Continent to the Other." "There ought to be a Stand made," he added, noting that McDougall's leadership was central in his partisans' attempts to gain a foothold. "I rejoice that McDougall is imprisoned for the Cause as the like best way to bring things to a Crisis." And of the DeLanceys' attempts to curtail McDougall's supporters, the diner encouraged perseverance and resolution, as well as more radical methods, noting that he sought to "git the Government rid of such, partial self interested, and Iniquitous Rulers."[45]

At this stage, with their leader imprisoned, McDougall's supporters were considering means to force Colden to dissolve the assembly and call for another election. Some, it seems, wanted to replace the elected DeLancey candidates— John Cruger, Jacob Walton, James Jauncey, and James DeLancey—whose behavior toward McDougall, they believed, compromised or least questioned their republicanism. McDougall's trial was also on the horizon, and some were concerned about who would represent him. Even as early as February it was rumored that Boston's James Otis Jr. would travel down. Unfortunately for McDougall, Otis was incapable of traveling to New York. What's more, the DeLanceys were not oblivious to the growth of McDougall's support base.[46]

In the same issue of Holt's *New-York Journal* that reported the commemorations in Hampden Hall, it was reported the forty-five members of the DeLanceyite Chamber of Commerce visited Lt. Gov. Cadwallader Colden to offer "their Thanks for granting them Letters of Incorporation." Without listing the members who visited Colden, the DeLanceys were clearly attempting to undermine and discredit McDougall's appropriation of the '45. Another writer also questioned whether forty-five virgins visited McDougall, alleging that it was only twenty-eight. Another writer reported that although "300 People, *gentle* and *simple*, may have dined at Hampden-Hall," "no more than about 126, including Gentlemen, Freeholders, Freemen and *Boys*, dined and *paid* for their Dinners." The suggestion here was that McDougall and his high-ranking supporters had treated most of the diners at Hampden Hall, inferring that most of the men who dined there were not economically independent, and some were only children—individuals who held no political or economic agency or independence. Thus, when McDougall's supporters claimed it was above three hundred people, they were lying, which, in turn, showed that they lacked virtue and were not the kind of people New Yorkers should associate with to secure their economic independence. As the DeLanceys put it, "it resembles too closely their *Fraud* and *Deceit*." The DeLanceyite author also alleged McDougall's supporters were not truly loyal to George III—in other words, they were not Britons. One of McDougall's supporters, writing as "HAMPDEN," responded in Holt's *New-York Journal*, denigrating the DeLanceyite as a misguided, misinformed partisan. McDougall's jail-cell politicking prompted James Duane to write "A Defence of the GENERAL ASSEMBLY" in his "Dougliad" series, writing that they had advanced the city's "*internal OEconomy*," that is, its political economy. McDougall, on the other hand, had "*betrayed the common Cause*" and through his advancement of "The furious Zeal

of Party Spirit," he sought only "to damn to ever-lasting Ignominy the unsul-
lied Reputation of the *Colony*, keenly pursued under the Mask of *public Spirit*."
Simply put, McDougall was a liar. He was everything he said the DeLanceys
were.[47]

The back-and-forth between McDougall's supporters and the DeLanceys was
tiring and distracting. Indeed, as they went back and forth about how many
New Yorkers dined where, on March 24 British soldiers tried to destroy the
newly erected liberty pole. Their attempts were foiled after two attempts, in
part because New Yorkers forced them off. After retreating to Hampden Hall,
its proprietor, Henry Bicker, repelled the soldiers with a fixed bayonet. What
a sight Bicker must have presented, defending his establishment. For almost
every night thereafter, the liberty pole was closely guarded.[48]

But partisanship remained. Essays filled the city's weekly newspapers.
Broadsides were published with regularity, often simply reprinting newspaper
essays, and they were likely pasted onto the windows and walls of the city's
taverns and coffeehouses. In a way, it was probably harder to avoid the partisan arguments than not. People heard the same arguments day after day after
day, and those arguments like reinforced partisans' views to the near-total ex-
clusion or all other ideas. Indeed, eighteenth-century New Yorkers almost
certainly frequented places and read publications that aligned with and reinforced their views. John Holt's *New-York Journal*, for example, was considered
a radical newspaper, and it was well known that the DeLanceys enjoyed dining at Abraham Montayne's tavern. McDougall's supporters, on the other
hand, had Hampden Hall. Indeed, as New Yorkers' partisanship drove them
further away from their opponents, it brought like-minded New Yorkers closer
together.

There was little respite for New Yorkers, engaged or otherwise. McDougall was brought before a grand jury on April 25. The jurors were likely familiar to him, too. They included partisans Charles McEvers and George
Brewerton Jr. Of the eighteen people on the jury, one New Yorker noted that
only three were "likely to shew any tenderness for one who flagitiously flies
into the face of Government." The odds were stacked against McDougall, particularly when seen alongside his indictment. McDougall, it read, sought to
challenge New York's government and foment disorder through unfounded
allegations that New Yorkers "were in the utmost Peril and danger of being
Subverted and overturned by the evil measures" of the assembly and Colden.[49]

But the Scottish immigrant was not intimidated by the indictment or the
occasion. According to William Smith Jr., who was arguably the most prominent Livingston still active in public life, when McDougall came before the

grand jury he was accompanied by "An immense Multitude." Smith added, "He spoke with vast Propriety & awed and astonished Many." McDougall also retained John Morin Scott as counsel, and William Livingston served as associate counsel. It was to be a trial in which the DeLanceys and McDougall and the Livingstons went head-to-head. More importantly, though, McDougall's performance as he went from the New Gaol to the courtroom mobilized further support. "He . . . added I believe to the Number of his Friends," wrote Smith. By then, McDougall was a "republican idol." But when the trial began it quickly became obvious that the evidence against McDougall was murky, at best. James Parker's apprentices were questioned about McDougalls. In total, three apprentices testified, but none offered conclusive evidence that McDougall wrote *To the Betrayed Inhabitants* and the grand jury did not have enough evidence to convict. Given that his trial was brought before the colony's supreme court on its final day for the term, the trial was postponed until the following July. McDougall was released on bail. This time, with the help of Philip Livingston and Nicholas Bayard, he paid it.[50]

James Parker died on July 2, 1770, in Burlington, New Jersey, shortly before McDougall's trial was set to resume. Described by John Holt as "eminent in his Profession" and of "sound Judgment, & extensive Knowledge," Parker was the chief witness in the case against McDougall. With him gone, the case collapsed. And although the New York government, led by the DeLanceys, tried to secure a prosecution and subsequently imprisoned McDougall once again, he was released in the spring of 1771. He was never convicted of writing *To the Betrayed Inhabitants*.[51]

In a letter written earlier in 1770, Peter R. Livingston described McDougall as "a Man of Worth," someone who "acts from a true Spirit of Liberty." Livingston also noted that his faction was "indeavouring to make Capt. McDugalls Cause as popular as possible that in case he should be Convicted the fine may be light, and the more we git the other Colonies to take the Alarm the greater the probability to git him Cleared." In another letter, Livingston wrote of the "Surprizing Coalition" between Colden and the DeLanceys, which, he believed, drove the attempted prosecution of McDougall. Livingston recognized that New York City's political arena had evolved between McDougall's emergence in December of 1769 and his trial in the late spring of 1770. The Livingston faction had thrown its support behind McDougall. So, too, had the city's lawyers. William Smith Jr., a member of the Royal Council, drafted a letter in which he labeled McDougall a "gallant Son of Liberty." He also drafted another, arguing that everything McDougall said in his broadside was accurate. Elites and non-elites were working together against the DeLanceys and Colden. Two coherent, politically motivated groups had emerged in New York City, both of whom referred to themselves as the *"true* Sons of Liberty." These groups fed off each other, using the other's partisanship and political economy to reinforce their own ideas and their own interests.[52]

Not all New Yorkers sought participation in these two groups. Others maintained active lives outside of them. But for those whose political personae were articulated through the *"Club"* or alongside McDougall, their association served as an effective means to develop a distinct civic and political identity. For some, these identities had long-term political implications. But despite both groups' claims that they embodied New Yorkers' sentiments, their ability to mobilize further broad-based support was contingent upon their continued attempts to bring New Yorkers into their orbit. What New Yorkers did not realize was that further opportunities to encourage partisanship were on the horizon—and McDougall was on the streets, ready to mobilize supporters. Within the course of a few years, McDougall established himself as the most important figure within New York City politics, and he did so without being elected to the assembly, being nominated to the Royal Council, or serving in any other position sanctioned by Parliament.

CHAPTER 5

Liberty and No Importation
Popular Politics and Associationism

Alexander McDougall's rise within New York City's political world was unexpected. Compared with the historic, long-lasting financial and political clout of the DeLanceys, as well as the Livingstons, almost everything about McDougall was new: his money, his status, his political support. His heritage as a Scotsman does not appear to have affected his ascension, either—something that was unusual, for much of the eighteenth century, anti-Scottish sentiment was widespread in Britain and its colonies. Many believed the Scots posed a threat to the country's political and economic security, as well as its national identity and traditional gender roles. Scotophobia was also present in New York City. During the Stamp Act riots of 1765, New Yorkers dressed up Lt. Gov. Cadwallader Colden as a Jacobite drummer and burned him in effigy. But McDougall's rise within the city's popular political framework was welcomed. He was the so-called Wilkes of America. He challenged not only the traditional political establishment in New York but Scotophobia, as well.[1]

For many, McDougall represented political liberty and the city's freedom as he continued to advocate for colonial autonomy. He, like many others, including the DeLanceys, sought the repeal of the Townshend Acts, but by the spring of 1770 McDougall and the DeLanceys advocated different means through which to secure their goal. By this stage, the DeLanceys and many of their supporters were moderate or establishment Whigs. Their equivalents in Britain were the likes of Charles Watson-Wentworth, second Marquis of Rockingham, and Edmund Burke, member of Parliament (MP) for Wendover and Rockingham's private secretary. These metropole-based political figures believed that even if Parliament had the right to tax its colonies, doing so was not always a good idea. The DeLanceys held a similar view. As James DeLancey told Rockingham, colonists "have the Right of giving away their own Money and cannot conceive with what Equity the house of Commons should in Ease to themselves and their Constituents burthen the Colonies with all much Taxes as they may think proper to Impose." "It would have been happy for Great Britain and America, if this Controversy on the Rights of Taxation had never began." What was more important for the DeLanceys and their supporters was encouraging and securing colonial economic growth, something that had been the primary argument during the elections of 1768 and 1769 and had defined their behavior during winter of 1769 and 1770. It also inspired their thinking for the creation of the Chamber of Commerce and the Marine Society as they sought to increase production and consumption.[2]

Alexander McDougall and his supporters' equivalents in Britain were different. They included likes of the "Great Commoner" William Pitt the Elder, first Earl of Chatham; the one-eyed Irish MP Isaac Barré; William Petty, second Earl of Shelburne; and John Wilkes, McDougall's political namesake. Together, these men represented a form of eighteenth-century political thought that fully embraced republican ideas about individual freedom and the public good. Their social and political worlds were governed by ideological convictions that prioritized individual liberty and checks against government corruption. The DeLanceys' apparent alliance with Lt. Gov. Cadwallader Colden, coupled with their subsequent actions toward McDougall, made it appear to some New Yorkers that their local concerns were of little importance or consequence to the colony's institutional governance and, by extension, to its political economy.[3]

The interplay between local and imperial concerns worsened as McDougall sat in his jail cell. Between mid-1767 and mid-1769 Parliament passed a series of reforms that became known as the Townshend Acts. Its reasoning was threefold: to enhance its position within its colonies, to raise more revenue from the East India Company, and to better enforce trading regulations. Above all, in New York and the colonies, the Townshend Acts' most important effect was that they levied taxes on colonial imports of British paper, lead, paint, glass, and East India Company tea. The money that was raised from the duties would be used to defray the salaries of colonial judges and governors, a consequence of which was that they would dramatically reduce the power of colonial assemblies, including New York's. Since the administration of George Clark (1736–1743), the assembly controlled when the governor was paid. In the colony's not-too-distant past, the assembly's control over the governor's salary had become a point of contention. In the 1740s George Clinton, who was then governor, complained to Colden and others about the power the assembly held over the appropriation of his salary, prompting Clinton to note, "The Offices of the Govern^t are become Dependent on the Assembly." Colden, who acted as Clinton's chief minister throughout much of his gubernatorial tenure, thought it was a serious problem, too, writing, "All our party Politicks is laid on the assembly's granting money for the Support of Government." With the passage of the Townshend Acts, no more.[4]

The acts were named after Britain's newly appointed chancellor of the exchequer, Charles Townshend, a tory politician who sought to advance George Grenville's extractive imperialism. As chancellor, Townshend oversaw His Majesty's Treasury as well as trade, but because Pitt was ill for much of his tenure as prime minister, Townshend controlled much of the government and its business. For him, the duties were the beginning of a larger slate of fiscal reforms to better incorporate Britain's colonies into its vast empire. He sought a *"real American revenue,"* one that would bring a modest £65,000, roughly 10 percent of the cost of American garrisons, to ensure that colonial officials received their salaries without having to deal with colonial legislatures. Equally important, though, Townshend believed the amount coming in from the duties and later reforms could bring in as much as £1 million per annum. He also believed that the duties would be met with little to no opposition. Townshend, who went against all his fellow cabinet members when introducing the reforms, believed the money raised from his duties and later reforms would balance Britain's books.[5]

Charles Townshend was determined not to fail, as Grenville had done in 1765. But he and others misjudged how colonists would respond to his legislation. Opposition was widespread, and although Townshend's death in September 1767 ensured he remained unaware of the impact his duties had, many believed the legislation was designed to subjugate Britain's colonies and reassert Parliament's absolute sovereignty. As James DeLancey put it, the duties were "unnecessary Restrictions on the American Trade." DeLancey's political associates in Britain agreed; for instance, Edmund Burke described Townshend's legislation—the duties and the Restraining Act, which prevented the assembly from legislating—as a "confusion of ideas." Despite this, the legislation easily passed the House of Commons. (Shortly before the legislation was passed into law, Charles Townshend was granted the freedom of the City of London, in part because of his imperial legislation.) The opposition to the duties was fierce and long-lasting. The day-to-day impact of the Townshend

Acts and New Yorkers' competing political economies governed how they lived their daily lives.[6]

The Townshend Acts and Nonimportation

Debates over the Townshend Acts emerged before the DeLanceys' rise in the New York legislature. But New Yorkers' responses did little to incite the kind of broad-based, violent opposition that appeared when news of the Stamp Act arrived in Manhattan. Instead, the strongest opposition to the Townshend Acts appeared outside New York, coming from a Philadelphia lawyer named John Dickinson.

Dickinson, like the DeLanceys, was an advocate of a consumption-based growth policy for the colonies. He believed that the economic prosperity of colonial British America, as well as Great Britain, was contingent upon commercial success. The Townshend Acts, Dickinson believed, threatened the colonial prosperity of the entire British Empire. In his mind, the duties were illegal, and so he took up his pen to author a twelve-part series titled "Letters from a Farmer in Pennsylvania," which were published in Pennsylvania newspapers between December 1767 and February 1768. Dickinson's essays were reprinted in each of New York's three biweekly newspapers, as well as in almost every newspaper in colonial British America, making them among the most widely read anti-parliamentary rhetoric until the Revolutionary War. The average delay for John Holt to publish the letters was ten days; for James Parker it was eleven days; and for Hugh Gaine it was twelve. In other words, when the letters arrived in New York, the printers likely mobilized their types and apprentices, publishing them as soon as they could. Indeed, the only newspapers in the colonies that republished the letters sooner were those in Philadelphia. New Yorkers and almost everyone in an urban center could not avoid Dickinson's letters. They were the most widely circulated pieces of political propaganda during the imperial crisis. (They were also published in pamphlet editions.) The impact of the letters was considerable. One New Yorker believed Dickinson's writings had revealed the duties' problems "very ingeniously," noting that they did not have to add anything in their own works because they were "fully treated" in Dickinson's series. Indeed, Dickinson successfully captured colonists' feelings toward the Townshend Acts. More importantly, though, the letters reinforced intercolonial communication and political networks; not only were the letters reprinted for financial reasons—people wanted to read them, printers printed them—but the letters were also reprinted to mobilize support against the Townshend Acts. In doing so, printers, as well as those who read and distributed the essays, brought politically engaged colonists closer together.[7]

New York's opposition occurred at the local level. Instead of inciting violence to promote their repeal, as many did during the Stamp Act riots, New Yorkers focused their attentions on changing how they lived their daily lives, hoping that their collective action would secure the repeal of the Townshend Acts. (Between 1768 and 1775 three riots occurred.) To do this New Yorkers focused on where the Townshend Acts affected them most: the city's marketplace.[8]

In the winter of 1767, some rebranded the Society for the Encouragement of Arts, Agriculture, and Economy; the Society for Promoting Arts encouraged New York–made goods, particularly homespun manufactures, in an attempt to bolster the city's economy, provide employment for the city's non-elites, and force Parliament's hand. The society also provided financial assistance to those in need and, in February 1768, declared that none of its member would eat lamb, noting, "It would promote Industry, and assist in Clothing our numerous Poor." The society reasoned that the textile materials lambs yielded were too important to the city's local economy. Their example was successful. Other groups and societies, including the Sons of Liberty, agreed not to eat lamb until the summer.[9]

The Chamber of Commerce was founded to promote the DeLanceys' political economy within New York City, but its leaders—James DeLancey, Jacob Walton, James Jauncey, and John Cruger, the chamber's inaugural president—were aware of New Yorkers' concerns about the city's marketplace. They knew that more and more New Yorkers were falling into poverty; the DeLanceys' election was partly due to their campaign messaging about lifting their constituents into a better economic situation, and, as has already been discussed, they championed economic mobility—and their messages resonated with voters. (Hundreds of people were in the city's poorhouse, and church wardens assisted hundreds outdoors, as well. Poverty, one newspaper article claimed, was "infectious.") The DeLanceys moved forward with implementing opposition to the Townshend Acts. After receiving a letter from Boston merchants calling for the intercolonial nonimportation agreement, in its inaugural meeting, founding members of the chamber discussed the possibility of New York's entry into such an agreement if their urban counterparts in Massachusetts and Philadelphia did the same.[10]

On August 27, 1768, New York adopted a nonimportation agreement. It was adhered to by almost all the city's merchants, each of whom signed their name to a lengthy parchment agreeing that all orders sent after August 15 would be retracted and that, after November 1, no goods would be imported until the Townshend Acts were repealed. The city's tradespeople and artisans soon adopted a similar agreement. Together, New Yorkers attempted to force Parliament's hand by affecting how much money the Townshend Acts would raise. By signing their names to lists, colonists showed Parliament the power of popular politics.

New York's nonimportation agreement came into effect shortly before the 1769 election. As we have seen, the DeLanceys' skillful use of the Massachusetts circular letter enabled them to mobilize enough support to secure a commanding electoral victory in early 1769. James DeLancey, for one, was described as "the Oracle of the Sons of Liberty" in December. And for much of that year the nonimportation agreement enjoyed popular support. Even though New Yorkers still pushed for the repeal of the Townshend Acts, many believed that the reorientation of the city's consumer marketplace would promote its long-term growth.[11]

Parliament enforced the duties, leaving little room for compromise. Frederick North, second Earl of Guilford, who succeeded Townshend as chancellor of the exchequer, believed the duties were essential to Britain's economic future. Others disagreed. "The affairs in N. America tend more and more to confusion," wrote the Marquis of Rockingham. In another letter, Rockingham described the reaction to the Townshend Acts as "the dangerous madness." In January 1770, however, Grafton lost key members of his cabinet, whom he was unable to replace. On January 30, he left office, and was replaced by George III's longtime friend, the thirty-eight-year-old Lord North. North also enjoyed broad-based support throughout Britain. He, like Townshend, was an authoritarian—someone who sought to centralize the British Empire, increasing the power of Parliament and reducing the power of colonial legislatures—and he was among those cabinet members who rejected Grafton's efforts to repeal the Townshend Acts. But North was also pragmatic and a skilled politician. Amid increasing opposition to the duties, culminating in the Boston Massacre of March 5, 1770, he withdrew British troops from Boston, overrode the Currency Act of 1764, and pushed for the repeal of the duties. He also renewed the Quartering Act of 1765 without amendment, despite opposition in Britain and New York, and George III promoted Thomas Gage to lieutenant general, after which he was one of the most senior figures in the British Army.[12]

In April 1770, North secured the partial repeal of the Townshend Acts. From the following December the taxes on glass, lead, paint, and paper would be no more. Parliament responded meekly to the colonists' demands. A tax on tea was retained. North was more conciliatory toward the colonies than most of his recent predecessors, but he still believed in Parliament's absolute, indivisible sovereignty over the colonies; the tax on tea remained, and it was expected to bring in about £20,000, which was less than the sum generated by duties that were already in place on calicoes that were sent to the colonies. What's more, the following month Parliament permitted the colony to print the £120,000 that the DeLancey legislature had pushed for, in an albeit heavily amended form that the assembly did not accept until February 1771, largely thanks to the colony's agent of over two decades, Robert Charles, in his final acts as New York's representative. New Yorkers, and colonists more generally, no doubt recognized the paltry sum the Townshend Acts created, and once news of the partial repeal and parliamentary authorization to print money reached Manhattan, it prompted a series of debates about nonimportation and, more important, New York's place within the British Empire.[13]

In May 1770 news of the partial repeal of the Townshend Acts arrived in New York. The city's printers—Huge Gaine, James Parker, and John Holt—published multiple reports from Parliament and the other colonies in each their respective newspapers. Reaction was swift. Both the DeLanceys and McDougall and his supporters made their feelings known: the former wanted to resume trading; the latter did not, believing the tax on tea was unconstitutional because it originated from Parliament and not the New York Assembly. As Holt put it in his issue of May 17, maintaining the nonimportation agreement was *"the only affectual means, to ward off inglorious Bondage, and obtain a redress of all our grievances,"* namely, the repeal of the final duty on tea.[14]

For Alexander McDougall, as for Holt, giving up nonimportation was misguided, if not absurd. Their reasons were practical and ideological. They appreciated how effective the agreement had been and the impact it was having on British trade and commerce. Nowhere was the agreement more effective than in New York. The colony's agreement had a greater financial impact than any other colony in British America. Francis Bernard, the despised governor of Massachusetts, reported to the authoritarian Wills Hill, first Earl of Hillsborough, secretary of state for the colonies and president of the Board of Trade, "A Gentleman from New York tells me that the Merchants there continue very stout in Non-exportation." Holt, having aligned himself with McDougall, wanted like-minded New Yorkers to realize the positive impact the nonimportation agreement was having on their cause. In an issue of his newspaper, he printed the comparative value of New York's trade from 1768 to 1769, showing that in a single-year period the value of the colony's trade fell by 85 percent, from £482,000 to £74,000. The success of the nonimportation agreement can partly be explained by how rigorously it was enforced. In March 1769, a committee was formed to oversee the city's trade and commerce, and it decreed that anyone who violated the agreement "should be deemed Enemies to this Country."

Some goods still arrived, but the guilty individuals often pleaded ignorance, giving up their goods to the committee, and those who willfully violated it were set straight. Since Parliament had repealed most of the duties because of commercial pressure, the continuation of the nonimportation agreement made sense: it would push British legislators to repeal the remaining duty on tea because the economic impact was too great.[15]

The practical impact of the nonimportation agreement was also complemented by its ideological infrastructure, and its continuation was a means through which those who supported Alexander McDougall's political economy could mobilize and reinforce support. McDougall did not believe that a free-working marketplace was legitimate if the people's welfare—that is, the public good—was under threat, and his stance was grounded in the belief that the remaining, financially unprofitable duty on tea was designed to subjugate New Yorkers' welfare, and if they submitted to it they were abrogating their rights as Britons and rubber-stamping Parliament's authority to tax the colonies, whenever it wanted, in the future.[16]

When news of the partial repeal of the Townshend Acts arrived, McDougallites responded quickly, hoping to convince colonists that New York's agreement should remain in place, as in the other colonies. But they also realized that they needed to show people why their political economy was the correct path for New York. In doing so they had to overcome people's worries over the city's struggling economy. To do this they advocated a town-meeting style of politics, encouraging non-elites' attendance and participation in the proceedings and promoting the polarization of city politics, ostensibly hoping that people's partisanship would cloud, if not overcome, the good-faith arguments that both sides articulated.

McDougallites argued that New Yorkers' liberties were dependent on the continued enforcement of the nonimportation agreement. In an essay entitled "LIBERTAS ET NATALE SOLUM" (Liberty and my Native Soil), "CATO" outlined the McDougallites' view, linking the continuation of the nonimportation agreement with the maintenance of New Yorkers' liberties: their commitment to nonimportation was the only way to "recover our freedom." "CATO" implicated the DeLanceys in the discussion, arguing that if New Yorkers listened to those "selfish and insidious persons" who sought only to promote "their private advantage," they would be moving against the "common weal." Other essays reinforced the McDougallites' view. McDougall and his supporters printed of a diverse range of materials to broadcast their message, which was one of unity and collective mobilization. "A CARD" urged New Yorkers to *"unite and stand BY YOUR INTEGRITY"* by supporting those *"BRAVE and WISE"* men who would represent and protect *"the sacred Cause of Liberty deeply rooted in your*

Hearts." Another essayist argued that if the nonimportation agreement was lifted, it would "entail infamy upon this province," encouraging the establishment of political "slavery upon the whole continent."[17]

But to mobilize broad-based support required more than words. It required action, too—and the McDougallites took their politics out onto the streets to do just that. On May 30, 1770, after the widespread dissemination of news from the other colonies that they would maintain nonimportation, McDougallites called for a meeting at City Hall, at the intersection of Broad Street and Wall Street. According to Alexander McDougall, a small broadside was distributed "in the most public Places" around the city: coffeehouses, taverns, market-places, churches, wharves—places where New Yorkers not only worked but also socialized. The advertisement was for New Yorkers "of all Ranks," too, and it called upon those "Friends of Liberty of all Ranks" to meet to discuss "Measures to support the Liberties of this Country." It was reported that "a considerable Number of the Inhabitants" attended and they resolved to cease any form of engagement—economic, political, social—with individuals who and colonies that went against the nonimportation agreement. New York would not import goods; those who did were "Enemies to the Liberties of North-America." "To the utmost of" their ability, they declared, New York would "preserve the Non-Importation Agreement . . . until the Act aforesaid is totally repealed." They also agreed to reach out to other colonies to try to persuade their inhabitants to adopt comparable resolutions. The McDougallites, it seemed, had mobilized support within Manhattan. But they were not finished. They were looking beyond Wall Street, beyond the Foundry, and beyond Nicholas Bayard's, Leonard Lispenard's, and the DeLanceys' estates. Alexander McDougall had their sights set on intercolonial political mobilization, believing he was protecting not only New Yorkers' liberties but the liberties of all colonists in North America.[18]

The McDougallites' resolutions were agreed to without the sanction of the city's Committee of Inspection. The committee, which was set up in 1769 and later reorganized, had one aim: to enforce the nonimportation agreement in New York. Most of its members were DeLanceys. Because the meeting was held "without the Knowledge of the Committee," its "irregular Proceeding[s]" necessitated further deliberation on nonimportation—discussions that they had to be present for. The committee thus rejected and disregarded the McDougallites' resolutions. They would reach their own conclusions the following day.[19]

Following a meeting that New Yorkers were prohibited from attending, the committee added nine new members: Miles Sherbrooke, Charles McEvers, John Alsop, Thomas W. Moore, Isaac Sears, John Broome, Sampson Simpson, Peter Vandervoort, and Theodorus Van Wyck. Simpson, Sears, and Vandervoort held political ties to the McDougallites, and Sherbrooke, McEvers, and Alsop had ties to *"the Club"* through voting for the DeLanceys in 1769, belonging to the Chamber of Commerce or the Marine Society, or by participating in the March 1770 celebration at Abraham Montayne's tavern. (Theodorus Van Wyck was the defeated Livingston candidate in 1769).[20]

The new committee moved quickly to consider New York's response to nonimportation. To thwart the McDougallites' ability to mobilize support, it also proposed that the fate of the city's nonimportation agreement would be decided by New Yorkers through ward-by-ward polls, which offered both groups an opportunity to mobilize support, almost making it a public statement on whose vision for the city's short- and long-term future captured the needs of the city. The DeLancey-led committee also dispatched a letter to merchants in other urban centers, asking whether they would consider ending their nonimportation agreements on everything except tea. They refused.[21]

The city's population was being courted by both groups. This was not entirely dissimilar to what happened during the election, but in this instance New Yorkers' mobilization was not for institutional purposes. It was more than that; their mobilization was truly popular, outside of the traditional boundaries of the colony's assembly and the city's Common Council, and they were being called to decide on an issue that the assembly had no control over—a significant step in bringing politics into people's parlors and the city's taverns and coffeehouses, as well as its streets. When New Yorkers cast their votes, they made a public statement that had both local and imperial consequences; after all, what was imported affected how they lived their lives. It affected what they wore, what they ate and drank, how they furnished their homes, and more. Did they want to continue without many of the goods they had grown accustomed to? British exports had fallen from £2.5 million in 1768 to £1.6 million a year later—a difference that New Yorkers contributed to—and the citywide polls tested their sentiments, political and practical.[22]

Polls were taken on June 11, 1770. Partisans hustled through the city streets, knocking on doors, canvassing opinion. Having known of the partial repeal for a month, some twelve hundred New Yorkers voted to amend the city's agreement: all goods except tea were agreed to be imported. Parliament had repealed almost all the duties. Their protests worked. And thus, letters were dispatched informing their Bostonian and Philadelphian counterparts of their decision. Then, New Yorkers were told that "if this Agreement should be rejected by the other Colonies, the Sense of the Town will again be taken." Alexander McDougall hotly disputed results of the poll, believing that his opponents unfairly mobilized their partisan supporters to ensure victory. He alleged that the poll was carried out by "selfish, mercenary importers, and a few mechanicks," adding that they were all "tools of a party."[23]

Following allegations of corruption, two outspoken McDougallites, Isaac Sears and Peter Vandervoort, resigned from the Committee of Inspection. They reported that by amending the nonimportation agreement, the committee had "counteract[ed] the very Design of our Appointment." That is, by importing goods, they would be moving against the public welfare. The ideological divisions were widening and becoming even more apparent as the two groups' competing political economies clashed in the city's public sphere, governing not only the city's institutional politics but its popular iterations, as well.[24]

Indeed, the city's political ecosystem became increasingly polluted over the coming weeks, largely due to other urban centers' decisions about nonimportation. Each group offered an ideologically based vision for the city's future. In early July 1770, representatives from Boston and Philadelphia outlined their opposition to New York's decision to amend their nonimportation agreement. Upon hearing the news, a private meeting took place to discuss the future of the city's trade and commerce; it was attended by the Committee of Inspection and a handful of other colonists, most of whom were associated with "the Friends to Liberty and Trade." Of the twenty-three attendees, sixteen voted for DeLancey candidates in 1769; thirteen dined in Montayne's tavern in March 1770; and seven were also members of either the Chamber of Commerce or the Marine Society. The only man who did not have positive ties with the DeLanceys was McDougall. Without enough political clout to overcome the DeLanceys' voices, the attendees determined that a second ward-by-ward poll was required to determine how the city would respond to nonimportation. This time, however, it would be DeLancey partisans who collected the signatures, all but ensuring the outcome they desired.[25]

For the DeLanceys, their ideas remained important, but it became clear that their interests affected their behavior. They did not want to be outmaneuvered by McDougall or lose face. The date set for what essentially became a partisan roll call was Saturday, July 7, 1770. Both the DeLanceys and McDougall gathered close to one another before canvassing support—McDougall was at City Hall, the DeLanceys at Montayne's tavern. As votes were collected, it became clear that most New Yorkers supported the resumption of trade. But the McDougallites thought the election was rigged in the DeLanceys' favor, and they would not be outdone. As they quickly surmised the vote was going against them, they moved forward "at the expence of blood" to stop those DeLancey partisans who were collecting votes. They "insulted and abused" them and even attempted to tear "their papers"—that is, New Yorkers' votes.

They had also commissioned a sailmaker to produce a flag embroidered with *"Liberty and no Importation, In Union with the other Colonies."* They had political badges made, too, before marching around New York's streets with "musick, colors, and staffs." They chanted, *"No Importation."* It was an emphatic display of partisanship and politics. But it was not enough. Two days later, after the polling ended, the sentiment of New Yorkers was quantified: 792 had publicly voted for the resumption of trade; 462 advocated the agreement's continuation. New Yorkers were likely aware of the sentiments of those voters in their lives: family members, neighbors, their shopkeeper, the person who sits near them in church. But if they needed further evidence, James Parker provided it, printing the names of everyone who voted in two consecutive issues of his newspaper. Columns and columns of names publicized and further politicized the voters' sentiments; everyone who had access to the newspaper could learn of their vote—New Yorkers, Bostonians, those in Parliament. Lt. Gov. Cadwallader Colden also reported that only "about 300 were neutral or unwilling to declare their sentiments," adding that there were only "a few" New Yorkers of "distinction" who opposed the resumption of trade. The vote was local, but it had vast consequences for the imperialism of the British Empire and New York City's place within it.[26]

For the DeLanceys, the election results reinforced their confidence in their popularity and political economy. It also reinforced their partisanship and opposition to Alexander McDougall and his supporters. Take Charles McEvers's vote, for example. Born in 1739, McEvers was a Manhattan merchant based on Dock Street, a short walk from Cruger's Wharf, where he traded in dry goods, teas, alcohol, and Irish exports. McEvers's family was well versed with New Yorkers' views on where they placed in the British Empire. Charles's brother James was infamously appointed and later resigned as the city's Stamp Officer in 1765. By the early 1770s, Charles McEvers was a fierce DeLancey partisan. He voted for them in 1769. He was a member of the Chamber of Commerce and the Marine Society. In March 1770, he celebrated the repeal of the Stamp Act in Montayne's tavern. Moreover, Charles's sister Mary was married to DeLanceyite Charles Ward Apthorp, and his son Charles Jr. later married Mary Bache, Theophylact Bache's daughter, as DeLanceyite families came together. (Charles also named one of his children Bache and acted as a sponsor at Amelia Matilda Bache's baptism.) And of the nonimportation vote, he told a friend "that he signed to import goods in order to put an End to yᵉ Power of a Turbulent Party," namely, McDougall—and what he represented.[27]

Charles McEvers was not alone, either. Many New Yorkers used the vote to articulate and reinforce their partisanship. Four hundred and sixty-two colonists voted against the resumption of trade in New York. They represented a diverse group who represented the city's inhabitants: pewterers, doctors, merchants, shopkeepers, a hatter, a tavern-keeper, a joiner, a printer. De facto leadership was provided by the two former DeLancey supporters, John Lamb and Isaac Sears, as well as Alexander McDougall. (Additionally, though women were excluded from most formal aspects of institutional politics in pre-wartime New York City, when votes on nonimportation were taken, female merchants and shopkeepers were consulted. In this instance, three women voted "AGAINST IMPORTING.")[28]

An illustration of the group's associationism can be seen through their voting behavior in the 1769 election, showing clear opposition to the DeLanceys. Of the 462 signatories, 209 (42%) voted in the 1769 election, casting 826 votes between them: 591 votes (71.5%) were cast for the Livingston candidates and 235 votes (28.5%) were cast for the DeLancey candidates. The Livingston candidates received no less than 140 votes each; no DeLancey candidate received more than 66. The Livingstons also received more comprehensive votes than the DeLanceys. Of the 209 voters, 132 (63.1%) voted for two or more Livingstons and no DeLanceys. Forty-six (22%) voted for the DeLanceys. Thirty-one (14.8%) divided their votes between the two groups. McDougallites were tapping into those who held a weak state–subject relationship. The nonimportation dispute also led some of "the Friends to Liberty and Trade" to support Alexander McDougall. Of the 233 "Friends to Liberty and Trade" who dined in Abraham Montayne's tavern, in March 1770, only thirteen supported the nonimportation agreement's continuation, including the DeLanceyite propagandist, Isaac Corsa. Other New Yorkers representing the mercantile interest in March 1770 were also present; James Beekman was a well-known merchant, Daniel Dunscomb and Joseph Bull were dry-goods importers, and Francis Fowler was a ship's captain.[29]

Furthermore, those advocating nonimportation also drew some support from the Marine Society and the Chamber of Commerce. Of the Marine Society's seventy-three members, eight supported the continuation of the nonimportation agreement. More critically, of the eight members, four voted in the 1769 election. These men were not DeLancey supporters; two, Henry C. and Nicholas Bogart, were comprehensive Livingston voters, and William Heyer and Anthony Rutgers voted for three Livingston candidates and one DeLancey.[30]

Identifying the precise occupations of these individuals is difficult, but as is indicated in the newspaper, Nicholas Bogart and Isaac Sheldon were shopkeepers, David Dickson was a ship's captain, and Robert Ray was a dry-goods importer. More generally, given that they were members of the Marine Society, all of them were involved in trade. Similarly, ten members of the Chamber of

Commerce supported the agreement's continuation, and like those in the Marine Society, all the 1769 voters, except for Isaac Sears, were predominantly Livingston supporters.[31] The cohort of merchants and shopkeepers who were opposed to the resumption of trade indicates that, at least for these individuals, economic self-sufficiency was probably less important than their ideological conviction. Indeed, for some, including Bull and Dunscomb, the political decision that the nonimportation poll afforded allowed them to move away from the DeLanceys.

Of those 792 who voted for the resumption of importation, 259, or around a third, voted in the 1769 election, casting 1,025 votes between them. The advocates for importation were as diverse as their opponents. Alongside a handful of women, there were druggists, grocers, sailmakers, politicians, doctors, bakers. Many mercantile families were also represented, including the Beekmans, the Laights, the Ludlows, the Rhinelanders, and the Ten Eycks, who signed alongside well-known merchants like Theophylact Bache and Henry White. Leadership was provided by prominent DeLancey partisans: Isaac Low, Jacob Walton, and James Jauncey.

The overlap between the 1769 poll list and the 1770 importation list also shows that the long-standing supporters endorsed the DeLanceys' view on nonimportation. Of the 259 voters in 1769 who voted in the nonimportation poll, 194 (74.9%) voted for only DeLancey candidates in 1769. Only twenty-eight (10.8%) did not vote for a DeLancey candidate, and 37 (14.2%) divided their votes between both groups. Moreover, the correlation between the proponents of ending nonimportation and the March 1770 dining list is striking; 108 (46%) voted for the resumption of trade in New York.[32] Of those who advocated trade and voted in 1769, sixty-nine dined in Abraham Montayne's tavern in March 1770, and of the 121 DeLanceyites who voted in 1770, 89.3 percent supported the resumption of trade.

Members of the Marine Society and the Chamber of Commerce also advocated the resumption of trade. The political sentiment of these individuals in favor of importation offers further illustration of their coalescence into political associations by mid-1770. Twenty-four members of the Marine Society advocated the resumption of trade.[33] Thirty-nine members of the Chamber of Commerce did so, too. It must be remembered, too, that not all the members of the Marine Society voted and that some part of its membership included ship's captains who may not have been in New York at the time of the poll. Similarly, not all members of the Chamber of Commerce voted. But of those who did vote, 77.4 percent of the Marine Society's members and 81.3 percent of the Chamber of Commerce's supported importation.[34] Of those who were members of either the Marine Society or the Chamber of Commerce and had voted in 1769, all except one voted for the DeLancey ticket.[35]

As in previous political contests, voting in the nonimportation debates had long-term political consequences. Of the 792 New Yorkers who supported the resumption of trade, 281 (35.48%) became loyalists in the American Revolution. Predictably, sixty were merchants (21.35%), but there were a larger proportion of skilled artisans (72 individuals, 25.62%) who joined them as loyalists. Of the 462 New Yorkers who supported the continuation of nonimportation, only ninety-four (20.35%) became loyalists. Most of these individuals were merchants (fourteen individuals, 14.89%), but skilled artisans were well represented (twenty-two individuals, 23.4%).[36]

It is important to consider the political associations of these men. They offer insight into the long-term consequences of their mobilization. Some advocates of importation were long-standing supporters of the DeLanceys. There were 118 future loyalists who voted in both the 1769 election and the mid-1770 election. Of these men, 110 (93.2%) voted for at least one DeLancey candidate in 1769. Of the 102 future loyalists who voted for the DeLancey ticket in 1769, 52 (50.1%) voted for the resumption of trade. The political connections are evident in other areas, as well. Of the 125 future loyalists who dined in Montayne's tavern, sixty-nine (55.2%) advocated the resumption of trade and forty-five (36%) voted for at least one DeLancey candidate. Of these forty-five DeLancey voters, twenty-seven (60%) voted for each DeLancey candidate. Moreover, of the twenty-four members of the pro-DeLancey Marine Society who supported the resumption of trade, nineteen (79.1%) became loyalists, and thirty (76.9%) members of the pro-DeLancey Chamber of Commerce became loyalists, too. Upon cross-examination, it becomes apparent that the political associations and connections these men formed during the preceding two-year period proved important arbiters of their political behavior in the American Revolution. These were long-standing, committed supporters of the DeLanceys. This core group of New Yorkers had been active political participants for several years, remaining on the same side throughout, and their pre-wartime dispositions, it seems, helped guide their political action in the years to come.

The McDougallites' response to the nonimportation agreement is also revealing. On July 25, 1770, McDougall published "A Protest" against the resumption of trade, a final attempt to mobilize support. In the essay, McDougall entered a lengthy critical discussion against the resumption of trade and "the Friends to Liberty and Trade." He argued that because tea was still subject to parliamentary duties, it was "a Test of the Parliamentary Right to tax us." It was "a Repetition of the Evils . . . we groaned during the Existence of . . . the Stamp Act." The McDougallites sought the *"preservation of American Liberty,"* and it was "the *Common Interest* of all the Colonies" to act together to secure the repeal of the tax on tea by perpetuating the nonimportation agreement. Following his classical republicanism, McDougall claimed that only through the full repeal of the Townshend Acts would New Yorkers be able to advance the public welfare. When McDougall's essay was published, it was noted that it had been *"signed by a considerable Number"* of New Yorkers, but it did not list their names. But in McDougall's personal papers the extant, though partially mutilated, manuscript copy of the essay is adorned with eighty-three signatures—and the vellum manuscript offers a basic muster roll of all those associated with Alexander McDougall in pre-wartime New York City: John Lamb, Isaac Sears, Gershom Mott, Peter R. Livingston, Peter Van Brugh Livingston, William Livingston, Hugh Hughes. None of these individuals were associated with the DeLanceys. None became loyalists in the American Revolution. They all became patriots—prominent ones, too.[37]

Despite his efforts, McDougall's attempts at reversing the result of the poll failed. The nonimportation agreement was lifted. Once again, the DeLanceys successfully cultivated broad-based support, mobilizing long-standing and new supporters despite the McDougallites' attempts to intimidate voters through violence. The DeLanceys' political economy held greater social, political, and economic relevance to ordinary New Yorkers, offering New Yorkers more opportunities. Removing the constraint of nonimportation enabled them to advance their—and the city's—economic stability. And by promoting economic independence, New Yorkers were able to bring more money into their pockets; and in so doing, they were protecting their property and projecting their masculinity within the political public sphere. After years of penny-pinching, ending nonimportation was a simple choice for many New Yorkers. Lifting the agreement was attractive because it presented opportunities for New Yorkers to secure their property through economic individualism. It served their common interests: to participate in the rehabilitation of New York City.[38]

The Ideas and Interests of Everyday Life

The political divisions—DeLanceyite and McDougallite—that emerged between 1769 and 1770 remained in place through 1775. Equally important, these divisions did not concern or involve only the elite. New Yorkers of all ranks were involved, and elite and non-elite New Yorkers, from both sides, worked together. From mid-1770, both groups adopted inward-looking characteristics that defined their public political lives and pushed them further apart and brought those within each group closer together. Their affiliation created a sense of commonality within the groups that transcended social cleavages. Two political groups had mobilized in pre-wartime New York City: one largely became loyalist, the other revolutionary or patriot. Between 1770 and 1775, these individuals shaped each other's political identity within New York City's political framework. Individual, family, and work-based networks interacted within the city's civic spaces voluntarily to create a sense of community with one another. It is difficult to decide whether bonds of friendship or political sentiment were more important. It is certain that they complemented and reinforced one another.[39]

Indeed, although McDougall lost popular support and relevance, the consequences of his rise on the DeLanceys' everyday lives was significant. With their almost-incessant campaigning against the Scotsman and his supporters, those who associated with the DeLanceys created a network of like-minded individuals. As they dined and campaigned together, they forged closer bonds and became more entrenched in one another's lives. These relationships became important arbiters of political sentiment not only in the early 1770s but during the American Revolution.[40]

Following the decision by New York's colonists to resume trading in July, the DeLanceys occupied a dominant position within the city's partisan public sphere. They held majorities in the New York Assembly as well as the Royal and Common Councils, and popular feeling in the city had moved against the McDougallites. It seemed as if their time had passed. As "LÆLIUS" wrote, "The noise of faction has dwindled into gentle murmurs," adding that the McDougallites had "vanished into thin air!" The prospect of the DeLanceys and their allies dominating New York City politics for years to come seemed altogether more likely as disputes over imperial issues subsided. Between 1770 and 1773, the British government did not pass any new measures that provoked opposition, pushing the McDougallites from the public limelight. Without the ability to mobilize support, their ideas lost political relevance and they were unable to continue public opposition to the remaining duty on tea. Popular opinion sided with the DeLanceys: they enacted nonimportation to push for the repeal of the Townshend Acts and lifted it when Parliament relented. They also secured the issuance of paper currency, showing those in Manhattan that they were following through on their principal election idea of 1768 and 1769. But the decline of popular partisanship was not entirely their doing. It was aided by the behavior of Gov. William Tryon, who was sworn into office on

July 9, 1771, after impressing as North Carolina's governor. Soon after assuming his role, Tryon kept "as clear as possible of the Parties," focusing instead on advancing the public good as the king's representative in New York.[41]

With cooling attitudes toward the imperial relationship, then, New Yorkers lived their lives. They interacted with their friends, their relations, and their colleagues, drawing on the networks they had developed over the previous few years. Networking in eighteenth-century New York City was an everyday practice. People saw each other regularly. As has already been noted, the city's narrow streets, numerous taverns, churches, and coffeehouses, and bustling wharves created a face-to-face culture. The increasing associationism of the DeLanceys brought them closer together, supporting and enhancing how these people lived their lives. As ships came and went, the constant presence of your DeLanceyite companion in your life became increasingly important. By 1775 DeLanceyites were intertwined in each other's lives through politics, business, and family to such an extent that their lives revolved as much around their interpersonal relationships as their shared politics. Three men—Frederick Rhinelander, Evert Bancker Jr., and Charles Nicoll—represent the formation and development of a partisan political identity that began in the late 1760s and lasted through the American Revolution, and by analyzing their networks it shows how ideas can affect interests and vice versa.[42]

Frederick Rhinelander

A twenty-seven-year-old storekeeper based at the corner of Burling's Slip at the tip of what is now John Street, Frederick Rhinelander dealt in "crockery and other merchandise." He was the eldest son of William Rhinelander, and in 1765 he married Mary Speeder, who was one year his senior. Frederick Rhinelander had two younger brothers, William Jr., born in 1753, and Philip, born in 1756. His sister Sarah was born in in 1755, and with his brothers he operated a successful business. Rhinelander's interactions have been analyzed from his business records—order-, memo-, and day-books—and land petitions and probate records.[43]

Network analysis for individuals like Rhinelander—and the individuals who follow—can be particularly helpful in understanding personal relationships and how they developed. Interactions throughout a set period are dynamic—people come in and out of each other's lives—but through sustained interaction it is possible to identify turning points and interpret friendships and loyalties over time. More critically, when networks are cross-examined and combined, the results can bring people together, showing interconnectivity between groups. This type of analysis is helpful when there is a dearth of correspondence between individuals in an area. And in New York City, where its inhabitants had no reason to write to one another, going beyond epistolary networks makes it possible to etch out not only DeLanceyite sociability in pre-wartime New York City but the various types of networks that operated simultaneously within a single urban center: familial, intellectual, religious, business.[44]

For this book, I analyzed Frederick Rhinelander's engagements with future loyalists as recorded in his memo- and order-book of 1772–1773. These sources are often messy. They were not designed to by read by anyone other than Rhinelander and his associates; they are filled with notation and hastily made edits. It is also difficult to determine how "strong" Rhinelander's relationships were using these sources. That is, just because somebody was, say, a "regular" customer, it does not mean their relationship with Rhinelander was necessarily stronger than someone else's. These kinds of sources are informative, however. They show who interacted with Rhinelander and when, and upon examination it becomes clear that Rhinelander interacted with many of his political associates. During this short period, eighteen future loyalists entered Rhinelander's store. He noted when they came in, what they bought, and how much it cost. The tavern-keeper and DeLanceyite David Grim and yeoman farmer John Davis were the two colonists who came into Rhinelander's store most frequently. On the three occasions Grim came in toward the end of the year, he purchased numerous items that were likely for his patrons, including enameled and agate pots. Davis's purchases were similar: crockery, pitchers, and engraved wine glasses. After Grim and Davis, six other colonists came in on two occasions, including DeLanceyites Edward and William Laight, Morris Earle, Philip Roe, Joshua Pell, and Joseph Thorne. Following this group were a series of other colonists who perhaps entered Rhinelander's store en route to another location.

Daybooks provide a more accurate insight into the daily lives of storekeepers. Until the American Revolution, Rhinelander's were characteristically meticulous. Every time a customer came into his store and purchased an item, not only did Rhinelander note the date, what they purchased, and how much they paid, he routinely assigned customers unique identification numbers. Rhinelander's daybook extends from 1774 to 1777. Engagements were analyzed from 1774 to 1775, revealing several differences from the social interactions recorded in his memo- and order-book of 1772–1773. The first is the increased number of interactions. As documented in his memo- and order-book, Rhinelander engaged with eighteen future loyalists. In his daybook, he interacted with sixty-three, an increase of 150 percent. The closest individual in Rhinelander's network was his brother, William Rhinelander Jr. Throughout this period, they interacted in Frederick's store seventeen times. This is not surprising; they worked together. Other future loyalists who also featured in Rhinelander's daily life who could be described as regular customers were James Rivington, Silas Purdy, Walter Franklin, Edward and William Laight, David Grim, John Roome, William Rhinelander Sr., Israel Seaman, and Jacob Brewerton. Each of these colonists engaged with Rhinelander between four and eight times. Colonists who did business with Rhinelander two to three times included Job Willets, James Mott, Israel Hallet, William Field, Nicholas Bogart, Thomas Buchanan, Walter Buchanan, Oliver DeLancey, Thomas Lynch, John Tabor Kempe, Samuel Carman, William Ustick, and Jacobus Lefferts. Other less-regular customers were also members of *"the Club,"* including Joseph Allicocke, William Walton, Charles Nicoll, Edward Nicoll, and Charles McEvers. What is particularly revealing are the type of people Rhinelander was engaging with: they were all linked to the DeLanceys, through voting for them in 1769, dining in Montayne's tavern, supporting importation in 1770, or familial ties. William Walton, for instance, was James DeLancey's uncle, and Jacob Walton was married to John Cruger's granddaughter, Mary Cruger. Rhinelander's store also acted as a focal point that brought these people together; Charles Nicoll, for instance, was in business with Edward Laight throughout much of the 1760s. These future loyalists' engagements with Rhinelander complemented their political connections. Not all future loyalists in Rhinelander's daybook were "Friends to Liberty and Trade." The high number of men who were indicates that Rhinelander's store might have been a hub of political debate, which might have influenced other future loyalists' political sentiments later.[45]

Outside of his store, Rhinelander engaged with other future loyalists through the acquisition of land. There had been a long-standing dispute between New York and New Hampshire over land in the western region of the Connecticut River. In 1764, however, George III and the Privy Council ruled in favor of New York, and land grants were regularly issued throughout the 1760s. By 1776, a total of 2,115,610 acres had been granted in one hundred patents and an additional township. Future loyalists, including Frederick Rhinelander, were among the grantees. William Laight, one of Rhinelander's friends, described him as "a Connoisseur" of land grant–related matters.[46]

On November 13, 1774, Frederick Rhinelander and twenty-two others petitioned the Royal Council for "a Tract of Land . . . by the name of Westford." Of the twenty-two, at least fifteen became loyalists. From those individuals whose allegiances have been determined, several also engaged with Rhinelander in his store: William Rhinelander Jr., William Rhinelander Sr., Philip Rhinelander Sr., James Mott, and Charles Doughty.[47]

In November 1775, these same individuals submitted further petitions for other townships. In their petitions they included information on how they would divide the land into separate lots, which were reserved for the Church of England minister and the establishment of a local school. One would be for the Society for the Propagation of the Gospel (SPG), another for the SPG minister, one for the joint use of the minister and the Church of England, and another to be used by a schoolmaster who would educate the children of the township. By investing in land that was close or adjacent to each other, the association formed from the transactions when petitioning for this land would likely have further cemented bonds among Frederick Rhinelander and his friends.[48]

Another way in which Rhinelander engaged with other future loyalists was through the mutual ownership of vessels. Rhinelander owned a one-third stake in the sloop *Prince William*, with John Healey, William Bayard, and William Pagan, all of whom became loyalists. Pagan and Rhinelander were also connected through the schooner *Buck*, which they owned with Robert Dale and Samuel Pearce, who also became loyalists. Rhinelander also owned stakes in several other vessels with future loyalists: the *Swift*, with Edward and William Laight and James Hallett; the *Prince of Wales* with William Laight and Linus King; and a brig with William Price, William Pagan, and Robert Pigeon.[49]

Through his land and maritime partnerships, Rhinelander established enduring ties with future loyalists. Mundane social interactions in his store were routine and transient, whereas the ties formed through land grant partnerships, by virtue of the partners sharing capital and resources, endured, at least on paper, until the partnership was dissolved. To enter into these kinds of agreements with other people required a degree of trust, and the bonds created did indeed last until partners died. In 1809, when Frederick's brother William died, he bequeathed a considerable amount of his personal estate to his "highly Valued friend James Mott Esquire." Mott was a regular customer at Frederick's store. They also jointly owned land and vessels. When William died, he bequeathed to Mott his gold watch and chain "together with a Gold mourning ring which I hope he will wear as a mark of my firm friendship and attachment to him."[50]

When Rhinelander's various partnerships are combined with his commercial networks in New York City, the number of future loyalists within his overall network increases. Whereas from 1772 to 1773 he interacted with eighteen future loyalists, when the other networks are added to the networks cultivated in his store, it increases to seventy-nine. It can be inferred that, following the polarization of New York society in mid-1770, Rhinelander turned to several like-minded men, including associates in *"the Club"* and the independent militia company in which Rhinelander was enlisted. As he gravitated toward like-minded New Yorkers during moments of crisis, he established bonds that transcended their political origins. He began to interact with his fellow militiamen and associates in *"the Club"* with greater frequency in his store and in other aspects of his life. But what is most significant is that the developments in Rhinelander's networks did not occur in isolation. Other future loyalists' networks followed a similar trajectory.

Evert Bancker Jr.

Evert Bancker Jr., a New Yorker of Dutch heritage, owned a shop beside John Holt's printing office near the Royal Exchange at the bottom of Broad Street. Like Rhinelander, Bancker kept records of his daily interactions, but instead of using day- or account-books, Bancker's extant records are blotters, invoice-books, and a well-kept journal, which can be used to reconstruct his network.[51]

On March 30, 1771, Evert Bancker Jr. started a journal "Containing all my Dealings." Like Rhinelander, every time a customer came into his shop, he too noted down the date, what they purchased, and how much it was sold for. For the purposes of this study, those customers who would become loyalists have been documented and tracked using the same methodology as applied to visitors to Rhinelander's store. From 1771 to 1774, Bancker engaged with twenty-four future loyalists. His most frequent customer was John Marston, a Dutch New Yorker whose family was connected to the DeLanceys. Bancker's customers were well connected with the DeLanceys, including Peter Berton, Grove Bend, Charles McEvers, John Tabor Kempe, Gabriel H. Ludlow, Jacobus Lefferts, and Jarvis Roebuck. Also, when Rhinelander's network and Bancker's are combined, the crossover between them illustrates the levels of connectivity between them.

After collating Bancker's ties with Frederick Rhinelander's, two interesting observations can be made. First, nine individuals were customers of both Bancker and Rhinelander. Most of the individuals engaging with them both are merchants; only Leonard Lispenard, William Field, and John Tabor Kempe were not.[52] Second, some of the individuals represented in Rhinelander's circle who are not connected to Bancker in the above image were actually extremely close to Bancker, including DeLanceyites Peter Berton, William Walton, Samuel Carman, Thomas Buchanan, Gabriel H. Ludlow, Joseph Allicocke, and Charles Nicoll. Nicoll and Allicocke were linked to Bancker in ways unrecorded in his journal. For instance, on October 20, 1772, Bancker married Nicoll's niece, Ann(a) Nicoll Nuttell Taylor, and after their marriage, Bancker borrowed money from Nicoll. He also engaged in regular, lighthearted correspondence with Allicocke. He developed relationships with both Nicoll and Allicocke, as well as other DeLanceyites, which went beyond the page. Both Allicocke and Edward Laight, for instance, helped settle a dispute regarding Charles Nicoll's estate after he died, and Bancker, who was an executor for Nicoll's will, described them as "good friends." (Allicocke, moreover, was a witness.) Such omissions are reminders that although Bancker's journal—or any other comparable source—might offer an insight into his network, findings that may be drawn remain inferential instead of conclusive.[53]

The inferences that can be drawn from Bancker's network indicate that it reflected his political persuasions. The culture of sensibility—that is, a capacity for feelings that often emerge in response to or in empathy with others' emotions—and friendship played important roles in the establishment and evolution of community in 1760s and 1770s colonial British America.[54] In Bancker's case, he established a complementary support network with individuals outside of his store that strengthened his network. The ties that Allicocke and Bancker shared with Nicoll, however, went beyond friendship and kinship. Like Rhinelander, they, too, invested jointly in land. On June 18, 1771, the trio, along with fellow DeLanceyite Isaac Heron, petitioned the council for four thousand acres in Albany County. They later submitted another petition with twenty-six other individuals for thirty thousand acres by the Connecticut River with the aim of building a township. Of the twenty-six petitioners, nine became loyalists, including William Pagan, James Moran, John Slidell, and John Woods—individuals who also engaged with Frederick Rhinelander or Bancker in their stores. Last, this same group, led by Nicoll, Bancker, and Heron, submitted another petition where they outlined the location of the township.[55]

Evert Bancker Jr.'s network followed a similar trajectory to Frederick Rhinelander's, and it included a number of individuals who acted as bridges to bring them together.

Charles Nicoll

Charles Nicoll's network is the final and most significant case study. Nicoll was a wine-seller in New York throughout the imperial crisis, and his network offers the most suggestive outline for the development of future loyalists' sociability prior to the American Revolution. A close reading of Nicoll's account book, which runs from 1768 to 1776, supports the inference extrapolated from Rhinelander's and Bancker's networks that future loyalists who developed strong social bonds with each other prior to the American Revolution were also political associates.[56]

Charles Nicoll was a long-standing supporter of the DeLanceys. Under their leadership, he joined the Sons of Liberty in opposition to the Stamp Act and dined with them on several occasions. During the 1768 and 1769 elections, he was a DeLancey voter. Moreover, as a "Friend to Liberty and Trade," in March 1770, he dined at Montayne's tavern. Before mid-1770, however, Nicoll's base of customers was not indicative of any sense of group consciousness. From 1768 to July 1770, Nicoll engaged with twenty-seven future loyalists, including DeLancey supporters Joseph Allicocke, Evert Bancker Jr., James Rivington, Willet Taylor, and Leonard Lispenard. His most frequent and sustained custom came from Allicocke, who came into his store fourteen times to purchase items such as Madeira wine, oil, and claret. Taylor came in six times, Lispenard came in twice, and Bancker, who had not yet married Nicoll's niece, came in twice. James Rivington purchased items from Nicoll only once. What is most revealing about Nicoll's daybook is the lack of regular customers. The only individual who came in as part of his daily life was Allicocke. The rest of his engagements appear somewhat arbitrary. Yet there were like-minded individuals present, including DeLancey supporters John Harris Cruger, Thomas Doughty, Edward Laight, Abraham Walton, John Watts, and John Wetherhead. After the nonimportation debates of July 1770, these men and other DeLancey supporters became regular customers of Nicoll. It is possible, therefore, that the customers' propensity to shop with Nicoll bore some relation to their common political views and opposition to the continuation of nonimportation.

Furthermore, after the nonimportation agreement was removed, in July 1770, and "the Friends to Liberty and Trade" established broad-based support, Nicoll's customer-base expanded. Between July 1770 and April 1775, Nicoll's network came to include 114 future loyalists. Like Nicoll, Bancker, and Rhinelander, many of these future loyalists were DeLanceyites, including George Brewerton, Thomas Buchanan, Isaac Low, Jarvis Roebuck, Miles Sherbrooke, Jacob Walton, and Henry White, among others. Equally important, the number of sustained interactions that Nicoll had with future loyalists also increased. Allicocke visited Nicoll's store fourteen times between November 1768 and January 1770; from October 1770 to December 1771, he visited twenty-four times; and from January 1772 to March 1773, he visited twenty-three times. Overall, from mid-1770 to April 1775, Allicocke visited Nicoll's store 108 times, spending between 4s. and £287.2s.6d. In 1775, moreover, Allicocke and Nicoll served as executors to James Carr's estate. Alongside Allicocke, future loyalists Henry Van der Ham, Waldron Blauu, John Turner, and John Taylor became regular customers for Nicoll as they often visited his store three or four times per month. From 1769 to mid-1770, Van der Ham interacted with Nicoll in his store nine times. But from April 1772 to October 1773, he interacted with him thirty-three times, and he continued interacting with him beyond 1775. From mid-1770 more future loyalists entered Nicoll's life and became regular customers to create a heretofore unknown sense of familiarity within it. Of his new customers, only 18 percent would interact with him once, and 58 percent interacted with him more than four times. By sustaining relationships with his new customers, it can be assumed that Nicoll was cognizant of their views and they his, influencing each other to some degree.[57]

The increased numbers within Frederick Rhinelander's and Charles Nicoll's networks suggest that what would become a loyalist consciousness was forming between mid-1770 and 1775 in New York. Overall, twenty-eight future loyalists acted as bridges to link the networks together, including men like Allicocke, DeLancey, Kempe, the Laights, McEvers, and Pagan. These men were all DeLanceyites, and their face-to-face interactions complemented and reinforced their political sentiments.

Personal relationships within the private sphere complemented colonists' military service and their partisanship. It reinforced their political actions, whereby their shared sentiment influenced how they behaved and, more important, their allegiance in the American Revolution.[58] Indeed, Frederick Rhinelander, Evert Bancker Jr., and Charles Nicoll were politically like-minded New Yorkers. Comparative analyzes of their networks indicate that their political action should not be subsumed into the public and private sphere. Instead, their sociability prior to the American Revolution reinforced their partisanship and association, putting their relationships and networks within the political culture of New York City. These "Friends to Liberty and Trade" were individuals who held long-standing relationships with each other, cultivated over a period of sustained interaction. In the case of Rhinelander, Bancker, and Nicoll, it came through their support of the DeLanceys' election in 1768 and 1769, the March 1770 celebration and the nonimportation debates of mid-1770.

After the emergence of the McDougallites, their social relationships became more important to their political consciousness. And between mid-1770 until March 1777, these people coalesced to form a coherent association. But it was not only social engagements that brought them together; political events influenced the course of their lives, allowing them to reaffirm their partisanship and commitment to one another. Their shared interpretation of provincial politics helped shape the ways in which they understood revolutionary developments. Their political network, filled with elites and non-elites, was their social, economic, familial network—and more.[59]

CHAPTER 6

The Mob Begin to Think and Reason

Tea and Popular Mobilizations

Conditions in New York City improved following the resumption of trade. Imports from Britain doubled, popular political meetings stopped, and people went about their daily lives, shopping in stores, drinking in taverns and coffeehouses. The demand for British goods had not ended with the nonimportation agreement. Consumption habits changed as New Yorkers, adhering to their agreement, simply chose not to acquire British goods. And thus with the ban lifted, the backlog of demand gripped the city's economy as money flowed in and out of the city's port. The colony had also acquired a degree of imperial stability. On December 27, 1770, Rockingham Whig Edmund Burke was appointed as the colony's agent in Parliament. After accepting the position the following June, Burke regularly corresponded with James DeLancey, who had initially recommended him. In their letters Burke often wrote "fully and confidentially" about maintaining a positive, economically fruitful relationship between the colonies and Britain—something he had championed since at least 1765. He, like the DeLanceys, sought to remove what they viewed as restrictive legislation that hurt Britain and its colonies. He also appreciated the importance of New York's assembly in conjunction with his role in advancing its interests—and therefore the interests of all voting New Yorkers. He described himself as *"an agent for the House of Representatives only."* Burke was, therefore, New Yorkers' representative in Parliament.[1]

Others in Manhattan also felt that the city's political problems were a distant memory. Lt. Gen. Thomas Gage highlighted the city's "domestic tranquility," and William Smith Jr. noted the political independency of the colony's governors in the 1770s, beginning with John Murray, fourth Earl of Dunmore, who briefly succeeded Sir Henry Moore in 1770, and then William Tryon. Both men, Smith commented, sought to separate themselves for the colony's institutional politicking—a notable difference from Moore and Cadwallader Colden, who both sought to curry favor with the assembly's factions. Both Dunmore's and Tryon's official correspondence with Hillsborough was largely focused on settling boundary disputes and the dispersal of land throughout the colony. They sent large vellum deeds, petitions, maps, and lengthy descriptions of land grants, and in Britain's official government records the size of the volumes containing relevant correspondence thickened in size as more and more pages were folded and stuffed in. Picking sides was not in their remit. "I will be your *independent* governor," Tryon stated.[2]

But Manhattan's place as an imperial outpost ensured that neither Dunmore nor Tryon nor the colony's inhabitants could avoid or ignore the political economy of the British Empire and Parliament's imperialism. Indeed, the duty on tea from the Townshend Acts remained as a symbol of Parliament's ability to legislate over the colonies. Between 1770 and 1773 colonists discussed Parliament's powers and their place within the British Empire. This was likely partly spurred on by the single tea duty. Indeed, from 1770 to 1773, colonists paid duties on 787,000 pounds of East India Company tea. It still could not keep up with the East India Company's expenses.[3]

What's more, most New Yorkers acquired their tea through smugglers from the Dutch East Indies (now Indonesia). Smuggling was so pervasive that up to fifteen hundred chests of Dutch tea arrived in the city per year; the city's port thus acted as a colonial gateway for smuggled tea to be sold in other colonies. As such, colonists' consumption habits inevitably impacted how much East India Company tea that was sold in the colonies. Even though the three-penny duty was paid on nearly a million pounds of tea, over eighteen million pounds lay unsold in the company's London warehouses. Some British politicians believed the company was mismanaged—it had accumulated about £1 million of debt—but a severe famine in Bengal and collapsing stock value following an empire-wide credit slump simply made matters worse, especially in Manhattan. Tradespeople and artisans closed their stores. Merchants were unable to survive without longer credit, including some of Manhattan's most prominent houses. Philip Livingston and Broome and Co. faced ruin, and Robert and John Murray's mercantile firm collapsed. Many laborers and artisans also lost much-needed employment, forcing them to turn to the city's poorhouse. In March 1772, the house contained 425 paupers, which was over 20 percent more than in February 1771. The winter of 1772 to 1773 did not make matters any easier. It was unusually severe, freezing the East River and enabling New Yorkers to walk to Brooklyn. Sickness, crime, and prostitution worsened, too. More New Yorkers than ever before could not live without assistance. Across the Atlantic, the East India Company's administrators had approached the North administration for financial assistance. On May 10, 1773, Parliament passed the Tea Act, which loaned the company £1.4 million and enabled it to export tea directly to the colonies, removing the 10 percent duty it previously paid and undercutting all other mercantile operations, including smugglers. The Tea Act also allowed the company to appoint colonists as tea consignees, who were tasked with overseeing company business wherever its tea was sold. New York's consignees were Benjamin Booth, Abraham Lott, and Henry White, three of the city's most prominent merchants.[4]

News of the Tea Act reached Manhattan in September. New Yorkers quickly recognized its consequence: the East India Company could sell its tea at a cheaper price as those who smuggled it into the city. Lord North, who despised smuggling and calculated that colonists paid one-fiftieth the taxes of a Briton, thought this would all but guarantee success. He noted that he doubted colonists "would resist at being able to drink their tea at nine-pence in the pound cheaper." The prime minister was so confident that neither he nor the British Treasury informed his stepbrother William Legge, second Earl of Dartmouth, who had replaced Hillsborough as secretary of state for the colonies in August 1772, about the change. Dartmouth's governors, therefore, were given no warning of the legislation and unfortunately for the prime minister and despite tea's incredible popularity, he was wrong. The Tea Act sparked uproar.[5]

The Tea Act

"A New Flame is apparently kindling in America," William Smith Jr. wrote in his "Historical Memoirs." "I suppose we shall repeat all the Confusions of 1765 & 1766," he continued, adding, "our Domestic Parties will probably die, & be swallowed up in the general Opposition to the Parliamentary Project of raising the Arm of Government by Revenue Laws."[6]

Colonists recognized that the Tea Act was part of Parliament's imperial reforms to show that it held ultimate legislative supremacy over the colonies. Some also believed that it was a political ploy to trick colonists into paying, and thus legitimizing, the original Townshend duty on tea. New York mercantile partners Pigou & Booth, which was contractually obliged to import East India

Company tea, anticipated problems from the start. Local smugglers, they wrote, "be able to raise a considerable mob" in opposition to the legislation. Benjamin Booth added that smugglers would be leading the opposition, writing, "The only persons who are suspected of making opposition are the smugglers." They were "all professed Sons of Liberty," Booth added. More importantly, though, at this stage the Liberty Boys were aligned with Alexander McDougall. In the days and months to come, they consolidated their relationship.[7]

To show their opposition to the Tea Act, the McDougallites authored a series of essays that were published in newspapers and as broadsides in which they argued that the Tea Act threatened colonists' liberties because it gave the company a monopoly in the tea trade. They also compared the city's appointed East India tea consignees to the "STAMP OFFICERS" of 1765, alleging that they would "operate . . . against the freedom of America." What's more, the DeLanceys were associated with Booth, Lott, and White, and the McDougallites used their opponents' relationships with the East India Company to depict them—and, by implication, their political colleagues—as men who aimed to force New Yorkers into political slavery. They were, the McDougallites declared, the "base and cruel instruments" of parliamentary oppression. In other words, the DeLanceys were part of Parliament's authoritarian imperial reforms.[8]

By arguing that the act threatened the public welfare, the McDougallites articulated a refreshed iteration of their political economy. For them, the Tea Act threatened the public good and the people's welfare. It was not only about forgoing the three-penny duty, either. The act gave the East India Company a monopoly over the tea trade in New York; the fact that New Yorkers would save money did not matter to them. Their belief that the public good was in jeopardy was more important. As such, their critiques of the act—and by extension all those who were associated with it—targeted not just Parliament but all those colonists who were associated with it. They also criticized the DeLanceys' political economy, showing that economic advancement did not always advance or even protect the public good. On the contrary, the McDougallites used the Tea Act to depict their opponents as self-interested and corrupt. As "A TRADESMAN" argued, the Tea Act would "sap the Foundations of Liberty," enabling "a few Men" to reap large "Profits" as the majority suffered. All told, the act was further evidence of Parliament's goal: to subjugate its American colonies and force them to accept its supremacy.[9]

The McDougallites' rhetoric had a demonstrable impact upon colonists' sentiments. As Governor Tryon opined to Dartmouth, "It is with real regret I acquainted your Lordship of the ferment of the Minds of many . . . since the Arrival here of . . . intelligence of the East India Company's Intention to ship Tea on their own Account to America." Of the McDougallites' publications,

Tryon wrote, they were "productions calculated to sow Sedition and to support and make popular the cause of those who are deepest concerned in the illicit Trade." Dartmouth knew that the McDougallites had been without broad-based support since early 1770, and he was hopeful that the DeLanceys would thwart the McDougallites' attempts to mobilize support. He wrote to Tryon that "the Authors & Abettors of such unwarrantable proceedings will be met with Disappointment & Disgrace." Maj. Gen. Frederick Haldimand, who was then acting commander-in-chief of British forces in North America, agreed, writing to Dartmouth, "I canot but think however but that the mercantile interest will prevail."[10]

The DeLanceys did not let the McDougallites' writings go unanswered, either. Writing as "POPLICOLA" in James Rivington's newly established *New-York Gazetteer* and in broadsides, Anglican minister John Vardill authored a series of essays to counter the McDougallites' attempts to mobilize support. A graduate of King's College and close colleague and friend of prominent New York City Anglicans Myles Cooper and Charles Inglis, Vardill, described as "the Pope, Milton, Addison & Swift" of America, was in his early twenties when he composed this series. By drawing on the DeLanceys' political economy as the means of best advancing colonists' economic independence, he argued that the East India Company's regulation of the tea trade would stabilize the city's economy and advance the public good. Vardill's series was thus an articulation and defense of the DeLanceys' political economy. Vardill, who was the son of a ship's captain, also noted that if the East India Company collapsed it would "be fatal to our trading interest," but if it averted bankruptcy New Yorkers would "not only promote the common good, but your own particular interest also." "The importance of modern states," Vardill went on, was largely based on "their *commercial advantages*." "Every good citizen will be inclined from duty as well as interest, to love his country, and to be zealous in advancing its welfare," Vardill continued, because it would be for "the good of the *whole society*" and colonists' "*common happiness*." Moreover, it was not the DeLanceys who were corrupt and self-interested. It was McDougall and his supporters—the "giddy cabal" who were "actuated by self interest," determined to assume "*judicial* and *executive* power." If colonists mobilized in support, Vardill alleged, they would "become *enslaved* by *dangerous* tyrants." Other attempts inspired by the DeLanceys to immobilize the McDougallites were more simplistic but no less effective. In one broadside, for instance, "ISAAC VAN POMPKIN" argued that because East India tea was of higher quality than smuggled Dutch tea, the act should be supported.[11]

Meanwhile, James DeLancey predicted the issues the Tea Act would raise, recognizing how it was part of Parliament's imperial reforms to limit institutional power in the colonies while taking more from them. Parliament's continued attempts to alter the British imperial state developed in contrast to DeLancey's imperial political economy, which was based on continued commercial relations and a colonial legislature that operated in support of Parliament, levying taxes and providing men whenever necessary. Writing to New York agent Edmund Burke in the spring of 1773, DeLancey sensed that Parliament was moving "to render every Person immediately dependent on the Crown for the offices that are held under Government." In another letter to Burke, DeLancey reiterated his concern, writing, "I am astonished at the infatuation of the people on your side of the Atlantic relative to the affairs of the India Company and think they seem determined to punish the Directors to give an Influence to the Crown." The consequences, DeLancey predicted, would "in the end be fatal to the liberties of the Nation." DeLancey was resolute in his establishment Whig view of Parliament's legislation, believing it was unwise, and so he wrote to the Marquis of Rockingham to encourage his friend and political ally to push for its repeal. "Even America," DeLancey wrote in October 1773, "is not likely to escape the gripping News of the hungry Ministry." "Tea must be sent to this county," he continued, adding, "yet it may serve as precedent for future Taxes." "I imagine it will cause as much noise as the Stamp Act did."[12]

With the DeLanceys mobilizing printers' types as well as their epistolary and political networks, Alexander McDougall was relentless in his attempts to rally New Yorkers in opposition to the Tea Act. Reemphasizing their association with English parliamentarian John Hampden in a five-part series titled "*The* ALARM," McDougall, as "HAMPDEN," called Vardill "the *deceitful*, LYING, *infamous* POPLICOLA." He declared that the Tea Act would make colonists "pregnant with Chains," turning them into "the most miserable of mortals." McDougall blamed the DeLanceys and their political economy for the Tea Act. He argued that because they had not sought the complete repeal of the Townshend Acts, they had instead legitimized the idea of Parliament "raising a revenue in America," one that, he wrote, "will rob the colony, in a commercial view, of near twenty nine thousand pounds currency per annum." Other critiques also questioned the DeLanceys' behavior. "A TRADESMAN" illustrated his bewilderment at "POPLICOLA"'s essays. He found it "Strange" that a person "who . . . [had] resided so long" in New York would "take the Inhabitants for perfect Ideots!"[13]

The McDougallites continued their published criticism of the DeLanceys, but they also attacked them in another way—they burned one of their members in effigy. William Kelly was a prominent merchant in New York and a DeLancey voter in 1769. The McDougallites alleged that Kelly had solicited a position as an East India Company consignee because he was a partner of

Abraham Lott. Moreover, of New Yorkers, it was reported that Kelly had told Lord North that Tryon would "cram the Tea down their throats." This behavior, McDougallites argued, was indicative of the DeLanceys' individualism and their self-interest. It showed that their political economy did not operate to advance New Yorkers' interests. Instead, it was entirely "inimical to the Liberties of America." With thousands in attendance, an effigy of Kelly, with labels affixed to his breast and back that read "The just Reward of that black and horrid Crime, Ingratitude" and "a disgrace to my country," was symbolically burned on November 5, 1773, Pope's Day. Burning Kelly's effigy associated him, as well as the DeLanceys and their political economy, with corruption and tyranny—the antitheses of republican ideals. Though the McDougallites authored several political publications, they kept a constant theme. As "CASSIUS" argued, "the FRIENDS of LIBERTY, and COMMERCE" worked against the public good. They were "infamous, sordid, and parasitical." Writing as "Brutus," McDougall reminded New Yorkers that they would continue the tea boycott. More importantly, though, the McDougallites' collective action was successful in mobilizing people to their cause. Gov. William Tryon witnessed popular sentiment shift in New York City during this period, noting that McDougall had "enflame[d] the passions" of New Yorkers to "make popular the Cause."[14]

Later that month, the McDougallites circulated fifteen hundred copies of "the ASSOCIATION of The Sons of Liberty." They distributed them to "the principal gentlemen of the city, merchants, lawyers, and other inhabitants of all ranks"—individuals whom they sought to bring into their orbit. Colonists were called to "ASSOCIATE WITHOUT DISTINCTION," sign their names, and publicly declare that "no taxes be imposed upon them but by their own consent"; otherwise, they would "bid adieu to American liberty." Through this public declaration, the signatories bound themselves together in opposition to not only the Tea Act but the DeLanceys and Parliament's absolute authority over them. The likes of McDougall, John Lamb, and Philip Livingston signed the document, as well as a host of ordinary New Yorkers. According to William Smith Jr., the DeLanceys recognized McDougall's rise in popularity. They were concerned that popular opinion could permanently move against them—and so they "fell in with the Multitude to save [their] Interest." As such, multiple DeLanceyites signed the Association.[15]

To mobilize further support, the McDougallites likely commissioned the publication of one of the few political caricatures that was published in colonial British America. Titled "Liberty triumphant; or, the Downfall of OPPRESSION" and later attributed to New York engraver Henry Dawkins, the illustration attacked those who created, instituted, and supported the Tea Act. William Kelly was labeled "The infamous K—y" and is pictured with the Devil, who is whispering to Kelly, "Speak in favour of yᵉ Scheme now's the time to push your fortune." Kelly, with the Devil gripping his arms and directing his body, is speaking to the reviled John Stuart, third Earl of Bute, stating, "Govʳ· T—n will cram the Tea down the Throats of the New Yorkers," solidifying the rumor that Kelly had said this. Bute, in turn, responds with a broad Scottish accent that Kelly—and thus all supporters of the Tea Act—must respond to colonists' protests with great spirit. The unidentified Vardill is speaking with the East India Company director, Maj. Gen. Robert Clive, first Baron Clive. "I have prostituted my reason and my Conscience to serve you, and therefore am entitled to some reward," to which Clive responds, "If we had succeeded, you should have been provided for." Across the Atlantic, the colonies are "represented by a Woman" and the Sons of Liberty are "represented by the Natives of America, in their savage garb." Both are directing arrows toward Lord North, with America noting, "Aid me my Sons, and prevent my being Fetter'd," to which they are responding, "We will secure your freedom, or die in the Attempt," "Lead us on to Liberty or Death," and "Lead on, Lead on." Underneath, colonists who supported the Tea Act are represented, and it is likely that these individuals represent popular beliefs surrounding the DeLanceys and their relationship to William Kelly and the Tea Act. One notes, "The People have discover'd our design to divide them, & we shall never be able to regain their confidence." This individual, perhaps James DeLancey, is speaking to a smaller, heavier-set man who has two faces and is holding McDougall's Association. "We must now make a Virtue of necessity & join against landing the Tea" (see figures 6.1, 6.2, 6.3).[16]

FIGURES 6.1–3. *Liberty Triumphant; or the Downfall of Oppression*, and details, ca. 1774, [by Henry Dawkins], Miriam and Ira D. Wallach Division of Art, Prints and Photographs, New York Public Library

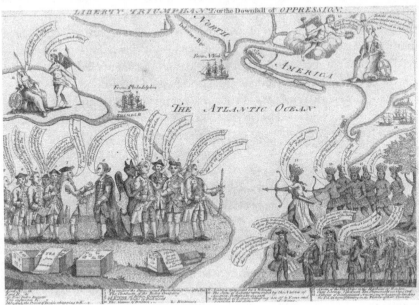

FIGURES 6.1–3. (continued)

With the wide circulation of materials against the Tea Act, the pressure that McDougallites had placed on East India Company consignees Henry White, Abraham Lott, and Benjamin Booth proved too much. On December 1, a day after the Association was published, they petitioned Tryon to resign, citing the "general and spirited Opposition" to the Tea Act. William Smith Jr. also helped the East India consignees, helping them draft a letter to any "Captain of Tea Ship" in late December. Smith, who was also counseling Governor Tryon at this point, likely exerted considerable editorial control over the letter's contents. He was a careful, thoughtful individual, someone who took his time to weigh his words and his options. People trusted his judgment and valued his opinion—officials, assemblymen, East India consignees. Smith's draft, held within his personal papers, is filled with adjustments and notations, much like many of his drafts. In the letter, the agents encouraged the anonymous "Captain" not to make port in Manhattan and instead find "a Way of Escape." "The whole Continent," the agents went on, "is thrown into a Ferment by Consequences this last Act of Parliam^t," the purpose for which was "establishing a Revenue for the Support of a Government in this Country, totally independent of us & yet maintained at our own Expence." This evolution toward an extractive British imperial state, the agents noted, was strongly opposed by those in New York City and elsewhere. "Such an Establishment will plunge them into a most abject Slavery." Whether or not this letter was ever delivered is unknown, but the "Ferment" Smith and the agents described had an effect. The colony's government agreed to handle any imported tea. Fortunately for Governor Tryon, tea did not arrive until the following April. By then, however, other events had polarized the city's political world even further.[17]

On December 16, 1773, the *Dartmouth* sailed into Boston Harbor. Bostonians, like New Yorkers, fiercely opposed the Tea Act. But unlike New York's governor, Gov. Thomas Hutchinson, whose sons were East India Company consignees, insisted that the act be enforced. Hutchinson was insistent that he would not permit the *Dartmouth* to leave without offloading its tea. Fifty Bostonians, disguised as Mohawks, had other ideas, dumping 340 chests of tea, totaling ninety thousand pounds and worth nearly £10,000, into the harbor in what later became known as the Boston Tea Party.[18]

Boston silversmith Paul Revere arrived in Manhattan on December 21 with news of the protest. Four days later, up to three thousand New Yorkers protested the Tea Act at City Hall. For New Yorkers, the events in Boston "astonished the Town." Local merchant John Thurman Jr. summarized New Yorkers' position on tea: they would "perish Reather than suffer it to be Landed." News of the Bostonians' actions astonished those in Parliament, too, including Rockingham, who told Edmund Burke, "The conduct of the American's can not be justified" despite "the folly and impolicy of the provocation." But Lord North's cabinet and others were more forthright. North and other members of Parliament sought to firmly reassert Britain's authority. Between March and June 1774, Parliament passed the Coercive Acts, which closed Boston Harbor, enabled the British Army to suppress rioting, and gutted Massachusetts's charter. North attracted supporters for his response, too. In 1774 a general election took place, resulting in the reorientation of the House of Commons: those who supported North's hardline approach to the colonies, as well as the British Empire, were returned. Moreover, the Boston Tea Party brought King George III into the imperial crisis. "The colonists," George III stated, "must be reduced to absolute obedience, if need be, by the ruthless use of force." Like many others, he strongly endorsed North's approach, and he was pleased that the Coercive Acts, which were known in the colonies as the Intolerable Acts, were met with little opposition. As North put it, for Parliament, as well as for him and George III, it was about "whether we have or have not any authority in that country."[19]

The North administration's response to the Boston Tea Party intensified the dispute between the colonies and Britain's imperial system. Colonists protested the authoritarian imperialism. Colonists could not accept Parliament legislating for them, without any input. Nor could they tolerate a political economy in which their money funded the British Empire and legislation that they could not support. After news of the Boston Tea Party reached Manhattan and following considerable institutional deliberations, Gov. William Tryon agreed that any tea that arrived in New York Harbor would not be unloaded. He also agreed that the British Royal Navy ships would not protect any vessel with tea as its cargo. As such, New Yorkers, led by McDougall, agreed that vessels could be resupplied prior to their return voyage. Tryon also implored British officials to stop taxing the American colonies. The compromise between the colony's government and its popular leaders was well supported, and many New Yorkers were delighted in Tryon's response. (When Tryon departed New York for Britain on April 7, 1774, due to ill-health, his departure was marked by the largest commemoration ever held in the colony for a departing governor.)[20]

With Tryon gone, Lt. Gov. Cadwallader Colden reassumed the governorship temporarily. The departing governor predicted that Colden would "do little" to affect colonial affairs. He was right. Old, weary, and relatively uninterested in the political squabbles that dominated his earlier gubernatorial tenures, Colden was physically and likely mentally ill-equipped to deal with the political and imperial issues that soon dominated popular politics in Manhattan. But despite his willingness for a peaceful return to gubernatorial affairs,

Colden had a knack for bad timing. On April 18, the *Nancy* and its cargo of tea sailed into New York's harbor. Four days later, the *London* arrived, it too filled with tea. New Yorkers—particularly those who signed the Association— had waited for this moment for nearly five months. After Capt. Benjamin Lockyer of the *Nancy* refused to unload his cargo, Capt. James Chambers of the *London*, who had also brought the hated stamps to the colony in 1765, tried to bluff his way into port. Unsuccessful, Chambers was forced to apologize publicly at Fraunces Tavern. Worse, at 8 p.m. on April 22, New Yorkers dumped the *London*'s eighteen chests of tea, as well as twenty boxes of Chambers's private collection, into the East River in their own tea party. Colden, aged eighty-seven, did nothing. Assembly speaker John Cruger reported that New Yorkers were "Agitated against the Importation of Tea Subject to a duty."[21]

At 8 a.m. the next day, following the large-scale distribution of a handbill from the city's Committee of Inspection, all of Manhattan's churches rang their bells in unison. The collective clanging pierced every part of Manhattan, deafening those walking the streets and bringing people out. "About 9," one newspaper reported, "the greatest Number of People were collected at and near the Coffee-House, that was ever known in this City." Thousands upon thousands poured into the streets to show their opposition to the Tea Act and, by extension, Parliament's authority over them. Witnessing the spectacle, Captain Lockyer was concerned, believing "some Mischief" might come his away. He was led through the crowd and back to the *Nancy*. He received "loud Huzza's, and many Guns were fired, expressive of their Joy at his Departure." The circumstances surrounding Lockyer's departure, as well as the destruction of the East India Company tea, represented an important step in the participatory nature of popular politics in Manhattan. Across the British Empire, church bells were often tolled to commemorate important historical events within the British calendar—George III's accession and birthday, for instance— but this moment marked another instance: colonists indicated their differences from those in Britain. Opposition to the Tea Act was growing and so, too, was New Yorkers' opposition to the increasingly extractive imperial state that Lord North and his government was crafting. These interactions on the streets created new and reinforced established networks, many of which were based on opposition to Parliament and those who supported its measures. Yet political mobilization often occurs in fits and spurts, usually in response to something. Without the necessary catalyst, it is often difficult to keep people interested, enthused, and together. McDougall had experienced firsthand how political interest can fizzle out, particularly among those who are interested in living their daily lives instead of involving themselves in the humdrum of everyday popular politics, which, to be sure, represented the majority of New

Yorkers. McDougall and others no doubt hoped that the Tea Act would be repealed; they had sent a strong message to Parliament, one that Captain Lockyer and Captain Chambers would take to London. But that would take time; it took up to three months to cross the Atlantic, depending on the weather, and as many coming back. New Yorkers only had to wait a few weeks for another opportunity for new mobilizations to occur.[22]

The Coercive Acts

News of the Boston Port Act arrived on May 11, 1774, informing New Yorkers of the removal of the city's customs officers and the closure of its port. A day later, a complete copy of the act came to hand. "There never was," one report lamented in reference to the Glorious Revolution, "perhaps, since the *revolution*, so important a crisis in the constitution of this country as the present state of American affairs." "The FATE OF A GREAT EMPIRE" was at stake, it continued. Four days later, Hugh Gaine's *New-York Gazette* addressed the issue, printing an appeal from "A British American, who is a Lover of Peace, as well as a Hate of every Species of Tyranny," calling for New Yorkers to donate however much they could afford so they could "RAISE IMMEDIATELY, by Subscription, a Sum equal to the estimated Value of the DROWNED TEAS."[23]

McDougall, no doubt, had been gauging political sentiment within Manhattan. In a small, hastily composed scrapbook of "Political Memorandums," the Scotsman privately noted his thoughts about New York City and the Boston Port Act. For him, as well as his associates, the act represented the most severe piece of legislation ever passed over the colonies. Their radical Whig political economy was grounded in a firm belief in a republican government that put Parliament and its colonial equivalents on a comparable, if not an identical, footing. The Boston Port Act was a march toward imperial tyranny. Governmental interests in London were being placed above those in Manhattan, reducing the colonies to the periphery, subverting their supposed equal status as Britons, and effectively guaranteeing that neither Britain nor New York would be as commercially successful as both might have been. Put simply, the Boston Port Act, as well as the other Coercive Acts, signaled to McDougall that Parliament was not protecting or enhancing the public good. Instead, it would impoverish New York City—and British North America.[24]

McDougall and his supporters had grown increasingly radical in their politics. They lost whatever faith they had in the DeLancey-led assembly, pushing instead for a new popular political institution that could represent New Yorkers' ideas and defend their interests. This view—that the assembly did not represent New Yorkers—had been brewing within Manhattan for several months. In early January, one writer, perhaps somewhat tongue-in-check, proposed that the colony should replace Gov. William Tryon with their own appointee, who would be referred to as "Lord Protector of that part of America formerly called the province of New-York" and would only rule as long as they had popular support. The writer also proposed that there would be monthly meetings of "all persons," who would be designated the "Council of State." This council, the writer continued, would "rid" New York "of the expence and trouble of employing ASSEMBLYMEN." Within McDougall's "Political Memorandums," he documented the city's views about institutional representation, political economy, and everyday life, capturing discussions about the colony's governorship and assembly beyond the pages of a newspaper. On May 12, McDougall wrote news of the Boston Port Act "was received with Great abhorence & indignation by the Sons of Freedom." "The officers of Govern[t]," McDougall went on, "endeavour to divide the People." A day later McDougall was confronted with one of the DeLanceys' fiercest partisans, Oliver DeLancey, who allegedly declared that he "would rather spend away every Shilling of his Fortune than that the Boston Port Bill be complied with." David Johnston, another DeLanceyite, reputedly declared that any Bostonians who complied with the act deserved to be "Hanged & Quartered." The DeLanceys, McDougall knew all too well, were skilled at political mobilization, and he had a dull view of their motives during this meeting. "This," McDougall wrote of DeLancey's and Johnston's actions, "is to amuse the Sons of Liberty to get their confidence." It was nothing but "deceit & Hipocrisy."[25]

With such strong feelings toward Parliament's legislation, Isaac Sears took the lead in rallying for a meeting in which the city's popular leaders would discuss how New York, as a major trading hub, should respond to the Boston Port Act. On May 15, the DeLanceys agreed to a meeting the next night at Fraunces Tavern, one in which the attendees would establish a committee that would determine the colony's course of action. At most, the DeLanceys had twenty-four hours to prepare—but it was more than enough time to rally their supporters to their cause.[26]

During the Fraunces Tavern meeting, McDougall and his associates reaffirmed their ardent desire to quickly implement a trade boycott. The DeLanceys disagreed. They had not forgotten the tough years of a few past. Understandably, they appreciated that a trade boycott, however severe, would inhibit the colony's commercial progress. Some DeLanceyites quickly made their feelings known. Gabriel H. Ludlow, for instance, stated "openly & insolently" two days before the Fraunces Tavern meeting that he would not support nonimportation. The DeLanceys were not solely concerned with the money in their and their associates' pockets. Many of the DeLanceyites, although sympathetic toward those in Boston, fundamentally disagreed with the way they responded to the arrival of East India Company tea. Destroying it was, in their view, a step too far, and many believed that, as Haldimand put it shortly after news of the Tea Party reached Manhattan, Bostonians should "be made to pay for" the destroyed East India tea.[27]

In Manhattan, debates about whether the East India Company should be compensated largely occurred within DeLanceyite spaces. Their opposition to the act was real; they believed in the reciprocity of the British Empire, where the colonies and Britain both advanced through shared commercial interests. The Boston Port Act went against that. They also believed the act was unconstitutional. The Fraunces Tavern meeting, however, was a difficult situation for them. The assembly was not then in session, meaning that they could not petition George III or Parliament for at least several weeks. They did not have that much time. Alongside mobilizing support in New York, McDougall and Sears had also written to Samuel Adams, the prominent radical in Massachusetts, about coordinating opposition to Parliament. The DeLanceys, then, fell back on their tried-and-tested methods of political mobilization. It was not solely about self-interest and maintaining their position atop the pyramid of New York politics. Instead, they sought to shape how the colony responded. They mobilized hundreds of their supporters to Fraunces Tavern. McDougall noted that they "were at great pains all day to collect every tool who was under their influence as well as those in Trade as out of it." Men like Edward Laight, Charles Nicoll, Isaac Low, "all the Waltons," and "a number of merchants, clerks" came out to support them. William Smith Jr. noted something similar, writing, "The De Lanceys urged their Friends to attend." There were so many people that the meeting had to be moved from Fraunces Tavern to the Royal Exchange at the foot of Broad Street. Open since 1752 and also known as the Merchants' Exchange, it was designed in the DeLanceys' political economy: it embraced commerce and the social good. It had a gambrel roof and cupola, and on its first floor was an arcaded floor, leaving the lower part open for a marketplace. On the second floor was an ornate long room with twenty-foot ceilings. It was an ideal spot for balls and dances—as well as political meetings.[28]

The May 16 meeting was a loud, hot affair. Hundreds of people filtered into the exchange's long room. They hustled together to set up and seize their own spaces within the room, a place where they would announce their views. Indeed, in those spaces New Yorkers gathered in their groups, with their associates, to publicly articulate their opposition to the Boston Port Act and, more significant, Parliament's ultimate authority over their lives. As more and more people filtered and huddled into the room, temperatures rose both in the air and on the ground. There were likely more DeLanceys than McDougallites in the room that day, and they used their numerical advantage to seize control. Isaac Low was appointed chair of the meeting—and he orchestrated affairs.

A DeLancey voter in 1768 and 1769 and a diner at Montayne's tavern in 1770, Low was born in 1735 at Raritan Landing, near New Brunswick, in New Jersey. He was a smart choice as chair. During the colony's last trade boycott, he served on the committee of inspection that oversaw its implementation. He was a smart appointee then, too. Low was one of Manhattan's most respected merchants, and his family was well connected to the DeLanceys: his sisters married Irish emigres Hugh and Alexander Wallace, DeLanceyite merchants. With one of their own overseeing proceedings, DeLanceyites no doubt had no issue speaking their minds.[29]

With Low dictating who could speak, he called early on DeLanceyites who believed that if the East India Company tea were paid for, relations between Britain and its American colonies would return to normal. Repayment would "open the Port of Boston," McDougall wrote, who also complained in his "Political Memorandums" that nonimportation was a nonstarter. The DeLanceys were not interested. McDougall believed his opponents did not want to take the lead in opposing the Port Act; instead, they wanted to determine the "Sense of the other Colonies" before acting or receive instruction from Boston. DeLanceyites in the meeting were skeptical about whether trade boycotts would be well received in Manhattan, and they did not want to further deplete their support levels—and if Boston paid for the tea, the idea of a trade boycott made little to no sense. With a decision on nonimportation delayed, the next topic of conversation was about the size of the colony's Committee of Inspection, or Committee of Correspondence. This proved to be a source of bitter debate. McDougall and his supporters wanted a committee of fifteen. The DeLanceys wanted fifty, thinking a larger committee would be more representative of the people and thus better able to advance their interests. With Low as chair and the support of cartmen and other non-elites, the DeLanceys were able to win the day. Low, a skilled political operator, repeatedly called on his associates to deliver their opinions and, after the larger committee was agreed to, nominations. Tempers likely increased as the forty-three-year-old Low turned to his friends again and again as his associates were nominated again and again. According to the Scotsman from Islay, assemblyman James Jauncey was nominated to the committee "without a vote" as they were effectively shut out of the committee.[30]

McDougall was furious. "The whole of the Business of this meeting," wrote McDougall, "so far as the Delancy[s] had an agency in it, Evidenced a design to get such a Com^e nominated as would be under their direction." To confirm the nominations of May 16, the committee was subjected to a popular vote within Manhattan, scheduled to take place three days later. Newspapers advertised the meeting, with hopes to attract at least as many as had attended the meeting in the exchange. Two of the city's printers—Holt and Rivington, who published on the same day—dedicated space within their papers to advertise the meeting at the coffeehouse at 1 p.m. A broadside was printed, as well. Perhaps the timing was ill-suited, the weather was too warm, or people were simply uninterested, but for whatever reason, the turnout was not as high as expected. McDougallites stayed home, possibly because on May 17, McDougall had received supportive letters from Boston that he quickly brandished around the coffeehouse. This celebration of the Bostonians' agreement likely emboldened the McDougallites, who felt confident that New York's committee could not postpone discussions of nonimportation, whatever the DeLanceys felt. More importantly, though, on the day of the meeting, McDougall was absent, citing illness. Without his presence Isaac Sears led his association's cause as best he could, but without his colleagues and political associates, the DeLanceys dominated once more. Low and the Waltons who were present stopped Sears from publicly reading letters from Boston that supported nonimportation and instead moved quickly to confirm the nominations. Sears realized the situation he was in. There were not enough of his associates to win the day. In what can only be described as a desperate attempt to gain the upper hand, he demanded that he go to City Hall to obtain signatures to determine the committee's composition. Sears also sought those who could not ordinarily vote in the colony's elections, alleging that the Boston Port Act affected all New Yorkers and not only its freeholders and freemen. Unfortunately for Sears, however, those in attendance could not afford to take more time off work, lest they lose their day's wages or even their jobs. For these people, as for most people in colonial British America, political debates about Parliament and legislation were not the most important aspects of their lives. They might have felt strongly about a piece of legislation, but their interactions with the British Empire, and what those interactions meant, often did not take precedence above earning a wage and making ends meet. New Yorkers could not afford to sacrifice hours of their day squabbling over the details about selecting the committee—many simply wanted the committee to be organized so it could begin its work. After some typical factional back and forth, the committee was confirmed as it was proposed at the exchange; the only change was the addition of Francis Lewis, a sixty-one-year-old merchant and French and Indian War veteran who lived across the East River in Whitestone.[31]

Isaac Low, who was appointed chair, announced the committee to the public without delay, acknowledging that there were severe divisions within the city about how best to oppose the Boston Port Act. "The only difference amongst us is," he noted, "the mode of effecting it." "I mean the preservation of our just rights and liberties." The DeLanceys believed they had a won a key victory in the popular and extrainstitutional fight against the Boston Port Act. Others did, too. In a letter to the Earl of Dartmouth, Maj. Gen. Frederick Haldimand described the McDougallites as "violent enthusiasts" and "a few hotheaded & designing men." The DeLanceys, on the other hand, "entertained more loial and liberal ideas of Government." Lt. Gov. Cadwallader Colden echoed Haldimand's statements in his own letter to Dartmouth, describing the McDougallites as "hot Headed" and "the warmest Zealots." The DeLanceys, per Colden, opposed the Boston Port Act. They were, wrote Colden, "not displeased with the Clamour and Opposition that was shown against internal Taxation," but, Colden went on, they packed the Committee of Fifty-One with "the most prudent and considerate People of the Place." Moreover, Colden wrote that he had spoken with some prominent, though unnamed, New Yorkers, who assured him that nonimportation was not an option that the committee would consider. The DeLanceys, Colden explained in another letter to Dartmouth, were "Men of cool Tempers." They would "endeavour to avoid all extravagant and dangerous Measures."[32]

Neither Haldimand nor Colden were wrong that the Committee of Fifty-One was dominated by its DeLanceyite members. But this is not to suggest that their loyalty toward Britain or Parliament was overwhelming or determined their allegiances during the American Revolution. Almost certainly every DeLanceyite member opposed the Coercive Acts. Of the fifty-one members, thirty-three were DeLanceys, of whom thirty would become loyalists, including Theophylact Bache, Elias Desbrosses, Edward Laight, Miles Sherbrooke, and Charles McEvers, all of whom were well known to each other. Equally important, though, their loyalism did not, and should not, negate their opposition to the Coercive Acts, or their commitment to overturning or at least containing Parliament's move toward an extractive imperial state. Eighteen of the other members of the Committee of Fifty were McDougallites, including Peter Van Brugh Livingston, Henry Remsen, and David van Horne. The DeLanceys dominated the committee. Isaac Low was its chair, and ardent DeLanceyite Joseph Allicocke was appointed secretary. The DeLanceyites had "the Lead among the People," too, according to Colden, despite McDougall's protests.[33]

But the committee did not represent everyone's interests, and its evasion over nonimportation led a group of laborers and artisans to organize a Committee of Mechanics. Chaired by former DeLanceyite Daniel Dunscomb, who, along with John Broom and Joseph Bull, had moved toward the McDougallites because of their active support of nonimportation in 1770, the Committee of Mechanics pressured and often directly opposed the Committee of

Fifty-One. Its members were confident that they could dissolve the Fifty-One if its members "misbehaved." As one New Yorker put it on May 20, "The mob begin to think and reason." Most of the members of the Mechanics' committee remain unknown; there are no extant census-like documents showing who made up its membership. But it would not be unlikely if at least some of its members came from the tradesmen and laborers who could not sacrifice their afternoons to discuss the Committee of Fifty-One's members.[34]

The organization of the Committee of Mechanics was among the most significant moments in the history of British New York. For one of the first times in the city's history, its lower-class inhabitants were independent political actors, people whose support and views had to be acknowledged and recognized. These men represented a new kind of politician in colonial America, one that the continent had not seen before. Their activism appealed to people like them—shoemakers, coopers, shipwrights. Artisans who did not necessarily adhere to traditional forms of political deference. People who would champion their lifestyle because they lived it. For these Mechanics, the DeLanceys did not embody their ideas and interests, and many of them fully supported trade boycotts. They did not agree with how the Committee of Fifty-One was handling the situation. Even though many if not all of these individuals did not receive a comparable education to the likes of James DeLancey or Jacob Walton, these Manhattan Mechanics appreciated that the Boston Port Act, as well as the other Coercive Acts and especially the Massachusetts Government Act, represented a fundamental shift in the imperialism of the British Empire. The Committee of Fifty-One opposed the legislation, too, but, as with the local political disputes of the late 1760s and early 1770s, they did not agree with the Committee of Mechanics over how New York City—and, by extension, the colony—should respond.[35]

The Committee of Mechanics, then, operated parallel to the Committee of Fifty-One, monitoring and checking its actions. It is unclear whether their quasi-oversight made any difference, at least at first, but the Mechanics made sure that they offered it. On May 23, for instance, during the first sanctioned meeting of the Fifty-One, the Mechanics sent a letter consenting to the Fifty-One's composition. During that same meeting, the Fifty-One, of whom forty were present, drafted a letter to the Boston Committee of Correspondence, discussing how New York wanted to respond to the Coercive Acts. Getting to this point was, however, a drawn-out affair, something that Alexander McDougall tried to avoid. McDougall wrote that he told the committee "that no personal or Political difference with any member of that Com^e should induce any prejudice to whatever they advanced." In other words, committee members' opinions should not be challenged, or mocked, and those in attendance should consider the recommendations and not the people delivering them. Yet this hardly, if ever, happened in Manhattan politics. When the draft letter to the Boston Committee was presented, Theophylact Bache, Charles McEvers, and Charles Shaw—three prominent DeLanceyites—objected to the mentioning of an intercolonial congress. They were overruled, but others tried more extreme measures. Some merchants wanted to include the clause that "the People of Boston were not suffering in the Cause of American Liberty." This stance was considered conservative. It, too, was rejected, but it showed McDougall that some of his committee members were not likely to consider his. Moreover, James Jauncey reiterated the DeLanceyite position: if Boston compensated the East India Company for its tea, "the Port would be opened."[36]

For McDougall, statements like this reaffirmed his belief that the DeLanceys were not, and would likely never be, on the same page as him and his associates. With multiple assemblymen on the Fifty-One, Jauncey's assertion provoked John Broome to ask what the "Committee of Correspondence of the Assembly" was doing in response to the "present alarming Crisis." The assembly, then out of session, had formed a twelve-man committee on January 20, 1774, to discuss the colony's institutional response to the Coercive Acts. All the DeLanceyite assemblymen for New York City were in it. Almost all its other members were also DeLanceyites, and they had been busy. Four members had reached out to New York's agent Edmund Burke about the impending imperial crisis. On May 31, John Cruger, James Jauncey, Jacob Walton, and Kings County assemblyman Simon Boerum reported of the "great uneasiness throughout the Colonies" but offered nothing on the Tea Act or the Boston Port Act. Of the Administration of Justice Act, however, they described it as an "abhorrence." It was "one of the most flagrant violations" of the British Constitution.[37]

The assembly committee's opposition to the Coercive Acts is an often-overlooked aspect of New York City's imperial crisis. This is partly due to the committee's origins. It was an extension of a long-standing committee that corresponded with the colony's agent. In this case, however, the committee took on new importance. Its members were directly corresponding with a political ally who they believed could and would represent their interests in Parliament, as well as the interests of their constituents. Put differently, the committee believed that if the representative tiers of the British Empire worked as they should—with the assemblymen representing New Yorkers and the agent representing the assembly in Parliament—New Yorkers' concerns would be addressed. But transatlantic correspondence was slow. Letters from Massachusetts and elsewhere that encouraged quick decision-making arrived long before any letters from Burke. For instance, on June 6 the Committee of Fifty-One had to respond to a letter from Boston's committee, in which the Bostonians heartily supported trade boycotts. The Fifty-One had neither discussed trade boycotts, thinking it something to be discussed in an intercolonial congress, nor mentioned it in their letter. In the Fifty-One's reply on June 7, they flatly told their Bostonian equivalents, "You have made a mistake—for on revising our letter to you, so far from finding a word mention'd of a 'Suspension of Trade.'" "The Idea is not even conceived."[38]

The Fifty-One responded to letters from other committees in other colonies and towns in early June 1774, and in each of its letters talk of "a General Congress of Deputies from the different Colonies" was mentioned and widely supported. The assembly committee also corresponded with other colonies, agreeing to an intercolonial congress. Such a mobilization of colonial delegates had not taken place since the Stamp Act Congress of 1765, when delegates representing nine colonies gathered in Manhattan between October 7 and 25, 1765 to discuss how the colonies would oppose the Stamp Act. A few days after the congress ended, riots took place across colonial British America. Equally important, though, the Declaration of Rights and Grievances was not presented to the House of Lords and the House of Commons refused to even acknowledge it, noting that it came from an extralegal, unconstitutional assembly that Parliament neither sanctioned nor recognized. A little under ten years later, a similar prospect was on the horizon for New York—and many DeLanceyites likely appreciated that the colony would not be as deferential as it had been in 1765.[39]

The DeLanceyites believed that the New York Assembly was the only legitimate political institution in the colony, but they opposed the Coercive Acts with equal conviction and if there was to be an intercolonial congress, they wanted to control the appointment of New York's delegates. They recognized that if their men were appointed, they could control the colony's approach to the impending crisis. The moment to discuss delegates began on June 27. Alexander McDougall opened the debate but was quickly rebuffed as the DeLanceyite members reiterated their commitment to the assembly and its institutional legitimacy: they proposed that the assembly appoint delegates to the congress. But McDougall and others believed Lt. Gov. Cadwallader Colden would not recall the assembly in time.

And so, at 6 p.m. on June 29, 1774, in the Royal Exchange, McDougall proposed that the Fifty-One nominate five people in Manhattan to represent its inhabitants in a new colonial congress in New York or at the so-called "general Congress," which was scheduled to take place in Philadelphia in September. McDougall also proposed that the Fifty-One's nominations should be agreed to by the Committee of Mechanics.[40]

McDougall's proposal was a radical step toward overhauling the traditional organs of governance in New York—the colony and the city. Unsatisfied with the assembly's approach to the crisis, as well as Colden's inevitable inaction, McDougall had suggested that the Fifty-One set up, and thus legitimize, an alternative form of institutional governance. More, McDougall realized that by setting up another form of government, if albeit temporary, its organization would also legitimize the Continental Congress. Words carried across one of the exchange's rooms as the committee members debated the motion. Isaac Low called on member after member after member, one after the other, and the minutes went on and on. The debates likely centered on the nature of imperial governance in New York, and the DeLanceys were almost certainly firm opponents of McDougall's motion, which threatened not only their political ascendency within the assembly but, more important, their understanding of the imperial British state. If McDougall's proposal were to pass, the DeLanceys realized, it would undermine the assembly's committee's work with Edmund Burke as well as the institutional and imperial legitimacy of the assembly and the Fifty-One—the committee that was set up to capture and represent the will of New Yorkers.[41]

Low, tired from conducting the debates, called the meeting to a close. He scheduled another meeting for July 4. McDougall's motion quickly became the topic of discussion. In a partisan vote, it was determined that the Committee of Mechanics' consent was not required. DeLanceyite voters included longtime supporters Charles Nicoll, Charles McEvers, Edward Laight, and Theophylact Bache. McDougall's adherents included Francis Lewis, Isaac Sears, and Peter Van Brugh Livingston. Low, recognizing that his associates were on the front-foot and had the majority, then called on Bache, who proposed that the Fifty-One would nominate five people to represent Manhattan at the Continental Congress, who would then be confirmed by the city's freeholders and freemen, that is, its usual voting population. Bache also proposed the New York's other counties could appoint their own delegates. Sears appreciated the moment was getting away from him and his associates, and so he took the floor to nominate the delegates: Isaac Low, James Duane, Philip Livingston, John Morin Scott, and Alexander McDougall. Sears's nomination was bold. Livingston was an experienced politician and civic officer, Low was a prominent figure in the Fifty-One, and James Duane had become a prominent legal figure within the colony. These figures did not stimulate much discussion, but the nomination of the reviled Scott and the partisan McDougall was greeted with considerable opposition. The DeLanceyite members of the Fifty-One knew what their appointment would mean. They instead put forward John Jay, who had also married into the Livingston family, and John Alsop as replacements, people who were unlikely to propose a total overhaul of New York's government.[42]

A day later, however, the Committee of Mechanics rebuked the proposed delegates, proposing its own ticket, one that included Alexander McDougall and Leonard Lispenard, a Dutch innkeeper. Duane and Alsop were out, and the Mechanics called for New Yorkers to gather at the Fields on July 6, where they passed nine resolutions. Most important, they resolved that "the principal colonies" should "stop all importation from, and exportation to Great-Britain" and that the colony's deputies to the Continental Congress will be "instructed, empowered, and directed . . . to agree for this city, upon a non-importation" agreement until the Boston Port Act was repealed. Finally, it was ordered that the resolutions should be published in all of Manhattan's newspapers, which they were, and that they should be sent to other colonies for review. McDougall ran the meeting, start to finish. A broadside that was plastered around Manhattan prior to the meeting labeled people "The Enemies of America," presumably referring to some members of the Fifty-One; the broadside alleged they were against "the common Cause of this Country."[43]

Partisanship within Manhattan's streets and in its coffeehouses and taverns was fierce. Not for several years had two competing political economies been presented to the public in such stark fashion. Both supported sending delegates to the Continental Congress, but the Fifty-One were opposed to trade boycotts and the Mechanics were not. More important, the Mechanics were made up of almost entirely non-elites, people who lacked political agency and had often sided with the DeLanceys in previous crises. "The political Sky at this Place is cloudy," William Smith Jr. wrote around this time.[44]

The Fifty-One rebuked the Mechanics' meeting and the subsequent resolutions on July 7. "Such proceedings are evidently calculated to throw an Odium on this Committee," the Fifty-One ruled, "and to cause groundless Jealousies & suspicions of their Conduct, as well as disunion among our fellow Citizens." Then, the Fifty-One appointed a seven-person committee, including Low, McDougall, and Sears, to draft resolutions "expressing their Sense of the Boston Port Act." The Fifty-One's decision to appoint McDougall and some of his associates to the subcommittee was an ostensible olive branch, but coming after such a strong rebuke earlier in the meeting and the subsequent publication of that rebuke, any attempts at securing McDougall's support or faith were short-lived. On July 8, ten of McDougall's associates on the Fifty-One resigned: Francis Lewis, Isaac Sears, Peter Van Brugh Livingston, Leonard Lispenard, and others. McDougall resigned, too, citing their commitment to "the Public Interest" and the DeLanceys' commitment to promoting "disunion among us, which," they added, "must impede the public business." In what was likely a heated moment, *Rivington's Gazetteer* reported they "quitted the chamber in a rage, ordering their names to be struck off, and afterwards bawling along the streets, 'the Committee is dissolved; the committee is dissolved.'"[45]

But the Fifty-One had not been dissolved. Its remaining forty members, almost all of whom were DeLanceyites, were pushed into a perilous position. Their opponents clearly had considerable popular support from Manhattan's non-elites, and they were charging the DeLanceyites as factional, corrupt politicians who were actively working against the common the good. Worse, the McDougallites' parading through Manhattan's streets announcing the committee's dissolution could have forced it to happen. Some New Yorkers might have believed them, thinking the dissolution was a positive development. Rumors could spread quickly in a city like New York. Down by the city waterfront, the noise coming from the chaos of loading and unloading ships and the local shanty businesses and cartmen would have drowned out clarity; the alleged dissolution of the Fifty-One could have quickly resulted in not only its dissolution but the establishment of another committee or the newfound predominance of the Committee of Mechanics.

The DeLanceyite members of the Fifty-One had to get a grip of the situation before it truly got out of hand. One group, it seems, took a violent approach, attacking Isaac Sears, who, it was reported, received a "good drubbing." Others were more sensible. This group met at 6 p.m. at the Royal Exchange on July 13, and the remaining members of the subcommittee presented their resolutions. They were accepted and ordered for publication. Of the ten, the most significant, at least for the DeLanceyite members, was the Fifty-One's long-sought-after commitment to the incorporation of a nonimportation agreement, but it was a last resort and only to be agreed to if the Continental Congress adopted one. The Fifty-One reasoned that "nothing less than dire necessity can justify, or ought to induce the colonies to unite in any measure that might materially injure our brethren the manufacturers, traders, and merchants in great Britain."[46]

The resolutions were a total rearticulation of the DeLanceys' political economy and their vision of how the British Empire should, and hopefully would, work. They believed in a reciprocal marketplace where Britons and colonial Americans exchanged goods through a drawn-out process that involved those who made the goods, sold them, and transported them across the Atlantic. This commercial empire, as we have already seen, was consumption based, and through the adoption of that understanding of how an integrated commercial British Empire would work, the DeLanceys believed they had done enough to mobilize support. Such a view had worked before—why not again?[47]

The Fifty-One announced that at 2 p.m. on July 19, 1774, a public meeting would be held to vote on its resolutions and on the five delegates to the Continental Congress: John Alsop, John Jay, James Duane, Philip Livingston, and Isaac Low. New Yorkers had six days to go through the resolutions and the candidates and come to a decision. Unlike the colony's assemblymen, who represented their constituents by doing what they thought was right, and Edmund Burke, who represented what he thought was the assembly's interests in Parliament, the delegates to the Continental Congress would be tasked with following New Yorkers' instructions. The delegates represented New Yorkers' interests. If they did not follow through, they could be replaced. The six resolutions were printed as a broadside and distributed throughout Manhattan. Unfortunately for the DeLanceys, they were rejected. Perhaps because of the early afternoon meeting time or a lackluster attempt by the DeLanceys to get their people in the room, fewer people than expected attended the meeting. John Morin Scott, a gifted orator, attended, though, and his criticism of the Fifty-One's resolutions played an important role in its rejection. The only positive of the meeting for the Fifty-One was the confirmation of who the delegates would be to the Continental Congress.[48]

To consolidate support, the Fifty-One appointed another subcommittee to draft further resolutions. However, at a moment when unity was required, rifts emerged within the Fifty-One. DeLanceyite members refused to join the subcommittee, including Isaac Low, who surrendered his chairman duties to Peter Van Brugh Livingston. The DeLanceyites were on the back foot. On July 26, the McDougallites explicitly demanded to know whether the Fifty-One's delegates would pursue nonimportation. Almost all of them agreed. They had little to no choice. The DeLanceys were between Scylla and Charybdis; they made best of a bad situation, accepting that, as Holt put it in the New-York Journal, "a Non importation Agreement will be necessary."[49]

On July 28, then, New Yorkers voted on the delegates. The vote was open to the city's freemen, freeholders, and taxpaying inhabitants, and it was overseen not only by partisans of the Fifty-One and the Committee of Mechanics but also by Manhattan's Common Council, aldermen, and vestrymen. The assembly's committee of correspondence and Lt. Gov. Cadwallader Colden could do little, if anything, to stop it. Ward-by-ward voting was completed, and Fifty-One's candidates, whose names had been proposed for three weeks, were finally confirmed. Shortly thereafter, four other counties reaffirmed the decision, and in a few short weeks, they were off to Philadelphia to attend the Continental Congress.

Equally important, though, delegates from other colonies passed through New York City as they made their way south. These visits, if albeit sometimes brief, provided Alexander McDougall with further opportunities to broaden his support network and push his political economy against that of the DeLanceys.

Lt. Gov. Colden appreciated the development, too, and he believed that things were getting out of control. "Government here," he told Dartmouth in early August, "cannot prevent the frequent Meetings of the People." Colden added that although "moderate Men" were confirmed as delegates, "the most violent Men" still held sway within Manhattan and elsewhere. Perhaps it was time, Colden mused, to "lay aside the Right of raising Money on the subjects for America."[50]

CHAPTER 7

Unite or Die

Congresses, Clubs, and Conventions

John Holt was ready. By the summer of 1774, he was an ardent supporter of Alexander McDougall and his political understanding of what was going on in New York City and beyond. McDougall's objectives were his own, and Holt was fully aware of the role he could play in advancing their cause. His *New-York Journal* was one of the most partisan and widely read newspapers in Manhattan. Holt knew how to spread news with his and others' words, and he had had a history of success. With the Manhattan sun heating his press, types, and hands, Holt worked tirelessly to publish his issues on time. He went on without delay, meeting with those in his network who supplied essays, poems, and information, determining what was newsworthy—what merited inclusion during one of the most partisan periods in early American history. What's more, Holt contributed to the increased partisanship within Manhattan, and throughout 1774 and beyond, he continued to do so. But he used more than just words. He also used illustrations to bring people into his orbit—or push them away.[1]

In the June 23, 1774, issue of the *New-York Journal*, Holt gave New Yorkers a choice. "UNITE OR DIE," the illustration in the newspaper's nameplate read. The radical printer had changed his nameplate from the British Royal Coat of Arms, becoming the first printer during the imperial crisis to revive Benjamin Franklin's famous 1754 "Join, or Die" emblem by using a divided snake to depict all the colonies from north to south. (Other printers soon replicated

Holt's example, including Massachusetts' Isaiah Thomas.) Twenty years earlier, Franklin used the divided snake to call for a unified colonial response against the French and Native Americans. In 1774 Holt called for an intercolonial response against the Coercive Acts. Equally important, though, through his slight alteration of Franklin's words, Holt implored his readers to push for colonial unification. Joining together was not enough. Their concerted efforts could not be forced or coerced. Instead, they had to unite into a single, coordinated political body to achieve their goals.[2]

Holt firmly understood the power of symbols. He appreciated that an image could convey ideas that could be quickly understood, enabling him to be blunt and forthright. When the delegates to the First Continental Congress adjourned and its journal was printed, it was affixed with an emblem that included a column that was fixed on the pedestal "Magna Carta." On the top of the pedestal was a cap, signifying liberty, and twelve arms were both supporting the column and resting upon it. Around the outside of the emblem was a Latin motto that, when translated, read, "We uphold this, we lean upon this." This emblem embodied Holt's feelings about the congress and its objectives, too. On December 15, then, Holt again changed the *New-York Journal*'s nameplate. This time, he changed it to a similar emblem to the one adorning the *Journal of the Proceedings of the Congress*. The colonies, Holt argued, were united. Encircled around the image was a snake swallowing its tail, symbolizing eternity, with an inscription. "UNITED NOW ALIVE AND FREE AND THUS SUPPORTED EVER BLESS OUR LAND FIRM ON THIS BASIS LIBERTY SHALL STAND," it read. Holt, like the congress, was bringing the colonies together to articulate, and thus construct, a united group. The colonies were not yet a nation, and Holt defined their relationship as distinct, though closely connected, peoples. For people like Holt, you were with him or you were against him. There was little to no middle ground—and whatever was left was slowly moving away (see figures 7.1, 7.2, and 7.3).[3]

In Hanover Square, less than four hundred yards away from Holt's shop, forty-eight-year-old James Rivington was ready, too, and he was not impressed with Holt's antics. The *New-York Journal* was, according to Rivington, "a receptacle for every inflammatory piece that is published throughout the continent." Rivington also later used Virgil's *Eclogues* and Genesis to liken Holt's snake imagery as evil, reporting that Holt was among the "Sons of Sedition." Both Rivington and Holt published on Thursdays, each hoping that their newspaper would be New Yorkers' choice. As they went to press, both likely grabbed a copy of their rival's paper, not just for news and information but also to see how they were presenting their work. Rivington quickly appreciated the potential impact of Holt's nameplate changes—and he was forced to keep up with his rival's journalistic flair.[4]

When Rivington began publishing his *Gazetteer* in April 1773, he selected a two-masted schooner as the illustration on his nameplate, placing him as a firm advocate of the DeLanceys' political economy. Rivington was linking Manhattan to the British Empire. But in the fall of 1774 Rivington altered his nameplate. On November 3, he printed a newspaper without a nameplate. The nameplate simply read, "RIVINGTON's New-York GAZETTEER." But a week later, he made his stand: the nameplate he settled on was the British Royal Coat of Arms. New York, though protesting the Coercive Acts, sought compromise. Its allegiance was not in doubt (see figures 7.4, 7.5, and 7.6).[5]

Both Holt's and Rivington's newspapers reflected political sentiment within Manhattan and the Eastern Seaboard. But they were more than that—their newspapers also mobilized support. They did not simply maintain it. From mid-1774, New Yorkers' associations and loyalties were tested. Radical Whigs like Alexander McDougall and Holt often sided with those who described themselves as patriots. Those who were establishment or moderate Whigs were forced to determine if they would move toward radicalism or go in the other direction—one where they would be lambasted as "tories." A majority of the DeLanceys became loyalists, including the likes of Frederick Rhinelander, Charles Nicoll, Evert Bancker Jr., Joseph Allicocke, and William and Edward Laight, and despite their opposition to parliamentary taxation, their partisanship and political economy pushed them toward loyalism. "The right of Parliament to tax this Country," Rhinelander wrote in early 1775, "we all disapprove of." "But the Arbitrary and unjust Resolves of the Congress I must tell you we," he went on, "detest." Together, the DeLanceyites had formed what Rhinelander called "a small political Club," and it was their goal to promote "a speedy Reconciliation." But Rhinelander was intelligent. He had been involved in popular politics in Manhattan for close to a decade, and he appreciated that they had degraded into a bitter, factional contest. "If ever this Province fights," he went on, "it will be for the King." He and his associates would do whatever it took to "counteract" the McDougallites, referred to as "the Blues." Rhinelander's colorful characterization was historic in nature. In the seventeenth century, Scottish Presbyterians adopted the color blue against Charles I's and the royalists' red. It is unclear whether McDougall and his supporters conjured this characterization. It's possible; in their minds, they were resisting Parliament's arbitrary rule just as the Scots resisted Charles I's. As the *Gentleman's Magazine* put it in September 1762, they were "Honest true blues, a staunch, firm, chosen band." And McDougall was their leader. The DeLanceys, on the other hand, were "the Sons of Britain," and they were New York City's loyalists—loyal to their constituents, loyal to the city, loyal to the colony, and loyal to the king and, ultimately, Parliament.[6]

[THURSDAY, June 16, 1774.]   THE   [NUMBER 1641.]

NEW-YORK  JOURNAL;
OR,
THE
GENERAL   ADVERTISER.

Containing the freshest ADVICES,   *both* FOREIGN *and* DOMESTIC.

☞ PRINTED AND PUBLISHED BY JOHN HOLT, NEAR THE COFFEE-HOUSE.

[THURSDAY, June 23, 1774.]   THE   [NUMBER 1642.]

NEW-YORK  JOURNAL;
OR,
THE
GENERAL   UNITE OR DIE.   ADVERTISER.

Containing the freshest ADVICES,   *both* FOREIGN *and* DOMESTIC

☞ PRINTED AND PUBLISHED BY JOHN HOLT, NEAR THE COFFEE-HOUSE.

FIGURES 7.1–3. Mastheads from the *New-York Journal; or, the General Advertiser*, June 16 and 23 and December 15, 1774, Collection of The New-York Historical Society, courtesy American Antiquarian Society

FIGURES 7.1–3. (continued)

The General Congress

On September 5, 1774, the First Continental Congress was scheduled to convene in Philadelphia at Carpenters' Hall. Completed in 1771, the building was offered by the city's Carpenters' Guild, and it was a suitably grand venue. The time, place, location, and participants were set. Fifty-six delegates from twelve colonies soon ushered themselves into the space, into their wooden chairs, as colonists met as one for the first time in two decades. Sitting at their desks, looking around the room, the delegates likely realized the significance of what they were doing, not only in relation to the history of their colony but in their own lives. Many of them were farther away from their home than they had ever been, and they were interacting with people they did not know—individuals whose lifestyles were sometimes radically different than their own—for a cause that could potentially affect hundreds of thousands of people, the overwhelming majority of whom they did not know and would never meet.[7]

The sense of anticipation for the congress had grown larger since New York's delegates were announced. McDougall might have been disappointed at the somewhat moderate slate the colony was sending, but he did not let it affect his politicking. Far from it. McDougall realized that delegates from Connecticut, Rhode Island, and, most important, Massachusetts would likely pass through the city, and he further appreciated that by interacting with them in public spaces he could publicly show his support.

John Adams, Robert Treat Paine, and the rest of the Massachusetts delegation arrived in Manhattan on August 20, ten days after leaving Boston, and they remained there for six days—considerably longer than they stayed anywhere

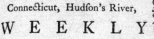

RIVINGTON's
NEW-YORK GAZETTEER;
THE
Connecticut, Hudson's River, New-Jersey, and Quebec
WEEKLY ADVERTISER.

PRINTED at his OPEN and UNINFLUENCED PRESS, fronting HANOVER-SQUARE.

RIVINGTON's
NEW-YORK GAZETTEER;
THE
Connecticut, Hudson's River, New-Jersey, and Quebec
WEEKLY ADVERTISER.

PRINTED at his OPEN and UNINFLUENCED PRESS, fronting HANOVER-SQUARE.

FIGURES 7.4–7.6. Mastheads from *Rivington's New-York Gazetteer*, October 27 and November 3 and 10, 1774, courtesy American Antiquarian Society

else on their journey. "This City will be a Subject of much Speculation to me," Adams wrote in a diary that he was keeping for the benefit of his wife, Abigail. Adams committed eighteen pages of his diary to his time in Manhattan. He enjoyed his time there. More importantly, though, McDougall and his associates targeted Adams and the delegation. They took them to places and put them in public spaces to claim those areas as their own. The McDougallites used the delegates to articulate their political power.[8]

When Adams arrived in New York City, his first stop was Hull's tavern at 10 a.m. on August 20. It was a Saturday. Hull's tavern was operated by Robert Hull, and it was located at roughly 115 Broadway, not far north of Trinity Church or far from the Oswego Market. Since the 1750s, various tavern-keepers had been the site's proprietor, and it was variously known as the Province Arms and New York Arms. When Hull took over, the building had been standing for over forty years—it was built in 1730 by James DeLancey's grandfather, Stephen DeLancey. By this stage, the two-floor space was widely recognized as among the finest and largest in the city, and various important meetings took place there, including meetings relating to the Stamp Act crisis of 1765, as well as social events— dances, concerts, political meetings. Hull was the final proprietor during the colonial era and as one of the most prominent taverns in the city, it provided the eastern delegation with a fitting entrance into Manhattan.[9]

Shortly thereafter, the delegation met Alexander McDougall and Jeremiah Platt. Platt, a merchant and partner in the firm Broome, Platt and Co., did not stay for long. McDougall, Adams wrote, "stayed longer." He "talk'd a good deal." Adams quickly realized that he shared similar views to McDougall, describing him as "a very sensible Man." Later that day, McDougall showed Adams and the delegation around the city, taking them to public places where they might be useful for partisan purposes: taverns, Fort George, the statue of George III, partisans' houses, and "up the broad Way." Places where they could be seen. Altogether, Adams went to nearly "every Part of the City." Along the way, McDougall introduced him to his like-minded colleagues and friends. It had to be an exhausting tour, one that involved lots of walking during one of the hottest months of the year. During a quiet moment, McDougall gave him a quick breakdown of political affairs in the city, noting that there were "two great Families" in New York "upon whose Motions all their Politicks turn." The Livingstons, associated with McDougall, held "Virtue and Abilities as well as fortune." The DeLanceys, Adams was assured, had "not much of either of the three." Associating himself with Alexander McDougall on the city's streets, as well as in its taverns, Adams and the other delegates united with the Scotsman, who impressed them with his "thorough Knowledge of Politicks."[10]

On August 23, McDougall took the delegation to John Morin Scott's home at what is now West Forty-Third Street between Eighth and Ninth Avenues. McDougall spoke candidly and without fear of reproach. Of those who "profess attachment to the American Cause," McDougall recommended Adams "avoid every Expression here." McDougall "says there is a powerfull Party here, who are intimidated by Fears of a Civil War, and they have been induced to acquiesce by Assurances that there was no Danger, and that a peacefull Cessation of Commerce would effect Relief." These people were the DeLanceys, individuals Adams and the delegation avoided entirely.[11]

The DeLanceys, however, were aware of McDougall's game, and they understood what he was doing. But they did not try to intercede. Instead, they jumped at the chance to parade the delegation from Connecticut, who arrived toward the end of August, around the town. According to one of their number, they did not even have the time to "shift out linen" before DeLancey partisans Charles McEvers, Theophylact Bache, and Miles Sherbrooke took them to a tavern. Like McDougall did, the DeLanceys confessed their support for the Continental Congress. The same observer told his wife that although "parties ran excessively high in the City" and he did not socialize with the prominent radicals—"the Broomes, Sears, McDougall, or any of them." Instead, he wrote that the DeLanceyites he dined with were "favorable to the Cause we were upon." McDougall did have a chance to meet the delegates, but the DeLanceys got there first.[12]

New Yorkers' contrasting actions toward two different congressional delegations offer an insight into Manhattan's political climate. Both the DeLanceyites and McDougallites were attempting to influence, even control, the city's public spaces. They wanted to show that it was they, and not their opponents, who merited popular support. Manhattan's printers played a role, too, but their contributions emphasize the calculated politicking of the city's partisans. Hugh Gaine announced the arrival of the Massachusetts delegation on August 22 and John Holt and James Rivington announced on August 25. The delegates were to be "entertain[ed]," Rivington said—and so they were. Away from private political meetings, Manhattan's partisans fought over who controlled the streets. Debate was spilling off the pages and into action. They were getting desperate. "They talk very loud, very fast, and altogether," Adams complained. Sometimes, their enthusiasm was too much.[13]

When New York's delegates departed for Philadelphia on September 1, they left a deeply divided city. But their exits from the city suggested otherwise. As Isaac Low made his way to Paulus Hook, he was escorted "by a considerable Number of respectable Inhabitants, with Colours flying, Music playing, and loud Huzzas." James Duane, Philip Livingston, and John Alsop traveled together, departing from the Royal Exchange. They were saluted by cannon fire and multiple huzzas, as they went on their way to *"defend their Rights"* in the name of *"the common Cause."* But when New York's delegates arrived and began their business on September 5, it quickly became clear that Low, Jay, Duane, and Alsop were among the most moderate in attendance.[14]

Alexander McDougall recognized that the DeLanceyite delegates might not follow through on their earlier declaration to pursue nonimportation. They might also outvote or overpower anything that Philip Livingston tried to do. Livingston, though an advocate for reconciliation, supported nonimportation as an effective means to seek redress. Equally important, the DeLanceyite delegates did not believe that the Continental Congress was a legitimate political body, that is, it was not an intercolonial government with the jurisdiction to enforce laws or resolutions. This DeLanceyite position, although constitutionally correct, ran contrary to those of more radical delegates who declared that government was "dissolved." (Similar problems plagued the Stamp Act Congress of 1765.) McDougall did not want New York's delegates to betray their earlier statements. In early September, he, too, traveled to Philadelphia. Given that he was not a delegate, he was not permitted to participate in or view the debates. Still, this did not stop the fiery Scotsman from leaving his mark. He socialized with those who shared similar views to him, including John Adams, Roger Sherman, and Charles Lee, to influence the debates to ensure that trade boycotts were incorporated. McDougall had also previously advised Adams to temper his actions in the congress regarding, what McDougall said some New Yorkers called, "the levelling Spirit of the New England Colonies." Sitting in Philadelphia's taverns, McDougall almost certainly discussed nonimportation and other items of debates—items he likely should not have been privy to—and he was surely delighted to discover that Duane and Jay, who were slowly moving away from the DeLanceyite position, supported a trade boycott, as they said they would.[15]

McDougall traveled back to Manhattan in early to mid-October. He brought with him news that the congress would almost certainly incorporate a trade boycott. Official news of the Continental Association came soon thereafter. Comprised of fourteen articles, the association was the most significant and impactful output of the First Continental Congress. Among the stipulations included a nonimportation agreement that would be incorporated on December 1, 1774; from March 1, 1775, British goods were to be passed over in favor of colonial goods, and from September 10, 1775, a nonexportation agreement would go into effect. People all over the colonies, from Manhattan to Richmond, were cut off from the transatlantic British marketplace. Behavioral prescriptions were also implemented. Colonists were expected to cast aside costly social activities as well as popular activities. According to William Smith Jr., "The Congress have played so bold a Card, that I think we are cast intirely upon the Magnanimity of the British Nation." Worried, Smith was concerned they were "pouring Oil into the Flames."[16]

With such a wide-ranging reach, the congress determined to reconvene in Philadelphia in May 1775 to discuss Parliament's hopefully positive response to their articles, where they hoped to lift the trade boycotts and return to political economic normalcy. But until then, the boycotts had to be enforced. To do this the Continental Association, as it was also called, stipulated that every town, city, and county had to form a committee of inspection to enforce the articles. Moreover, if they found anyone in violation of the articles, their names were to be published—they were to be named and shamed, publicly embarrassed and mocked, presented as working against the liberties not just of their neighbors but against every colonist in British America. Like the Committee of Mechanics had done earlier in the year, New York's committees mobilized hundreds of people, all of whom would have been white men, into a political movement against Parliament. Their work was not easy. The men patrolled wharves, inspecting the vessels that came into port, overseeing the path of every container inside. Everyday life was politicized, and Alexander McDougall's political economy was being put into practice in Manhattan and beyond. Parliament was being rebuked for its unjust taxation and overly extractive imperialism. Equally important, McDougall and his supporters had formed alliances with like-minded radical Whigs outside of their city walls, and it seemed as if Manhattan's committeemen were on his side, too. "You know what spirit prevailed in our Committee of 51 before the Congress had published their Resolves Laws &c," wrote William Smith Jr. "Their Delegates are become Converts to the prevailing Sentiments of the Congress." Smith was baffled, adding that he had "little Clue" about what had happened in Philadelphia. He was "not without Suspicions," too, but McDougall cared little. People were mobilizing to his cause.[17]

Thousands served in these committees of inspection. The level of political mobilization for colonists, elite and non-elite, was unprecedented. The Continental Congress could not, and did not, enforce policy; that fell to the local committees in rural hamlets, urban centers, towns, villages, and cities. Beyond Manhattan, many of those who served on the committees had likely served on one before—a committee that had been set up to counter the Stamp Act and the Townshend Acts, for instance—and they often reflected judicial bodies. To promote compliance, committees had colonists sign their names to the Continental Association as evidence that they supported the repeal of the Coercive Acts—that they were with them and those who did not sign were not.

The act of signing was meant to be voluntary, but often people felt pressured to sign. Others were undoubtedly forced to do so. In Manhattan, when the delegates brought news of the association and, to some people's surprise, indicated their support for it, it the Committee of Fifty-One announced on November 7, 1774, that eight people for each ward in New York City would be its committee. After some negotiation with the Committee of Mechanics, both the Fifty-One and the Mechanics were dissolved, and a new committee was set up to enforce the association. McDougallites were pleased with the development.[18]

The Committee of Sixty was formed on November 22. Lt. Gov. Cadwallader Colden thought it would have a difficult time, alleging to Dartmouth that the association was "generally disrelished." But this was far from the case. The association was well enforced in New York City, with adherents coming from both sides of the political spectrum. John Morin Scott noted that "Every Office [was] shut up," adding that New Yorkers were "all staunch Whigs now." Despite his positive feelings about New Yorkers, Scott remained anxious about the Continental Congress and any success it might have had. He thought the congress's petitions would "most probably [be] condemned," but he, like McDougall, was "prepared for the worst." "Who can prize life without liberty?" he asked.[19]

Scott's assessment about New Yorkers' behavior was accurate. Few wanted to show their opposition to such a measure lest they be denigrated as an individual who "whould favor Tyranny or arbitrary Power of any kind." Frederick Rhinelander, for instance, the noted DeLanceyite, abided by the association's terms. On June 2, 1774, he ordered twelve quart and pint glasses, six half-pint glasses, a sugar loaf decanter, eighteen "Gale tumblers," forty-eight tall punch glasses, and twenty-four wine glasses. Two months later Rhinelander ordered crockery from the same firm and then placed to further orders in late August. When these goods arrived in December 1774, along with a looking glass he ordered on June 27, 1774, they were clearly contrary to the terms of the association. Rhinelander had to justify his order, but because of the popular desire to "comply with the association," he handed over all his goods without hesitation or reservation.[20]

A major reason behind the Sixty's success was its composition. The former Committee of Mechanics was in an even greater position of power. Prior to the November 22 election, its members had negotiated with the former Fifty-One committeemen to agree upon a mutually agreeable list of people. The two committees had essentially operated alongside one another for most of the summer, but the Fifty-One's concession that a non-elite group of men could dictate the composition of Manhattan's Committee of Inspection was a dramatic step. Although some Fifty-One members retained their positions, the election of new members altered its political makeup. The DeLanceys were "outwitted and disgusted," wrote William Smith Jr., perhaps because only thirty or forty people were alleged to have turned up to vote.[21]

Twenty-nine members of the Committee of Fifty-One kept their seats, twenty-two lost theirs, and there were thirty-one new additions. The Committee of Sixty signaled a shift in the city's political arena: the DeLanceys were no longer in control of New York City's popular political sphere. Three of their most vocal partisans—Theophylact Bache, James Jauncey, and Charles McEvers—lost their places. So, too, did several prominent merchants, including John Thurman Jr. and Alexander Wallace. And although partisans like Edward Laight and Isaac Low kept their places, most of the new members were either McDougallites or were participating in the extrainstitutional political arena for the first time. Hugh Hughes, a prominent McDougallite, felt that the new McDougallite-led committee would stop "the Minds of Others from being poisoned by the Emissaries of Power." As Maj. Gen. Frederick Haldimand opined, an "alarming Spirit" was growing in the city. He was worried that "the growing evil" would not be "crush[ed] . . . in time."[22]

The Blues and the Provincial Convention

In Fort George, Lt. Gov. Cadwallader Colden watched on as governmental power dwindled away. He had not yet called the assembly into session, and the Royal Council did little. But he remained confident, telling Dartmouth that many New Yorkers "favour moderate and conciliatory Measures." He further added that some DeLanceyites had joined the Committee of Sixty out of concern for mob rule. They aimed to "protect the City from the ravages of the Mob," Colden wrote, even though they opposed some of the measures of the Continental Congress. They felt, he went on, "obliged at present to support" it because if they did not, the McDougallites would "take the Lead; and under pretense of executing the Dictates of the Congress, would immediately throw the City into the most perilous situation." With the situation worsening, Colden determined to call the assembly into session on January 10, 1775, with hopes that the assembly would regain popular political control and pursue "conciliatory Measures, and propose something that may be Countenanc'd by Administration." Everything was on the table for Colden, however unlikely, and he was certain of one thing: calling the assembly into session could not "make Matters worse than they are."[23]

William Smith Jr., ever present in the upper echelons of New York's political scene, then wrote to Gov. William Tryon about Manhattan's political developments. "Mʳ. Colden has thought fit to convoke the Assembly," he told the governor. Smith was confused at Colden's actions, and he felt he had to provide Tryon with an update about his lieutenant governor's actions. "What he expects from Members, that can sit but one full session more, I know," Smith wrote, adding that the McDougallites, whom he termed "the Patriots," planned "to get" the colony's assemblymen "to ratify" the Continental Congress's proceedings. Smith also added that such a plan "unluckily coincides with the Plan concerted by those, who aim at an Ascendancy over the Multitude, for private Ends." Colden, Smith thought, was "too old to discern or regard" such plans. Colden was well over his head. "I never so much regretted your Absence, as at this critical moment," Smith told him. According to Smith, many feared "the drawing of the Curtain." "America," he believed, must "be taught the Lesson, *that her Congress was not* infallible." The city and colony had experience politically disruptive moments before, and in this instance, it was all down to Cadwallader Colden.²⁴

In the period between the assembly going into session and the Continental Association's enforcement, and as Smith worked in the shadows, Anglican pamphleteers took the lead in opposing it in Manhattan. Led by Rev. Samuel Seabury and Rev. Isaac Wilkins, they each authored pamphlets that attacked and discredited the constitutional legitimacy and authority of the Continental Congress, almost all of which were advertised and published by James Rivington. Born in Jamaica, Wilkins was thirty-two years old in 1774. He was a graduate of King's College (now Columbia) and was married to Isabella Morris, the daughter of Lewis Morris, the wealthy estate owner who was disqualified from the assembly for nonresidence. And when Wilkins sat down at his writing desk to challenge the Continental Congress, he and Isabella had six children who were, directly and distantly, related to prominent DeLanceyite families: the Waltons, the DeLanceys, the Ludlows, the Philipses, the Lows. Wilkins might not have met all his relatives, but he was almost certainly aware of their shared ideas and interests—and he likely consulted family records to shore up his personal histories. Wilkins, like so many DeLanceyites, was a firm advocate of the assembly, of which he was a member for the Borough of Westchester, and its constitutional authority over New York. In *Short Advice to the Counties of New-York*, Wilkins stated that New York's assemblymen, and only they, were "the proper guardians of our rights and liberties." Adopting a similar message to Edmund Burke, Wilkins noted that they were "constituted our Representatives for that very purpose." Elsewhere, Wilkins labeled the Continental Congress and Committees of Inspection "illegal and disorderly," adding that they were "void of common sense" and were pursuing "ill-judged, tyrannical, and destructive measures." Seabury echoed Wilkins's claims, writing a handful of pamphlets into 1775 that mobilized radical New Yorkers and prompted replies, which Rivington also published, and violence. In one instance, a pamphlet was tarred and feathered.[25]

Alexander McDougall consumed these pamphlets and others like it, including Thomas Bradbury Chandler's *Friendly Address*, published in 1774. McDougall later lent a copy to Alexander Hamilton at some point between its publication and 1776. Moreover, McDougall probably sent pamphlets to John Adams, as well. As Adams later wrote, McDougall was "anxiously engaged to preserve the rights of" of "County." Naturally, McDougall disagreed with Chandler's arguments. So, too, did his supporters. (McDougall's copy that he lent Hamilton was lost, but Hamilton, then a student at King's College, bought him another.)[26]

Indeed, the actions of radical McDougallites pushed their opponents further away from them. When New Yorkers were violently defending the congress and its members, motives, and actions, those who were on the other end of the McDougallites turned toward their politically like-minded associates for comfort and redress. For instance, during the winter of 1774 and 1775 DeLanceyites Augustus Van Horne, Frederick Rhinelander, and William Laight turned toward one another in difficult moments. They met frequently and ensured that each other were kept well informed of, as Rhinelander put it in early January 1775 to John Vardill, who had recently been elected assistant minister and lecturer of Trinity Church and appointed Regius Professor at King's College, "Publick Matters." "The Old year is closed," Rhinelander added. "I wish disorder, confusion, and everything else had closed with it." DeLanceyites like Rhinelander and Laight grew increasingly tired of the McDougallites and the way they defended the Continental Congress. This is not to say, however, that these DeLanceyites supported colonial taxation. Far from it. As Rhinelander put it to Vardill, "The right of Parliament to tax this Country, I need not tell you we all disapprove of." Nevertheless, Rhinelander went on, he appreciated that his and the DeLanceys' political sentiments were increasingly disconnected not only from those in Manhattan but across the colony and the colonies. "The whole continent [is] against us," he wrote. McDougallites were defining who was with them and who was not—"who are Whigs and who Torys, or Rather who are friends to Liberty, and who Enemies to their Country," Rhinelander noted. One individual who they specifically targeted was printer James Rivington. People abused and mocked him as they passed his shop in Hanover Square. The verbal assaults Rivington suffered were so severe that subscribing to *Rivington's New-York Gazetteer* almost became synonymous with fighting against New Yorkers' rights and liberties. New Yorkers soon abandoned their subscriptions, at great personal cost to Rivington.[27]

But Rhinelander and his associates, who had formed "a small political Club" to discuss their views, remained confident in their assemblymen, James DeLancey, James Jauncey, John Cruger, and Jacob Walton. They shared his views. Indeed, the club Rhinelander helped establish included James Jauncey and James DeLancey, as well as other well-known DeLanceyites who held civic appointments, including assistant inspector of potash Joseph Allicocke, royal councilor and New York City chamberlain John Harris Cruger, Manhattan alderman George Brewerton Sr., and Thomas Jones, a justice of New York's supreme court. There were also lesser known DeLanceyites who were no less closely associated. There were DeLanceys, Waltons, Jaunceys, Ludlows, Banckers alongside Evert Bancker Jr., Isaac Heron, and Edward Laight. As they had been since the nonimportation crisis of 1771, they were together against the McDougallites, "the Blues." Indeed, the members for the club had been drawn from "the Old Amicable Society," a DeLanceyite organization that included the likes of Allicocke, Brewerton, Jauncey, Heron, Bancker, and John Harris Cruger, among others. And they knew the Blues would try to "instruct" the DeLancey assemblymen to approve of and adopt the Continental Congress's measures. "Our members are against it," Rhinelander wrote, adding "we will oppose." "Our highest wish is a speedy Reconciliation."[28]

But it would not be easy. "The heats are very Violent," wrote Oliver DeLancey to his son, Oliver Jr., adding, "if the forcible Councils persist I foresee horrid Carnage and immediate Ruin to America." DeLancey appreciated the efforts his associates had gone to in an effort to mobilize support. Political affairs, he believed, had "been kept cooler than in any other" province. "I pray for Moderate Measures," he wrote. DeLancey wrote on January 4, 1775, of his solution, which was similar to that of his nephew: "I pray . . . that Parliament will give America a just and equitable constitution and make England and America florish beyond the Power of its Enemies to injure."[29]

When the assembly convened in mid-January 1775, the DeLanceys had a plan to overcome the constitutional and political issues that the Continental Congress presented. DeLanceyites who opposed the Continental Association since its implementation had not been silent, and some inside and outside Manhattan believed New York would not adhere to the agreement. Their reasons were varied. Some opposed the agreement for personal reasons, others because they believed the congress was illegitimate. Some believed New York's assemblymen would determine the best path forward to send the ongoing dispute with Parliament. Whatever determined their course of action, DeLanceyite assemblymen and royal councilors fixed on a course of action to separate New York from the rest of the colonies—something Parliament had hoped New York would do. As Edmund Burke told James DeLancey, the "Ministry place their best hopes of dissolving the Union of the Colonies and breaking the present spirit of resistance, wholly in your Province." At 11 a.m. on January 5, then, Lt. Gov. Colden and most of his Royal Councilors met to discuss and draft Colden's opening address to the New York Assembly. He was scheduled to deliver it a few days later. William Smith Jr. was absent for at least the first hour of the meeting, but when he arrived and a rough draft was shoved into his hands, the reasons for his delayed invitation were clear. "I was against the whole of it," Smith later wrote, adding, "it would force the House to declare their Creed." Put differently, Smith thought Colden's draft was too aggressive. The language had been shaped by the DeLanceyite councilors. On the surface, their reasoning was decidedly partisan—namely, when the assemblymen discussed and then voted on a reply, they would be forced to declare their political sentiments. Moderation or neutrality would not be an option. Smith believed the DeLanceys wanted every member of the assembly to make their feelings known or argue with each other, which might force Colden to dissolve the assembly before its members could address the First Continental Congress or even consider the Second.[30]

After the draft was revised, albeit not to Smith's satisfaction, Colden delivered his opening address on January 13. Colden's statement was brief, only a couple of hundred words. It likely took him longer than most to make his way through it in an accent that was probably a combination of Scottish and Irish. By this stage of his life, he no longer wrote his own letters. Instead, he stamped his shaky signature at the end, relying on secretaries to articulate his ideas— ideas that he had communicated to colonial officials for over fifty years. In a recent letter to Dartmouth, Colden reflected on his career in the service of the British Empire. He wrote of "the Distress & Embarrassment" that he had recently been subjected to; he had been on the wrong end of "a popular Party" for a decade. Before that, he clashed with James DeLancey Sr. But he was resolute in his support of the British Empire and New York's central place within it. In another letter written the following day, he wrote of those New Yorkers "who promote Peace and discountenance Violence," and he was confident that those in the assembly would pursue this path.[31]

Colden opened his address with a call for action: "This Dispute between GREAT-BRITAIN and her AMERICAN DOMINIONS, is now brought to the most alarming Crisis." But it was not the Continental Congress that New Yorkers should look to, he declared, in what was the most significant address he had ever delivered:

It is to you, Gentlemen, in this anxious Moment, that your Country looks up for Counsel; and on you it, in a great Measure, depends to rescue Her from Evils of the most ruinous Tendency. Exert yourselves then with the Firmness becoming your important Office. If your Constituents are discontented and apprehensive, examine their Complaints with Calmness and Deliberation, and determine upon them with an honest Impartiality. If you find them to be well grounded, pursue the Means of Redress which the Constitution has pointed out: Supplicate the Throne, and our most gracious Sovereign will hear and relieve you with paternal Tenderness. But I entreat you, as you regard the Happiness of your Country, to discountenance every Measure which may increase our Distress: And anxious for the Re-establishment of Harmony, with that Power with which you are connected by the Ties of Blood, Religion, Interest and Duty, prove yourselves, by your Conduct on this Occasion, earnestly solicitous for a cordial and permanent Reconciliation.[32]

William Smith Jr. noted privately that Colden's address "shocked the house." It almost certainly did not shock the DeLanceyite members, who likely supported Colden's call to listen to their constituents and proceed accordingly. Smith was disappointed Colden chose to ignore his advice, but he was less concerned with Smith's thoughts or feelings—or anyone else's for that matter—than the prospect of "a civil War." His opening address set the tone of what was to come.[33]

And yet it took a while for the assembly to grapple with the political crises with which they were confronted. Not all members were in attendance. Some were at their estates, far from Manhattan, enjoying the warmth of their fires. James DeLancey remained confident, though, that he would guide New York through the storm, as his family had done for a generation. On January 20 the assembly presented its reply to Colden's opening address, stating: "Fully convinced that the Happiness of our Constituents depends greatly on the *Wisdom of our present Measures*, we shall exercise the important Trust they have reposed in us, with Firmness and Fidelity; AND WITH CALMNESS AND DELIBERATION, PURSUE THE MOST PROBABLE MEANS TO OBTAIN A REDRESS OF OUR GRIEVANCES." The DeLanceyite assemblymen planned to pursue redress themselves, as the colony's elected officials.[34]

The McDougallites thought differently, including Rensselaerswyck Manor assemblyman Abraham Ten Broeck. Born in 1734, Ten Broeck was a merchant from Albany. He had a high forehead and a long nose and a narrow face. He was related to Philip Livingston and had married into the Van Rensselaer family, one of the oldest and most powerful families north of Manhattan. He was active in local affairs, too. He had held commissions since the 1750s and had served in the assembly since 1761. By 1775 he had long been associated with Alexander McDougall and on January 27 his supporters packed the assembly's gallery to watch the debate. Ten Broeck proposed the assembly "take into Consideration the Proceedings of the Continental Congress." In a narrow, partisan vote, Ten Broeck's motion was defeated.[35]

McDougall took things a step further. The Scotsman believed that the New York Assembly, and especially its members from Manhattan, were not protecting the public good—and they never would. McDougall believed they were colluding with Parliament to deliberately inhibit New Yorkers' rights and liberties. For McDougall, there was one option: overturn the government and set up another that would represent New Yorkers' true interests and protect their liberties. As early as January 1775 McDougall called for the establishment of a separate colonial government in New York. A "Provincial Congress," he called it. He also believed that the colony should establish a separate militia to pursue and protection "the Common Cause." In a letter of January 29 to Samuel Adams, McDougall enclosed the recent assembly vote to show him "the true import of their determination," which he believed was to promote "disunion." "The true Friends of Liberty in and out of the House will leave no stone unturned to make the union of the Assemblies as Compleat as that of the Congress," McDougall wrote. The DeLanceys were "Parricides," and they were working against the place they were meant to protect.[36]

McDougall signed his letter to Adams "Marcus Brutus," a classical reference in which he represented himself as either Lucius Junius Brutus, the founder of the Roman republic who executed his sons to protect the commonwealth, or Marcus Junius Brutus, who assassinated Julius Caesar. Either way, McDougall was sacrificing his self-interest for the betterment of his country, something he had done since he first came to popular prominence within Manhattan in late 1769. Equally important, McDougall's signature shows that he believed that he was the Brutus of New York, possibly even of America, and only he could rise to the problems extractive British imperialism presented, which in this instance was symbolized by the DeLanceys, who were corrupt, possibly even Caesars.[37]

The assembly's behavior of the coming days, weeks, and months confirmed McDougall's beliefs and reinforced his conviction that the DeLanceyite assemblymen were in league with Parliament. On January 31, James DeLancey successfully moved that the assembly prepare memorials to the House of Lords, a "Representation and Remonstrance" to the House of Commons, and a petition to George III. On January 16, DeLanceyite assemblymen successfully voted down a motion from Philip Schuyler to have the assembly committee of correspondence's letters published. It did not stop there. A day later, they successfully voted down a motion from Suffolk County assemblyman Nathaniel Woodhull to thank New York's delegates to the First Continental Congress "for their faithful and judicious Charge of the Trust reposed in them." On February 21, they refused to thank "the Merchants and Inhabitants of this City and Colony" for adhering to the Continental Association and, most important, on the 23rd they refused to appointed delegates to the Second Continental Congress.[38]

But their opposition to addressing, dealing with, or appointing delegates to the Continental Congress was more than an overt display of partisanship. DeLanceyite Crean Brush, who represented Cumberland County, summarized their position. The Continental Congress "acted without any power or authority derived from this House." "We are the legal and constitutional Representatives of the people; to us the care of their liberties is," he added. Isaac Wilkins reinforced Brush's statements but was more forceful, describing the congress's actions "ill-judged, tyrannical, and destructive." Furthermore, when the assembly completed and dispatched their petitions, memorials, and remonstrance to Britain on March 25, it showed that the DeLanceys opposed external taxes. "No *Taxes* should be imposed on them without THEIR CONSENT given personally, or by their Representatives," they wrote, adding that they were writing on behalf of their *"Sister Colonies."* In another petition, they wrote that New Yorkers and all colonists were "entitled to EQUAL RIGHTS AND PRIVILEGES with their fellow Subjects in *Great-Britain.*" But they also condemned the Boston Tea Party and the "Mode[s] pursued for redressing the[ir] Grievances," perhaps including the Continental Congress.[39]

They hoped that would be the end of it—that their lengthy, elaborate dispatches to Parliament and George III, which were primarily written by James DeLancey, would bring an end New York's role in the crisis. When Edmund Burke presented the papers to Parliament, he soon found that Lord North approved of the assembly's actions, writing of the prime minister, "the Colony of New York had his hearty approbation." But the political responses they devised and executed were far more conservative than those advocated by New York's radicals. "We have not chosen Delegates to meet the next Congress," Alexander McDougall wrote, "waiting till we know whether the Assembly will do it or not." "If they don't," he went on, "we shall be able with more Ease to bring about a Provincial Congress." What McDougall was proposing was not entirely novel throughout colonial North America at this time, but McDougall's radicalism lay in his willingness to circumvent the New York Assembly, even though its members were debating and had debated the First Continental Congress.[40]

Despite the assembly's best hopes for their petition, memorial, and remonstrance, as well as North's ostensible approval, Burke was unable to present the remonstrance to the House of Commons. Establishment Whig George Montagu, fourth Duke of Manchester, was unable to present the assembly's memorial to the House of Lords, even with the assistance of political allies such as Charles Lennox, third Duke of Richmond, Charles Pratt, first Earl Camden, and even Rockingham himself. As to George III, by the summer of 1775 Burke had not yet heard if he had seen it. But even if he had, it was too late.[41]

The assembly adjourned on April 3, 1775, for a monthlong break, without appointing delegates to the Second Continental Congress. Instead, the Committee of Sixty acted. On March 1 it declared that a public vote would be held at the Royal Exchange on March 6, where *"the Freeholder and Freemen of the city and county of New-York"* would determine how to choose, and possibly select, delegates, all of which would occur without the purview of the assembly. A day after the announcement was made, DeLanceyites convened at Montayne's tavern to discuss how to respond. They determined that New Yorkers should postpone electing or selecting delegates until April 20, likely because they hoped Burke would have replied with positive news about the assembly's petitions. They distributed a broadside summarizing their beliefs. It was a moderate approach, one that was almost entirely out of touch with what was happening on the ground, where ordinary people—most of whom left no record behind—were deciding on how their government should act, what type of government it should be, and whom should it serve. Events inside and outside of Manhattan happened too suddenly for New Yorkers to accept the DeLanceys' approach, and even though those insiders and outsiders often had competing goals, many shared the goal of sending delegates to the Second Continental Congress—the intercolonial assembly that was made up of some of the most politically active and intellectually curious men in colonial North America, men who could launch, and perhaps lead, a civil war within the British Empire.[42]

The Committee of Sixty thus acted when the assembly would not. It adopted its government functions, becoming the institutional representatives for the people of the Manhattan and the colony. On March 4, they met at Van de Water's tavern, where they planned a public demonstration from the Liberty Pole, still untouched since 1770. They planned to hoist a "Union Flag" with a red field to show their proud support of "THE MEASURES OF THE CONGRESS" before marching to the Royal Exchange. The next night McDougall and his associates they hid weapons—clubs and staves—if emotions got out of control.[43]

Isaac Sears led the march to the Royal Exchange. With each step they were joined with the sound of trumps, drums, fifes, voices, picking up people as they went. The "Friends of Freedom," as John Holt described them, were led by two standard bearers. Instead of a British flag, their standard was a blue field that was inscribed on one side, "GEORGE III. REX AND THE LIBERTIES OF AMERICA. NO POPERY." On the other, it read, "THE UNION OF THE COLONIES, AND THE MEASURES OF THE CONGRESS." The standard was another means to mobilize New Yorkers, and it firmly showed where their allegiances lay—with George III and the other colonies, not Parliament, which they increasingly believed held little to no control over the American colonies. Moreover, the use of a standard, as well as the logistics of marching to a regimented chorus of fifes and drums militarized proceedings, marginalized those who were not marching with them or supported their political economy. There were likely elites and non-elites marching, singing, mobilizing together, as they loudly propagated that New Yorkers' political troubles—and thus the public good—could only be tackled and overcome at the Second Continental Congress. "When they arrived at the Exchange, around 12 noon, McDougall and the rest of the Sixty were waiting. Meanwhile, DeLanceyites met a short distance away, gathering at Montayne's tavern, and they brought as much civic clout as they could muster. Mayor Whitehead Hicks was there. So, too, was most of the Royal Council, members of the Royal Navy and the British Army, DeLanceyite assemblymen, and others who were reliant on them. When the groups met, they clashed. They exchanged verbal assaults, lambasting one another for their ill-conceived vision of New York's place within the crisis, and one DeLanceyite was robbed, had his clothes ripped off his back, and was hauled to the Liberty Pole, where he was thrown on his knees and told to damn George III. Later, he was dumped in a prison cell.[44]

Partisanship had evolved into violence. But when the voting commenced, it was clear that New Yorkers believed that a provincial convention should be organized and that the Sixty should nominate delegates to the Second Continental Congress to promote and protect their interests. Reports varied about how many supported the appointment of delegates, but whatever the numbers were, it did not look good for the DeLanceys. William Smith Jr. noted, "some say 10 some 5 some 3 to 1" in favor of McDougall's position. The DeLanceys' backs were against the wall. Isaac Low tried to make a stand, telling New Yorkers that he would not serve in a provincial convention or be sent to Philadelphia. His statements fell flat, but partisanship remained high. "The People here are much divided," one visitor remarked on March 11. "Party spirit is very high . . . nothing is heard of but Politics." Over the coming days New Yorkers continued chatting in taverns, coffeehouses, in the streets, on the docks and wharves, everywhere. A vote was held on March 15, and nearly one thousand men turned up to vote at City Hall. They delivered an extraordinary endorsement of the McDougallites' approach: 826 were in favor of a convention and only 163 were against it.[45]

Those who voted for a convention were a majority in each of Manhattan's seven wards. The city's diverse population was unevenly spread throughout the wards, and despite a population surge of between four thousand and six thousand between 1760 and 1775, the city boundaries did not measurably increase. Newcomers did not settle in the northern areas of Manhattan, either. Instead, more and more people—men, women, free and unfree—were packed into the existing seven wards. Most lived in the center of the city, usually within walking distance of Fort George at the tip of the island and closer to the East River. To deal a substantial increase in foot-traffic, streets were leveled and paved, particularly in the areas toward the west of Broadway and Dey (Dyes) Street. But most of the city laid their heads to rest in the East, North, and Montgomerie Wards, locations that also had churches for the city's Methodists, German Reformed, and Dutch Reformed as well as Baptist and Moravian meetinghouses. The city's wealthiest inhabitants lived in the Dock and East Wards, which were also the densest, most expensive, and most fashionable. Rents in those wards were sometimes double or three times as in other areas. The South Ward was home to the wealthy and fashionable, too, and those three wards also contained the highest number of enslaved blacks. Two of the poorer wards were Montgomerie and West, which were also the least densely populated. The West Ward, moreover, was the prostitution center of Manhattan, while the Out Ward was home to the city's poorest individuals, as well as two smelly tan yards, a public slaughterhouse, ropewalks, breweries, pottery kilns, and distilleries. It was not a popular spot to live; drainage was poor, and livestock trotted around the mucky, noisy streets, spreading disease. Put simply, some twenty-two thousand people lived in an area that was around four thousand feet wide and six thousand feet long.[46]

The ward-by-ward breakdown of the vote reveals with startling clarity the political and economic views of a section of Manhattan's white, male population. The so-called Anti-Congress Party, the DeLanceys, were overwhelmingly defeated. Only in the Dock Ward, where many of them lived, worked, and socialized, did they present a challenge—and they still received nearly 50 percent fewer votes. Perhaps most significantly, though, the city's poorest wards—Out, West, and Montgomerie—recorded some of the most significant results, almost uniformly calling for a provincial convention. Elites and nonelites, it seemed, had joined together. A provincial convention for the entire colony was scheduled for April 20, 1775, and eleven delegates were chosen for Manhattan, including Alexander McDougall, who had told Josiah Quincy Jr. around two weeks before voting that New York was with Massachusetts and the other colonies in "the Common cause." And so they were.[47]

The DeLanceys were understandably distressed at the situation. Their most prominent adherents—those in the assembly, for instance—had been depicted as working against the common good, against the people's needs, against their constituents' wishes. But even though the political tide was moving against them, they did not change their political conviction. They still opposed internal taxation. "I cannot," wrote William Laight, "allow the Parliament *every* Power, for it does not to me seem Reasonable that the *internal regulation* of this Country, & both with respect to *taxation & Police* should be within their jurisdiction." Laight was pleased with how the assembly acted, too, writing, "Should their conduct be the means of effecting an accommodation of the present dispute between G.B. & America, our Colony & Its Legislative Body will merit the thanks of Posterity for daring to act in a constitutional manner without relying, as all our neighbours have done, on Congresses & Committees." Others had made a similar point before; for instance, writing in January, Thomas Ellison Jr. noted, "Many here think the assembly should take no notice of what the Congress has done, but petition *themselves*, which would be the most likely means of healing the unhappy breach." But they had made a public misstep. Turning up to a crucial vote on the nature of New York's place within the British Empire with "Officers of the Crown," as William Smith Jr. put it, was politically suicidal. It confirmed for some New Yorkers everything that had been said about the DeLanceys before that they were "Anti Delegate Men [who] were only such as were in the Interest of Govt." They were "Dependt Tools," Smith added.[48]

Other DeLanceyites were not as levelheaded as William Laight. Some thought the forthcoming provincial convention wielded too much power, namely, its members' jurisdiction over who would represent New York in the Second Continental Congress. Frederick Rhinelander wanted to choose the delegates himself, thinking it was "rong to put it in the power of the Counties." He wanted his "Choise"—something DeLancey supporters had articulated since the elections of 1768 and 1769. Rhinelander wanted to consider and later approve of the people who would advocate for his interests in Philadelphia, but as he saw it, the way those delegates would be chosen would not allow for that. Unfortunately for Rhinelander, however, any public opposition to the provincial convention had consequences. In late March and early April 1775, he was condemned throughout Manhattan as "Unfriendly to Liberty," something that he wholeheartedly denied. Writing to William Elery, he wrote, "does this constitute me an Enemy to my Cuntry?" "If I have been represented to you as a person who whould not oppose the late oppressive acts of the British Parliament—as a person Whose principly whould favour Tryanny or arbitrary Power of any kind, I have been injured Sir in the highest degree." In another letter, written a few months later, things had only gotten worse for him. He was widely understood to be "a person unfriendly to the American Cause" and had lost considerable business as a result. Rhinelander was profoundly upset at the situation, adding, "I confess I could not approve of every measure adopted by the Congress, yet I profess to be as well attached to the interests of America, as any man in it." Neither Rhinelander's nor the DeLanceys' situation improved from March 1775.[49]

But John Holt was happy. In his mind New Yorkers came together on March 15. They overcame "every artifice" to defeat the DeLanceys' attempts "to prevent the election of the Deputies . . . and to frustrate the design of a Provincial Congress, and of sending Delegates . . . to the next General Congress." In Holt's next issue, he printed Isaac Low's March 16 statement about a provincial convention. The organization of such an institution was a radical step, but it did not supplant the New York Assembly. Its one and only mandate was to appoint delegates to the Continental Congress, especially if the colony was going to get what it wanted—the repeal of the Coercive Acts. "The preservation of our rights and liberties," Isaac Low noted, "depends on our acceding to the general union, and observing such a line of conduct as may be *firm*, as well as *temperate*." Unity, candor, and resolution were the way forward for New York's Committee of Sixty. Those who supported it needed plenty of all three in the days, weeks, months, and years to come.[50]

CHAPTER 8

The Din of War

Revolutionaries and Loyalists

By the late spring of 1775, many New Yorkers believed that Parliament's apparent unending march toward imperial authoritarianism had gone too far. By this time, many people had already taken a stand. People signed the Continental Association; others joined committees of safety and patrolled the streets securing additional signatures, often by force or extreme cajoling. Some joined what remained extralegal political institutions like the Provincial Congress, which by April had almost entirely usurped the power of New York's assembly. James DeLancey had long believed that Parliament's imperial authoritarianism had gone too far. Six years earlier, he had suggested to the Marquis of Rockingham that the colonies form "a Parliament in America." And in May 1774 he was resolute in his opposition to the British government's conduct toward the British American colonies. In 1775, as the crisis worsened, DeLancey took the distinctive approach of making his case for New York's colonial status in Britain.[1]

He left Manhattan in April 1775, determined to present his and his constituents' cases before Parliament, as well as any who might listen. In many ways, DeLancey's decision to travel to Britain captured his family and faction's political economy and their understanding of their place within the British Empire far better than their behavior over the preceding six months or so. Refusing to acknowledge the Continental Congress showed their conviction in the constitutional legitimacy of the New York Assembly, as well as their belief that the "General Congress" and any provincial conventions or congresses were illegal. Moreover, New York agent Edmund Burke's inability to convey the assembly's messages, many of which DeLancey wrote, likely emboldened his urge to travel across the Atlantic.[2]

DeLancey's behavior also offers a comparison to the behavior of Massachusetts's governor between 1771 and 1774 and, to use the words of the editor of his papers, "the most articulate spokesmen for the loyalist viewpoint," Thomas Hutchinson. Both men viewed their respective colonies—Hutchinson and Massachusetts, DeLancey and New York—as their colonial countries, and both felt that it was in their colonies' public and private interests to remain within the British Empire. Hutchinson departed the colonies in June 1774, and almost immediately initiated discussions with British ministers about Anglo-American relations. He was soon introduced to George III and Lord North, with aims of promoting reconciliation. It was his "special mission," according to one historian. But Hutchinson departed far earlier than James DeLancey, and he had no or little firsthand or secondhand knowledge of public attitudes toward the Coercive Acts. He could have little effect on what was happening. As news traveled across the Atlantic, Hutchinson was shocked at events transpiring in Boston, Philadelphia, and New York, but he could do nothing about it. Although he socialized with some New Yorkers in London and he may have dined with DeLancey on November 24, 1775, noting in his diary that he dined with a "Mr Delany of New York," Hutchinson became "a spectator." He was "a somewhat marginal figure." DeLancey, though unaware of Hutchinson's toil, risked a similar fate: irrelevance and an increasing likelihood that he could not return to his home, his country.[3]

Extant records surrounding DeLancey's departure from New York are scarce. Newspapers in New York City, the colony, or the continent, it seems, did not publicize his departure. He snuck out of the city. It is also possible, however, that DeLancey departed in haste or in as close to secret as he could manage. The New York assemblyman later reported that he had done almost everything he felt he could to mobilize support, and he felt disappointed in some of the responses he received, writing that he had "zealously exerted his Influence and Interest." But the DeLancey interest was flagging—and he was running out of options.[4]

James DeLancey traveled across the Atlantic more than most New Yorkers. He had connections in Britain that went beyond his enviable education. They were formed not just because of his status in New York but also because of his love of horseracing. DeLancey was the only colonial member of Britain's Jockey Club, then the country's preeminent horseracing organization. Founded in 1750, its members included Prince William Augustus, Duke of

Cumberland, and Prince Henry Frederick, Duke of Cumberland and Strathearn, as well as other prominent individuals like Charles James Fox, whom DeLancey was close to, and Augustus FitzRoy, third Duke of Grafton, the former prime minister and DeLancey's cousin. DeLancey's friend and colleague the Marquis of Rockingham was also a member. Away from the racecourse, members socialized in London in Euston and Pall Mall and on Bond Street and St. James's Street. Through this club, DeLancey had access to people of influence and stature, and he likely felt confident that he could successfully advocate for his constituents. The time of his departure was likely a conscious decision. Jockey Club members convened annually on June 3, the day before George III's birthday. When DeLancey departed Manhattan in April, he thought he would arrive in time for the dinner.[5]

Upon his arrival in Bath, the *Middlesex Journal* simply noted a "Mr. De Lancey" had arrived on July 5. The voyage had been slow. It was too late to make the Jockey Club dinner. But when DeLancey made it to London, undeterred, he quickly made his rounds. He pushed for reconciliation wherever he could. He also wrote to his associates of his father-in-law, William Allen, Pennsylvania's chief justice, encouraging them to push Continental Congress delegates to pursue reconciliation.[6]

Back in Manhattan, New Yorkers grappled with the fact that a provincial convention was going to take place and the colony would send delegates to the Second Continental Congress. Popular politics within Manhattan, ever so divisive, splintered further. In August 1774 McDougall told John Adams there were five parties within Manhattan. The first was made up of those who were "intimidated by Fears of a Civil War." The second despised "the levelling Spirit of New England." The third was largely religious in origin and was likely represented by Samuel Seabury, King's College president Myles Cooper, and Trinity Church assistant rector Charles Inglis. The fourth group, most of whom were almost certainly DeLanceyites, was "largely concerned in Navigation," that is, the commercial solidity of Manhattan within the British Empire. Last, McDougall said, there were those government officials who sought "Favours," that is, for example, Lt. Gov. Cadwallader Colden. But there was at least one other party, one that McDougall omitted—the one he represented and led. It contained many of the city's mechanics. William Laight, a loyal DeLanceyite, recognized McDougall's appeal, or his "zeal." New Yorkers were drawn to McDougall, and he welcomed them. Driven by "Ambition & Popularity," McDougall built a cohesive *"Set"* in New York City and beyond.[7]

From April 1775 through the spring of 1777, all these groups featured within popular politics in Manhattan. During this time, New Yorkers were often forced to determine who or what best represented their interests, if at all, whether it was Alexander McDougall, the DeLanceys, the Livingstons, or the assembly, Parliament, the provincial convention, the Second Continental Congress, or the church. But despite their differences, most shared one goal. "Every good man wishes that America may remain free," as Judge Robert Livingston Sr. noted on May 5, 1775. But New Yorkers disagreed on how to retain the colonies' freedoms. As it had been throughout much of the 1760s and 1770s, ideas and interests structured everyday life, political, social, economic. Between 1775 and 1777, amid difficult circumstances and whether they wanted to, Manhattan's residents had to determine what was important to them.[8]

The Battles of Lexington and Concord

On April 20, 1775, forty-three delegates from nine counties descended on New York's provincial convention. About half the colony had sent delegates. News of the convention was slow to reach Parliament. But it did not matter. By early 1775 British statesmen already believed that American affairs had gotten well out of hand. Some went so far as to argue that Britain's empire in North America was dwindling. Their solution was less about how to dampen Americans' convictions against Parliament than how hard British forces would strike to regain imperial control. As early as January 1775, William Pitt, first Earl of Chatham, informed Rockingham that Parliament and Britain's relationship with its colonies was "on the eve of the doom." The following month, Lord North, who failed to fully grasp the extent of colonists' resistance, reiterated his commitment to extracting revenue from America and reaffirmed his authoritarian interpretation of the British imperial state. On February 9, Massachusetts was declared to be in a state of rebellion. Around a month later, Edmund Burke delivered his renowned speech on reconciliation, in which he reoriented the moderate Whig approach to the imperial relationship. He shifted their stance away from imperial management to maintaining union, suggesting that the American colonies return to the relative independence they enjoyed within the British Empire prior to 1763. Only then, Burke argued, could Parliament overcome Americans' "stubborn spirit." But Parliament was against Burke and his view. His resolution was demolished, 270 votes to 78.[9]

In Manhattan, New York's provincial convention met for three days. Between April 20 and 23 they appointed delegates to the Second Continental Congress, including all the delegates who had traveled the previous September. But there was one significant exception. After defending his associates' decision not to recognize the Continental Congress, Isaac Low refused his nomination and election to the provincial convention, and in doing so he also resigned as a delegate to the congress in Philadelphia. He believed that the convention, and the congress, was unconstitutional. Others agreed. According to one report, "An inconsiderable number of persons" in the convention declared they would not participate. They stated that they would not "have anything to do with deputies and congresses." The proceedings were "illegal & unconstitutional." This was an almost identical view that Frederick Rhinelander had articulated earlier in April, one that was also replicated by over three hundred inhabitants of Westchester County. Led by Isaac Wilkins and Frederick Philipse III, third lord of Philipsburg Manor, they convened at the home of militia captain Abraham Hatfield, where they signed a "PROTEST" to declare their opposition to the provincial convention and Continental Congress's "illegal and unconstitutional proceedings." The signatories added that their political allegiance was owed to the "only true Representatives of the People, the General Assembly." Although signed in Westchester, the views represented many of those within Manhattan, including Rhinelander and his associates, and they were communicated en masse through publication in Hugh Gaine's and James Rivington's newspapers.[10]

Those who were elected as the colony's delegates—Philip Livingston, John Alsop, James Duane, John Jay, Simon Boerum, William Floyd, Henry Wisner, Philip Schuyler, Lewis Morris, Robert R. Livingston, Francis Lewis, and George Clinton—were given authority "to concert and determine upon such measures as shall be judged most effectual for the preservation and re-establishment of *American* rights and privileges, and for the restoration of harmony between *Great Britain* and the Colonies." DeLanceyites were distressed at the proceedings. William Laight believed Jay, his longtime friend and political associate, had deserted his friends and colleagues. As he put it, Jay had "turn'd in Politics, a rigid *Blue Skin.*" He was now aligned with McDougall, whose actions, Laight added, were solely motivated by "Ambition & Popularity."[11]

But whatever Laight believed McDougall's motives might have been, his understanding likely changed on April 23. In the same issue that Rivington announced New York's delegates to the Second Continental Congress, he printed news "that an action had happened between the King's troops and the inhabitants of Boston." Other items in his newspaper offered further information. The British Army "had killed eight or ten men," one piece reported. Another item from Worcester noted that six men had died and four were wounded. Another stated fifty colonists and 150 British soldiers had died. Other reports claimed that the entire town of Marshfield had been destroyed and all the soldiers had been "taken prisoners or killed." Nobody knew what had happened, except that British forces had clashed with colonists in Massachusetts—and some people might have died.[12]

What transpired on a damp April 19, 1775, in Lexington and Concord has gone down as one of the most significant days in the history of the western world. Lt. Gen. Thomas Gage, a tall man with bushy eyebrows and dark, piercing eyes, was then serving as the governor of Massachusetts as well as the commander-in-chief of British forces in North America. He had lived in America for two decades, and by then he was well versed in colonial affairs, particularly in New York City, where he lived in an opulent mansion on Broad Street with his wife, Margaret Kemble Gage. In April, far from home and surrounded by hostile Bostonians, Gage seized ammunition stores in Cambridge and Charlestown, after which he ordered some seven hundred British soldiers to follow suit in Lexington and Concord. Although they left Boston around 10 p.m., city inhabitants had a head-start to the eleven-or-so-mile journey. In Lexington, where the soldiers arrived at around 5 a.m., seventy armed minutemen tried to stop what they viewed as a British advance. Shots were fired on both sides; eight colonists and two soldiers fell. In Concord, as the British pressed on at around 12 noon, thousands of minutemen clashed with the British, hundreds of whom were killed. Twice as many soldiers fell as minutemen during Battles of Lexington and Concord, but colonists from over twenty Massachusetts towns died, stretching from Billerica to Brookline.[13]

News of the so-called Shot Heard Round the World quickly spread around New England, reaching Watertown and Boston at around 10 a.m. and Worcester a little after 12 noon. Colonists in Portsmouth, New Hampshire, heard in the early hours of the 20th. Those in Connecticut found out on the 20th, too. But those in Manhattan had to wait until between 2 p.m. and 4:30 p.m. on the 23rd, when twenty-three-year-old Israel Bissell frantically rode into town. Bissell, a Connecticut postrider, had traveled as fast he could down to Manhattan. At least one horse died from exhaustion on his journey, such was the intensity he demanded as he traveled southward.[14]

On the same day Bissell arrived in New York, Thomas Gage informed Secretary of State for the Colonies William Legge, second Earl of Dartmouth, about what had happened in Massachusetts. Dartmouth was sympathetic toward the Americans' demands, but he did not anticipate the severity and urgency of Gage's letter. "The Country are all Arming against His Majesty's Troops," Gage wrote. George III's colonists in Massachusetts—and possibly beyond—were "Rebels."[15]

The impact of the skirmishes in Massachusetts were felt quickly in New York. "The Town alarmed Yesterday with News from Boston," wrote William Smith Jr. on April 24. "Sundry Commotions here in consequence of it." Five days later, Smith returned to his "Historical Memoirs," where he was unable to accurately capture what was happening, writing, "It is impossible to fully describe the agitated State of the Town." He had never seen anything like it in his lifetime. As the conflicting reports and news of Bissell's arrival circulated, "Tales of all Kinds" were circulating around the city streets: "invented[,] believed, denied, discredited." Smith's characterization was accurate.[16]

On the evening of the 23rd, a few hours after Bissell came into the city, Isaac Sears, John Lamb, and Marinus Willett broke into the city's weapons arsenal in City Hall. They commandeered between five hundred and six hundred bayonets and cartridge boxes, all of which were ready for action. After carting them out, they chose to store them in an associate's garden for people to collect. When they did, McDougall, Sears, and Lamb had them sign their names to a quasi-muster roll, in which they acknowledged receiving weapons from the city, even though its Common Council had nothing to do with it. Manhattan, without the sanction of the Common Council, governor, Royal Council, or assembly, was at war. The soldiers were ordinary people—bakers, shoemakers, carpenters, curriers, saddlers, coopers, people who could only mark their name with an X. Sears and Lamb led them on military marches throughout the city, always beginning near Hampden Hall. And what an intimidating sight it must have been, especially for those who did not necessarily share their views. Letters were intercepted and read; people were threatened, Sears forcibly acquired the keys to the city's customhouse. The port of the City of New York was closed. As Robert R. Livingston noted on the 27th, Manhattan was "in a continual Bustle." "People hear are properly Fearless," he added. "I mean the Wigs." He was referring to the McDougallites—and he was confident in their resolve and prospects, writing, "Be assured the American cause from all appearance will be Victorious."[17]

The McDougallites also inventoried all the firearms and ammunition in Manhattan and established a military watch that prohibited the sale of firearms to people who they believe were their opponents. Others had their weapons sequestered, many of whom were DeLanceyites. For instance, Jarvis Roebuck had one pistol taken from him; Stephen Kibble, one cutlass and one cartouche box; William Ustick, one gun and bayonet, two hangers, and twelve sword blades; and Miles Sherbrooke had one gun barrel, one cutlass, one brass-barrel pistol, three silver swords, eight gilt swords, and fourteen muskets taken from him. Not all DeLanceyites gave up their weapons, though. Augustus van Horne and John Le Chevalier Roome refused to hand over their arms— and they were both imprisoned. McDougall and his supporters characterized what later became loyalism as an untenable position.[18]

Others were equally unamused with the McDougallites' actions. "The state of this City and province is very much altered," Charles Inglis wrote to John Vardill on May 2. The McDougallites had, Inglis went on, "breathed destruction to all the friends or order who they called Tories." New Yorkers were being forced "to accede to all the measures of the Provincial and Continental Congress's." "All Letters are opened & examined," he added. In an exhaustive letter, Inglis detailed the inescapable confusion of urban life in Manhattan and its imperial implications. Inglis, who often signed as *A Real Churchman* to avoid detection, observed, "The Empire seems now at stake," adding that the McDougallites were "American demagogues" who had been "seized" by an "Epidemic Phrenzy." They sought "exemption from the Jurisdiction of Parliam.ᵗ." In other words, Inglis thought, they sought independence. William Laight described them in similar terms: they were "Ambitious, Republican Demagogues."[19]

The next day, Lt. Gov. Cadwallader Colden wrote to Dartmouth. Filled with emotion and distress, Colden felt partly responsible for what had transpired in New York and in the colonies. "In all my correspondence," he began, "I have studied to give your Lordship an exact Idea of the real situation of the Province, and the most material transactions of the People." "The Accounts which I am now to give," he went on, "will almost entirely destroy the expectations you have had reason to entertain of the conduct which this Province would pursue." Then, Colden detailed the perilous situation he felt Manhattan was in, partly because the city was defended by one hundred British soldiers as well as the transport *Kingfisher*. It would not be enough. The government was "entirely prostrated." John Cruger agreed. Writing to New York agent Edmund Burke, he lamented, "The melancholy situation that this city and colony is in is beyond expression since the receival of the account from Boston," adding, "The cause of liberty has become general throughout America."[20]

Later that month, news of the battles of Lexington and Concord reached Britain. New York agent Edmund Burke was distraught, writing, "All our prospects of American reconciliation are, I fear, over." "Blood has been shed," he added. "The sluice is opened. Where, when, or how it will be stopped God only knows." Parliament and George III were determined to coerce the colonies into submission, but, like Dartmouth, Frederick North, second Earl of Guildford, pursued reconciliation, even though his actions had partly contributed to the increased crisis. North explored secret backchannels and third parties to diffuse the conflict, completely unbeknownst to and against the wishes of George III, who had recently described the colonists as "Deluded Americans." To reinvigorate parliamentary supremacy, the king and British government marched toward fighting a war across an ocean. In doing so, they reinforced their commitment to an increasingly authoritarian form of British imperialism, and Dartmouth took the extraordinary step of intercepting over two hundred pieces of colonists' mail to better understand what was happening. The secretary took an interest in New Yorkers' correspondence, and he was likely dismayed when reports of Lexington and Concord arrived. New Yorkers were together "in the general Cause," one person wrote. "The Colonies are more united than ever," wrote another. British officials increasingly believed the colonists were a foreign people and they would treat them as such. Appalled and unwilling to execute such a plan, Dartmouth resigned. But his replacement, Lord George Germain, was much more resolute in his determination to end the conflict quickly. It would be a unique civil war, where Britons fought against Britons but treated each other as foreigners.[21]

Revolution and Loyalism

Politics in Manhattan after McDougall distributed weapons were no less severe. On April 26, the Committee of Sixty resigned, unwilling and unprepared to do its job. It was replaced by the Committee of One Hundred and a new association was circulated throughout the city. By signing, New Yorkers once again publicly declared that they were either against the British or they were against other New Yorkers and colonists across the Eastern Seaboard. The new association was proposed by John Morin Scott and seconded by McDougall. Moreover, on April 26, twenty delegates had been elected to a provincial congress, instead of a convention, due to meet on May 22. To them, the traditional organs of governance in New York had failed—and their DeLanceyite assemblymen had failed them. New Yorkers turned to a provincial congress that would assume additional political responsibilities. As it was put in one broadside, the congress had to be formed to its congressmen could "deliberate upon, and from time to time direct such measures as may be expedient for our common safety." It would protect and advance New Yorkers' ideas and interests. Instead of choosing delegates to the Continental Congress, the Provincial Congress became the city's and the colony's government—and it would be sanctioned by the people, not by Colden, by Parliament, or by George III.[22]

This was arguably the most radical step that New Yorkers had made thus far. People had seldom if ever had confidence in Colden, who repeatedly prorogued the assembly throughout the spring and into the summer of 1775. Meanwhile, Gov. William Tryon remained absent in Britain, an almost forgotten character in their lives who was not instructed to return until May 4. More important, New Yorkers had lost confidence in the assembly, not least because its members had refused to do anything except wait for Parliament and George III to respond their remonstrance, petition, and memorial. The assembly's political inactivity was a grave misstep. New York's government was pushed aside, and one organized by and entirely for New Yorkers was established.

The Committee of One Hundred was primarily made up of New Yorkers who were closer to McDougall. Even if prominent DeLanceyites William Walton, Walter Franklin, Isaac Low, and John DeLancey were selected, there were Isaac Sears, John Lamb, John Morin Scott, Philip Livingston, John Jay, and Alexander McDougall. The DeLanceys had also lost several prominent voices— Charles Nicoll, Edward Laight, William Ustick, Charles Shaw—and those who held seats were often absent from or never attended meetings. Outspoken McDougallites seldom missed a meeting, if ever.[23]

Unsurprisingly, Alexander McDougall took the lead as he tried to bring more and more and more people into his orbit. "The Utmost Pains [are] taken to asswage the Multitude," William Smith Jr. wrote. The aggressive tactics worked, but they were helped by William Bradford's *Pennsylvania Journal*, who alleged in an article that John Holt reprinted in broadside that some New Yorkers, including many DeLanceys, were a "band of traitors." They were working to start "a civil war" and secure "New-York for the Ministry." The DeLanceyites involved included Oliver DeLancey, John Watts, and Henry White, all of whom felt compelled to sign the new association to appease the populace. White even went so far as to publish a broadside declaring his innocence.[24]

But this was not the end of the Bradford affair. On May 4, a few days after signing the association, John Watts departed Manhattan for Falmouth on the *Harriot*. As he made the three-thousand-mile journey, carrying hardly any possessions, he shared the company of Westchester assemblyman Isaac Wilkins and fellow royal councilor Roger Morris. Despite their high-ranking status, they each felt compelled to flee the city. As Wilkins later noted, because he had "Stood foremost in the Assembly against Congress" and acted "Uniformly against the measures," he had been made an outcast. His status as a "Tory" and someone who worked against the public good, he continued, "constrain'd him to fly."[25]

Rev. Myles Cooper, one of the others attacked in the *Pennsylvania Journal*, also fled the city. Signing the association was not an option for him—and he faced the consequences. Then the president of King's College and a double graduate of Queen's College, Oxford University, Cooper was attacked on the evening of May 10. Led by Isaac Sears and two of William Smith Jr.'s family members, hundreds of angry, well-lubricated colonists marched toward Cooper's residence at the college with clubs and hopes to tar and feather him. Cooper was only saved by the brave actions two former students. One, 1772 graduate Nicholas Ogden, raced ahead of the mob to warn Cooper. As soon as he arrived, sweating and out of breath, he urged Cooper to run. Another student, Alexander Hamilton, an immigrant from Nevis who formed a close bond with Cooper after matriculating, heard the commotion. When the mob arrived at Cooper's doorstep, Hamilton and his friend Robert Troup reputedly blocked the protesters, giving the president enough time to get away. He took refuge in a friend's home before settling on the *Kingfisher* in the harbor for the night. On May 25, Cooper fled to Britain on board the *Exeter*, where he was joined by friends and colleagues Rev. Thomas Bradbury Chandler and Rev. Samuel Cooke. Over a year later, writing in the *Gentleman's Magazine*, Cooper recalled "the din of war" that appeared on his doorstep. Like Wilkins, public attitudes toward Cooper and what he represented forced him to leave Manhattan, albeit temporarily in his mind.[26]

Cooper was not the only one who was assaulted, either, as the revolutionaries consolidated their popular and institutional power. On June 10, 1776, Scottish hairdresser James Deas was dragged out of his house by mob of around two hundred and assaulted. Later that day, the same crowd attacked Christopher Benson at his John Street home. Benson, a merchant, heard of the incoming threat and chose to welcome the mob at his door, sword in hand. Shouts rang out from the crowd that "they would kill him for a damned Tory" and they pelted him with stones and rocks, one of which hit him on the forehead. The blow temporarily stunned him. He lost his balance. He stumbled. Sensing their chance, the mob pounced, and ran toward his door. Frightened, Benson came to his senses and raised his sword once more. "The assailants stopped short," he later wrote, and dispersed. The mob tried again the next day but were again left disappointed. Benson was left astounded by their actions, and so he informed George Washington what had happened. Washington did not want to do anything, either for Benson or against the revolutionaries, telling the disgruntled merchant "that he had nothing to do with them, that he did not want to hear" of his complaints. Then, Benson heard someone near Washington mutter, "The best way would be to hang up to ten or a Dozen of the Tories like Dogs." "The Rascals would not be quiet without it." The strong actions of New York City's radicals were welcomed by those who shared their views.[27]

New York's Provincial Congress convened for the second time on May 22, 1775. It assumed, as Colden put it, "all the confidence and authority of a legal Government." Indeed, with the assembly prorogued, it was the government, and it was preparing Manhattan—and the colony—for war. Colden felt powerless to stop the complete revolution of governance in New York. "Congresses and Committees" had usurped his executive station. Many were unamused with the "unwarrantable claims and Pretensions of America," but hoped that Gov. William Tryon's return to North America would encourage reconciliatory sentiments. By "fully" explaining "the real Sentiments of Government here upon the present unhappy disputes," British officials believed Tryon could not only restore "the vigor of Government" but also encourage New Yorkers to regain "that good sense and good Humour" that had punctuated their earlier conduct. Without relying on brute force, Tryon was to use the power of persuasion to change people's minds. The pressure was on.[28]

Traveling across the Atlantic on the *Juliana*, Tryon possibly contemplated what and who awaited him. As the thirty-ninth governor of New York, he had endured difficult challenges before, particularly during his time as governor of North Carolina. But on this voyage, he received more troubling news. The *Juliana* stopped to exchange items and news with a ship that had sailed out of Maryland, and its master updated Tryon on colonial affairs after the Battles of Lexington and Concord. It was revolution. On June 25, Tryon arrived at Sandy Hook. He was greeted with appropriate levels of gubernatorial fanfare and celebration, but the moment was dampened because the newly commissioned general George Washington had arrived earlier in the day. Washington, a tall, firm, widely admired Virginian, had recently been appointed commander-in-chief of the Continental army. Delegates at the Continental Congress hoped his appointment would mobilize support in the north and south for the war effort, as they fought together against the British, their common enemy. In other words, the man tasked with defeating the British and their sympathizers arrived in Manhattan on the same day as the king's representative in New York, someone tasked with reasserting British control in the colony and beyond.[29]

Their arrivals were a simple, if historically notable, coincidence. Washington was traveling northward to the American camp in Cambridge. He departed Philadelphia on June 23 and arrived in Manhattan two days later at around 4 p.m. As he stepped off the ferry north of Sandy Hook and far enough from the British warship *Asia* and its guns, he was greeted by nine companies of recently mobilized militiamen, delegates to the Provincial Congress, and members of the Committee of One Hundred. This was not Washington's first time in New York City, either. In May 1773 he traveled to Manhattan with his stepson to visit King's College. During his time in the city, he visited multiple taverns, where he not only encountered Thomas Gage on multiple occasions but also dined with James DeLancey on at least one occasion. By then, moreover, Washington already knew DeLancey. They met two weeks earlier at a Philadelphia Jockey Club meeting, after which they possibly dined and almost certainly attended the mid-May horse races in Philadelphia, among the most important social events of the year. Tryon arrived four hours after Washington, and he was met by many of the same people. But he was quickly made aware of the Virginian's arrival. Not long after his return, he sought updates. He visited Hugh Wallace's home, where Wallace and other royal councilors brought the distressed governor up to speed on the perilous state of government in New York. Tryon quickly surmised the political shift and its severity. A day after his arrival, he told Gage that Colden had "little authority to transfer to me." A week or so later, he told Dartmouth there was a "General confederacy" among the colonies, one that he could do little to challenge or undermine. A "General Revolt" had taken place.[30]

Naturally, Alexander McDougall, now one of the most powerful colonial figures on the continent, felt differently. Writing to John Adams on June 5, 1775, he explained that his actions were "induced . . . from a Sincere desire to promote the common cause of America in this City" during what he labeled "the present interesting Struggle." McDougall and his supporters were given further reasons to defend their compatriots. On June 17, New Yorkers learned of the Battle of Bunker Hill, and Washington was in New York. An embarrassment for the British, Thomas Gage was soon replaced, prompting a reorientation of British military strategy in the war. William Tryon, trying to mobilize support and restore royal authority, struggled. Indeed, with the British focus initially in Massachusetts, people like Isaac Sears asserted near-total control in Manhattan. Around a week after Tryon's return, Sears revealed that he wanted to silence him to totally negate any impact he might have on the war effort. The radical patriot wanted to imprison the royal governor and send him to Connecticut. But it was not necessary. Tryon did little after his return, and he felt powerless. On July 4, he told Dartmouth he was in a "most degraded situation," describing his gubernatorial powers as "feeble." He also offered a candid assessment of the situation, writing, "Oceans of Blood may be spilt but in my opinion America will never receive parliamentary Taxation." Three days later, he asked to return to Britain, fearing for his health as well as that he would be "either taken Prisoner . . . or obliged to retire on board one of His Majestys Ships of War to avoid the insolence of an inflamed Mob." Tryon's request was permitted on September 6, but by the time he received the letter, he was already on board the *Dutchess of Gordon*, a merchant and passenger ship sitting in New York Harbor, trying to reestablish his government.[31]

Tryon was joined on the *Dutchess of Gordon* by others who sought to reestablish British control of New York, including John Thompson, a free African American New Yorker, and Chief Justice John Tabor Kempe. In a detailed letter to Cooper, Kempe reported on the almost complete usurpation of British authority in Manhattan. Pro-British publications, he added, could not be freely distributed. "The Liberty of the Press," he wrote, "is at an End." "Nothing can be got." Kempe was likely referring to Isaac Sears's successful seizure and imprisonment of Samuel Seabury and the destruction of James Rivington's types. In November, Seabury was taken prisoner by Sears and "about 100 Volunteers," who had "set out upon for New York &c . . . to disarm Tories." Alongside their attack on Seabury, they ransacked Rivington's printing office because he acted as Seabury's printer and had recently been appointed George III's printer. By their "taking away his Types," Rivington's publications would stop—and so, too, would his influence.[32]

Radicals like McDougall and Sears influenced, even controlled, sentiment within Manhattan during the early stages of the Revolutionary War. According to Washington, McDougall's "Zeal" was "unquestionable." Together, they created a community and a distinct identity that encouraged people to choose a side—revolutionary or loyalist—inciting fear and confusion. Tryon tried to mobilize support from the *Dutchess of Gordon* and it was difficult, if not impossible, to remain neutral or disaffected or articulate loyalism. Those who did not commit to the *right* side often faced the violent wrath of the revolutionaries. In constructing a new political order that emphasized their similarities—ideological, cultural, political, social, historical—radicals punished those who were different, those who did not conform to their quasi-national vision. For revolutionaries, anyone who did not uphold their legitimacy was a threat. And even though independence was not yet a realistic option, the imperial relationship, if restored, could not be the same as it once was. This complex situation affected everyday life, making it extremely difficult for those who had long-opposed men like Sears and McDougall. For those who had not accepted the new order, turning toward and fighting with the likes of McDougall was not a legitimate possibility, especially when men like him had espoused an interpretation of the past decade in which they—the DeLanceys, for instance—had worked against the public good and adhered to a political economy that worked against the needs of New York City. They were often branded as traitors, internal enemies, parricides, and worse.[33]

Similarly, those who tried to separate themselves from popular politics found it difficult. Dutch New Yorkers were among those who attempted to retain cultural and political independence. For much of the eighteenth century, they tried to maintain and protect their social and cultural practices. But even for them, among the most inward-looking in Manhattan, it was hard. Some voluntarily choose to enter the fray; Dutch New Yorkers are well represented among the list who received firearms after news of Lexington and Concord received Manhattan. Abraham Van Duersen, Peter Van Kleck, Jacobus Wynkoop, Renier Skaats, and representatives from other Dutch families—Quackenboss, Brevoort, Covenhoven, and Duryee—all received weapons. Kings County assemblyman John Rapalje also made his feelings known early. In May 1775, Rapalje, as well as other prominent Dutch New Yorkers and DeLanceyites Frederick Philipse III,

Daniel Kissam, and John Cruger, addressed Thomas Gage, expressing their desire for reconciliation. Others were forced to take a stand, and most stuck with their friends, family, and political associates. Their partisanship, as well as their ideas, influenced their behavior. In mid-1776 a British newspaper noted "The Persecution of the Loyalists continues unremitted" and cited the example of DeLanceyite Rem Rapalje, who was "cruelly rode on Rails." The article also noted that John Rapalje had been arrested. The Bancker family, too, was forced to engage. Abraham Bancker was eventually forced to decide, siding with the British. Evert Bancker Jr. sided with the British, too.[34]

As the war progressed, circumstances did not improve. On February 4, 1776, the situation for potential loyalists in New York City worsened with the arrival of Maj. Gen. Charles Lee. Lee was carried into the city on a stretcher, but it did not shake his resolve. Arriving with years of British and Polish military experience, as well as additional troops from Connecticut, Lee suppressed potential neutrals and ordered committees of safety to disarm any loyalists still withholding weapons. His approach was straightforward and unforgiving. Lee soon appointed Sears as lieutenant colonel and acting assistant adjutant general, shortly after which, on March 5, Lee ordered Sears to administer oaths of loyalty to Manhattan residents and those across the East River in Queens County. Of those who might refuse, Lee told Sears, it "must be construed in no more or less than an avowal of their hostile intention." Lee, who was acting without permission from Washington or the Continental Congress, ordered Sears to transport those who refused to Connecticut, "where they can no longer be dangerous." Reporting back, Sears noted he administered the oath "to four of the grate Torries," adding that "they swallowed [it] as hard as if it was a four pound shot, that they were trying to git down." Sears was in complete agreement with Lee about removing "the ringledors" to Connecticut. "Nothing else will do," he wrote.[35]

Lee was censured by the Continental Congress for his actions on March 9. The congress resolved that military officers could demand neither loyalty oaths nor tests of civilian populations. But the damage was done. A precedent had been set. For those who did not adhere to Sears's demands, he published their names for all to read. Others were indeed taken to Connecticut; some were taken to the subterranean Newgate Prison, where they worked at least seventy feet below ground in unsanitary conditions with close to one hundred other people at the Simsbury Mines. According to one captive, he was held prisoner for two years and he remained underground for over five months. Sears and Lee's tactics quelled any attempts at a large-scale countermobilization. According to Tryon, loyalists "suffer from committees, congresses, and minutemen, in their persons and property." The revolutionaries' behavior, Tryon went on, was "scarcely to be equalled in history."[36]

The impact of the revolutionaries' close monitoring of loyalists was significant. Not only did the revolutionaries' aggressive tactics show their commitment to reforming government, but they were equally committed to expelling their enemies and creating a state that included only like-minded associates. Those who did not fit in, voluntarily or otherwise, those who would not conform to what later became nationalism, were excluded. The likes of Myles Cooper and James DeLancey are obvious examples of those who did not belong in the political community the revolutionaries were creating. But there were others who could not accept the revolution in government. For instance, two DeLanceyites who had made their opposition to the Continental Congress known, Frederick Rhinelander and Benjamin Huggett, moved to what is now Englewood, New Jersey, to live in an area that became known as "the English Neighbourhood" in Bergen County. Christopher Benson, William Bayard, and others joined them, and the area soon became notorious, not because of its inhabitants' ancestry. George Washington described the area's inhabitants as "very Dangerous." They were "lurking," adding that he believed that Rhinelander and Huggett were orchestrating a loyalist countermobilization. But Rhinelander's assessment of the situation was simpler but no less severe. Writing to his mercantile suppliers in Britain, he lamented how he "was obliged to leave this City with my family after suffering many inconveniences & difficulties as great perhaps as you can conceive." If he had not left, he thought he would have become "a prisoner in New England," perhaps in the Simsbury Mines.[37]

Other people like Rhinelander left New York, as well. As the revolutionary government was established, New York's population plummeted. Houses were left empty. Streets, wharves, taverns, and coffeehouses were quiet. In September 1775, Tryon reported that "at least one third of the citizens had moved with their effects out of town," which equated to some eight thousand people. A year later, a further ten thousand had left. Two-thirds of New York City inhabitants had gone, including, for instance, Theophylact Bache, who fled to Flatbush in Brooklyn, where he "sincerely hope[d] for a reconciliation." Bache later went to Staten Island with his friend and political associate Augustus Van Cortlandt. DeLanceyite watchmaker Isaac Heron also left, fleeing to Staten Island and leaving his family, many of whom were severely ill. Prominent DeLanceyite Joseph Allicocke, who was threatened with murder and had his possessions pillaged, fled to Antigua, leaving his wife, Martha Jardine Allicocke, and five children behind. The mass exodus was painfully obvious to all those who stayed. The pastor of the city's Moravian church noted "some of the Streets look plague-stricken," adding, "so many houses are closed." Manhattan was a ghost town.[38]

Both elite and non-elite loyalists left, and others stayed. Their lives were difficult. With a pregnant wife, Charles Inglis stayed in Manhattan but soon found he was in a hopeless situation. "Violent threats" became a daily occurrence for the Anglican minister, who was lambasted as "a *Tory & Traitor.*" Throughout early 1776, Inglis dispatched numerous letters that conveyed the vulnerability of potential opponents to the revolutionary movement in New York City. "Down with the Tories is the cry," Inglis opined, adding, "The ruin we are already involved in makes us mad & I see nothing for the generality but such distress that will embitter all their days." Anglican minister John Milner offered similar sentiments. Writing to Inglis in mid-1776, Milner opined, "None dare to avow their Sentiments & America is at present one of the most disagreeable Countrys in the World—All who offend the new Laws (recommendations they are called) are gazetted & sent prisoners to the Barracks or a New England Camp." "Friends to Government," Milner continued, "are obliged to temporize or are awed into Silence." "Their Families are insulted & it is dangerous for them to be abroad at Night."[39]

Despite this opposition, Gov. William Tryon still believed he could reassert British imperial authority in New York. By October 1775, he was attempting to direct British action, undertaking frequent correspondence with Mayor Whitehead Hicks in which Tryon repeatedly attempted to obtain "security" from Hicks and the city's Common Council to enable him to safely return ashore where he could attempt to reestablish British authority. In a letter of October 13, Tryon warned Hicks that New York would be bombarded by the ships he commanded unless he was offered enough protection. Hicks, who had been mayor for close to a decade, and the Common Council demurred, assuring the governor that if he stepped ashore, his safety was not in question. But Tryon was unsatisfied with Hicks's assurances and moved to the *Halifax* packet in the harbor. His hopes of "do[ing] such business of the County" failed. Since the loyalists were without an effective means to channel political support, the revolutionaries remained in control.[40]

Tryon's impotence was reflective of the state of loyalism or counterrevolution in New York. With royal authority floating in the harbor, more people joined him. In early November, John Tabor Kempe wrote, "We have continually coming on board Numbers of Friends of Government, exasperated at the Tyranny they experience, and wishing for an Opportunity of acting against their Tyrants for the Restoration of Order and Government." Sat offshore without the means to mobilize broad-based support, neither Kempe nor Tryon nor any of their colleagues and friends could challenge the sovereignty of New York's revolutionaries. In late February 1776, the revolutionaries cut them off from the mainland. They prohibited "boat[s] of any kind" engaging with the *Dutchess of Gordon,* and on March 8, they ruled if a ship "armed Men of the Enemy on Board" the *Dutchess of Gordon,* or any of the other British ships, they were to launch a bombardment on the boat. They were, one person noted, "the designing children of the devil."[41]

Independence compounded their situation. One British minister lamented, "We were contending for the very existence of the Empire," adding that if those united states were victorious, they would soon "be a superior empire." The New York Provincial Congress instructed its delegation to the Continental Congress that they could not vote on "the important Question of Independency." But when the other colonies' delegates supported the resolution, independence galvanized revolutionary forces in New York City. On July 9, the day the declaration reached Manhattan, George Washington, who was then stationed in the city, stipulated that the declaration was to be read aloud in public spaces for all inhabitants to hear. "The Honorable Continental Congress," Washington wrote in his general orders, "impelled by the dictates of duty, policy and necessity, having been pleased to dissolve the Connection which subsisted between this Country, and Great Britain, and to declare the United Colonies of North America, free and independent STATES." The resolves were to be read at 6 p.m. that evening by someone with "an audible voice."[42]

Upon hearing the indictment of George III in the declaration, New Yorkers articulated whom and what they were loyal to. In 1770 they erected a gilded statue of the king at the Bowling Green as a token of their appreciation for the repeal of the Stamp Act in 1766. It was a towering equestrian statue, made by sculptor Joseph Wilton, which presented the young monarch in Roman clothing. Surrounding and protecting the statue was a wrought-iron fence, itself furnished with elaborate orbs surrounded by crowns on each individual post. When the statue arrived and had to be transported to its new location, James DeLancey and Jacob Walton footed the bill. They also paid to transport a statue of William Pitt, first Earl of Chatham, at the same time. Altogether, the two DeLanceyites paid over £808 to move the two giant, heavy statues. (They were reimbursed by the colony on February 16, 1771.) Six years later, after the declaration was read aloud for the first time, New Yorkers jumped atop its five-and-a-half-feet marble base and attacked the structure. They took chunks out of his face, his body, and his horse as they tried to bring it down. Others ordered their slaves to participate. Together, they threw rope around George III's outstretched arm and his body. Amid screams and shouts, they brought the statue to the ground. Once the horse's legs were ripped from the base, and they attacked it. Someone brandished an axe and cut of the king's head, as well as his nose and the wreath atop his head. New Yorkers also cut off the ornamental orbs on the surrounding fence, too, making room for George III's head, which was, as Charles Inglis reported, "stuck on the Top of an Iron Rail" before being carted throughout the city. (The fence still stands today.) The *Pennsylvania Journal* reported on July 17 that as the declaration was "received with loud huzzas, and the utmost demonstrations of joy," George III's statue, "which tory pride and folly raised," was "laid prostrate in the dirt; the just desert of an ungrateful tyrant!" The report went on, adding, "The lead wherewith this monument was made, is to be run into bullets, to assimilate with the brain of our infatuated adversaries, who, to gain a pepper-corn, lost an empire." Elsewhere, revolutionaries attacked comparable monarchical symbols. They tore down and burned portraits and signs, or turned them upside down, and attacked Anglican ministers. Royal authority was dead.[43]

After being transported to Litchfield, Connecticut, George III's roughly 4,000-pound statue was melted down. Its gilded lead was reworked and reshaped into 42,088 cartridges. An observer reported that they hoped the bullets would "make as deep impressions in the Bodies of some of his [George III's] red coated and Torie subjects." Other parts of the lead were used to create molds to fashion the bullets. A symbol of royal authority, destroyed in one colony and repurposed in another, would be fired back at those who were trying to reassert British control. The conflict had become a full-scale civil war within the British Empire. By then, the British Army had dispatched troops and the Royal Navy had deployed its vessels to conquer the continent. On July 9, the same day George III's statue came down, the Provincial Congress also declared its independency. No longer was it the "Provincial Congress of the Colony of New-York." It was "the Convention of the Representatives of the State of New-York."[44]

Loyalists in New York City lacked the necessary leadership or political means to encourage mobilization throughout almost all of 1775 through September 1776. The city's revolutionaries established popular control of New York. Its inhabitants' behavior was closely monitored and regulated. Neutrality became an untenable option for many. The revolutionaries had, one loyalist wrote, "seized all Government into their own Hands, & imprisoned & proscribed every Man who has been hardy enough to oppose them." "Neutrality is criminal." Another New York City inhabitant was equally distressed by the political temperament of New York, soliloquizing that if anyone breathed "a Siyllable against the Congress or their Measures," they would be "unanimously condemned."[45]

But what the loyalists did not realize was that throughout the summer of 1776, British forces gathered around Staten Island, a location the revolutionaries had not fortified. New York's revolutionaries had long feared the British approach. As early as March, Alexander McDougall wrote, "the Enemy has been momently expected, for some time." By April, the *Savage* and the *James* had anchored off the Island's north shore. The British were close.[46]

By July 1776, New Yorkers and McDougall's fears came to pass as they watched vessel after vessel after vessel come into view. William Howe and Richard Howe, brothers and commanders-in-chief of armed and naval forces in North America, finally arrived on July 12. William Howe was among the most highly rated generals in the British Army. He had assumed command of British forces on October 10, 1775, after Thomas Gage planned to depart for Britain, where he was widely criticized for his military conduct and misleading communications. The following July, William Howe was joined by his older brother Richard. They presented an imposing sight. Both were tall and muscular, and some believed they looked like George III. They each had prominent bulging, heavy-lidded eyes, and a long nose. (It was rumored that their mother was born out of wedlock, and George I was the father.) Alongside their physical presence, their military records were exceptional, and both were familiar with North America, having served during the French and Indian War. Equally important, though, the Howes were not only commissioned to defeat the revolutionaries. They were also peace commissioners; Richard Howe would not accept his command otherwise. Both commanders believed in reconciliation and thought it was possible.[47]

After the brothers united, they took stock of their forces—and what a sight it must have been. Together, they commanded 150 ships, ten thousand seamen, eleven thousand troops, and tens of thousands of guns. On August 1, they were joined by a further two thousand troops and forty-five ships. After eleven thousand more troops arrived, over 65 percent of the British Army and 45 percent of the Royal Navy were participating in the Revolutionary War, an astounding figure, particularly given that the Royal Navy was larger than the French and Spanish fleets combined. The expeditionary force was the largest Britain had ever dispatched.[48]

"Sir," Richard Howe began a letter to George Washington a day after his arrival. The letter was addressed "To George Washington, Esq., etc., etc., etc." Howe wanted to meet Washington in Manhattan to discuss reconciliation and peace. But his letter was never delivered. Howe had purposely omitted Washington's military title in both the salutation and the address, prompting one of Washington's aide de camps to tell Howe's emissary, "There is no such person in the army." William Howe began another letter to Washington on July 16 with "Sir," addressing it with "George Washington Esqr. &c. &ca." Again, it was never delivered. The Howes continually addressed Washington as "Sir," refusing to acknowledge his military title. It was a calculated move, one designed to undermine his legitimacy and, perhaps, lower his confidence.[49]

The Howes galvanized support. James Grant, British general and the former governor of East Florida, boasted that "if a good bleeding can bring those

Bible-faced Yankees to their senses—the fever of Independence should soon abate." On August 22, 1776, when British forces secured control of Long Island, and on September 15, when they secured New York City, the ensuing emergence of loyalism over the following years confirmed Grant's observations. Basil Feilding, sixth Earl of Denbigh, noted, "The Inhabitants receive our People with the utmost Joy, having been long oppress'd for their Attachment to Government."[50]

As British forces reasserted control, the Howes invited delegates from the Continental Congress to negotiate a peace settlement. The Staten Island Peace Conference, as it was known, was attended by Richard Howe and John Adams, Benjamin Franklin, and Edward Rutledge. A so-called Messenger of Peace, Howe informed Franklin that he wanted to "effect a lasting peace and reunion between the two countries' and end the war, and he told the delegates that he would not negotiate with them "as a Committee of Congress" but as "private Gentlemen of Influence." But as Howe quickly learned, his attempts would not be successful. The delegates' objectives varied widely from his. The men from Philadelphia refused to consider anything short of American independence. Howe's instructions from George III were inadequate, containing nothing of importance other than "granting pardons." The Americans' unexpected reluctance shifted the Howes' plans. They moved toward mobilizing New York's loyalists.[51]

Times were changing in Manhattan. The revolutionary government that had so closely monitored people's behavior was gone. So, too, were their printing presses. John Holt fled twice to avoid British capture, first to Kingston and then to Poughkeepsie. Both places were hardly ideal locations, and his business suffered. But not everybody followed Holt's nomadic path. Many stayed, and their reactions to the Howes' proclamations offer a useful paradigm from which to appreciate the contingent nature of allegiance in a society riven by distress and war. As British forces replaced American in New York, the Howes were aware of the volatile environment they entered. They recognized that local military events could have an important impact upon colonists' allegiance and subsequent behavior. In the royal proclamations, the Howes offered New York revolutionaries amnesty, indicating that they could return to their former posts without suffering any retribution. Bu their proclamations were widely criticized, especially by ardent loyalists and British officials. Ambrose Serle, William Howe's secretary, bemoaned that "Rebels in Prison . . . claimed the Benefit of the Proclamation," while "Some of the old Friends to Gov^t. are much displeased at its Publication." Serle was an avid critic of the Howes' leniency. He believed that revolutionaries' loyalism was disingenuous. "The People here," Serle argued, "of any and of all Professions, are not to be trusted to themselves, that their Attachment is precarious at the best to our Gov^t." Serle declared that the proclamations "violently offends all those who have suffered for their Attachment to Government."[52]

Charles Inglis also appreciated that revolutionaries would take advantage of the Howes' leniency. He noted that "they will all submit & lay hold of this professed mercy." Both Serle and Inglis were right. "The number of converts . . . is amazingly great," wrote one observer, adding that revolutionaries Henry Gilbert Livingston, William Alexander (Lord Stirling), and "Lott the hero" had also accepted the Howes' pardon. Other revolutionaries also took advantage of their leniency, including Leonard Lispenard, Peter Van Brugh Livingston, Peter Van Brugh Livingston Jr., and Peter T. Curtenius, among others. The signatories gave the Howes a sense of political optimism, not least because the signatures of these individuals were significant in the context of the Revolutionary War effort. Lispenard and Livingston had been elected to the extrainstitutional Provincial Congress, and Livingston had been elected its president. William Alexander and Henry Livingston were enlisted in the Continental army.[53]

Rightly or wrongly, the Howes believed they had converted noted revolutionaries to the British cause, giving them a sense of assurance that their role as military commanders and peace commissioners was effective. Their ostensible conversion established a veneer of confidence that validated the developing belief that most Americans were loyal or at least sought reconciliation. But for some, the reasons for revolutionaries pledging allegiance were clear: these were men of property who did not want to lose it and declared that they had been "deceived & led away" by the revolutionaries. These men were not loyalists.[54]

But the establishment of British rule in New York City also afforded an opportunity to mobilize support among committed loyalists. For instance, one commentator felt that "a respectable Number of loyalists" would emerge if called upon. "If there be one, among the confederate Colonies," one observer remarked, "that could Yet without Force, be brought back to Allegiance, it is New-York." The impact of loyalist leaders upon popular mobilization can be seen through two of New York City's loyalist declarations.[55]

Instead of publishing their addresses in the press, New York City loyalists mobilized on two separate occasions to furnish two "Declarations of Dependence," both of which were written by Charles Inglis. The first meeting took place on October 16 at City Hall. According to a newspaper report, "a very large Concourse of People" attended, including those "who were not driven away by the Hand of Violence, or sent [as] Prisoners to other Provinces." The declaration was left in a tavern for people to sign "every Day . . . till all had signed." The first "Declaration of Dependence" was signed by 936 New Yorkers, all of whom were male and almost certainly white. At the end of October, perhaps because of the popular support the address had attracted, William Tryon requested that Inglis draft another address. The second "Declaration of Dependence" was left on a table in Scott's Tavern on Wall Street for three days. In total, over seven hundred men signed their names. Some marked the manuscript "X." Many of the signatories of both documents were DeLanceyites and many signed their name to each document: Theophylact Bache, Alexander Wallace, Hugh Wallace, Isaac Low, Henry White, Frederick Rhinelander, Charles Nicoll, Evert Bancker Jr., Oliver DeLancey. And by the grouping of the signatories on both declarations, it is evident that people came in together. For instance, in the November declaration, Inglis's signature sits below fellow ministers Samuel Auchmuty and Benjamin Moore, and Charles Nicoll's is beside Augustus van Horne's and William Brownjohn's signatures, two of his friends. Similarly, in the October declaration, Jacob Walton's name is near Henry White's, Whitehead Hicks's, John Harris Cruger's, and John Wetherhead's. Families also signed each document together: there are multiple Brewertons, Bogarts, Brownjohns, Earles, Grims, Howells, Kippers, Laights, Nicolls, Pells, Rapaljes, and Rhinelanders. (No women signed the November declaration, either, and it is unlikely any of the signatories were free African Americans.) A parallel world was emerging in Manhattan, one in which George III remained at the center. Inglis, reflecting on the impact the document could have, felt that New York City's "Example . . . will be followed by every County in the Province."[56]

The presence of British forces encouraged the emergence of local loyalist leaders, providing the institutional and military framework that allowed locals to mobilize support. Manhattan's loyalists were not a leaderless group, lacking coherence and organization. Instead, as the necessary stages for political mobilization fell into place, hardline loyalists like Inglis filled the leadership vacuum that was created when people like James DeLancey left. Equally important, loyalists' declarations offer a crucial insight into the workings of counterrevolutionary political mobilization in New York during the early years of the Revolutionary War. After leaders had mustered popular support, the declarations that emerged were a starting of counterrevolutionary activity that brought loyalists together into a coherent, organized movement that was neither bottom-up nor top-down. It was both.[57]

Some clearly felt that the Howes' amnesty was unwise. Others were vocal in their opposition to it. Regardless, the Howes' approach encouraged loyalist sentiment between October and November 1776, and beyond. Between 1776 and 1778 William Tryon administered an oath of allegiance on at least three occasions. In Manhattan, the oath was offered between January 13 and February 26, 1777. When people took the oath, they offered their name and occupation.

Once the oath-taking was complete, Tryon had collected more than thirty half-sheets of paper. Thousands of names and occupations were listed. Tryon had a clerk or secretary alphabetize the names, and he submitted it to Lord George Germain in a letter of March 28, noting that the oath-takers had "taken the Oath of Fidelity and Allegiance to His Majesty and His Government." They had also renounced "all authority to Congresses and Committees." The packet Tryon submitted to Germain was over sixty pages long.[58]

Tryon was confident about the significance of oath-taking in revolutionary Manhattan. Even though his status was falling, he believed the oath of allegiance showed that New Yorkers, despite what happened earlier in the war, were loyal after all. In a letter to Germain, he wrote, "Large bodies of the People have already taken the benefit of the Grace therein offered them." Throughout the process of taking and administering oaths, Tryon, surrounded by the British Army, also admitted to Germain that he had gathered groups of people into circles and "took much pains" to explain to them "the iniquitous Arts &" of the revolutionaries to "Mislead them." As could be expected with military forces monitoring colonists' behavior, Tryon boasted that he "did not hear the least Murmur of discontent, but a general Satisfaction expressed at my coming among them." And why would they? Taking the oath of allegiance afforded a host of benefits: oath-takers were granted economic privileges—they could open commercial relations with people and firms in the West Indies, Europe, and other occupied cities; they were granted contracts to provide for the British Army and licenses to open and run taverns and inns; and they were afforded poor relief.[59]

Loyalism, then, provided multiple incentives for those willing to sign, and it was a successful approach. People returned to their everyday lives, at least as best they could. By February 1777, close to six thousand people in and around Manhattan had taken the oath of allegiance, some of whom were adopted New Yorkers who had created new lives for themselves. Indeed, thousands of loyalists had flocked to the city, seeking the protection the British Army provided, as the war was fought elsewhere, in other towns, cities, and colonies-turned-states. But those in Manhattan remained confident that reconciliation remained possible. "The Time in all probability for settling the Affairs of America is near approaching," wrote Charles Inglis. "Much indeed will depend on the Commissioners here," he went on, assigning primary importance to the Howes. "Now or never is our Time." But some refused to listen. "Pride & Obstinacy have hardened the Hearts of the Rebells & shutt their Ears against the Cries of a Country," wrote DeLanceyite John Wetherhead. Despite the British occupation, Wetherhead believed Manhattan had changed. There was "something contaminating the Air of that place," he wrote, adding, his some of his friends had "turned *Growlers*," and others were "Grumbletonian in Company." Wetherhead assigned blame to the British Army. "The general Opinion seems to be, that this Rebellion might have been crushed long ago" if Gage and the Howes had deployed all their forces "to annihilate the Whole power of the Rebells & so finish the Warr." Another observer reported echoed his sentiments, writing, "New York is no more the same City it was." They were right. The Revolutionary War had already exerted a considerable cost on Manhattan—political, economic, social, human—and the changing conditions of New Yorkers' lives had affected not only their ways of life but how they viewed each other and the city in which they lived. People's interests had been affected, and New York City was not the same.[60]

But many loyalists made the best of what was a bad situation. By June 1777, Frederick Rhinelander, who took the oath of allegiance and signed declarations of dependence, was happy to report to his British suppliers, "Trade is now carried on upon principles very different that it formerly was," adding, "we sell all for Cash & not a doubt of making £1000 by these Goods if they arrive in Season." Rhinelander had also recently approached new suppliers in Bristol and Birmingham to increase his business, and in his letters, he mentioned the names of those DeLanceyites whom he had associated with for close to a decade, including Edward and William Laight and Henry White. By the Revolutionary War, they were tories.[61]

The term "tory" became an increasingly popular insult in during the Revolutionary War. Its origins were older, dating back to the sixteenth and seventeenth centuries, but in revolutionary Manhattan, as elsewhere, it lacked political and historical nuance. There were almost certainly no tories in colonial British or wartime America—that is, genuine royalists who advocated, as Lord North put it, "to increase the prerogative." But being labeled a "tory" in 1775 and beyond carried that description, as well as several other historical and political connotations, almost all of which were negative. Revolutionaries castigated those who were not with them as "Tories," and those who were against the revolutionaries labeled them "rebels" or "traitors." As one New Englander put it, "The Government & AntiGovernment Subjects are now known by the old Names of Wig & Tory—as they were in the End of Q. Anne's Reign." In truth, however, the realities of life meant that colonists' political views occurred along a spectrum. Many likely agreed with some but not all the ideas being espoused from either side. There were not simply "revolutionaries" and "loyalists," or "traitors" and "Tories." Allegiance, and affiliation, was neither straightforward nor simple. As one colonist later put it, "different degrees of force" shaped colonists' views and actions. That is, political and historical labels were a neat way to mobilize support and push others out. It was the same across the Atlantic. In a speech before Parliament in which he defined "Whiggism" and "Toryism," Lord North declared of the revolutionaries, "Their language therefore was that of Toryism."[62]

But what North and others failed to fully understand was that most of Britain's North American colonists believed that Parliament was becoming, or had become, an arbitrary government, like those under the Stuarts. Colonists who protested the Coercive Acts and other pieces of legislation were not royalists; they believed George III should be a check on Parliament. Unlike the Scots after the Union of 1707 but like the Irish, Americans interpreted the imperial connection through George III, not Parliament—and he would protect their interests. After the Declaration of Independence was signed and publicized throughout the colonies, the ties were broken. Those who were "loyalists," or "tories," were left with few to no options. They had been castigated as outsiders. They had to acquiesce or face the consequences—and thousands did.[63]

Epilogue
Loyalist Americans beyond the Revolution

In early 1776, thinking of New York, John Adams described "the vast Importance of that City, Province, and the North River" to George Washington. He noted it was "the Nexus of the Northern and Southern Colonies, as a Kind of Key to the whole Continent, as it is a Passage to Canada to the Great Lakes and to all the Indians Nations." Across the Atlantic, in and around London, James DeLancey heard only rumors and gathered snippets of information and intelligence about what life was like in wartime Manhattan. DeLancey, formerly one of the wealthiest men in New York, almost certainly socialized in taverns and coffeehouses, including the New York coffeehouse at Sweeting's Alley near London's Royal Exchange. There, he was almost certain to run into other loyalist refugees, many of whom also socialized on Margaret Street. DeLancey, moreover, spent time with his friends the Marquis of Rockingham and Edmund Burke, who helped facilitate an introduction to Lord North, all with hopes to pursue further reconciliation and, perhaps, a return home to a city and colony whose importance he appreciated and recognized long before Adams did.[1]

As the war worsened for the British, however, it soon became clear to DeLancey that returning to Manhattan, or New York, was not an option. He became desperate and erratic. Burke worried about him. He thought DeLancey was behaving foolishly. But DeLancey's actions were understandable. Without having done anything except travel across the Atlantic to plead his and his constituents' cases, he was branded a traitor, legally and institutionally, and he lost everything. In 1779 all his estate, real and personal, was confiscated as per the Act of Attainder, which was originally written by his old foe John Morin Scott. Other estates that DeLancey knew and possibly visited were also confiscated, including those of his longtime friends, family members, and associates Hugh and Alexander Wallace, Henry White, Frederick Philipse III, David Colden, Christopher Billop, James Jauncey, Thomas Jones, William Bayard, Isaac Low, John Wetherhead, Oliver DeLancey, and others. These DeLanceyites were "for ever banished" from New York—their home—and if they were ever caught within state lines they would be "declared guilty of felony, and shall suffer death as in cases of felony, without the benefit of clergy." They would be executed.[2]

With such a threat looming, many other DeLanceyites joined James in London—the Wallaces, White, Low, Philipse, Colden. It was not easy for them. Philipse endured a difficult time leaving his manor and home in what is now Yonkers, New York. In an oral history that was conducted long after the Revolutionary War, it was reported that Philipse and others "cried bitterly" as he departed New York. "I must leave my country!" Philipse exclaimed, prompting the tears of those who knew him. It was a difficult decision for all involved, but when they arrived in London, they were often not short of company. Many lived close to one another. Isaac Low, for instance, lived in Mortlake with his wife, Margaret, near Philipse, who later relocated to Bath (where James DeLancey lived and died), and the Wallaces, both of whom had married Low's sisters. David Colden, meanwhile, lived in Soho for the sole reason of being close to his friends.[3]

New York loyalists built new lives in London, and they continued to socialize with like-minded associates. But it was near-impossible to replicate those they had in Manhattan. As William Bayard reported to Myles Cooper, "the Confusion, the Deviltry, the Every thing that was bad, Amongst the Cursed Rebells of our once happy Country, has Divested me totally, of all, Which was at least, a Competence, If not Affluence, & left me at this Day, without one shilling of Income." People like Bayard had left behind intricate networks that they and their family members had woven together over decades. In July 1783, the British government appointed a five-man Loyalist Claims Commission to investigate loyalists' situations and determine if they merited financial compensation. The commission was based in Lincoln's Inn Fields, and over three thousand people submitted claims, most of whom were New Yorkers, partly thanks to James DeLancey, who was selected as the colony's agent and chief negotiator. DeLancey, a man of and for the people, fiercely advocated for loyalists' rights. At one point, he even wrote to William Pitt the Younger, then chancellor of the exchequer, to support loyalists who had fought alongside or in the British Army. Pitt accepted DeLancey's proposals. A popular leader in Manhattan and in Britain, James DeLancey maintained some social prominence in Britain, and it was based around his family and networks. In 1791, printer James Rivington wrote to him at the home of Charles FitzRoy, first Baron Southampton, the British noble who had married his cousin and someone whom DeLancey later named in his will.[4]

Other DeLanceyite loyalists went elsewhere. Rev. Charles Inglis settled in Canada, where he became the first bishop of the Diocese of Nova Scotia, and in an interesting twist of fate, Rev. Samuel Seabury, the loyalist who was imprisoned in Connecticut, returned to the United States and became the first American Episcopal bishop and the first bishop of Connecticut. Other loyalists went to other locations in the Maritimes. Some went to Jamaica, the Bahamas, India, Sierra Leone, and beyond.[5]

For those who stayed in Britain, their families often remained intertwined with the British Empire. John DeLancey, James DeLancey's eldest son, was captain in the King's Royal Rifle Corps, also known as the Sixtieth (Royal American Regiment). James DeLancey's second son, who was also named James, became collector of customs on Crooked Island in the Bahamas. He also had a son who served in the Royal Navy and a daughter who married Sir Jukes Granville Clifton of Nottinghamshire County. Other DeLancey children also served in the British Army and the Royal Navy. Frederick Philipse III's son Philip was commissioned an officer in the Royal Artillery. Another son, John, was killed during the Battle of Trafalgar in 1805.[6]

Others found it harder to assimilate into British life. Isaac Low and his wife departed New York on the final evacuation ship that was bound for London. Although he was near friends and associates, the financial compensation he was afforded by the British government for his loyalism fell far short of what he had hoped to receive. Awarded £1,700, he considered himself "a ruined Man." With hopes to change his fortunes, Low sought clarification about his dividend. "I found on my own previous Examinations," wrote Low to his brother, "that my having been in Committee and Congress, was a great stumbling block." Low's attempts to receive financial compensation were indeed plagued by his activism. John Wetherhead, though also a DeLanceyite, was closer to the likes of John Tabor Kempe and Rev. Myles Cooper than Low. He noted that Low was "very forward in all disturbances," adding that he was "the leader of the Mob." As such, Wetherhead continued, Low was referred to as "Prolocutor." As he had been labeled a loyalist and a tory in New York, across the Atlantic, Low struggled to distance himself from his political activism, and he felt cheated for the remainder of his life.[7]

Isaac Low and others may have endured a difficult journey into British life, but the passage back into Manhattan society was, in theory, harder for those DeLanceyites who stayed. The Rhinelanders, the Laights, the Nicolls, the Banckers. Some even purchased some of James DeLancey's confiscated estate, and Evert Bancker Jr. was the person who surveyed it for sale. Their loyalism during the Revolutionary War was seldom questioned, particularly after the British Army assumed control of Manhattan and made the city its headquarters. Frederick Rhinelander's mercantile business in china, glass, and earthenware flourished. He enjoyed "good fortune" during the war, and after receiving a recommendation from Gov. William Tryon, he provided tableware to military leaders in the army. He also served in the city's vestry and oversaw housing and poor relief, among other duties. In July 1783, however, Rhinelander's estate was confiscated by the state. His behavior was deemed treasonous, and, like many others, he had to face the consequences for his loyalty to Britain. Rhinelander adjusted. He reoriented his business dealings, and he was successful in doing so.[8]

Other loyalists' properties were also confiscated by the state. But they were generally not subjected to mob violence or political estrangement. They returned to their normal lives, partly thanks to the efforts of those who had previously mobilized against them. Some, especially those who breathed new life into the Chamber of Commerce—Theophylact Bache, William Laight, Augustus van Horne, and others—increased their fortunes. The Rhinelanders became one of the wealthiest and most prominent families in New York City from the antebellum onward, going up to the twentieth century. When Frederick Rhinelander died in 1805, he was described in multiple newspapers as "a worthy and highly respected citizen." The apotheosis of the Rhinelanders was not limited to Frederick alone, either. On March 6, 1785, William Rhinelander sponsored the baptism of Hercules Mulligan Jr., the son of the prominent Revolutionary War spy who later provided George Washington with clothing during his presidential administration. Other former loyalist families flourished, including the Banckers, Goelets—and even the Coldens. Cadwallader Colden's grandson, Cadwallader David Colden, was New York City's mayor between 1818 and 1821, after which he served in the US House of Representatives.[9] The Waltons' residence on Pearl Street, moreover, was used as an early home of the Bank of New York. Alexander McDougall, the man who fought harder than almost anyone against the DeLanceyite Waltons, was its inaugural president, and he opposed much of the anti-loyalist sentiment. Nicholas Low, Isaac's brother, who also purchased nearly $10,000 of loyalists' estates, was a director. Similarly, Alexander Hamilton vehemently defended loyalists during his early legal career. So, too, did John Jay. James Duane, the erstwhile DeLanceyite propagandist, became New York City's mayor. Many simply wanted to return to, as Robert R. Livingston put it, "the usual tranquility."[10]

Historians often argue that there were more loyalists in New York than anywhere else in the colonies. New York was the loyalist center during the Revolutionary War, a place where those loyal to the crown could seek refuge, support, and possibly even advancement. New York City was, indeed, a loyalist center during the war. After all, it was the British Army's headquarters from 1776 until 1783. Loyalist petitions and statements were printed in the press, and Rev. Charles Inglis authored multiple declarations that were adorned with hundreds of signatures. Gov. William Tryon, moreover, administered the oath of allegiance to thousands of New Yorkers in Manhattan, on Long Island, and probably elsewhere, and he submitted the lists to British officials to visually demonstrate the extent and the numerical strength of New Yorkers' loyalism.

Such views, however, are narrow and do not fully recognize the complex origins of loyalism in Manhattan. Many people who signed Inglis's documents were not from New York, and those to whom Tryon administered the oath were coerced. Equally important, the British Army's occupation of the city did not lead to a productive partnership that reinforced New Yorkers' loyalism. Rather than supporting the loyalists' roles, the British instead instituted martial law in the city and never fully appreciated or recognized any loyalist leaders. New Yorkers were pushed aside. This is, perhaps, why the likes of Rhinelander, Bancker, and Nicoll remained in the city. Their vision for Manhattan's place within the empire was never going to be fully realized, especially as the war worsened for the British, and they likely came to accept that they would never fully adjust to life outside Manhattan.

And so they remained, building new lives in a new city, in a new state, in a new country. The associationism of the 1760s and 1770s, cultivated and stewarded by the DeLanceys, endured after the Revolution, despite the loyalist exodus, with many of the same people and families occupying key roles. Of the "old," pre-Revolutionary families, the DeLanceys suffered the most. Other loyalist families stayed, and those who were primarily on the other side—Livingstons, Schuylers, Van Cortlandts, Clintons, and so on—jostled with them for position and power. Alongside new political actors who emerged during and after the Revolution, they engaged in heated, loud partisan debates about what kind of city, state, and nation they wanted to build.

Much of this was possible because of the broad-based political mobilization of New York City's white male population during the 1760s and 1770s.

Thousands of politically like-minded New Yorkers rallied around one another to articulate and reinforce their beliefs and ideas within what became an increasingly political public sphere. More critically, these years witnessed the emergence of an enthusiastic, politically engaged population. Non-elites sought to participate in New York City's urban political framework. This new constituency articulated their political sentiment by the means of their partisanship and associationism. Through their voluntary mobilization, New Yorkers developed bonds with one another that not only solidified their belief in their ideas but also validated their opposition to those individuals who argued against them. In New York City, between 1768 and 1775, partisanship and associationism flourished within its urban environment. New Yorkers met in the assembly's viewing gallery and in committees and associations, as well as in taverns and coffeehouses, on the streets, in each other's homes and shops, and to complete business transactions. Everywhere they formed and developed identities that distinguished them within the city's urban political framework. Through their sociability within these public and private venues, their behavior eludes neat categorization within the public-private binary. The relationships these men cultivated—political, economic, familial—enabled them not only to make political statements in the public sphere, but as they began to interact more frequently, their private interactions became a political statement as well. In the period between mid-1770 and the American Revolution, for at least those New Yorkers who became loyalists, their social networks began to mirror their political sentiments as their everyday, private interactions soon became a statement of their individual and joint political intent.

Colonists' political mobilization performed important social functions at the community level. New Yorkers came to rely on long-standing supporters at moments of political division, while at the same time encouraging the broad-based mobilization of like-minded individuals whereby the correlation of New Yorkers' political, social, economic, ideological, and military interests became part of an interactive mechanism in which white men identified and associated with one another in both private and public spheres. As they looked to one another for support, they reinforced their partisanship and associationism. The imperial crisis and the opportunities for large-scale political mobilization on an institutional and popular level enabled New Yorkers to redefine the boundaries of the city's face-to-face, urban framework. The various crises these people faced brought them together and facilitated the development of interpersonal ties that were made possibly by what became shared political persuasions.

The consequences of these DeLanceys' political and social associationism and activities during the 1760s and 1770s reveal some of the short- and long-term consequences of loyalism during the American Revolution. They also show that loyalism, as a sociopolitical phenomenon, cannot be overhomogenized. Many mobilized in opposition to the Townshend Duties, the Tea Act, and almost every other piece of parliamentary legislation alongside those who became revolutionaries. But each group, as well as those not featured here, navigated these crises differently. Many shared the same goal, but as the imperial crisis offered new opportunities for political activities and mobilizations, those who became revolutionaries joined forces with their like-minded associates in other colonies. They adopted an intercolonial outlook and approach to managing and eventually challenging their relationship with Parliament and Britain. Manhattan's loyalists, however, remained largely focused on their political situation. The DeLanceys might have sincerely felt they were representing and advocating for their constituents, reinforcing their beliefs in the process, but in doing so they also appeared insular and short-sighted. Their opponents reoriented the political map to suit their political and ideological needs, and as they did so, it led to the eventual creation of a new civic identity. Their social, political, economic, and familial networks reinforced and developed their views of how and where they wanted to live their lives. Many of these networks were forged during the imperial crisis of the 1760s and 1770s.

The colony's political infrastructure helped make this happen. In the late 1740s and early 1750s, Peter Kalm, a Swedish botanist, visited colonial North America. He kept an extensive diary that he later prepared for publication in his native Sweden. Between 1753 and 1761, three volumes appeared, in Swedish, and between 1770 and 1771, an English translation was published. During his travels, he socialized with many prominent scientific figures, including Benjamin Franklin and Lt. Gov. Cadwallader Colden. He also kept detailed notes on the places he visited. Of Manhattan, Kalm noted New Yorkers did not like their city to be compared to Boston or Philadelphia "with regard to its fine buildings, its opulence, and extensive commerce." Theirs were grander. Kalm described the city's bendy streets, its horticulture, its "strong and neat" houses, and its "several churches," as well as its "good" port. More importantly, though, when describing the colony's political structure, Kalm's depiction encapsulated the DeLanceys' vision of the assembly. It was, Kalm noted, "a parliament or dyet in miniature." With their broad-based mobilization of New Yorkers to secure their election, the DeLanceys sought to create an inclusive assembly that advocated and protected the public good. In doing so, the political mobilization and subsequent development of popular associations, which were predicated on their political economy, constituted many New Yorkers' political coming-of-age. They discarded gradations of rank and privilege and came together because of their shared sentiments. Consequently, New York's political public sphere widened, at least for white men, whereby their participation in it was no longer dependent on their place within the social pyramid. Instead, it was dependent on their willingness to participate and promote, as James DeLancey put it, "Life Liberty & Commerce."[11]

APPENDIX

Identifying the Loyalists

Determining who the loyalists were has been a focus of historical research since the eighteenth century. From John Adams's well-known division of loyalties into thirds to Lorenzo Sabine's two-volume *Biographical Sketches*, interest in identifying those who were against the American Revolution remains high. More recently, historians often note that loyalists, including those in New York, were a diverse group, one that represented the overall diversity of colonial North America. Most rely on the compensation claims that were submitted to the British government after the Revolutionary War—but such sources are notoriously unreliable, and they are not a representative profile of loyalists during the Revolutionary War. But how can one identify a comparable record of sources to offer plausible information of who the loyalists were?[1]

By merging a variety of documents of varying size and specificity, it is possible to offer a reasonable, and more accurate, account of who the loyalists were. First, the most useful records for identifying loyalists were declarations and petitions and oaths of allegiance. Oaths of allegiance also sometimes listed occupations and ages, as well as familial and social connections. With these records, most of which have never been fully analyzed before, it is possible to identify thousands of elite and non-elite loyalists: gentlemen as well as rum-tasters and chocolate-makers, lawyers, merchants, and shopkeepers as well as cartmen, tobacconists, farmers, and weavers. Another vital source is probate records, which document familial connections and real and personal wealth and sometimes include estate inventories. There are also sources that document religious affiliation, education, occupation, associationism, and kinship, all of which are useful, and reference works can be insightful, including the loyalist claims.[2]

As a result of this approach, I identified 9,338 loyalists from the counties of New York, Kings, Queens, Suffolk, and Westchester. Every individual whom I identified signed a loyalist petition or declaration or were administered the oath of allegiance by Gov. William Tryon.

Occupations

Occupations were identified for 6,257 loyalists. The largest group were artisans, people often of lower and middling means. They represented around 27 percent of those whose occupations were identified, indicating that loyalism had considerable appeal to those of lower and middling rank and status. Among those artisans were Isaac Heron, an Irish watchmaker who moved to Manhattan in the early 1760s and quickly established himself, and Thomas and William Brown john, druggists who were based in Hanover Square. Artisans also used their trades to articulate their loyalism, something that other occupations could not do. For instance, Charles Oliver Bruff was a jeweler who was based in Maiden Lane. From September 1776, Bruff catered to the British Army and the Royal Navy. Two years later, he offered engravings of George III on swords, noting he sold "the most elegant sword pattern that has ever made its appearance in America." He also sold shoe buckles that were "suitable for all loyalists" and swords that were engraved with "Success to the British arms."[3]

The most numerous single occupation, however, was farmers, who represented around 22 percent of all occupations. Moreover, 46 percent of all farmers and yeomen were fifteen years old or younger. They were also ethnically diverse. Jacques Cortelyou, for instance, was a Dutch farmer from Kings County, and he signed a loyalist document alongside two members of his family, Peter and Isaac. The Cortelyou family was well established in the colony. Jacques's ancestor was a surveyor in New Amsterdam, and he was the first to produce a map of the city—the Castello Plan. William Brown, in contrast, was a farmer who fought in the French and Indian War and chose to remain in New York. He settled on the "great Road from New York to Boston," where he made small improvements to his family home until the Revolutionary War broke out. Similarly, Gilbert Pugsley of Philipse Manor in Westchester County was forced to sell his farm because he refused to acquiesce to the revolutionaries. He moved to New Brunswick.[4]

Wealth

In determining colonists' wealth, tax lists are an integral source, one that other scholars have used.[5] But there are none that remain extant for New York during the imperial crisis or the Revolutionary War. Many potentially useful sources for determining loyalists' wealth have been lost or destroyed. The New York State Archives, however, holds a large number of probate records relating to this period.[6] After consulting Ray C. Sawyer's *Index of New York State Wills* (New York, 1932), Kenneth Scott's *Genealogical Data from Administration Papers from the New York State Court of Appeals in Albany* (New York, 1972), Berthold Fernow's *Calendar of Wills on File and Recorded in the Offices of the Clerk of the Court of Appeals* (Baltimore, 1967), and other published and online sources, I discovered that a large proportion of the wills that were available were for individuals in Kings, Queens, and Westchester Counties. Without comparable sources for Manhattan and Suffolk County, I identified as many probate records as possible for those loyalists who died between 1775 and 1785 by cross-examining probate records with the 9,338 loyalists I identified. When a match was located, I took note of the volume and page numbers.[7]

Probate records were sampled for 227 loyalists, most of whom were in Kings and Queens Counties and around 168 of whom could be used for a substantive analysis. From a detailed, multilevel analysis of their records, I determined that 49 percent of New York's loyalists possessed person wealth of £200 sterling or less. Most of them were not wealthy, but there was considerable variation between them. Take, for instance, the probates of Benjamin Barker and Thomas Betts. Barker's personal wealth was worth £5 sterling. Upon his death in 1782, he bequeathed his children varying sums of money, ranging from 5s. to £5, but included nothing else relating to personal property. Thomas Betts, a yeoman from Newtown, Queens County, bequeathed his nephew Anthony £10, while his wife, Sarah, received £100 one year after his death. She also received the finest room in Betts's home as well as firewood and the privilege of being allowed to keep foals, geese, ducks, or turkeys. Alternatively, while some loyalists were poor, others were among the wealthiest in New York. For example, when Abraham Furman died in early 1779, without any funds available for family members, he stipulated that his executors were to sell all his moveable estate "but the Grain on the Ground." In contrast, when Walter Franklin died in 1780, his total estate was valued at over £17,000 and he bequeathed numerous items to members of his family that indicated his elite status. Franklin's wife, Mary, received his "best Carriage or Chariot," two horses, all his household and kitchen utensils, and over £1,000. His daughters, Maria and Sarah, both received over £2,250 as well as his mansion and four other pieces of property. Overall, seventeen loyalists' estimated personal wealth was less than £22 sterling, and sixteen left more than £2,231 sterling. They represented all levels of society.

Age

No historian has previously examined loyalists' ages with any degree of specificity. Of the 9,338 loyalists I identified, I was able to determine the dates of birth for 3,263. Two, Daniel Horsmanden and David Hains, were eighty-four years old at the start of the Revolutionary War. Six others were also born in the seventeenth century. Elderly loyalists—those between sixty-three and eighty-four—account for about 5 percent of the population. At the other end of the spectrum, eighty-one were twelve years old in 1775.[8]

The largest age group among this study, some 480 loyalists, were aged between twelve and sixteen years old in 1775. They represented around 15 percent of the total. The second largest group represented 14 percent of the total, and loyalists at or under twenty-one years of age account for about 29 percent, indicating that fathers and sons might have signed lists together and family networks encouraged loyalist voluntarism. Over 84 percent of the colony's loyalists, per this sampling, were aged fifty-two or under. But it would be incorrect to assume that the colony's loyalists were middle-aged, as they tended to be in Massachusetts.[9] Around 56 percent were between twenty-two and fifty-two years old.

This can be further broken down to reveal two groups: those between twenty-two and thirty-six years old (1,071), who account for about one-third of the complete total (32.83%), and those aged between thirty-seven and sixty-two (1,083), who account for another third (33.2%) of the total. The near-equitable distribution of frequencies among three age groups (29% under twenty-one years old, 33 percent between thirty-two and thirty-six and 33 percent between thirty-seven and sixty-two) indicates that loyalism was not a generational phenomenon. Colonists of all ages became loyalists. And because a significant proportion of loyalists were dependent or semidependent on their families—that is, those under twenty-one years of age—it is probable that family allegiances were the most influential.

For instance, in Brookhaven, Suffolk County, the sixty-five-year-old Alexander Hawkins signed alongside his family members: thirty-two-year-old Simeon Hawkins, twenty-six-year-old Jonas Hawkins, twenty-three-year-old Benjamin Hawkins, and nineteen-year-old Thomas Hawkins. Family networks were important outside Suffolk County, too. In New York City, Benjamin and Edward Buckbee took the oath of allegiance. So, too, did Edward and Wil-

Table 1   New York Loyalists' Age Ranges

AGE RANGE	NO. OF LOYALISTS	% OF WHOLE	CUMULATIVE %
12–16	480	14.71	14.71
17–21	457	14.01	28.72
22–26	364	11.16	39.87
27–31	372	11.4	51.27
32–36	335	10.27	61.54
37–41	304	9.32	70.86
42–46	210	6.44	77.29
46–51	240	7.36	84.65
52–56	205	6.28	90.93
57–61	124	3.8	94.73
62–66	87	2.67	97.40
67–71	55	1.69	99.08
72–76	25	0.77	99.85
77–81	3	0.09	99.94
82–87	2	0.06	100.00
TOTAL	3,263	100.00	100.00

liam Laight and Frederick, William Sr., William Jr., and Philip Rhinelander. In Kings County, Isaac, Garret, and Joris Martinsey were administered the oath of allegiance, as were members of the Hegeman, Ditmars, Suydam, Wyckoff, Stryker, Lefferts, and Lott families. In Westchester County, twenty-eight members of the Purdy family signed a loyalist petition. So did thirteen members of the Gidney family, eleven members of the Underhill family, nine members of the Haines family, eight members of the Hart and Tompkins families, seven members of the Merritt family, and, among others, five members of the Storm family. Family networks were important in Queens County, too. Sixty-one surnames were represented by five or more individuals, many of whom were Dutch. There were, for example, more than five Brinkerhoffs, Rapaljes, Remsens, Schencks, Snedekers, Suydams and Van Nostrandts.

Education

Formal education in eighteenth-century British America was the domain of elites. Although children's schools were established in local towns and cities, once a child reached adulthood, further educational opportunities were largely restricted to elite or upper-middling social status. By 1775 the colonies had nine academic institutions: Harvard College, the College of William and Mary, Yale

College, the College of New Jersey (Princeton), the College of Philadelphia (University of Pennsylvania), the College of Rhode Island (Brown), Queen's College (Rutgers), Dartmouth College, and King's College (Columbia). Of those listed, Harvard (1636), Yale (1701), and Dartmouth (1769) were Congregationalist; the College of William and Mary (1693) and King's College (1754) were Anglican; the College of New Jersey (1746) was Presbyterian; the College of Rhode Island (1764) was Baptist; and Queen's College (1766) was Dutch Reformed. Only the College of Philadelphia (1751) was nonsectarian.

This study has found that seventy-five loyalists out of 9,338 attended higher education institutions before the American Revolution. In this study's analysis of records from British and colonial universities and colleges, it has been found that New York loyalists' access to higher education was far more limited than loyalists in Massachusetts. The backgrounds of these educated New York loyalists reveal that a significant number (sixty-one) attended college in New York and that of the remaining fourteen who attended institutions outside New York, most (eight) attended college in another colony. Notable loyalists who were educated at higher institutions in Britain included Samuel Seabury and Charles Inglis, both awarded degrees by the University of Oxford even though they did not matriculate. The Buchanans, a wealthy Scottish mercantile family, sent Thomas Buchanan to study at the University of Glasgow in the 1740s before he relocated to New York. Another loyalist, Peter Middleton, was awarded an MD from the University of St. Andrews.

Of those who attended institutions in the colonies, the future mayor of New York City, David Mathews, was the only loyalist graduate of the College of New Jersey; Samuel Seabury and Edmund Fanning were Yale alumni; and Fanning, Samuel Auchmuty and Robert N. Auchmuty completed degrees at Harvard. There were no New York loyalist graduates from the College of Philadelphia or the College of William and Mary. (John DeLancey matriculated at Philadelphia in 1762 but did not graduate.) No loyalists have been found to have attended Queen's College or Dartmouth.

Most New York loyalists who attended university were graduates of King's College in New York City. Over 81 percent of New York's higher-educated loyalists were graduates of King's College. Alongside its sixty-one graduates and its president, ten of its governors became loyalists, as well. Unlike Harvard, King's College students' matriculation was not always moderated by rank or status. The future occupations of these graduates indicate that men of both lesser as well as greater means attended the college: twelve became merchants, eight became gentlemen, seven were Anglican ministers, three were lawyers, and three were public officials or doctors. Graduates whose vocations were associated with lower social status included two druggists, five yeomen, a brewer, a cartman, a cooper, a coppersmith, an innkeeper, a mason, and a tailor.[10]

Religion

Historians have often made a correlation between loyalism and Anglicanism in the American Revolution. In *The King's Friends*, Wallace Brown suggested that "there was an Anglican tinge to Loyalism" across the northern colonies. But Anglican loyalists were not found only in the northern colonies; they were across the continent. In Georgia, Maryland, and North Carolina, as well as in Delaware, Connecticut, Massachusetts, New York, and Rhode Island, Anglicanism played a role in determining its colonists' allegiance. Also, there is a consensus in the literature that Anglican Loyalists were more numerous in New York than in the other colonies. Philip Ranlet argued that all New York loyalists "were either Anglicans or those of other faiths who were influenced by an Anglican minister or some other staunch Tory." Brown also suggested that the "bulk" of New York's loyalist population were Anglican. Others have argued the Revolutionary War was based on religious differences.[11]

Nevertheless, recent work has emphasized loyalists' religious pluralism.[12] But despite this, or perhaps because of it, few have moved beyond a framework centered on clergymen and elites. As such, what remains unclear is the religious diversity of the rank and file, which this analysis focuses on to determine the correlation between loyalism and religion in New York City and County only, where most records are extant.

Anglicans were a minority in New York, but they constituted most of its loyalist population. In total, 850 loyalists out of the 1,251 whose religion could be identified were Anglican. This study has identified 489 loyalists who married in an Anglican Church between 1746 and 1785. Most of these individuals were married by the time of the American Revolution (59.68%). Often, they were married by an Anglican minister who became a loyalist.

Baptismal records complement this analysis. Between 1775 and 1785, 442 loyalists had children baptized in an Anglican church. Most were baptized in Trinity Church, but some were baptized in St. Paul's. Only one child was baptized in 1775; in 1776 and 1777, no children were baptized. Between 1778 and 1783, however, birth rates changed. Eighty-three percent of identified Anglican loyalists had a child baptized. This may have been due, in part, to the security British control afforded them, thereby indicating that it became a means through which to strengthen British imperialism. Indeed, baptisms showed colonists' political commitment on an Atlantic scale. It was more than a rite of admission to the Christian community. It was a demonstration of loyalists' commitment to the rule of the king, both as head of state and head of the English Church. For example, October 1, 1778, William Sutherland baptized his son Henry Clinton Sutherland, naming him after the commander-in-chief of the British Army. Another loyalist whose allegiance was articulated through their child's name was David Buchanan. A Scotsman, Buchanan had his daughter baptized on February 21, 1781, as Anne Britannia Buchanan, naming her after Queen Anne, the reigning monarch during the Act of Union.[13]

Quakers were the second most numerous denomination identified during this study. In total, 157 loyalists have been identified as belonging to the Society of Friends. Given that Quakers represented a tiny portion of New York's population, their loyalism indicates their focus on moderation, reconciliation—their pacifism. New York Quakers' loyalism thus became a form of political accommodation that enabled them to continue practicing their religion. As one post-Revolutionary report stated, though "a large number of Inhabitants . . . left their Homes" between 1775 and 1776, Quakers "generally kept their places." They "Chose rather to hazard all than omit the attendance of their Religious Meetings." Elias Hicks, an inhabitant of Long Island, validated this view, writing, those "who stood faithful to their principles did not meddle in the controversy, had, after a short period at first, considerable favor allowed them."[14]

I also identified loyalists who were Dutch Reformists, Presbyterians, Lutherans, German Reformists, and Moravians. Seventy-nine were Dutch Reformists, sixty-seven were Presbyterians, forty-one were Lutherans, twenty-six were German Reformists, and eleven were Moravians. In total, then, 69 percent of New York City's loyalists were Anglican, nearly 13 percent were Quakers, 6 percent were Dutch Reformists, 5 percent were Presbyterians, 3 percent were Lutherans, 2 percent were German Reformists, and under 1 percent were Moravians.

Although the number of Dutch Reformed members is low, it should be remembered that this project has sampled only New York City; it was Kings County that was populated by Dutch-speaking inhabitants. If we assume that its loyalists were, for the most part, Dutch Reformists, then their numbers would increase significantly. Contemporaries also appreciated the number of loyalists from the Dutch Church. As the historian Thomas Jones remarked, it was "next in rank" to the Anglican Church. It is possible, therefore, and a subject for future research to confirm, that Dutch Reformists, and not Quakers, were the second most influential denomination of New York's loyalists.[15]

The data concerning the other Protestant denominations are also significant. Given that Presbyterians were the second most politically influential religious group in New York City before the Revolution, their small numbers suggests that there was no correlation between Presbyterianism and loyalism. It could be inferred that most New York City Presbyterians were revolutionaries.

What emerges are tentative correlations between loyalism and religion in New York City. This strong association was unique. Several historians have argued that there was no correlation between rank-and-file loyalism and Anglicanism in Virginia, while Colin Nicolson put forward this same argument when examining Massachusetts. However, in New York City, there is clear evidence of a strong correlation between loyalism and Anglicanism. The link between loyalism and Anglicanism also transcended the societal gap between the elite and the non-elite inhabitants of New York City. Alongside elite Anglican assemblymen like James DeLancey, Frederick Philipse III, and Jacob Walton, were merchants like William Bayard and Theophylact Bache, shopkeepers like Christopher Blundell and Samuel Murgatroyd, a cordwainer, Isaac DeLaMater, a ship-chandler, Adam DeGrushee, and a tailor, Emmanuel Rinedollar. With these men was a breeches-maker, Cornelius Ryan, and a yeoman, Israel Underhill, among a range of other elite and non-elite Anglican loyalists who represented the occupational diversity of New York City.[16]

New York's Loyalists

Although historians have moved beyond outdated depictions of loyalists as wealthy, royal officeholders, too much reliance has been placed on Wallace Brown's *The King's Friends*. This study complements and builds on *The King's Friends*, which largely focused on New Yorkers outside of the city. This study also complements Robert Michael Dructor's unpublished, often overlooked 1975 doctoral dissertation, in which he noted that most merchants "chose loyalty over independence." Dructor also showed that most loyalists were Anglicans, and they were evenly dispersed throughout the city.[17]

New York's loyalists were skilled artisans, owning both real and personal estate. These were individuals involved in the everyday lives of hundreds of their fellow colonists as their livelihoods depended upon their business with other members of their society. After growing up in a period of imperial and provincial expansion, living through numerous wars, these men had cemented themselves and their relationships within the developing social and economic framework of their society in the years leading up to and through the imperial crisis. Most of them were not wealthy, university-educated, royally connected New Yorkers. They were carpenters, shoemakers, bakers, or cordwainers. Most were Anglicans, but there were also Quakers, Dutch and German Reformists, Lutherans, Presbyterians, Moravians, and more. Most were uneducated and under forty years of age. In almost every demographical marker, New York's loyalists represented the diversity of the colony in the years leading up to the American Revolution.

But these analyses, as well as Brown's and Dructor's, fail to account for every loyalist in New York City, the colony, or the continent. Information for "ordinary" individuals, particularly women and minorities, is difficult to obtain, and the source base used within this study has favored white men. The fact is that no sources can detail perfectly who eighteenth-century loyalists were, but they can indicate trends like what has been offered here, showing New York loyalists' similarities and their differences and giving a focused, though albeit conservative, insight into American identity prior to and during the American Revolution.

NOTES

Prologue

1. *Diary and Autobiography of John Adams*, ed. L. H. Butterfield and others, 4 vols. (Cambridge, MA: Harvard University Press, 1961; hereafter, JA, *D&A*), 2:101.

2. JA, *D&A*, 2:102. See also Richard Alan Ryerson, *John Adams's Republic: The One, the Few, and the Many* (Baltimore: Johns Hopkins University Press, 2016), 83–84.

3. Adams to Tudor, 24 June 1776, in *The Papers of John Adams*, ed. Robert J. Taylor, Gregg L. Lint, Sara Georgini, and others, 21 vols. published to date (Cambridge, MA: Harvard University Press, 1977– ; hereafter, JA, *Papers*), 4:335–336.

4. Tudor to Adams, 7 July 1776, in JA, *Papers*, 4:367–368.

5. Washington to Joseph Reed, in 14 January 1776, in *The Papers of George Washington: Revolutionary War Series*, ed. Philander D. Chase, Frank E. Grizzard Jr., Edward G. Lengel, David R. Hoth, and others, 30 vols. to date (Charlottesville: University of Virginia Press, 1985– ; hereafter, Washington, *Papers, Rev. War Series*), 2:406–407.

6. Adams to Abigail Adams, 22 September 1776, in *Adams Family Correspondence*, ed. L. H. Butterfield, Marc Friedlaender, Richard Alan Ryerson, Margaret A. Hogan, Sara Martin, Hobson Woodward, and others, 15 vols. published to date (Cambridge, MA: Harvard University Press, 1963–), 2:132; Ruma Chopra, *Unnatural Rebellion: Loyalists in New York City during the Revolution* (Charlottesville: University of Virginia Press, 2011), 51–52. For others who believed the British occupation of New York would be its high point or otherwise insignificant to the war effort, see Arthur Lee to C. W. F. Dumas, 23 September 1776, in *The Diplomatic Correspondence of the American Revolution*, ed. Jared Sparks, 12 vols. (Boston: Nathan Hale and Gray & Bowen, 1829–1830), 9:285; committee of secret correspondence to William Bingham, 21 September 1776, in *The Papers of Benjamin Franklin*, ed. Leonard W. Labaree, William B. Willcox, Claude A. Lopez, Barbara B. Oberg, Ellen R. Cohn, and others, 43 vols. to date (New Haven, CT: Yale University Press, 1959–), 22:615–620.

7. Adams to Vergennes, 13 July 1780, in JA, *Papers*, 9:521.

8. Following George Bancroft, in the early to mid-twentieth century, for instance, came the likes of J. Franklin Jameson, Carl L. Becker, Merrill Jensen, and Charles Beard—the Progressives—and the Imperial school of Charles M. Andrews and Leonard W. Laberee. Then, after World War II, came the Consensus school, which was later joined by the neo-Whig school of Bernard Bailyn, Gordon S. Wood, and others, all of whom explored the history of ideas during the Revolution with greater depth and nuance than their predecessors. The neo-Whig school has probably offered the most dominant and long-lasting assessment of the Revolution's origins. Despite the emergence of

other schools, as one scholar put it in 2017, "most of the books published in the decades after [Bernard Bailyn's] *Ideological Origins* responded to it in some way." See Mary Beth Norton et al., "Bernard Bailyn's Ideological Origins at Fifty," *Harvard University Press Blog* (19 April 2017), https://harvardpress.typepad.com/hup_publicity/2017/04/bernard -bailyns-ideological-origins-at-fifty.html#norton (accessed 9 August 2020). The neo-Whig school was joined by the New Social History school from the mid-1960s until the late 1980s, during which time neo-Progressives such as Gary B. Nash, Jesse Lemisch, and Alfred F. Young, among others, confronted the neo-Whigs' assessment through a particular focus on non-elites. Sometimes, the debates were strong and personal. "Boom! . . . Boom! What is that noise?" wrote Lemisch in the *Radical History Review*. "It's the sound of cannon around the Charles Warren Center at Harvard," Lemisch continued, adding that "Bernard Bailyn has retreated into his secret underground bunker . . . to protect him from *those* crazed maniacs—the STUDENT RADICALS," that is, those adopting a neo-Progressive approach. Lemisch's witty but fierce critique was not, however, confined to his school. In 1975 Bailyn attacked those who studied "the mob," "the helpless and inarticulate," and enslaved people as mostly "hopelessly presentist" or motivated by "extreme and political presentism." This is not to say, however, that "ideas" were not discussed or explored in American historiography related to the American Revolution. Other historians had also explored the history of ideas, including John C. Miller and Merrill Jensen. See Lemisch, "Bailyn Besieged in His Bunker," *Radical History Review* 3 (Winter 1977): 72–83, https://doi.org/10.1215/1636545-1977-13-72; Bailyn, "Lines of Force in Recent Writings about the American Revolution" (paper presented at the Fourteenth International Congress of Historical Sciences, San Francisco, 1975), 8–20, 24–34. See also Lemisch, "What Made Our Revolution?" *New Republic* (25 May 1968), 25–28. For Miller's and Jensen's work, see Mark Peterson, "The Social Origins of *Ideological Origins*: Notes on the Historical Legacy of Bernard Bailyn," *Reviews in American History* 49, no. 2 (2011): 360–387, https://doi.org/10.1353/rah.2021.0034. See also Alfred F. Young and Gregory H. Nobles, *Whose American Revolution Was It? Historians Interpret the Founding* (New York: New York University Press, 2011).

9. *A National Program for the Publication of Historical Documents* (Washington, DC: US Government Printing Office, 1954), iii.

10. *National Program for the Publication of Historical Documents*, vi, viii.

11. *National Program for the Publication of Historical Documents*, 1–2.

12. Washington to Samuel Tucker, 7 August 1776, in Washington, *Papers, Rev. War Series*, 5:616.

13. See, for example, Robert M. Calhoon, *The Loyalists in Revolutionary America, 1760–1781* (New York: Harcourt, Brace, Jovanich, 1973); Robert M. Calhoon et al., *Tory Insurgents: The Loyalist Perception and Other Essays* (Columbia: University of South Carolina Press, 2010); Maya Jasanoff, *Liberty's Exiles: American Loyalists in the Revolutionary World* (New York: Knopf, 2011); *The Loyal Atlantic: Remaking the British Atlantic*, ed. Jerry Bannister and Liam Riordan (Toronto: University of Toronto Press, 2012); Wallace Brown, *The King's Friends: The Composition and Motives of the American Loyalist Claimants* (Providence, RI: Brown University Press, 1965); Bernard Bailyn, *The Ordeal of Thomas Hutchinson* (Cambridge, MA: Harvard University Press, 1976); James W. St. G. Walker, *The Black Loyalists: The Search for a Promised Land in Nova Scotia and Sierra Leone* (New

York: Dalhousie University Press and Holmes and Meier, 1976); Harvey Amani Whit-field, *North to Bondage: Loyalist Slavery in the Maritimes* (Vancouver: University of British Columbia Press, 2016). For recent assessments on the state of loyalist studies, see also *The Consequences of Loyalism: Essays in Honor of Robert M. Calhoon*, ed. Rebecca Brannon and Joseph S. Moore (Columbia: University of South Carolina Press, 2019).

14. See Eugene R. Fingerhut, "Uses and Abuses of the American Loyalists' Claims: A Critique of Quantitative Analyses," *William and Mary Quarterly* (hereafter, *WMQ*) 25, no. 2 (1968): 245–258, https://doi.org/10.2307/1919094.

15. Colin Nicolson, *The "Infamas Govener": Francis Bernard and the Origins of the American Revolution* (Boston: Northeastern University Press, 2000); Ray Raphael, *The First American Revolution: Before Lexington and Concord* (New York: New Press, 2002); T. H. Breen, *American Insurgents, American Patriots: The Revolution of the People* (New York: Hill & Wang, 2011). See also Mary Beth Norton, *1774: The Long Year of Revolution* (New York: Knopf, 2020), xvi; Steven Pincus, Tiraana Bains, and A. Zuercher Reichardt, "Thinking the Empire Whole," *History Australia* 16, no. 4 (2019): 612, https://doi.org/10.1080/14490854.2019.1670692; Patricia U. Bonomi, "New York: The Royal Colony," *New York History* 82 (2001): 22, https://www.jstor.org/stable/42677750.

16. Roger J. Champagne, "New York's Radicals and the Coming of Independence," *Journal of American History* (hereafter, *JAH*) 51, no. 1 (1964): 21–40, https://doi.org/10.2307/1917932; Roger Champagne, "Family Politics versus Constitutional Principles: The New York Assembly Elections of 1768 and 1769," *WMQ* 20, no. 1 (1963): 57–79, https://doi.org/10.2307/1921355.

17. Alan Tully, *Forming American Politics: Ideas, Interests, and Institutions in Colonial New York and Pennsylvania* (Baltimore: Johns Hopkins University Press, 1994), 401.

18. For instances of when New Yorkers came together during the Revolutionary War, see Judith L. Van Buskirk, *Generous Enemies: Patriots and Loyalists in Revolutionary New York* (Philadelphia: University of Pennsylvania Press, 2002).

19. See, for instance, Bernard Bailyn, *The Ideological Origins of the American Revolution* (Cambridge, MA: Harvard University Press, 1967); Gordon S. Wood, *The Creation of the American Republic, 1776–1787* (Chapel Hill: University of North Carolina Press, 1969); Pauline Maier, *From Resistance to Revolution: Colonial Radicals and the Development of American Opposition to Britain, 1765–1776* (New York: Knopf, 1972); J. G. A. Pocock, *The Machiavellian Moment: Florentine Political Thought and the Atlantic Republican Tradition* (Princeton, NJ: Princeton University Press, 1975); Joyce O. Appleby, *Liberalism and Republicanism in the Historical Imagination* (Cambridge, MA: Harvard University Press, 1992); John Phillip Reid, *Constitutional History of the American Revolution*, 4 vols. (Madison: University of Wisconsin Press, 1986–1993); Jack P. Greene, *Peripheries and Center: Constitutional Development in the Extended Polities of the British Empire and the United States, 1607–1788* (Athens: University of Georgia Press, 1986); Robert A. Gross, *The Minutemen and Their World* (New York: Hill and Wang, 1976); Gary B. Nash, *Urban Crucible: Social Change, Political Consciousness, and the Origins of the American Revolution* (Cambridge, MA: Harvard University Press, 1979). See also Patrick Spero, "Introduction," in *The American Revolution Reborn*, ed. Patrick Spero and Michael Zuckerman (Philadelphia: University of Pennsylvania Press, 2016), 3; Joshua Canale, "Violent Divisions and New Directions," *Reviews in American History* 46, no. 2 (2018): 183, https://doi.org/10.1353/rah.2018.0028.

20. See Edmund S. Morgan, "The American Revolution: Revisions in Need of Revising," *WMQ* 14 (1957): 3–15, https://doi.org/10.2307/1917368; T. H. Breen, "Ideology and Nationalism on the Eve of the American Revolution: Revisions Once More in Need of Revising," *JAH* 84 (1997): 13–39, https://doi.org/10.2307/2952733.

21. See, for instance, Albrecht Koschnik, *"Let a Common Interest Bind Us Together": Associations, Partisanship, and Culture in Philadelphia, 1775–1840* (Charlottesville: University of Virginia Press, 2007); David Waldstreicher, *In the Midst of Perpetual Fetes: The Making of American Nationalism, 1776–1820* (Chapel Hill: University of North Carolina Press, 1997); Johann N. Neem, *Creating a Nation of Joiners: Democracy and Civil Society in Early National Massachusetts* (Cambridge, MA: Harvard University Press, 2008); John L. Brooke, "Ancient Lodges and Self-Created Societies: Voluntary Association and the Public Sphere in the Early Republic," in *Launching the "Extended Republic": The Federalist Era*, ed. Ronald Hoffman and Peter J. Albert (Charlottesville: University Press of Virginia, 1996), 273–377; Catherine Kaplan O'Donnell, *Men of Letters in the Early Republic: Cultivating Forums of Citizenship* (Chapel Hill: University of North Carolina Press, 2008); Andrew M. Schocket, *Founding Corporate Power in Early National Philadelphia* (DeKalb: Northern Illinois University Press, 2007). Mary Beth Norton framed loyalism as a negative movement in her *The British-Americans: The Loyalist Exiles in England, 1774–1789* (Boston: Little, Brown, 1972). See also Staughton Lynd, "Tories and Neo-Whigs," *Reviews in American History* 1, no. 2 (1973): 201–208, esp. 204, https://doi.org/10.2307/2701035.

22. Tully, *Forming American Politics*, 402, 403; Steven Pincus, Tiraana Bains, and A. Zuercher Reichardt, "Reconnecting the Global British Empire: Response to Critics," *History Australia* 16, no. 4 (2019): 654, https://doi.org/10.1080/14490854.2019.1670700; Nash, *Urban Crucible*.

23. John A. Garraty, Mark C. Carnes, and Paul Betz, eds., *American National Biography*, 24 vols. plus supplement (New York: Oxford University Press, 1999–2002; rev. ed., www.anb.org); Henry C. Van Schaack, *Henry Cruger: The Colleague of Edmund Burke* (New York: C. Benjamin Richardson, 1859), 1–6; Joseph Outerbridge Brown, *The Jaunceys of New York* (New York: Thitchener & Glastaeter, 1876), 15–18; Edward Countryman, "The Uses of Capital in Revolutionary America: The Case of the New York Loyalist Merchants," *WMQ* 49, no. 1 (1992): 17–18, https://doi.org/10.2307/2947333. For Oliver DeLancey's correspondence and engagement with Otis and Hancock, see William Tudor, *The Life of James Otis, of Massachusetts* (Boston: Wells and Lilly, 1823), 33–34. DeLancey tried—and failed—to engage Otis's legal services on his behalf of his sister.

24. *Journal of the Votes and Proceedings of the General Assembly of the Colony of New-York*, Charles Evans and others, *American Bibliography: A Chronological Dictionary of All Books, Pamphlets and Periodical Publications Printed in the United States of America* [1639–1800], 14 vols. (Chicago and Worcester, MA, 1903–1959; rev. ed., www.readex.com), no. 12158.

25. Justin du Rivage, *Revolution against Empire: Taxes, Politics, and the Origins of American Independence* (New Haven, CT: Yale University Press, 2017); Steve Pincus, *The Heart of the Declaration: The Founders' Case for an Activist Government* (New Haven, CT: Yale University Press, 2016).

26. Samuel Seabury to Myles Cooper, 1 August 1775, in *The Cause of Loyalty: The Revolutionary War Correspondence of Myles Cooper*, ed. Christopher F. Minty and Peter W. Walker (forthcoming); Charles Inglis to John Vardill, 2 May 1775, Egerton MS, 2135, British Library.

1. Outwrote as well as Outvoted

1. Robert Livingston Jr. (of Clermont) to Robert Livingston Jr. (3d Lord of the Manor), 21 February 1768, Livingston Family Papers, Gilder Lehrman Institute, on deposit at New-York Historical Society (hereafter, NHi); Don R. Gerlach, *Philip Schuyler and the American Revolution in New York 1733–1777* (Lincoln: University of Nebraska Press, 1964), 137; Nicholas Varga, "Election Procedures and Practices," *New York History* (hereafter, *NYH*) 41 (1960), 256–257, https://www.jstor.org/stable/23154475; Alan Taylor, "'The Art of Hook & Snivey': Political Culture in Upstate New York during the 1790s," *Journal of American History* (hereafter, *JAH*) 79 (1993), 1376–1380, https://doi.org/10.2307/2080209; James McLachlan, Richard A. Harrison, Ruth L. Woodward, Wesley Frank Craven, and J. Jefferson Looney, *Princetonians: A Biographical Dictionary*, 5 vols. (Princeton, NJ: Princeton University Press, 1976–1991), 1:274, 275–276; Sung Bok Kim, *Landlord and Tenant in Colonial New York: Manorial Society, 1664–1775* (Chapel Hill: University of North Carolina Press, 1977), 107–108, 109, 114, 127, 418; Patricia U. Bonomi, *A Factious People: Politics and Society in Colonial New York* (New York: Columbia University Press, 1971), 289, Appendix C.

2. William Smith Jr., *The History of the Province of New-York*, ed. Michael Kammen, 2 vols. (Cambridge, MA: Harvard University Press, 1972), 1:226.

3. Mike Rapport, *The Unruly City: Paris, London, and New York in the Age of Revolution* (New York: Basic, 2017), xx–xxi; Joseph S. Tiedemann, *Reluctant Revolutionaries: New York City and the Road to Independence, 1763–1776* (Ithaca, NY: Cornell University Press, 1997), 13, 16–17, 20–25; Andrew Burnaby, *Travels through the Middle Settlements in North-America* (London, 1775), 105–115; Edwin G. Burrows and Mike Wallace, *Gotham: A History of New York City to 1898* (New York: Oxford University Press, 1999; hereafter, *Gotham*), 194; Carl Bridenbaugh, *Cities in Revolt: Urban Life in America, 1743–1776* (New York: Knopf, 1955), 16, 42; Alan Taylor, *American Revolutions: A Continental History, 1750–1804* (New York: W. W. Norton, 2016), 56, 66.

4. Ruma Chopra, *Unnatural Rebellion: Loyalists in New York City during the Revolution* (Charlottesville: University of Virginia Press, 2011), 11.

5. John A. Garraty, Mark C. Carnes, and Paul Betz, eds., *American National Biography*, 24 vols. plus supplement (New York: Oxford University Press, 1999–2002; rev. ed., www.anb.org; hereafter, *ANB*); C. A. Weslager, *The Stamp Act Congress* (Newark: University of Delaware Press, 1976), 81–82; Cynthia A. Kierner, *Traders and Gentlefolk: The Livingstons of New York, 1675–1790* (Ithaca, NY: Cornell University Press, 1992), 163–164; Joyce D. Goodfriend, *Before the Melting Pot: Society and Culture in Colonial New York City, 1664–1730* (Princeton, NJ: Princeton University Press, 1992), 173; Bayard Claim, AO 12/20, f. 130–148, National Archives of the United Kingdom (hereafter, UK-KeNA); *Biographical Directory of the United States Congress, 1774–2005* (Washington, DC, 2005; rev. edn., bioguide.congress.gov); Bonomi, *Factious People*, 240.

6. Conrad Edick Wright, *Revolutionary Generation: Harvard Men and the Consequences of Independence* (Amherst: University of Massachusetts Press, 2005), 66; Milton M. Klein, "The Rise of the New York Bar: The Legal Career of William Livingston," *William and Mary Quarterly* 15 (1958): 334–358, https://doi.org/10.2307/1915621; Gregory Afinogenov, "Lawyers and Politics in Eighteenth-Century New York," *NYH* 89 (2008): 142–162, https://www.jstor.org/stable/23183447; *Catalogue of the John Adams Library in the Public Library of the City of Boston* (Boston: Published by the Trustees, 1917).

7. Clarkson to John Bennett, 28 December 1765, Letter-book of David Clarkson, f. 4, Huntington Library, San Marino, CA (hereafter, CSmH); Clarkson to Unknown, 6 January 1766, Letter-book of David Clarkson, f. 4, CSmH; John Watts to Isaac Barré, 28 February 1762, *Letter Book of John Watts: Merchant and Councillor of New York* (New York: Printed for the Society, 1928), 27; Watts to Nathaniel Paice, 11 August 1765, *Letter Book of John Watts*, 367; Tiedemann, *Reluctant Revolutionaries*, 49–54; Afinogenov, "Lawyers and Politics," 144, 145, 156–157; Klein, "Rise of the New York Bar," 353; *ANB*.

8. Bonomi, *Factious People*, 56–102, esp. 60, 66, 72–74; Leopold S. Launitz-Schürer Jr., *Loyal Whigs and Revolutionaries: The Making of an American Revolution in New York, 1765–1776* (New York: New York University Press, 1980), 1–21; Yates, Notes for a History of New York, Abraham Yates Jr. Papers, box 6, Manuscripts and Archives Division, New York Public Library (hereafter, NN); Smith to John Reid, [1770] William Smith Jr. Papers, box 1, f. 5, NN; Jill Lepore, *New York Burning: Liberty, Slavery, and Conspiracy in Eighteenth-Century Manhattan* (New York: Knopf, 2005), 218.

9. Philip Ranlet and Richard B. Morris, "Richard B. Morris's James DeLancey: Portrait in Loyalism," *NYH* 80 (1999): 185–210, https://www.jstor.org/stable/23182484; Julian Gwyn, *The Enterprising Admiral: The Personal Fortune of Admiral Sir Peter Warren* (Montreal: McGill-Queen's University Press, 1974), 102, 203; Leslie Stephen and Sidney Lee, eds., *The Dictionary of National Biography*, 21 vols. plus supplements (New York and London, 1885–1901; repr. Oxford: Oxford University Press, 1959–1960; rev. ed., www.oxforddnb.com hereafter, *DNB*); Joyce D. Goodfriend, *Who Should Rule at Home? Confronting the Elite in British New York City* (Ithaca, NY: Cornell University Press, 2017), 3; Bonomi, *Factious People*, 143; David E. Narrett, *Inheritance and Family Life in Colonial New York City* (Ithaca, NY: Cornell University Press, 1992), 124; James DeLancey Claim, AO 12/19, f. 205–206, 209, 212, 213, UK-KeNA. For more on DeLancey's estates, see Bancker Plans, NN.

10. *The Papers of Benjamin Franklin*, ed. Leonard W. Labaree, William B. Willcox, Claude A. Lopez, Barbara B. Oberg, Ellen R. Cohn, and others, 43 vols. published to date, 16:130; Bonomi, *Factious People*, 294; Annette Townsend, *The Walton Family of New York, 1630–1940* (Philadelphia: Historical Publication Society, 1945), 36; Simon Middleton, *From Privilege to Rights: Work and Politics in Colonial New York City* (Philadelphia: University of Pennsylvania Press, 2006), 212, 289; Martha J. Lamb, *History of the City of New York*, 3 vols. (New York: Valentine's Manual, Inc., 1877–1896), 2:683–685; Walter Barrett, *The Old Merchants of New York*, 5 vols. (New York: Thomas R. Knox and Co., 1885), 1:104; I. N. Phelps Stokes, *The Iconography of Manhattan Island, 1498–1909*, 6 vols. (New York: R. H. Dodd, 1915–1928; hereafter, Stokes, *Iconography*), 6:32; David W. Dunlap, "In Drawing, Guide to Past of Gracie Mansion Site," *New York Times*, 22 October 2007, https://www.nytimes.com/2007/10/23/nyregion/23gracie.html?smid=url -share. For a contemporary reference to Belview, see *Rivington's New-York Gazetteer*, 18 August 1774. The *Norfolk Chronicle*, 23 November 1776, reported that Walton's estate was "beautiful" and "at Horneshook, near Hell Gate."

11. Joseph O. Brown, *The Jaunceys of New York* (New York: Thitchener & Glastaeter, 1876), 3–4, 15–16; Lorenzo Sabine, *Biographical Sketches of Loyalists of the American Revolution*, 2 vols. (Boston: Little, Brown and Co., 1847–1864), 1:572; John Austin Stevens Jr., *Colonial New York. Sketches Biographical and Historical 1768–1784* (New York: John F. Trow and Co., 1867), 138; Edward Countryman, *A People in Revolution: The American Revolu-*

tion and Political Society in New York, 1760–1790 (Baltimore: Johns Hopkins University Press, 1981), 112; *New York Genealogical and Biographical Record* 26 (1895), 187.

12. Barbara Clark Smith, *The Freedoms We Lost: Consent and Resistance in Revolutionary America* (New York: New Press, 2010), 4–5, 6–15.

13. Joseph M. Adelman, *Revolutionary Networks: The Business and Politics of Printing the News, 1763–1789* (Baltimore: Johns Hopkins University Press, 2019), 83; Hugh Gaine Receipt Book, NN.

14. Brian Cowan, *The Social Life of Coffee: The Emergence of the British Coffeehouse* (New Haven, CT: Yale University Press, 2005), 99–105; Benjamin L. Carp, *Rebels Rising: Cities and the American Revolution* (New York: Oxford University Press, 2007), 64, 68; David S. Shields, *Civil Tongues & Polite Letters in British America* (Chapel Hill: University of North Carolina Press, 1997), 20; Thomas E. Brennan, *Public Drinking and Popular Culture in Eighteenth-Century Paris* (Princeton, NJ: Princeton University Press, 1988), 297; Vaughn Scriber, *Inn Civility: Urban Taverns and Early American Civil Society* (New York: New York University Press, 2019), 3, 15, 28; Serena R. Zabin, *Dangerous Economies: Status and Commerce in Imperial New York* (Philadelphia: University of Pennsylvania Press, 2009), 57–58, 62–65, 136–137.

15. Jeffrey L. Pasley, *"The Tyranny of Printers": Newspaper Politics in the Early American Republic* (Charlottesville: University Press of Virginia, 2001), 6–7; Robert G. Parkinson, *The Common Cause: Creating Race and Nation in the American Revolution* (Chapel Hill: University of North Carolina Press, 2016), 14–15, 43–45; *New-York Mercury*, 15 March 1762; *New-York Gazette; or, the Weekly Post-Boy* (hereafter, *NYGP*), 12 February 1770.

16. J. Paul Hunter, *Before Novels: The Cultural Contexts of Eighteenth-Century English Fiction* (New York: W. W. Norton, 1990), 83; Narrett, *Inheritance*, 223–24, 225.

17. *New-York Journal; or, the General Advertiser* (hereafter, *NYJ*), 11 February 1768; *NYGP*, 15 February 1768; *New-York Gazette; and the Weekly Mercury* (hereafter, *NYGM*), 15 February 1768.

18. Gordon S. Wood, *The Creation of the American Republic, 1776–1787* (Chapel Hill: University of North Carolina Press, 1969), 53–65; Justin du Rivage, *Revolution against Empire: Taxes, Politics, and the Origins of American Independence* (New Haven, CT: Yale University Press, 2017), 5–6, 8–11; Joyce O. Appleby, *Liberalism and Republicanism in the Historical Imagination* (Cambridge, MA: Harvard University Press, 1992), 177–78; Taylor, "'Hook & Snivey,'" 1374–1376.

19. Cowan, *Social Life of Coffee*, 84, 86–88; Goodfriend, *Who Should Rule at Home?* 60–64.

20. *A CARD* (New York, 1768), Charles Evans and others, *American Bibliography: A Chronological Dictionary of All Books, Pamphlets and Periodical Publications Printed in the United States of America* [1639–1800], 14 vols. (Chicago and Worcester, MA, 1903–1959; rev. ed., www.readex.com; hereafter, Evans), No. 10848; Graham Russell Hodges, *New York City Cartmen, 1667–1850* (New York: New York University Press, 1986), 55–56; *The Political Works of James Harrington*, ed. J. G. A. Pocock (New York: Cambridge University Press, 1977), 163; Kevin J. Hayes, *The Library of John Montgomerie, Colonial Governor of New York and New Jersey* (Newark: University of Delaware Press, 2000), 40, 107.

21. *A CARD* (New York, 1768), Evans, No. 10849; Hodges, *New York City Cartmen*, 55; Allan Kulikoff, "Silence Dogood and the Leather-Apron Men," *Pennsylvania History* 81 (2014): 364–374, https://doi.org/10.5325/pennhistory.81.3.0364; Simon P. Newman,

"Benjamin Franklin and the Leather-Apron Men: The Politics of Class in Eighteenth-Century Philadelphia," *Journal of American Studies* 43 (2009): 161–175, https://www.jstor.org/stable/40464376.

22. *A Word of Advice* (New York, 1768), Evans, No. 11125; *A WORD OF ADVICE* (New York, 1768), Evans, No. 11126; Bernard Bailyn, *The Ideological Origins of the American Revolution* (Cambridge, MA: Harvard University Press, 1967), 232–246.

23. Thomas M. Truxes, *Defying Empire: Trading with the Enemy in Colonial New York* (New Haven, CT: Yale University Press, 2008), 172, 173; *Gotham*, 191–94; Michael Kammen, *Colonial New York: A History* (New York: Charles Scribner's Sons, 1975), 332.

24. Cathy Matson, *Merchants & Empire: Trading in Colonial New York* (Baltimore: Johns Hopkins University Press, 2003), 282; Gwyn, *Enterprising Admiral*, 36, 40, 48, 49–50; Gary B. Nash, *Urban Crucible: Social Change, Political Consciousness, and the Origins of the American Revolution* (Cambridge, MA: Harvard University Press, 1979), 250; Thomas L. Purvis, *Colonial America to 1763* (New York: Facts On File, 1999), 226; *DNB*.

25. Middleton, *Rights to Privileges*, 199–200; Varga, "Election Procedures and Practices," 262–263; Nash, *Urban Crucible*, 143; John Livingston to Robert Livingston, 28 August 1750, quoted in Milton M. Klein, *The American Whig: William Livingston of New York* (New York: Garland, 1993), 202–3, 453.

26. Quoted in Hodges, *New York City Cartmen*, 55; Ross J. S. Hoffman, *Edmund Burke: New York Agent* (Philadelphia: American Philosophical Society, 1956), 87; *A Political Creed for the Day* (New York, 1768), Evans, No. 11047; *A Better Creed than the Last* (New York, 1768), Evans, No. 10832; *To the Worthy Freeholders and Freemen* (New York, 1768), Evans, No. 11091; *NYJ*, 3 March 1768; Launitz-Schürer, *Loyal Whigs*, 55–56. For the Information of the Publick (New York, 1768), Evans, No. 10898; *NYJ*, 20 February 1768; *To the Freeholders and Freemen of the City and County of New-York* (New York, 1768), Evans, No. 41892.

27. *A Few Observations on the Conduct of the General Assembly* (New York, 1768), Library of Congress; Craig Bruce Smith, *American Honor: The Creation of the Nation's Ideals during the Revolutionary Era* (Chapel Hill: University of North Carolina Press, 2018), 207; Kim, *Landlord and Tenant*, 347, 389, 396.

28. *NYJ*, 25 February 1768; Philanthropos, *To the Freeholders and Freemen of the City and County of New-York* (New York: John Holt, 1768), Evans, No. 11040.

29. *THE OCCASIONALIST* (New York, 1768), Evans, No. 11017; *A PORTRAIT* (New York, 1768), Evans, No. 11048.

30. *The Voter's New Catechism* (New York, 1768), Evans, No. 11108; *NYJ*, 4 March 1768.

31. *Voter's New Catechism*; *NYJ*, 4 March 1768.

32. Kate Haulman, *The Politics of Fashion in Eighteenth-Century America* (Chapel Hill: University of North Carolina Press, 2011), 2–3, 4; Receipt, James DeLancey Papers, box 1, NHi; Zara Anishanslin, *Portrait of a Woman in Silk: Hidden Histories of the British Atlantic World* (New Haven, CT: Yale University Press, 2016), 70–73.

33. Anishanslin, *Portrait*, 72–76; Geoffrey Treasure, *The Huguenots* (New Haven, CT: Yale University Press, 2013), 370–371.

34. *Gotham*, 183; Brennan, *Public Drinking and Popular Culture*, 7, 135, 187; Carp, *Rebels Rising*, 77; W. Harrison Bayles, *Old Taverns of New York* (New York: Frank Allaben Genealogical Co., 1915), 114–115, 141; Stokes, *Iconography*, 4:715.

35. *NYGP*, 15 February 1768. This was also released as a broadside: *From Parker's New-York Gazette* (New York: James Parker, 1768), Evans, No. 10908.

36. Stout to DeLancey, 7 March 1768, DeLancey Family Papers, box 1, NHi.

37. Stout to DeLancey, 7 March 1768, DeLancey Family Papers, box 1, NHi; Peter Thompson, *Rum Punch & Revolution: Taverngoing and Public Life in Eighteenth-Century Philadelphia* (Philadelphia: University of Pennsylvania Press, 1998), chaps. 4–5; Charles Hemstreet, *Nooks and Corners of Old New York* (New York: Charles Scribner's Sons, 1889), 48; Tea Water Pump, New York City Misc. Mss. Collection, box 9, f. 1, NN; Alvin F. Harlow, *Old Bowery Days: The Chronicles of a Famous Street* (New York: D. Appleton, 1931), 104–105; James Nevlus, "The Ever-changing Bowery: New York City's Oldest Street Is More than Its Skid Row Reputation," ed. Sara Polsky, 4 October 2017, https://ny.curbed.com/2017/10/4/16413696/bowery-nyc-history-lower-east-side, accessed 12 May 2018; Gerard T. Koeppel, *Water for Gotham: A History* (Princeton, NJ: Princeton University Press, 2000), 34, 36.

38. Grim and Fareley Receipts, James DeLancey Papers, box 1, NHi; *MERCHANTS'-HALL* (New York, 1768), Evans, No. 10974; Launitz-Schürer, *Loyal Whigs*, 57.

39. *NYGM*, 14 March 1768; *NYGP*, 14 March 1768; *NYJ*, 17 March 1768. Bayard's votes were not printed in the local newspapers. The *NYGM* and *NYJ* both reported that there were 1,929 voters, and the *NYGP* reported there were "no less than 1960 Voters."

40. Roger J. Champagne, "Liberty Boys and Mechanics of New York City, 1764–1774," *Labor History* 8 (1967): 132, https://doi.org/10.1080/00236566708584011; Barbara Clark Smith, "Beyond the Vote: The Limits of Deference in Colonial Politics," *Early American Studies: An Interdisciplinary Journal* 3 (2005): 362, https://www.jstor.org/stable/23546526; *NYJ*, 3 March 1768; Hodges, *New York City Cartmen*, 55–56.

41. *A Copy of the Poll List, of the Election for Representatives for the City and County of New-York, 1761, 1768, and 1769* (New York: Francis Hart & Co., 1880; hereafter, *Copy of the Poll List*), 1768, 3, 10, 26, 28, 30, 50–52, 56; Judith L. Van Buskirk, *Generous Enemies: Patriots and Loyalists in Revolutionary New York* (Philadelphia: University of Pennsylvania Press, 2002), 188; *NYGP*, 22 February 1768; *Minutes of the Common Council of the City of New-York, 1675–1776*, 8 vols. (New York: Dodd, Mead, 1905), 7:127; *Ustick Family Register* (Dubuque, IA: William W. Ustick, 1894), 4; *NYJ*, 27 August 1767, 1 September 1768.

42. Nash, *Urban Crucible*, 365.

43. *Copy of the Poll List*, 1761, 1768.

44. James Vaughn, for instance, uses the terms "liberal" and "conservative" in *Politics of Empire*. For a critique, see Max Skjönsberg's review in *Parliamentary History* 39, no. 2 (2020): 354–357, https://doi-org.proxy01.its.virginia.edu/10.1111/1750-0206.12495.

45. Wetherhead to Johnson, 14 March 1768, in *The Papers of Sir William Johnson*, 2nd ed., rev. and exp., 20 vols. (Albany, NY: University of the State of New York, 1921–1965, 2008; hereafter, Johnson, *Papers*), 6:151–152; Charles Inglis to Samuel Johnson, 22 March 1768, quoted in Carl Bridenbaugh, *Mitre and Sceptre: Transatlantic Faiths, Ideas, Personalities, and Politics, 1689–1775* (New York: Oxford University Press, 1962), 261–262; Morris quoted in Bonomi, *Factious People*, 244–245.

46. Kim, *Landlord and Tenant*, 418; Bonomi, *Factious People*, 246, Appendix C; Marc Egnal, *A Mighty Empire: The Origins of the American Revolution* (Ithaca, NY: Cornell University Press, 1988), 181; Colden to the Earl of Hillsborough, 25 April 1768, in *N.Y. Col. Docs.*, 8:61; Mary Lou Lustig, *Privilege and Prerogative: New York's Provincial Elite, 1710–1776* (Madison, NJ: Fairleigh Dickinson University Press, 1995), 146; Gerlach, *Philip Schuyler*, 142–43; Michael D. Hattem, "'As Serves our Interest best': Political Economy

and the Logic of Resistance in New York City, 1765–1775," *NYH* 98 (2017): 55, https://doi.org/10.1353/nyh.2017.0037.

47. Klein, *American Whig*, 457, 517; J. G. A. Pocock, *The Machiavellian Moment: Florentine Political Thought and the Atlantic Republican Tradition* (Princeton, NJ: Princeton University Press, 1975), 390.

2. Too Much Power over Our Common People

1. *Journal of the Votes and Proceedings of the General Assembly of the Colony of New-York* (hereafter, *Assembly Journal*), 1, 10, 11, 12, Charles Evans and others, *American Bibliography: A Chronological Dictionary of All Books, Pamphlets and Periodical Publications Printed in the United States of America* [1639–1800], 14 vols. (Chicago and Worcester, MA, 1903–1959; rev. ed., www.readex.com; hereafter, Evans), No. 11007; *The Papers of George Washington: Revolutionary War Series*, ed. Philander D. Chase, Frank E. Grizzard Jr., Edward G. Lengel, David R. Hoth, and others, 30 vols. published to date), 5:292; Thomas Jones, *History of New York during the Revolutionary War*, 2 vols. (New York: Printed for the New-York Historical Society, 1879), 1:507; Patricia U. Bonomi, *A Factious People: Politics and Society in Colonial New York* (New York: Columbia University Press, 1971), 277.

2. *The Papers of Sir Francis Bernard*, ed. Colin Nicolson, 6 vols. (Charlottesville: Colonial Society of Massachusetts and the University of Virginia Press, 2007–2022; hereafter, Bernard, *Papers*), 4:359–362; Justin du Rivage, *Revolution against Empire: Taxes, Politics, and the Origins of American Independence* (New Haven, CT: Yale University Press, 2017), 151.

3. Bernard, *Papers*, 4:149–152; Hillsborough to the colonial governors, 21 April 1768, CO 5/241, f. 56–57, National Archives of the United Kingdom (hereafter, UK-KeNA); Andrew D. M. Beaumont, *Colonial America and the Earl of Halifax, 1748–1761* (New York: Oxford University Press, 2014), 4; Moore to Hillsborough, 7 July 1768, in *Documents Relative to the Colonial History of the State of New-York*, ed. E. B. O'Callaghan and Berthold Fernow, 15 vols. (Albany, NY: Weed, Parsons and Co., 1853–1887; hereafter, *N.Y. Col. Docs*), 8:80; du Rivage, *Revolution against Empire*, 148–149, 156; Joseph S. Tiedemann, *Reluctant Revolutionaries: New York City and the Road to Independence, 1763–1776* (Ithaca, NY: Cornell University Press, 1997), 128–129.

4. *Assembly Journal*, 8, 16, Evans, No. 11007; *Papers of John Adams*, ed. Robert J. Taylor, Gregg L. Lint, Sara Georgini, and others, 21 vols. published to date (Cambridge, MA: Harvard University Press, 1977–   ; hereafter, JA, *Papers*), 1:222–223; William Smith, *Historical Memoirs of William Smith*, ed. William H. W. Sabine, 3 vols. (New York: New York Times, 1969; hereafter, Smith, *Memoirs*), 1:46; Bernard, *Papers*, 4:133; *New-York Gazette; or, the Weekly Post-Boy* (hereafter, *NYGP*), 21 November 1768; *New-York Journal; or, the General Advertiser* (hereafter, *NYJ*), 17 November 1768.

5. *NYJ*, 1 December 1768.

6. T. H. Breen, *The Marketplace of Revolution: How Consumer Politics Shaped American Independence* (New York: Oxford University Press, 2004), 25; Livingston quoted in Tiedemann, *Reluctant Revolutionaries*, 130; Leopold S. Launitz-Schürer Jr., *Loyal Whigs and Revolutionaries: The Making of an American Revolution in New York, 1765–1776* (New York: New York University Press, 1980), 59–60.

7. *Assembly Journal*, 73–75, 79–80, Evans, No. 11007; Milton M. Klein, *The American Whig: William Livingston of New York* (New York: Garland, 1993), 460, 517; Tiedemann, *Reluctant Revolutionaries*, 120–122, 130–131.

8. Roger Champagne, "Family Politics versus Constitutional Principles: The New York Assembly Elections of 1768 and 1769," *William and Mary Quarterly* (hereafter, *WMQ*) 20, no. 1 (1963): 59, https://doi.org/10.2307/1921355; Bernard Friedman, "New York Assembly Elections of 1768 and 1769," *New York History* (hereafter, *NYH*) 45 (1965): 8, https://www.jstor.org/stable/23162463; Steve Pincus, *The Heart of the Declaration: The Founders' Case for an Activist Government* (New Haven, CT: Yale University Press, 2016), 18–19.

9. Christopher F. Minty, "Republicanism and the Public Good: A Re-examination of the DeLanceys, c. 1768–1769," *NYH* 97 (2016): 65–69, https://www.jstor.org/stable/90018206; *Minutes of the Common Council of the City of New-York, 1675–1776*, 8 vols. (New York: Dodd, Mead, 1905), 7:144–146; Jessica Choppin Roney, *Governed by a Spirit of Opposition: The Origins of American Political Practice in Philadelphia* (Baltimore: Johns Hopkins University Press, 2014), 76–77; Benjamin L. Carp, "Fire of Liberty: Firefighters, Urban Voluntary Culture, and the Revolutionary Movement," *WMQ* 58 (2001): 782, 785–787, 791–792, https://doi.org/10.2307/2674500.

10. Minty, "Republicanism and the Public Good," 69–72; Klein, *American Whig*, 458; *Assembly Journal*, 54, Evans, No. 11007; Don R. Gerlach, *Philip Schuyler and the American Revolution in New York 1733–1777* (Lincoln: University of Nebraska Press, 1964), 153–157; Cynthia A. Kierner, *Traders and Gentlefolk: The Livingstons of New York, 1675–1790* (Ithaca, NY: Cornell University Press, 1992), 175, 186. Alan Tully also writes that elections were held "infrequently." The 1768 and 1769 elections complicate this interpretation. See Alan Tully, *Forming American Politics: Ideas, Interests, and Institutions in Colonial New York and Pennsylvania* (Baltimore: Johns Hopkins University Press, 1994), 401.

11. Klein, *American Whig*, 491; Patricia U. Bonomi, *Under the Cope of Heaven: Religion, Society, and Politics in Colonial America* (New York: Oxford University Press, 2003), 51–54; Ruma Chopra, *Unnatural Rebellion: Loyalists in New York City during the Revolution* (Charlottesville: University of Virginia Press, 2011), 13.

12. James B. Bell, *Empire, Religion and Revolution in Early Virginia, 1607–1786* (Basingstoke: Palgrave, 2013), 165–166; Bell, *The Imperial Origins of the King's Church in Early America, 1607–1783* (Basingstoke: Palgrave, 2004), 214–215; Peter M. Doll, *Revolution, Religion, and National Identity: Imperial Anglicanism in British North America, 1745–1795* (Madison, NJ: Fairleigh Dickinson University Press, 2000), 35–65; Leslie Stephen and Sidney Lee, eds., *The Dictionary of National Biography*, 21 vols. plus supplements (New York and London, 1885–1901; repr. Oxford: Oxford University Press, 1959–1960; rev. ed., www.oxforddnb.com; hereafter, *DNB*).

13. Johnson to Secker, 30 October 1752, in *Samuel Johnson, President of King's College: His Career and Writings*, ed. Carol Schneider and Herbert W. Schneider, 4 vols. (New York: Columbia University Press, 1929) 1:163; *DNB*.

14. L. F. S. Upton, *The Loyal Whig: William Smith of New York & Quebec* (Toronto: University of Toronto Press, 1969), 62–63; *The Papers of Benjamin Franklin*, ed. Leonard W. Labaree, William B. Willcox, Claude A. Lopez, Barbara B. Oberg, Ellen R. Cohn, and others, 43 vols. published to date (New Haven, CT: Yale University Press, 1959– ;

hereafter, Franklin, *Papers*), 4:72; JA, *Papers*, 1:214; Chandler quoted in Carl Bridenbaugh, *Mitre and Sceptre: Transatlantic Faiths, Ideas, Personalities, and Politics, 1689–1775* (New York: Oxford University Press, 1962), 247.

15. Livingston to Welles, 2 February 1768, box 18, Johnson Family Papers, Sterling Memorial Library, Yale University (hereafter, CtY).

16. Klein, *American Whig*, 490, 507; Chandler to Johnson, 5 March 1768, in *The Papers of Sir William Johnson*, 2nd ed., rev. and exp., 20 vols. (Albany, NY: University of the State of New York, 1921–1965, 2008; hereafter, Johnson, *Papers*), 6:133; Heron Claim, AO 13/65, f. 508, UK-KeNA; Inglis to Johnson, 22 March 1768, quoted in Klein, *American Whig*, 487.

17. Parker to Benjamin Franklin, 18 April 1768, in Franklin, *Papers*, 15:100–102; same to same, 30 May 1769, in Franklin, *Papers*, 16:137–140; Andrew Eliot to Thomas Hollis, 18 April 1768, in *Collections of the Massachusetts Historical Society*, 79 vols. (Boston: Published by the Society, 1792–1939), 4:425; Ross N. Hebb, *Samuel Seabury and Charles Inglis: Two Bishops, Two Churches* (Madison, NJ: Fairleigh Dickinson University Press, 2010), 29; *New-York Mercury*, 4 April 1768.

18. Bonomi, *Under the Cope of Heaven*, 205–206; Bridenbaugh, *Mitre and Sceptre*, 298, 299.

19. Livingston to Noah Welles, 7 December 1754, Johnson Family Papers, CtY; Brendan McConville, *These Daring Disturbers of the Peace: The Struggle for Property and Power in New Jersey* (Ithaca, NY: Cornell University Press, 1999), 47–50; William Livingston to Peter R. Livingston, 10 November 1758, William Livingston Family Papers, reel 1, Massachusetts Historical Society.

20. *New-York Weekly Journal*, 13 February 1749; *Independent Reflector*, 22 March, 1, 12 April 1753; NYGP, 15, 29 February 1768; NYJ, 18 February 1768.

21. *New-York Gazette; and the Weekly Mercury* (hereafter, NYGM), 4 April 1768; Chandler to Johnson, 4 March 1768, in Johnson, *Papers*, 6:132–133.

22. NYGP, 2, 9 January 1769.

23. NYGP, 23 January 1769.

24. [Livingston], *REASONS For the present glorious combination of the dissenters in this city* (New York: James Parker, 1769), Evans, No. 11436; *New-York Mercury*, 8 September, 6 October 1755; NYGP, 16 January 1769; Bridenbaugh, *Mitre and Scepter*, 172; McConville, *Daring Disturbers*, 48.

25. NYGP, 16 January 1769; Bridenbaugh, *Mitre and Sceptre*, 120–127, quotes at 123, 127; John Webb Pratt, *Religion, Politics, and Diversity: The Church-State Theme in New York History* (Ithaca, NY: Cornell University Press, 1967), 40–47; Ned C. Landsman, "Roots, Routes, and Rootedness: Diversity, Migration, and Toleration in Mid-Atlantic Pluralism," *Early American Studies: An Interdisciplinary Journal* 2 (2004): 282–283, https://doi.org/10.1353/eam.2007.0042.

26. *REASONS*.

27. *REASONS*; Charles W. Baird, "Civil Status of the Presbyterians in the Province of New York," *Magazine of American History* 3 (1879): 593–628; Bridenbaugh, *Mitre and Sceptre*, 168, 208–209, 260–261.

28. John Langdon Sibley, Clifford K. Shipton, Conrad Edick Wright, Edward W. Hanson, and others, *Biographical Sketches of Graduates of Harvard University and Cambridge, Massachusetts*, 18 vols. published to date (Cambridge and Boston: C. W. Sever, Harvard

University Press, and the Massachusetts Historical Society, 1873–), 14:183–190; Peter R. Livingston to Oliver Wendell, 19 January 1769, Livingston Family Papers, Museum of the City of New York (hereafter, NNMus); John Wetherhead to Johnson, 9 January 1769, in Johnson, *Papers*, 6:575; John Morin Scott, Peter Van Brugh Livingston, and Theodorus Van Wyck, *To the Freeholders and Freemen of the City and County of New-York* (New York, 1769), Evans, No. 11456; *Advertisement* (New York, 1769), Evans, No. 11378.

29. *NYJ*, 5, 12 January 1769; Duane to Robert Livingston Jr., 1 June 1769, quoted in Launitz-Schürer, *Loyal Whigs*, 64.

30. *To the Freeholders and Freemen of the City and County of New-York* (New York, 1769), Evans, No. 11496; *Whereas a great Handle . . .* (New York, 1769), Evans, No. 11376; *NYGM*, 9 January 1769; *NYJ*, 5 January 1769.

31. Livingston, *To the Freeholders and Freemen, Of the City and County of New-York* (New York, 1769), Evans, No. 11311; *NYGM*, 9, 16 January 1769; Cruger, DeLancey, Jauncey, and Walton, *To the Freeholders and Freemen, of the City and County of New-York* (New York, 1769), Evans, No. 11229. See also *NYJ*, 12 January 1769.

32. Michael Kammen, *Colonial New York: A History* (New York: Charles Scriber's Sons, 1975), 330; C. A. Weslager, *The Stamp Act Congress* (Newark: University of Delaware Press, 1976), 81; John Austin Stevens Jr., *Colonial New York. Sketches Biographical and Historical 1768–1784* (New York: John F. Trow and Co., 1867), 6–8; Craig Steven Wilder, *Ebony & Ivy: Race, Slavery, and the Troubled History of America's Universities* (New York: Bloomsbury, 2013), 47, 52–53, 60; *DNB*.

33. Graham Russell Hodges, *New York City Cartmen, 1667–1850* (New York: New York University Press, 1986), 53.

34. Kierner, *Traders and Gentlefolk*, 74, 174, 256; Franklin Bowditch Dexter, *Biographical Sketches of the Graduates of Yale College with Annals of the College History*, 6 vols. (New York: Henry Holt and Co., 1885–1912), 1:422, 430–431, 571, 583–585; Walter S. Dunn Jr., *The New Imperial Economy: The British Army and the American Frontier, 1764–1768* (Westport, CT: Praeger, 2001), 125; Wilder, *Ebony & Ivy*, 58, 68–69, 104. For Philip Livingston's slave trading, see Eric Foner, "Columbia and Slavery: A Preliminary Report," 9–10, available at https://columbiaandslavery.columbia.edu/sites/default/files/content/Spread sheets/PreliminaryReport.pdf (accessed 9 July 2018).

35. Cuyler Reynolds, comp., *Genealogical and Family History of Southern New York and the Hudson River Valley*, 3 vols. (New York: Lewis Historical Publishing Co., 1914), 3:1402; *Year Book of the Sons of the Revolution in the State of New York* (New York: Exchange Printing Co., 1893), 310; *Portrait and Biographical Record of Suffolk County* (New York: Chapman Publishing Co., 1896), 958; Joyce D. Goodfriend, *Who Should Rule at Home? Confronting the Elite in British New York City* (Ithaca, NY: Cornell University Press, 2017), 57; *Minutes of the Common Council*, 6:86, 383; Edwin G. Burrows and Mike Wallace, *Gotham: A History of New York City to 1898* (New York: Oxford University Press, 1999), 187; Morrison H. Heckscher and Leslie Greene Bowman, *American Rococo, 1750–1775: Elegance in Ornament* (New York: Distributed by Harry N. Abrams, 1992), 110–111.

36. *NYJ*, 12, 26 January1769; *NYGM*, 16, 20 January 1769; Lester C. Olson, *Emblems of American Community in the Revolutionary Era* (Washington, DC: Smithsonian Institution Press, 1991), 21; Jay to Robert R. Livingston, January 1769, *The Selected Papers of John Jay*, ed. Elizabeth M. Nuxoll and others, 7 vols. (Charlottesville: University of Virginia Press, 2010–2021; hereafter, Jay, *Selected Papers*), 1:56–58; *Memorial History of the City of New-York*,

ed. James Grant Wilson, 4 vols. (New York: New-York History Co., 1892–1893), 2:467; Duane quoted in Bonomi, *Factious People*, 252.

37. *NYJ*, 12 January 1769.

38. *NYJ*, 19 January 1769; *The Querist, To the Freeholders and Freemen, of the City and County of New-York* (New York, 1769), Evans, No. 11431. See also *The Examiner, Addressed to the Freeholders and Freemen, of the City of New-York* (New York, 1769), Evans, No. 11253; *The Querist, To the Freeholders and Freemen, of the City and County of New-York* (New York, 1769), Evans, No. 11432; *A CARD* (New York, 1769), Evans, No. 11198; *A CARD* (New York, 1769), Evans, No. 11199.

39. *A Contrast* (New York, 1769), Evans, No. 11223.

40. *A Contrast* (New York, 1769), Evans, No. 11223; Jessica Choppin Roney, "'Effective Men' and Voluntary Associations in Philadelphia, 1725–1775," in *New Men: Manliness in Early America*, ed. Thomas A. Foster (New York: New York University Press, 2011), 157; John L. Brooke, "Ancient Lodges and Self-Created Societies: Voluntary Association and the Public Sphere in the Early Republic," in *Launching the "Extended Republic": The Federalist Era*, ed. Ronald Hoffman and Peter J. Albert (Charlottesville: University Press of Virginia, 1996), 283.

41. *NYGM*, 16 January 1769; *NYJ*, 19 January 1769; Albrecht Koschnik, "Voluntary Associations, Political Culture, and the Public Sphere in Philadelphia, 1780–1830" (PhD diss., University of Virginia, 2000), 234–237. For other DeLanceyite responses to Livingston, see A MEMBER OF THE CHURCH OF ENGLAND, *Observation on the Reasons . . .* (New York, 1769), Evans, No. 11394; THE FREEHOLDER, *Answer to the Reasons* (New York, 1769), Evans, No. 11260; THE FREEHOLDER, *A Continuation of the Answers, To the Reasons* (New York, 1769), Evans, No. 11261; THE FREEHOLDER, *Conclusion of the Answers, To the Reasons* (New York, 1769), Evans, No. 11262.

42. THE FREEHOLDER, *A Continuation of the Answers, To the Reasons*, Evans, No. 11261; *A Political Catechism*, which was attached to the rear of THE EXAMINER, *Addressed to the Freeholders and Freemen, of the City of New-York* (New York, 1769), Evans, No. 11254.

43. *Zutzliche Gegen Nachricht . . .* (New York, 1769), Evans, No. 11390; *Nun Will ich Valediciren Nun So Will ich* (New York, 1769), Evans, No. 11389.

44. Tessa Watt, *Cheap Print and Popular Piety, 1550–1640* (New York: Cambridge University Press, 1991), 5; Natascha Würzbach, *The Rise of the English Street Ballad, 1550–1650*, transl. Gayna Walls (New York: Cambridge University Press, 1990), 2, 228.

45. Hamilton, "Itinerarium," 57, Huntington Library, San Marino, CA; *NYJ*, 26 January 1769; *A SONG* (New York, 1769), Evans, No. 11472; *Nun Will ich Valediciren Nun So Will ich* (New York, 1769), Evans, No. 11389; Moses Coit Tyler, *The Literary History of the American Revolution 1763–1783* (New York: G. P. Putnam's Sons, 1905), 239.

46. Gordon S. Wood, *The Creation of the American Republic, 1776–1787* (Chapel Hill: University of North Carolina Press, 1969), 68; *NYGM*, 23 January 1769.

47. *NYJ*, 2 February 1769; *NYGM*, 6 February 1769; Watts and Duane quoted in Bonomi, *Factious People*, 253–254; Peter R. Livingston to Oliver Wendell, 30 January 1769, Livingston Family Papers, NNMus.

48. Bonomi, *Factious People*, 244–245; Milton M. Klein, "Democracy and Politics in Colonial New York," *NYH* 40, no. 3 (1959): 244–245, https://www.jstor.org/stable/23153664; Mary Lou Lustig, *Privilege and Prerogative: New York's Provincial Elite, 1710–*

1776 (Madison, NJ: Fairleigh Dickinson University Press, 1995), 149; Roger J. Champagne, "Liberty Boys and Mechanics of New York City, 1764–1774," *Labor History* 8 (1967): 132, https://doi.org/10.1080/00236566708584011; Hodges, *Cartmen*, 56–57. See also *A Copy of the Poll List, of the Election for Representatives for the City and County of New-York, 1761, 1768, and 1769* (New York: Francis Hart & Co., 1880), 1768, 1769.

49. Moore to Hillsborough, 21 January 1769, in *N.Y. Col. Docs.*, 8:148; Jack P. Greene, *The Quest for Power: The Lower Houses of Assembly in the Southern Royal Colonies, 1689–1776* (Chapel Hill: University of North Carolina Press, 1963), 3–50, esp. 11.

50. *NYGM*, 30 January 1769; *NYJ*, 2 February 1769; *NYGP*, 30 January 1769; Peter Van Schaack to Henry Van Schaack, 27 January 1769, in Henry C. Van Schaack, *The Life of Peter Van Schaack* (New York: D. Appleton and Co., 1842), 10.

3. The Minions of Tyranny and Despotism

1. *New-York Gazette; and the Weekly Mercury* (hereafter, *NYGM*), 6 February 1769; *The Livingston Family in America and Its Scottish Origins*, comp. Florence Van Rensselaer (New York: s.n., 1949), 85; Patricia U. Bonomi, "New York: The Royal Colony," *New York History* (hereafter, *NYH*) 82 (2001): 7, https://www.jstor.org/stable/42677750.

2. Leslie Stephen and Sidney Lee, eds., *The Dictionary of National Biography*, 21 vols. plus supplements; rev. ed., www.oxforddnb.com (New York and London, 1885–1901; repr. Oxford: Oxford University Press, 1959–1960; hereafter, *DNB*); George Wilson Bridges, *The Annals of Jamaica*, 2 vols. (London: John Murray, 1827–1828), 2:91–97, 105; Trevor Burnard, *Mastery, Tyranny, and Desire: Thomas Thistlewood and His Slaves in the Anglo-Jamaican World* (Chapel Hill: University of North Carolina Press, 2004), 10, 151, 171.

3. Moore to Hillsborough, 13 April 1769, CO 5/1100, f. 136–137, National Archives of the United Kingdom (hereafter, UK-KeNA); Moore to Hillsborough, 3 June 1769, CO 5/1100, f. 215–216, UK-KeNA; Moore to Hillsborough, 21 January 1769, in *Documents Relative to the Colonial History of the State of New-York*, ed. E. B. O'Callaghan and Berthold Fernow, 15 vols. (Albany, NY: Weed, Parsons, 1853–1887; hereafter, *N.Y. Col. Docs.*), 8:148–149; John Austin Stevens Jr., *Colonial New York. Sketches Biographical and Historical 1768–1784* (New York: John F. Trow and Co., 1867), 35–36; Colden, "Comments on Government in Gen.," n.d., Unpublished Scientific and Political Papers and Notes, reel 2, Colden Papers, New-York Historical Society (hereafter, NHi); Bonomi, "New York," 12–13; Leonard W. Labaree, *Royal Government in America: A Study of the British Colonial System before 1783* (New York: Frederick Ungar, 1930), 339.

4. Cynthia A. Kierner, *Traders and Gentlefolk: The Livingstons of New York, 1675–1790* (Ithaca, NY: Cornell University Press, 1992), 189–190; Joseph S. Tiedemann, *Reluctant Revolutionaries: New York City and the Road to Independence, 1763–1776* (Ithaca, NY: Cornell University Press, 1997), 136.

5. *Journal of the Votes and Proceedings of the General Assembly of the Colony of New-York* (hereafter, *Assembly Journal*), 7, 8, 24–25, 26–27, 39–40, 45, 63–65, 67, Charles Evans and others, *American Bibliography: A Chronological Dictionary of All Books, Pamphlets and Periodical Publications Printed in the United States of America* [1639–1800], 14 vols.; rev. ed., www.readex.com (Chicago and Worcester, MA, 1903–1959; hereafter, Evans), No. 11365; William Smith, *Historical Memoirs of William Smith*, ed. William H. W. Sabine, 3 vols. (New York: New York Times, 1969; hereafter, Smith, *Memoirs*), 1:52–53;

Leopold S. Launitz-Schürer Jr., *Loyal Whigs and Revolutionaries: The Making of an American Revolution in New York, 1765–1776* (New York: New York University Press, 1980), 78; Moore to Hillsborough, 26 May 1769, in *N.Y. Col. Docs.*, 8:167–168; Moore to Hillsborough, 3 June 1769, in *N.Y. Col. Docs.*, 8:170.

6. Launitz-Schürer, *Loyal Whigs*, 75–76; Kierner, *Traders and Gentlefolk*, 183–184; *Assembly Journal*, 70–71, Evans, No. 11365; Tiedemann, *Reluctant Revolutionaries*, 138; Edward Countryman, *A People in Revolution: The American Revolution and Political Society in New York, 1760–1790* (Baltimore: Johns Hopkins University Press, 1981), 82, 91–92. For the assembly disqualifying Livingston in 1769, see *Assembly Journal*, 8–9, Evans, No. 11774; Smith, *Memoirs*, 1:66, 69; George Dangerfield, *Chancellor Robert R. Livingston of New York 1746–1813* (New York: Harcourt, Brace, 1960), 42–43.

7. Francis D. Cogliano, *Emperor of Liberty: Thomas Jefferson's Foreign Policy* (New Haven, CT: Yale University Press, 2004), 9–10.

8. *DNB*; Smith, *Memoirs*, 1:67–68; Philip Peter Livingston to Hillsborough, 11 September 1768, in *N.Y. Col. Docs.*, 8:187; *New-York Chronicle*, 7–14, 14–21 September 1769; *NYGM*, 18 September 1769; *An Elegy* (New York, 1769), Evans, No. 11245.

9. Hugh Ledlie to John Lamb, 15 January 1788, John Lamb Papers, NHi; Colden to Henry Seymour Conway, 13 December 1765, in *The Letter Books of Cadwallader Colden*, 2 vols. (New York: Printed for the New-York Historical Society, 1877–1878; hereafter, Colden, *Letter Books*), 2:66–68; Colden to Jeffery Amherst, 24 June 1766, in Colden, *Letter Books*, 2:110–113; *The Montrésor Journals*, ed. G. D. Scull (New York: Printed for the New-York Historical Society, 1882), 351, 354; Clarkson to Unknown, 23 November 1765, Letter-book of David Clarkson, f. 3, Huntington Library, San Marino, CA (hereafter, CSmH).

10. Bonomi, "New York," 21–22; Anne Grant, *Memoirs of an American Lady* (Albany, NY: Joel Munsell, 1876), 266; A List for the Invitation to the Funeral of His Excellency Sir Henry Moore, Livingston Papers, NHi.

11. John M. Dixon, *The Enlightenment of Cadwallader Colden: Empire, Science, and Intellectual Culture in British New York* (Ithaca, NY: Cornell University Press, 2016), 148; Philip Ranlet, *Cadwallader Colden, 1688–1776: A Life between Revolutions* (Lanham, MD: Hamilton Books, 2019), 268; Bernard to Lord Barrington, 7 February 1768, in *The Papers of Sir Francis Bernard*, ed. Colin Nicolson, 6 vols. (Charlottesville: Colonial Society of Massachusetts and the University of Virginia Press, 2007–2022), 4:93.

12. *NYGM*, 21 May 1770.

13. *Assembly Journal*, 1, 14–15, Evans, No. 11774; *Assembly Journal*, 4, Evans, No. 11365.

14. Clinton to Pelham (in Colden's hand), 8 December 1757, George Clinton Papers, box 2, f. 10, William L. Clements Library, University of Michigan (hereafter, MiU-C); Clinton, State of the Province, George Clinton Papers, box 2, f. 12, MiU-C.

15. *Assembly Journal*, 1, 14–15, Evans, No. 11774; *Assembly Journal*, 4, Evans, No. 11365; *NYGM*, 4 December 1769; *New-York Gazette; or, the Weekly Post-Boy* (hereafter, *NYGP*), 4 December 1769; *New-York Journal; or, the General Advertiser* (hereafter, *NYJ*), 7 December 1769; Hillsborough to Colden, 18 January 1770, CO 5/1101, f. 16–17, UK-KeNA; Colden to Hillsborough, 4 October 1769, in *N.Y. Col. Docs.*, 8:189; Philip Peter Livingston to Hillsborough, 11 September 1769, in *N.Y. Col. Docs.*, 8:188–189; Smith, *Memoirs*, 1:68; Colden to Hillsborough, 4 October. 1769, in Smith, *Memoirs*, 8:189; Ranlet, *Cadwallader Colden*, 358; Stefan Bielinski, "Harmanus Schuyler," New York State Museum,

https://exhibitions.nysm.nysed.gov/albany/bios/s/harschuyler.html (accessed 25 December 2019).

16. Smith, *Memoirs*, 1:68–69; Bonomi, "New York," 14.

17. Smith, *Memoirs*, 1:69; David Clarkson to Unknown, 22 December 1769, Letterbook of David Clarkson, f. 78, CSmH; Bonomi, "New York," 14.

18. Justin du Rivage, *Revolution against Empire: Taxes, Politics, and the Origins of American Independence* (New Haven, CT: Yale University Press, 2017), 112; Steven Pincus, "The Rise and Fall of Empires: An Essay in Economic and Political Liberty," *Journal of Policy History* 29 (2017): 305–318, doi:10.1017/S0898030617000070; Virginia D. Harrington, *The New York Merchant on the Eve of the American Revolution* (New York: Columbia University Press, 1935), 317, 318, 323.

19. *Assembly Journal*, 14, 86–87, Evans, No. 11365; Moore to Hillsborough, 29 May 1769, CO 5/1100, f. 158–159, UK-KeNA; Hillsborough to Moore, 15 July 1769, CO 5/1100, f. 224–225, UK-KeNA Moore to Hillsborough, 9 September 1769, CO 5/1000, f. 269, UK-KeNA; Colden to Hillsborough, 11 September 1769, CO 5/1100, f. 270, UK-KeNA; Colden to Hillsborough, 16 October 1769, CO 5/1100, f. 275–276, UK-KeNA.

20. *Assembly Journal*, 26–27, Evans, No. 11774; Benjamin L. Carp, *Rebels Rising: Cities and the American Revolution* (New York: Oxford University Press, 2007), 177, 182, 194–195.

21. *Assembly Journal*, 26–27, Evans, No. 11774; Mary Patterson Clarke, *Parliamentary Privilege in the American Colonies* (New Haven, CT: Yale University Press, 1943), 173, 175, 177–178.

22. *NYJ*, 21 December 1769.

23. James Duane to John Dickinson, 12 November 1770, quoted in Alan Tully, *Forming American Politics: Ideas, Interests, and Institutions in Colonial New York and Pennsylvania* (Baltimore: Johns Hopkins University Press, 1994), 366.

24. Peter R. Livingston to Robert Livingston Jr., 14 May 1769, quoted in Patricia U. Bonomi, *A Factious People: Politics and Society in Colonial New York* (New York: Columbia University Press, 1971), 258–259; Peter R. Livingston to Schuyler, 27 February 1769, Philip Schuyler Papers, box 23, Manuscripts and Archives Division, New York Public Library (hereafter, NN); Hugh Wallace to Sir William Johnson, 7 January 1769, in William Johnson, *The Papers of Sir William Johnson*, 2nd ed., rev. and exp., 20 vols. (Albany, NY: University of the State of New York, 1921–1965, 2008; hereafter, Johnson, *Papers*), 6:570–571.

25. John Gilbert McCurdy, "From Fort George to the Fields: The Public Space and the Military Geography of Revolutionary New York City," *Journal of Urban History* 44 (2018): 637–638, https://doi.org/10.1177%2F0096144218759028; John W. Shy, *Toward Lexington: The Role of the British Army in the Coming of the American Revolution* (Princeton, NJ: Princeton University Press, 1965), 187; du Rivage, *Revolution against Empire*, 152–153; Rohit T. Aggarwala, "'I want a Packet to arrive': Making New York City the Headquarters of British America, 1696–1783," *NYH* 97 (2017): 7–39, https://www.jstor.org/stable/90018770; John Gilbert McCurdy, *Quarters: The Accommodation of the British Army and the Coming of the American Revolution* (Ithaca, NY: Cornell University Press, 2019), 175; *NYGP*, 14 August 1766.

26. Hector Bolitho and Derek Peel, *The Drummonds of Charing Cross* (London: Allen & Unwin, 1967), 56–58; Correspondence from James McEvers relating to Drummonds

North American Pay Agency, DR/464/1/12, Royal Bank of Scotland Archives; Correspondence from Charles McEvers, DR/464/1/14, Royal Bank of Scotland Archives; Joseph S. Tiedemann, "Interconnected Communities: The Middle Colonies on the Eve of the American Revolution," *Pennsylvania History* 76, no. 1 (2009): 20, https://www.jstor.org/stable/27778871.

27. Bolitho and Peel, *Drummonds*, 58; Correspondence from Messrs. Watts and McEvers, DR/464/1/15–16, Royal Bank of Scotland Archives; *A Copy of the Poll List, of the Election for Representatives for the City and County of New-York*, 1761, 1768, and 1769 (New York: Francis Hart & Co., 1880), 1769, 15; Peter Goelet Papers, Special Collections Research Center, William & Mary; *NYGM*, 7 March 1768, 16 January 1769.

28. Correspondence from Messrs. Watts and McEvers, DR/464/1/15, Royal Bank of Scotland Archives; A List of Sundry Bills drawn by John Watts and Charles McEvers, DR/464/3/5, Royal Bank of Scotland Archives.

29. Steve Pincus, *The Heart of the Declaration: The Founders' Case for an Activist Government* (New Haven, CT: Yale University Press, 2016), 2–4, 7, 26–27; Steven Pincus, Tiraana Bains, and A. Zuercher Reichardt, "Thinking the Empire Whole," *History Australia* 16, no. 4 (2019): 625, 627, https://doi.org/10.1080/14490854.2019.1670692. For Watts and McEvers's thoughts on the economy and the role the British Army could play, see Correspondence from Messrs. Watts & McEvers in New York, DR/464/1/15, Royal Bank of Scotland Archives.

30. *NYGP*, 12 February 1770.

31. *Assembly Journal*, 86–87, Evans, No. 11365; Roger J. Champagne, *Alexander McDougall and the American Revolution* (Schenectady, NY: New York State American Revolution Bicentennial Commission/Union College Press, 1975), 18; Evert Bancker and Gerard Bancker, Barrack Master Accounts, 1768–1774, NN; Pincus, "Rise and Fall of Empires," 310; *NYJ*, 21 January 1768; Steven Pincus, *1688: The First Modern Revolution* (New Haven, CT: Yale University Press, 2009), 376.

32. *Assembly Journal*, 43–44, Evans, No. 11774; Colden to Hillsborough, 16 December 1769, CO 5/1101, f. 10–11, 12–13, UK-KeNA; Don R. Gerlach, *Philip Schuyler and the American Revolution in New York 1733–1777* (Lincoln: University of Nebraska Press, 1964), 202–203.

33. Moore to the Duke of Richmond, 23 August 1766, in *N.Y. Col. Docs.*, 7:867; Smith, *Memoirs*, 1:67.

34. Smith, *Memoirs*, 1:67; *NYGP*, 12 February 1770.

35. *Middlesex Journal*, 30 January–1 February 1770.

36. Private Association, 12 November 1769, Private Owner, 2021.

37. *Biographical Directory of the United States Congress, 1774–2005* (Washington, DC, 2005; rev. ed., bioguide.congress.gov); Richard M. Ketchum, *Divided Loyalties: How the American Revolution came to New York* (New York: Henry Holt, 2002), 99; Launitz-Schürer, *Loyal Whigs*, 80–84; Tiedemann, *Reluctant Revolutionaries*, 141–143; Tully, *Forming American Politics*, 251; *NYJ*, 10 May 1770; Bonomi, "New York," 18. See also Liam Riordan, "A Loyalist Who Loved His Country Too Much: Thomas Hutchinson, Historian of Colonial Massachusetts," *New England Quarterly* 90, no. 3 (2017): 344–388, https://doi.org/10.1162/tneq_a_00624.

38. John A. Garraty, Mark C. Carnes, and Paul Betz, eds., *American National Biography* (New York: Oxford University Press, 1999–2002; 24 vols. plus supplement; rev. ed., www

.anb.org); Champagne, *Alexander McDougall*, 5–6; Kierner, *Traders and Gentlefolk*, 192–193; Herbert L. Osgood, ed., "The Society of Dissenters founded at New York in 1769," *American Historical Review* 6 (1901): 500, https://doi.org/10.2307/1833513.

39. *NYGP*, 12 February 1770; *To the Betrayed Inhabitants of New York* (New York: [James Parker,] 1769), Evans, No. 11319; Champagne, *Alexander McDougall*, 12–14; Bonomi, *Factious People*, 268.

40. Gordon Bond, *James Parker: A Printer on the Eve of Revolution* (Union, NJ: Garden State Legacy, 2010), 483–484; Nan A. Rothschild, *New York City Neighborhoods: The 18th Century* (Clinton Corners, NY: Percheron Press, 2008), 78; *Gotham*, 175.

41. McCurdy, *Quarters*, 64; *NYGM*, 25 December 1769; *NYJ*, 10 May 1770.

42. Kierner, *Traders and Gentlefolk*, 192–194.

43. Bonomi, *Factious People*, 260–262.

44. Du Rivage, *Revolution against Empire*, passim, esp. 8, 44–52.

45. Tiedemann, *Reluctant Revolutionaries*, 143.

46. Colden, *By the Honourable Cadwallader Colden* (New York, 1769), Evans, No. 11362; Colden, *By the Honourable Cadwallader Colden* (New York, 1769), Evans, No. 11363; *Assembly Journal*, 45–49, Evans, No. 11774; Gerard Bancker to William Alexander, 19 December 1769, William Alexander Papers, NHi (accessed on microfilm at David Library of the American Revolution [now at American Philosophical Society], reel no. 404).

47. Return of Small Beer, New York City Misc. Mss., box 9, NHi; Evert Bancker Jr., Blotter, 1770, Bancker Family Papers, NHi; Paul E. Kopperman, "'The Cheapest Pay': Alcohol Abuse in the Eighteenth-Century British Army," *Journal of Military History* 60 (1996): 445–470, https://www.proquest.com/docview/195635761; David Hackett Fischer, *Liberty and Freedom: A Visual History of America's Founding Ideas* (New York: Oxford University Press, 2005), 37–49; Yvonne Korshak, "The Liberty Cap as a Revolutionary Symbol in America and France," *Smithsonian Studies in American Art* 1 (1987): 52, 54–56, 57.

48. McCurdy, "From Fort George to the Fields," 635–637.

49. *NYJ*, 1 March 1770; *NYGP*, 5 February 1770; Lee R. Boyer, "Lobster Backs, Liberty Boys, and Laborers in the Streets: New York's Golden Hill and Nassau Street Riots," New-York Historical Society, *Quarterly* 57, (1973): 289–292; Carp, *Rebels Rising*, 67, 90–92; *News from the Liberty-Pole; or a Friday Morning's Conversation* (New York, 1769), Evans, No. 11387; *The Procession with the Standard of Fiction: A Cantata* (New York, 1770), Evans, No. 11827; McCurdy, "From Fort George to the Fields," 637.

50. Carp, *Rebels Rising*, 67; Smith, *Memoirs*, 1:72; Resolution of the Inhabitants of the City of New York, New York City Misc. Mss., box 9, no. 23, NHi; *NYJ*, 18, 25 January 1770; [Lamb], *To the PUBLIC* (New York, 1770), NHi; Boyer, "Lobster Backs," 286; Philip Ranlet, *The New York Loyalists* (Knoxville: University of Tennessee Press, 1986), 30–31.

51. McCurdy, "From Fort George to the Fields," 637; McCurdy, *Quarters*, 195–196; Henry B. Dawson, *The Sons of Liberty in New York* (New York, 1859), 112–116; Isaac Q. Leake, *Memoir of the Life and Times of General John Lamb, an Officer of the Revolution* (Albany, NY: Joel Munsell, 1857), 54–59; Sixteenth Regiment of Foot, *God and a Soldier all Men doth adore* (New York, 1770), Evans, Nos. 11936, 43033; *NYGP*, 5 February 1770; *NYJ*, 1 March 1770; Hicks, *To the Inhabitants* (New York, 1770), Evans, No. 11776; *Gotham*, 211; Boyer, "Lobster Backs," 281–307; Shy, *Toward Lexington*, 178–190; Colden to

Hillsborough, 21 February 1770, in *N.Y. Col. Docs.*, 8:208–211; Macleod to Johnson, 24 January [1770], in Johnson, *Papers*, 7:351–352.

52. *The Correspondence of Thomas Gage*, comp. and ed. Clarence Edwin Carter, 2 vols. (New Haven, CT: Yale University Press, 1931), 1:246; Boyer, "Lobster Backs," 282, 283; McCurdy, "From Fort George to the Fields," 637; Inglis to Johnson, 28 March 1770, in Johnson, *Papers*, 7:509.

53. *Minutes of the Common Council of the City of New-York, 1675–1776*, 8 vols. (New York: Dodd, Mead, 1905), 7:203–204.

54. *Minutes of the Common Council*, 7:203–204; *Copy of the Poll List*, 1768, 9, 17, 21, 24, 25; *Copy of the Poll List*, 1769, 7, 16, 19; McCurdy, *Quarters*, 196; Tiedemann, *Reluctant Revolutionaries*, 148–149; I. N. Phelps Stokes, *The Iconography of Manhattan Island, 1498–1909*, 6 vols. (New York: R. H. Dodd, 1915–1928), 4:805.

55. Stokes, *Iconography*, 4:805; *NYGM*, 5 February 1770; *To the Sons of Liberty in this City* (New York, 1770), Evans, No. 11891; *NYJ*, 8 February 1770; *New-York American*, 20 May 1833; Macleod to Johnson, 5 February 1770, in Johnson, *Papers*, 7:371; *Gotham*, 211; Leake, *Memoir*, 58–59; Martha J. Lamb, *History of the City of New York*, 3 vols. (New York: Valentine's Manual, Inc., 1877–1896), 1:747; Smith, *Memoirs*, 1:73; Fischer, *Liberty and Freedom*, 46–47. For DeLancey members of the Common Council at this time, see *Minutes of the Common Council*, 7:193.

56. *Gotham*, 211; Smith, *Memoirs*, 1:73–76; Bonomi, *Factious People*, 269; Colden to Hillsborough, 21 February 1770, in *N.Y. Col. Docs.*, 8:208; Benjamin Young Prime to Petrus Tappen, 20 April 1770, in *New York City during the American Revolution* (New York: Privately Printed, 1861), 50–51, 52.

4. All the Sons of Liberty

1. Edward Hagaman Hall, *The Old Martyrs' Prison* (New York: American Scenic and Historic Preservation Society, 1902), 6–7, 8–13; *A Copy of the Poll List, of the Election for Representatives for the City and County of New-York* (New York: Francis Hart & Co., 1880), 1768, 31; *Copy of the Poll List*, 1769, 23.

2. Joseph S. Tiedemann, *Reluctant Revolutionaries: New York City and the Road to Independence, 1763–1776* (Ithaca, NY: Cornell University Press, 1997), 76; Nick Bunker, *An Empire on the Edge: How Britain Came to Fight America* (New York: Knopf, 2014), 209–210; Leopold S. Launitz-Schürer Jr., *Loyal Whigs and Revolutionaries: The Making of an American Revolution in New York, 1765–1776* (New York: New York University Press, 1980), 33–34; Patricia U. Bonomi, *A Factious People: Politics and Society in Colonial New York* (New York: Columbia University Press, 1971), 235; Roger J. Champagne, "New York's Radicals and the Coming of Independence," *Journal of American History* (hereafter, *JAH*) 51, no. 1 (1964) 21–40, esp. 21, https://doi.org/10.2307/1917932. A notable exception, however, is Roger J. Champagne, *Alexander McDougall and the American Revolution* (Schenectady, NY: New York State American Revolution Bicentennial Commission/Union College Press, 1975), 13.

3. Jill Lepore, *New York Burning: Liberty, Slavery, and Conspiracy in Eighteenth-Century Manhattan* (New York: Knopf, 2006), 20, 66–67, 221–223; Champagne, *Alexander McDougall*, 27–28.

4. *New-York Journal; or, the General Advertiser* (hereafter, *NYJ*), 15 February 1770.

5. *NYJ*, 15 February 1770.

6. *NYJ*, 15 February 1770; *Historical Memoirs of William Smith*, ed. William H. W. Sabine, 3 vols. (New York: New York Times, 1969; hereafter, Smith, *Memoirs*), 1:74–75; Benjamin Roberts to Sir William Johnson, 12 February 1770, in *The Papers of Sir William Johnson*, 2nd ed., rev. and exp., 20 vols. (Albany, NY: University of the State of New York, 1921–1965, 2008; hereafter, Johnson, *Papers*), 7:389; Macleod to Johnson, 19 February 1770, in Johnson, *Papers*, 7:397–398.

7. Bruce Mann, *Republic of Debtors: Bankruptcy in the Age of American Independence* (Cambridge, MA: Harvard University Press, 2002), 86; *NYJ*, 15 February, 8 March 1770; Tiedemann, *Reluctant Revolutionaries*, 151; Mary Lou Lustig, *Privilege and Prerogative: New York's Provincial Elite, 1710–1776* (Madison, NJ: Fairleigh Dickinson University Press, 1995), 154; Colden to Hillsborough, 21 February 1770, in *Documents Relative to the Colonial History of the State of New-York*, ed. E. B. O'Callaghan and Berthold Fernow, 15 vols. (Albany, NY: Weed, Parsons and Co., 1853–1887), 8:208.

8. Lustig, *Privilege and Prerogative*, 153–154; Pauline Maier, "John Wilkes and American Disillusionment with Britain," *William and Mary Quarterly* (hereafter, WMQ) 20 (1963): 373–395, https://doi.org/10.2307/1918953; *Boston Gazette*, 26 February 1770. For more on Scots in New York, see Stephen Saunders Webb, *Marlborough's America* (New Haven, CT: Yale University Press, 2013), 322–323; Joyce D. Goodfriend, *Before the Melting Pot: Society and Culture in Colonial New York City, 1664–1730* (Princeton, N.J.: Princeton University Press, 1992), 142–144.

9. *The Watchman* (New York: John Holt, 1770), Evans, Nos. 11916, 11917, 11919, 11920, 11921; Tiedemann, *Reluctant Revolutionaries*, 151; Champagne, *Alexander McDougall*, 28. Some thought that Benjamin Young Prime was the author of the series, and Prime felt compelled to carry weapons as he walked the streets. See I. N. Phelps Stokes, *The Iconography of Manhattan Island, 1498–1909*, 6 vols. (New York: R. H. Dodd, 1915–1928), 6:31.

10. Daniel J. Hulsebosch, *Constituting Empire: New York and the Transformation of Constitutionalism in the Atlantic World, 1664–1830* (Chapel Hill: University of North Carolina Press, 2005), 125–127.

11. *New-York Gazette; or, the Weekly Post-Boy* (hereafter, NYGP), 12, 16 February, 8 March 1770; Luke John Feder, "The Sense of the City: Politics and Culture in Pre-Revolutionary New York City" (PhD diss., State University of New York at Stony Brook, 2010), 150–191; Maier, "John Wilkes," 386.

12. *NYGM*, 16 April 1770; *NYGP*, 12 March 1770.

13. Edmund S. Morgan, *Prologue to Revolution: Sources and Documents on the Stamp Act Crisis, 1764–1766* (Chapel Hill: University of North Carolina Press, 1959), 134–142; Justin du Rivage, *Revolution against Empire: Taxes, Politics, and the Origins of American Independence* (New Haven, CT: Yale University Press, 2017), 108–109, 138–141.

14. See especially Daniel T. Rodgers, "Republicanism: The Career of a Concept," *JAH* 79, no. 1 (1992): 11–38, https://doi.org/10.2307/2078466.

15. *NYJ*, 22 March 1770; *NYGM*, 26 March 1770.

16. *NYJ*, 22 March 1770; *NYGM*, 26 March 1770; DeLancey to Rockingham, 4 February 1769, Wentworth Woodhouse Muniments, Sheffield City Archives and Local Studies Library (hereafter, UkSh); DeLancey to Rockingham, 8 November 1765, Wentworth Woodhouse Muniments, UkSh. The Stamp Act was repealed on 18 March 1766, but because 18 March 1770 fell on the Sabbath, New Yorkers held their celebrations the

following day. John Holt printed a list of the diners in his newspaper, stating that 233 men were present. See *NYJ*, 12 April 1770.

17. John Austin Stevens Jr., *Colonial Records of the New York Chamber of Commerce, 1768–1784* (New York: John F. Trow and Co., 1867), 14, 21, 46–48, 56–57, 62, 67–68, 71, 74, 82. For instances when the chamber announced its aims, see *NYGM*, 10 July 1769; *NYJ*, 3 October 1769.

18. Martha J. Lamb, "The Golden Age of Colonial New York," *Magazine of American History* 24 (1890), 17, 19. Isaac Low, a DeLancey supporter and a merchant, proposed incorporation on 5 December 1769. See Stevens, *Colonial Records*, 1, 29, 67, 79–82; R. J. Bennett, *Local Business Voice: The History of Chambers of Commerce in Britain, Ireland, and Revolutionary America, 1760–2011* (New York: Oxford University Press, 2011), 133, 136; Lee Friedman, "The First Chamber of Commerce in the United States," *Bulletin of the Business Historical Society* 21 (1947): 137–143, doi:10.1017/S0007680500009727.

19. Benjamin Roberts to Sir William Johnson, 26 February 1770, in Johnson, *Papers*, 7:416; Oscar Handlin and Mary F. Handlin, "Origins of the American Business Corporation," *Journal of Economic History* 5 (1945): 1–23; Jessica Choppin Roney, "'First Movers in Every Useful Undertaking': Formal Voluntary Associations in Philadelphia, 1725–1775" (PhD diss., Johns Hopkins University, 2008), 113–123.

20. Ben Marsh, "The Meanings of Georgia's Eighteenth-Century Seals," *Georgia Historical Society Quarterly* 96 (2012), 195, 196, 200, 203, https://www.jstor.org/stable/23622209.

21. *The Book of Mottos* (London: Henry Washbourne, 1841), non.

22. Joseph Spence, *Polymetis* (London: Printed for R. Dodsley, 1747), 104, 146, 108; David Hackett Fischer, *Liberty and Freedom: A Visual History of America's Founding Ideas* (New York: Oxford University Press, 2005), 61–67; Matilde Battistini, *Symbols and Allegories in Art* (Los Angeles: J. Paul Getty Museum, 2005), 60–61; Steven Olderr, *Symbolism: A Comprehensive Dictionary*, 2nd ed. (Jefferson, NC: McFarland, 2012), 50, 58, 67, 81.

23. *The Marine Society of the City of New York, in the State of New York* (New York: Printed for the Society, 1877), 17–23.

24. Spence, *Polymetis*, 103; Battistini, *Symbols*, 128–132, 294–309; Marsh, "Meanings of Georgia's Eighteenth-Century Great Seals," 204, 206–207; Marina Warner, *Monuments & Maidens: The Allegory of the Female Form* (New York: Wiedenfeld and Nicolson, 1985), 213–328; Olderr, *Symbolism*, 38.

25. Paul A. Gilje, "The Rise of Capitalism in the Early Republic," *Journal of the Early Republic* 16 (1996): 164–165, https://doi.org/10.2307/3124244; Pauline Maier, "The Revolutionary Origins of the American Corporation," *WMQ* 50 (1993): 51–84, https://doi.org/10.2307/2947236; Stanley Elkins and Eric McKitrick, *The Age of Federalism* (New York: Oxford University Press, 1993), 451, 453–455, 456; Joyce Appleby, *Capitalism and a New Social Order: The Republican Vision of the 1790s* (New York: New York University Press, 1984), 55–56, 66. Quotes taken from *NYJ*, 8 November 1770, 25 July 1771; *NYGP*, 30 November 1769, 29 November 1770.

26. The DeLancey voters were John Alsop, Theophylact Bache, Joseph Bull, John Cruger, John Harris Cruger, Gerardus Duyckink, James Jauncey, Edward Laight, Leonard Lispenard, Isaac Low, Gabriel H. Ludlow, Abraham Lynsen, Thomas Marston, Charles McEvers, Lewis Pintard, Thomas Randall, Isaac Sears, John Thurman Sr., Augustus Van Horne, Samuel Verplanck, Gerard Walton, Jacob Walton, Thomas Walton,

William Walton, John Wetherhead, Henry White, and Thomas White. Van Zandt, Mc-Donald, and Bogart voted for all the Livingston candidates, but Sharpe voted only for John Morin Scott. See *Copy of the Poll List*, 1769.

27. These men were *John Alsop, Theophylact Bache,* Gerard W. Beekman, *Joseph Bull, John Cruger, John Harris Cruger,* William Imlay, *James Jauncey, Edward Laight, Leonard Lispenard, Isaac Low, Gabriel H. Ludlow,* George W. Ludlow, John Moore, Thomas W. Moore, Miles Sherbrooke, *John Thurman Sr., Augustus Van Horne, Samuel Verplanck,* Alexander Wallace, *Jacob Walton, Thomas Walton,* and *William Walton.* Those who voted for the DeLanceys in 1769 are in *italics.* See *Copy of the Poll List*, 1769.

28. *NYJ*, 12 April 1770.

29. These voters and members were Theophylact Bache, John Harris Cruger, Robert Dale, Nicholas Fletcher, Linus King, Henry Law, Leonard Lispenard, Isaac Low, James Jauncey, Charles McEvers, Thomas Randall, Daniel Stiles, Willet Taylor, William Thompson, Normand Tolmie, Samuel Verplanck, Henry White, Jacob Walton, and William Walton. James Jauncey and Jacob Walton stood in the election—and were elected—and thus could not vote for the entire DeLancey ticket because they did not vote for themselves. See *Copy of the Poll List*, 1769.

30. *NYJ*, 12 April 1770.

31. *NYJ*, 12 April 1770; Carl L. Becker, *The History of Political Parties in the Province of New York, 1760–1776* (Madison, WI: [s.n.], 1909), 8; Isaac Q. Leake, *Memoir of the Life and Times of General John Lamb, an Officer of the Revolution* (Albany, NY: Joel Munsell, 1857), 4; Benjamin L. Carp, *Rebels Rising: Cities and the American Revolution* (New York: Oxford University Press, 2007), 91, 92; Emma Hart, *Building Charleston: Town and Society in the Eighteenth-Century Atlantic World* (Charlottesville: University of Virginia Press, 2010), 11.

32. Dirk Hoerder, *Crowd Action in Revolutionary Massachusetts, 1765–1780* (New York: Academic Press, 1977); Gary B. Nash, *Urban Crucible: Social Change, Political Consciousness, and the Origins of the American Revolution* (Cambridge, MA: Harvard University Press, 1979); Richard Alan Ryerson, *The Revolution is Now Begun: The Radical Committees of Philadelphia, 1765–1776* (Philadelphia: University of Pennsylvania Press, 1978); Jessica Choppin Roney, *Governed by a Spirit of Opposition: The Origins of American Political Practice in Philadelphia* (Baltimore: Johns Hopkins University Press, 2014).

33. *NYGP*, 29 February 1768; *NYJ*, 15 June 1769; *NYGM*, 13 November 1769.

34. *NYGM*, 5, 12, 19, 26 February, 5, 12 March 1770.

35. Simon P. Newman "'The Friends of Equality and of the French Revolution': Toasts and Popular Opposition to George Washington's Foreign Policy," in *L'Amérique: Des colonies aux républiques,* ed. Lucia Bergamasco and Marie-Jeanne Rossignol (Paris: Institut d'Éudes Anglophones, 2005), 131–162; Benjamin Irvin, *Clothed in Robes of Sovereignty: The Continental Congress and the People Out of Doors* (New York: Oxford University Press, 2011), 146–147.

36. *NYJ*, 12 April 1770; Albrecht Koschnik, "Fashioning a Federalist Self: Young Men and Voluntary Association in Early Nineteenth-Century Philadelphia," *Explorations in Early American Culture* 4 (2000): 244, https://www.jstor.org/stable/23549301; Peter Thompson, *Rum Punch & Revolution: Taverngoing and Public Life in Eighteenth-Century Philadelphia* (Philadelphia: University of Pennsylvania Press, 1998), 111–144.

37. Roney, "'First Movers,'" 35–37; *NYJ*, 22 March, 12 April 1770; *NYGM*, 26 March 1770.

38. *NYJ*, 12 April 1770; *NYGM*, 30 April 1770; Thomas Jones, *History of New York during the Revolutionary War*, 2 vols. (New York: Printed for the New-York Historical Society, 1879), 1:27.

39. Virginia D. Harrington, *The New York Merchant on the Eve of the American Revolution* (New York: Columbia University Press, 1935), 349.

40. For issues of allegiance, see Christopher F. Minty "'Of One Hart and One Mind': Local Institutions and the American Revolution," *Early American Studies: An Interdisciplinary Journal* 15 (2007): 99–132, https://www.jstor.org/stable/90000337; Donald F. Johnson, "Ambiguous Allegiances: Urban Loyalties during the American Revolution," *JAH* 104 (2017): 610–631, https://doi.org/10.1093/jahist/jax311.

41. *NYGM*, 19 February 1770; Normand Macleod to Sir William Johnson, 19 February 1770, in Johnson, *Papers*, 7:398; Becker, *History of Political Parties*, 103–107; Tiedemann, *Reluctant Revolutionaries*, 146–153; Carp, *Rebels Rising*, 103–107; Leake, *Memoir*, 62; Stokes, *Iconography*, 4:807.

42. *NYJ*, 8, 15, 22 February, 1, 8, 15 March 1770; *Twenty-fifth Annual Report of the American Scenic and Historic Preservation Society, 1920* (Albany, NY: J. B. Lyon, 1920), 146.

43. *NYJ*, 15 February, 22, 29 March 1770; *NYGM*, 12, 26 March 1770; *The following PATRIOTIC TOASTS . . .* (New York, 1770), Evans, No. 49255. See also David Waldstreicher, *In the Midst of Perpetual Fetes: The Making of American Nationalism, 1776–1820* (Chapel Hill: University of North Carolina Press, 1997); Jeffrey L. Pasley, "The Cheese and the Words: Popular Political Culture and Participatory Democracy in the Early American Republic," in *Beyond the Founders: New Approaches to the Political History of the Early American Republic*, ed. Jeffrey L. Pasley, Andrew W. Robertson, and David Waldstreicher (Chapel Hill: University of North Carolina Press, 2004), 40–41; McDougall quoted in Stokes, *Iconography*, 4:808.

44. J. G. A. Pocock, "Virtue and Commerce in the Eighteenth Century," *Journal of Interdisciplinary History* 3 (1972): 132, https://doi.org/10.2307/202465; Gordon S. Wood, *The Radicalism of the American Revolution* (New York: Knopf, 1992), 83–89; Elkins and McKitrick, *Age of Federalism*, 17; Roney, "'First Movers,'" 279–280; Drew R. McCoy, *The Elusive Republic: Political Economy in Jeffersonian America* (Chapel Hill: University of North Carolina Press, 1980), 17–32; Michael D. Hattem, *Past and Prologue: Politics and Memory in the American Revolution* (New Haven, CT: Yale University Press, 2020).

45. *NYJ*, 29 March 1770; Jonathan Langdon to Robert Morris, 24 March 1770, quoted in Bonomi, *Factious People*, 272–273.

46. Benjamin Roberts to Sir William Johnson, 26 February 1770, in Johnson, *Papers*, 7:416

47. *NYJ*, 29 March, 5, 12 April 1770; *NYGM*, 28 May 1770.

48. Stokes, *Iconography*, 4:808; Carp, *Rebels Rising*, 92.

49. *NYJ*, 3 May 1770; James Rivington to Sir William Johnson, 23 April 1770, in Johnson, *Papers*, 7:578–579; Copy of Indictment for Libel, McDougall Papers, reel 1, New-York Historical Society (hereafter, NHi); "King Agt Alexr. M'Dougal," John Tabor Kempe Papers, box 2, f. 1, NHi.

50. Smith, *Memoirs*, 1:81; Evidence against McDougall, McDougall Papers, reel 1, NHi; *NYJ*, 3 May 1770; Milton M. Klein, *The American Whig: William Livingston of New York* (New York: Garland, 1993), 530–531; Bonomi, *Factious People*, 274; Marc Egnal, *A*

Mighty Empire: The Origins of the American Revolution (Ithaca, NY: Cornell University Press, 1988), 185.

51. *NYJ*, 5 July 1770.

52. Bonomi, *Factious People*, 274–275; Launitz-Schürer, *Loyal Whigs*, 86; Livingston to Oliver Wendell, 17 February 1770, Livingston Family Papers, f. 13, Museum of the City of New York (hereafter, NNMus); Draft [1770?], Livingston Family Papers, f. 13, NN-Mus; Livingston to Wendell, 15 February 1770, Livingston Family Papers, f. 13, NN-Mus; L. F. S. Upton, *The Loyal Whig: William Smith of New York & Quebec* (Toronto: University of Toronto Press, 1969), 70–71; "Extract of a Letter," 24 February 1770, William Smith Jr. Papers, Manuscripts and Archives Division, New York Public Library.

5. Liberty and No Importation

1. George Rudé, *Wilkes and Liberty: A Social Study of 1763 to 1774* (Oxford: Oxford University Press, 1962); John Brewer, *Party Ideology and Popular Politics at the Accession of George III* (Cambridge: Cambridge University Press, 1976); Linda Colley, *Britons: Forging the Nation, 1707–1837* (New Haven, CT: Yale University Press, 1992), esp. 101–131; Kathleen Wilson, *The Sense of the People: Politics, Culture and Imperialism in England, 1715–1785* (New York: Cambridge University Press, 1995), 212–228; Andrew Hook, *Scotland and America: A Study of Cultural Relations* (Glasgow: Blackie & Sons, 1975), 47–72; Adele Hast, *Loyalism in Revolutionary Virginia: The Norfolk Area and the Eastern Shore* (Ann Arbor: UMI Research Press, 1982), 10–13; Timothy Worth, "Transatlantic Scotophobia: Nation, Empire and Anti-Scottish Sentiment in England and America, 1760–1783" (PhD diss., University of Southampton, 2016); John M. Dixon, *The Enlightenment of Cadwallader Colden: Empire, Science, and Intellectual Culture in British New York* (Ithaca, NY: Cornell University Press, 2016), 162–163.

2. DeLancey to Rockingham, 4 February 1769, Wentworth Woodhouse Muniments, Sheffield City Archives and Local Studies Library (hereafter, UkSh); James M. Vaughn, *The Politics of Empire at the Accession of George III: The East India Company and the Crisis and Transformation of Britain's Imperial State* (New Haven, CT: Yale University Press, 2019), 196.

3. Justin du Rivage, *Revolution against Empire: Taxes, Politics, and the Origins of American Independence* (New Haven, CT: Yale University Press, 2017), 7, 8–9, 10, 15, 156–157; Caroline Robbins, *The Eighteenth-Century Commonwealthman* (Cambridge, MA: Harvard University Press, 1959), 7; Gordon S. Wood, *The Creation of the American Republic, 1776–1787* (Chapel Hill: University of North Carolina Press, 1969), 14–15; Jack P. Greene, *The Constitutional Origins of the American Revolution* (New York: Cambridge University Press, 2010); Steve Pincus, *The Heart of the Declaration: The Founders' Case for an Activist Government* (New Haven, CT: Yale University Press, 2016), 85.

4. Patricia U. Bonomi, *A Factious People: Politics and Society in Colonial New York* (New York: Columbia University Press, 1971), 134, 294; Stanley N. Katz, *Newcastle's New York: Anglo-American Politics, 1732–1753* (Cambridge, MA: Harvard University Press, 1968), 43, 156–157, 168–169; Clinton to the Duke of Bedford, 24 February 1748/49, Colden Papers, box 4, New-York Historical Society (hereafter, NHi); Clinton to Henry Pelham, 8 December 1746, George Clinton Papers, William L. Clements Library, University of Michigan

(hereafter, MiU-C); "Comments on Government in General," Colden Papers, box 2, NHi; Jonathan Eacott, *Selling Empire: India and the Making of Britain and America, 1600–1830* (Chapel Hill: University of North Carolina Press, 2016), 189; Pincus, *Heart*, 89.

5. Du Rivage, *Revolution against Empire*, xiv, 151; Patrick Griffin, *The Townshend Moment: The Making of Empire and Revolution in the Eighteenth Century* (New Haven, CT: Yale University Press, 2017), 116–121, 124–126, 128–129, 132–139; Brendan Simms, *Three Victories and a Defeat: The Rise and Fall of the First British Empire, 1714–1783* (New York: Basic, 2007), 551; Vaughn, *Politics of Empire*, 206, 210; John Gilbert McCurdy, *Quarters: The Accommodation of the British Army and the Coming of the American Revolution* (Ithaca, NY: Cornell University Press, 2019), 116; Townshend to [Adam Smith], [November/December 1766], Townshend Papers, MiU-C; *Autobiography and Political Correspondence of Augustus Henry Third Duke of Grafton*, ed. William R. Anson (London: John Murray, 1898), 126; Shelburne to Chatham, 1 February 1767, *Correspondence of William Pitt, Earl of Chatham*, 4 vols. (London: John Murray, 1838–1840), 3:184–185. Charles Townshend also oversaw and orchestrated the successful passage of the Restraining Act, for which see Griffin, *Townshend Moment*, 124–126.

6. Du Rivage, *Revolution against Empire*, xiii, xiv, 151, 156–157; Griffin, *Townshend Moment*, 121, 129–132; DeLancey to Rockingham, 4 February 1769, Wentworth Woodhouse Muniments, UkSh; Richard Bourke, *Empire and Revolution: The Political Life of Edmund Burke* (Princeton, NJ: Princeton University Press, 2015), 306–307, 312 (Burke quoted at 306).

7. *New-York Journal; or, the General Advertiser* (hereafter, *NYJ*), 21 December 1767; Steven Pincus, "The Rise and Fall of Empires: An Essay in Economic and Political Liberty," *Journal of Policy History* 29 (2017): 312, doi:10.1017/S0898030617000070; Eacott, *Selling Empire*, 190; Joseph M. Adelman, *Revolutionary Networks: The Business and Politics of Printing the News, 1763–1789* (Baltimore: Johns Hopkins University Press, 2019), 82, 85–91, 112. For a recent interpretation of Dickinson's letters, see Michael D. Hattem, *Past and Prologue: Politics and Memory in the American Revolution* (New Haven, CT: Yale University Press, 2020).

8. Edward Countryman, *A People in Revolution: The American Revolution and Political Society in New York, 1760–1790* (Baltimore: Johns Hopkins University Press, 1981), 37–45.

9. *NYJ*, 4, 11 February, 26 March, 13 April 1768; Zara Anishanslin, *Portrait of a Woman in Silk: Hidden Histories of the British Atlantic World* (New Haven, CT: Yale University Press, 2016), 303. See also Laurel Thatcher Ulrich, *The Age of Homespun: Objects and Stories in the Creation of an American Myth* (New York: Knopf, 2001).

10. For poverty in New York, see *NYJ*, 7, 14 January 1768; Raymond A. Mohl, "Poverty in Early America, A Reappraisal: The Case of Eighteenth-Century New York City," *New York History* 50 (1969): 12, 16–17, https://www.jstor.org/stable/23169029; *New-York Gazette; and the Weekly Mercury* (hereafter, *NYGM*), 22 February 1768; Carl L. Becker, *The History of Political Parties in the Province of New York, 1760–1776* (Madison, WI: [s.n.], 1909), 60–61.

11. Pincus, *Heart*, 89–90; du Rivage, *Revolution against Empire*, 157, 165; *Historical Memoirs of William Smith*, ed. William H. W. Sabine, 3 vols. (New York: New York Times, 1969; hereafter, Smith, *Memoirs*), 1:48; *NYJ*, 3 August 1769; *New-York Chronicle*, 22 June 1769.

12. George Thomas, *Memoirs of the Marquis of Rockingham and his Contemporaries*, 2 vols. (London: Richard Bentley, 1852), 2:76, 80; du Rivage, *Revolution against Empire*, 162,

164, 165–166; Leslie Stephen and Sidney Lee, eds., *The Dictionary of National Biography*, 21 vols. plus supplements; rev. ed., www.oxforddnb.com (New York and London, 1885–1901; repr. Oxford: Oxford University Press, 1959–1960; hereafter, *DNB*); George III to North, 23 January 1770, GEO/MAIN/932, Windsor Castle, The Royal Archives; Peter D. G. Thomas, *Lord North* (London: Penguin, 1976), 69–72; Andrew Jackson O'Shaughnessy, *The Men Who Lost America: British Leadership, the American Revolution, and the Fate of the Empire* (New Haven, CT: Yale University Press, 2013), 30, 49, 51; McCurdy, *Quarters*, 204, 205–206.

13. O'Shaughnessy, *Men Who Lost America*, 49, 50; Thomas, *Lord North*, 69; Eacott, *Selling Empire*, 190; Joseph S. Tiedemann, *Reluctant Revolutionaries: New York City and the Road to Independence, 1763–1776* (Ithaca, NY: Cornell University Press, 1997), 154; Nicholas Varga, "Robert Charles: New York Agent, 1748–1770," *William and Mary Quarterly* 18 (1961): 234–235, https://doi.org/10.2307/1918544; *The Papers of Benjamin Franklin*, ed. Leonard W. Labaree, William B. Willcox, Claude A. Lopez, Barbara B. Oberg, Ellen R. Cohn, and others, 43 vols. published to date (New Haven, CT: Yale University Press, 1959– ; hereafter, Franklin, *Papers*), 17:168–172; McCurdy, *Quarters*, 209–210.

14. Mary Lou Lustig, *Privilege and Prerogative: New York's Provincial Elite, 1710–1776* (Madison, NJ: Fairleigh Dickinson University Press, 1995), 161; O'Shaughnessy, *Men Who Lost America*, 51–52; NYGM, 20 April, 14 May, 4, 11, 25 June, 23 July; *New-York Gazette; or, the Weekly Post-Boy* (hereafter, *NYGP*), 7 May, 4 June 1770; NYJ, 17, 24 May, 7 June; Notes on Nonimportation, 15 May 1770, McDougall Papers, reel 1, NHi.

15. Bernard to Hillsborough, 8 May 1769, Jared Sparks Collection of American Manuscripts, MS Sparks 4, vol. 7, f. 163, Houghton Library, Harvard University; *Connecticut Journal*, 2 June 1769; *Boston Evening-Post*, 5 June 1769; NYJ, 27 July 1769; NYGM, 15 May 1769.

16. Hattem, *Past and Prologue*.

17. *NYGP*, 11, 18, 25 June 1770.

18. *Advertisement* (New York, 1770), Charles Evans and others, *American Bibliography: A Chronological Dictionary of All Books, Pamphlets and Periodical Publications Printed in the United States of America* [1639–1800], 14 vols. (Chicago and Worcester, MA, 1903–1959; rev. ed., www.readex.com; hereafter, Evans), No. 11781; NYGM, 11 June 1770; Notes on Nonimportation, 30 May 1770, McDougall Papers, reel 1, NHi; T. H. Breen, *The Marketplace of Revolution: How Consumer Politics Shaped American Independence* (New York: Oxford University Press, 2004), 247.

19. *NYGP*, 11 June 1770; *Advertisement* (New York, 1770), Evans, No. 11782. Members of the Committee of Inspection were predominantly associated with the DeLanceys. Those in *italics* voted for the DeLanceys in 1769, those in **bold** dined with "the Friends to Liberty and Trade" in March 1770, and those in ***bold italics*** did both. The committee included ***Theophylact Bache***, ***Gerard W. Beekman***, ***Joseph Bull***, ***John Harris Cruger***, Peter T. Curtenius, James Desbrosses Jr., ***Daniel Dunscomb***, Thomas Franklin Jr., Walter Franklin, ***Edward Laight***, ***Isaac Low***, ***John Murray***, Henry Remsen Jr., ***John Thurman Jr.***, **Hubert Van Wagenen**, and Jacob Watson. Members of the committee obtained from *Advertisement* (New York, 1770), Evans, No. 11782. The committee was reformed in November 1769 and included DeLanceyites John Harris Cruger, Jacob Walton, Anthony Van Dam, Charles McEvers, Benjamin Booth, Theophylact Bache, and Edward Laight, as well as Isaac Sears and Peter T. Curtenius, among others. See Private Association, 12 November 1769, Private Owner, 2021.

20. Notes on Nonimportation, 1 June 1770, McDougall Papers, reel 1, NHi.

21. Notes on Nonimportation, 11 June 1770, McDougall Papers, reel 1, NHi; *NYJ*, 28 June 1770; *New York Gazette; or, the Weekly Post Boy*, 2 July 1770.

22. Alan Taylor, *American Revolutions: A Continental History, 1750–1804* (New York: W. W. Norton, 2016), 112.

23. *NYGM*, 18 June 1770; *New-York* (New York, 1770), Evans, No. 11784; *NYJ*, 1 June 1770; Roger J. Champagne, *Alexander McDougall and the American Revolution* (Schenectady, NY: New York State American Revolution Bicentennial Commission/Union College Press, 1975), 36; *NYGP*, 2 July 1770; *A CARD, NUMBER 1* (New York, 1770), Evans, No. 11594.

24. *NYJ*, 21 June, 12 July 1770; Wood, *Creation of the American Republic*, 53–70, 418–420; Steven Rosswurm, *Arms, Country, and Class: The Philadelphia Militia and "Lower Sort" During the American Revolution, 1775–1783* (New Brunswick, NJ: Rutgers University Press, 1987), 194–199.

25. *NYGM*, 23 July 1770; *Advertisement* (New York, 1770), Evans, No. 11785; Notes on Nonimportation, 26 June 1770, McDougall Papers, reel 1, NHi; *NYJ*, 28 June 1770; *NYGM*, 2 July 1770. Those in *italics* voted for the DeLanceys, those underlined were members of either the Chamber of Commerce or Marine Society, and those in **bold** dined in March 1770. Those whose names are left unformatted took no part in the events, and no other information has been located. The individuals present were *Theophylact Bache*, *Henry Brevoort*, *Thomas Doughty*, *Gilbert Forbes*, *Peter Goelet*, Abraham Kipp, Isaac Kipp, *Leonard Kipp*,* *Edward Laight*, *Jonathan Lawrence*, *Gabriel Ludlow*, *William Ludlow*, *Thomas Ludlow*, Alexander McDougall, **John McKenny**, **Frederick Rhinelander**, *Jarvis Roebuck*, *William Ustick*, *Augustus Van Horne*, *Baltus Van Kleeck*, **Peter Berton**, *Thomas Walton*, and Jacob Watson. *Leonard Kipp voted for John Cruger, Jacob Walton, John Morin Scott, and Theodorus Van Wyck. Taken from Notes on Nonimportation, 7 July 1770, McDougall Papers, reel 1, NHi. See also *Boston Evening-Post*, 16 July 1770; *Boston Gazette*, 16 July 1770.

26. *NYGM*, 23 July 1770; *NYGP*, 16, 23, 30 July 1770; *Boston Gazette*, 16 July 1770; *Boston Evening-Post*, 16 July 1770; Champagne, *Alexander McDougall*, 38–39; Benjamin L. Carp, *Rebels Rising: Cities and the American Revolution* (New York: Oxford University Press, 2007), 80; Colden to Hillsborough, 7 July 1770, in *Documents Relative to the Colonial History of the State of New-York*, ed. E. B. O'Callaghan and Berthold Fernow, 15 vols. (Albany, NY: Weed, Parsons and Co., 1853–1887; hereafter, *N.Y. Col. Docs.*), 8:217.

27. John Austin Stevens Jr., *Colonial New York. Sketches Biographical and Historical 1768–1784* (New York: John F. Trow and Co., 1867), 149; *The Papers of Sir William Johnson*, 2nd ed., rev. and exp., 20 vols. (Albany, NY: University of the State of New York, 1921–1965, 2008; hereafter, Johnson, *Papers*), 13:555; Franklin, *Papers*, 16:264; McEvers, cited in Notes on Nonimportation, 17 July 1770, McDougall Papers, reel 1, NHi; Alexander Colden to Anthony Todd, 11 July 1770, in *N.Y. Col. Docs.*, 8:219; *NYGP*, 23, 30 July 1770. For Bache McEvers and Amelia Matilda Bache, see registers of the Parish of Trinity Church, https://registers.trinitywallstreet.org/ (accessed 28 December 2019).

28. These women were Elisabeth Breese, Florus Bancker, and "*Mrs. Davis.*" Breese and Bancker were shopkeepers; "*Mrs. Davis*" was a dry-goods importer.

29. These men were James Beekman, Joseph Bull, Isaac Corsa, John Dalley Sr., Daniel Dunscomb, James Dunscomb, Francis Fowler, John Johnson, Thomas Lawrence, John Lockhart, William Miller, Benjamin Moore, and Anthony Rutgers.

30. The seven men were Henry C. and Nicholas Bogart, David Dickson, William Heyer, William Poole, Robert Ray, Anthony Rutgers, and Isaac Sheldon. In the 1769 election, Heyer voted for Jacob Walton (DeLancey), Philip Livingston (Livingston), John Morin Scott (Livingston), and Theodorus Van Wyck (Livingston). See *A Copy of the Poll List, of the Election for Representatives for the City and County of New-York* (New York: Francis Hart & Co., 1880), 1769.

31. The ten members of the Chamber of Commerce who supported the nonimportation agreement were Samuel Bayard, James Beekman, Henry C. Bogart, Joseph Bull, Walter Franklin, William Neilson, Garret Rapalje, Isaac Roosevelt, Isaac Sears, and Jacobus Van Zandt. Of these men, Bayard, Bogart, Rapalje, Roosevelt, Sears, and Van Zandt voted in 1769. Except for Sears, who was then a firm DeLancey supporter, the Livingstons received their comprehensive support. See *Copy of the Poll List*, 1769.

32. Andrew and Thomas Barclay and George Stanton signed under the name of their businesses, *"Barclay Andrew and Son"* and *"Stanton, Miss and Co."*

33. According to the list of those "FOR IMPORTING," a "William Heyer" voted, but because there were two further William Heyers in New York City who were supportive of the Livingstons and nonimportation, the individual found here has been omitted from further analysis (here and below).

34. William Seton signed under his company's name, *"Seton and Curson."* Moreover, two Samuel Bayards appear: Samuel Bayard and Samuel Bayard Jr. Given that a "Capt. Samuel Bayard" voted in 1769, appears on the nonimporters' list, and was a member in the Chamber of Commerce, his preference in relation to nonimportation was deemed historically robust and has been included in this analysis. For his voting behavior, see *Copy of the Poll List*, 1769, 4; *NYGP*, 30 July 1770.

35. These individuals were Theophylact Bache, John Cruger, John Harris Cruger, Robert Dale, James Jauncey, Linus King, Edward Laight, Isaac Low, Thomas Marston, Charles McEvers, Thomas W. Moore, Willet Taylor, John Thurman Sr., Augustus Van Horne, Jacob Walton, Gerard Walton, Thomas Walton, Jacob Walton, Henry White, and Thomas White. The one exception was Richard Sharpe, who voted for John Morin Scott.

36. For a similar analysis in Boston, see John W. Tyler, *Smugglers & Patriots: Boston Merchants and the Advent of the American Revolution* (Boston: Northeastern University Press, 1986), esp. 167–168.

37. Notes on Nonimportation, 25 July 1770, McDougall Papers, reel 1, NHi; *NYGP*, 30 July 1770.

38. Joyce Appleby, *Capitalism and a New Social Order: The Republican Vision of the 1790s* (New York: New York University Press, 1984).

39. J. Franklin Jameson, *The American Revolution Considered as a Social Movement* (Princeton, NJ: Princeton University Press, 1973), 12; Michael Kammen, *Colonial New York: A History* (New York: Charles Scribner's Sons, 1975), chap. 11; Edward Countryman, *A People in Revolution: The American Revolution and Political Society in New York, 1760–1790* (Baltimore: Johns Hopkins University Press, 1981), 13.

40. Lindsey O'Neill, *The Opened Letter: Networking in the Early Modern British World* (Philadelphia: University of Pennsylvania Press, 2015), 2–3; David Hancock, "The Trouble with Networks: Managing the Scots' Early-Modern Madeira Trade," *Business History Review* 79 (2005): 470–473, https://doi.org/10.2307/25097068.

41. *A Letter to the Celebrated Patriot of New-York* (New York, 1770), Evans, No. 11697; *DNB*; James Corbett David, *Dunmore's New World: The Extraordinary Life of a Royal Governor in Revolutionary America—with Jacobites, Counterfeiters, Land Schemes, Shipwrecks, Scalping, Indian Politics, Runaway Slaves, and Two Illegal Royal Weddings* (Charlottesville: University of Virginia Press, 2013), 41; Tryon to Hillsborough, 4 June 1772, CO 5/1103, f. 188–189, National Archives of the United Kingdom (hereafter, UK-KeNA).

42. O'Neill, *Opened Letter*, 4; Claude Grigon, "Commensality and Social Morphology: An Essay on Typology," in *Food, Drink and Identity: Cooking, Eating and Drinking in Europe since the Middle Ages*, ed. Peter Scholliers (New York: Berg, 2001), 27; Susan Clair Imbarrato, *Declarations of Independency in Eighteenth-Century American Biography* (Knoxville: University of Tennessee Press, 1998), 40–85.

43. Lorenzo Sabine, *Biographical Sketches of Loyalists of the American Revolution*, 2 vols. (Boston: Little, Brown and Co., 1847–1864), 2:570–571; Arlene Palmer Schwind, "The Ceramic Imports of Frederick Rhinelander, New York Loyalist Merchant," *Winterthur Portfolio* 19 (1984): 21–36, https://doi.org/10.1086/496162; George Norbury Mackenzie, *Colonial Families of the United States*, 7 vols. (Baltimore: Genealogical Publishing Co., 1966), 1:431–432.

44. O'Neill, *Opened Letter*, 6, 7.

45. Frederick Rhinelander daybook, Rhinelander Family Papers, NHi; John Austin Stevens Jr., *Colonial Records of the New York Chamber of Commerce, 1768–1784* (New York: John F. Trow and Co., 1867), 140; Joseph Alfred Scoville, *The Old Merchants of New York City*, 5 vols. (New York: T. R. Knox, 1885), 1:108; Thomas M. Truxes, *Defying Empire: Trading with the Enemy in Colonial New York* (New Haven, CT: Yale University Press, 2008), 220; Arthur W. North, *The Founders and the Founding of Walton, New York* ([Walton, NY: Walton Reporter Co., 1924]), 5.

46. David, *Dunmore's New World*, 39–40; Richard Francis Upton, *Revolutionary New Hampshire* (Port Washington, NY: Kennikat, 1970), 168, 189, 194–195. For reference to Rhinelander's skills as a land speculator, see Laight to John Vardill, 27 March 1775, AO 13/105, UK-KeNA.

47. Petition of William Rhinelander and others, 13 November 1774, Applications for Land Grants, 1642–1803, vol. 34, 140, New York State Archives (hereafter, N-Ar). John Buxton, Elijah Cock, Charles Doughty, Edward Eastman, Benjamin Hugget, Joseph Hull, James Mott, Jacob Rhinelander, William Rhinelander Jr., William Rhinelander Sr., Philip Rhinelander Jr., Philip Rhinelander Sr., Willet Weeks, and Charles White. Those whose allegiance has not been identified were Henry Franklin, Joshua Franklin, Thomas Hawxhurst, Tidignam Hull, John Kirk, William Lupton, and Harrison Palmer.

48. For the petitions and images, see Petition of Rhinelander, Applications for Land Grants, November 1775, vol. 35, 106, 107, N-Ar. The petition for Underhill had the additional grantee of Stanson Palmer, whose allegiance has not been determined.

49. Account of Warrants issued by Gov. Tryon, CO 5/1109, f. 82, 107, 125, UK-KeNA.

50. Will of William Rhinelander Jr., August 1809, Probated Wills, 1671–1815, vol. 48, 214, N-Ar.

51. For the Bancker family, see Howard James Banker, comp., *A Partial History and Genealogical Record of the Bancker or Banker Families of America* (Rutland, VT: Tuttle Co., 1909). Evert's father was named Gerardus, but he was referred to as Evert Jr. to distinguish him from his cousin, Evert Bancker, a son of Christopher Bancker. See Banker, *Partial History*, 250–251, 281–282.

52. Lispenard was a distiller, Field was a shopkeeper, and Kempe was New York's attorney general.

53. Genealogical Chart, Misc. Mss. Bancker, Jas., NHi; Allicocke to Bancker, 7 April 1770, Evert Bancker Jr. Papers, Correspondence, 1770 folder, NHi; Determination of E. Laight and J. Allicocke concerning the house, Estates and Misc. Papers, Bancker Plans, Manuscripts and Archives Division, New York Public Library.

54. Richard Godbeer, *The Overflowing of Friendship: Love between Men and the Creation of the American Republic* (Baltimore: Johns Hopkins University Press, 2009); Sarah Knott, *Sensibility and the American Revolution* (Chapel Hill: University of North Carolina Press, 2009).

55. Those in italics became loyalists. The petitioners were *John Antill*, Thomas Austin, Frederick Bassett, Samuel Boyer, Benjamin Buit, Richard Hatfield, Strafford Jones, Henry H. Kip, Valentine Lower, *Thomas Lupton*, *James Moran*, Peter Ogilvie, *William Pagan*, *John L. C. Roome*, *John Slidell*, Hezekiah Spelman, Thomas Stevenson, Thomas Stewart, William Stewart, *John Woods*, Isaac Henry Van Vleck, Richard Varick, John Wigram, John *Jacob Wilkins*, William Willard, and *Samuel Wright*. Petition of Charles Nicoll and others, Applications for Land Grants, 18 June 1771, vol. 30, 86; November 1774, vol. 34, 34, 62, N-Ar.

56. Daybook, 1768–1776: Wines and Liquor, Charles Nicoll Account Books, NHi. Interactions have been analyzed until April 1775.

57. *NYGM*, 27 February 1775; Anya Jabour, "Male Friendship and Masculinity in the Early National South: William Wirt and His Friends," *Journal of the Early Republic* 20 (2000): 83–111, https://doi.org/10.2307/3124831.

58. Karen V. Hansen, "Rediscovering the Social: Visiting Practices in Antebellum New England and the Limits of the Public/Private Dichotomy," in *Public and Private Thought and Practice: Perspectives on a Grand Dichotomy*, ed. Jeff Weintraub and Krishan Kumar (Chicago: University of Chicago Press, 1997), 270.

59. Joanna Innes, "II Representative Histories: Recent Studies of Popular Politics and Political Culture in Eighteenth and Early Nineteenth-Century England," *Journal of Historical Sociology* 4 (1991): 182–211, esp. 206, https://doi.org/10.1111/j.1467-6443.1991.tb00103.x; Appleby, *Capitalism and a New Social Order*, 56.

6. The Mob Begin to Think and Reason

1. Alan Taylor, *American Revolutions: A Continental History, 1750–1804* (New York: W. W. Norton, 2016), 112–113; Richard B. Sheridan, "The British Credit Crisis of 1772 and the American Colonies," *Journal of Economic History* 20 (1960): 170, https://www.jstor.org/stable/2114853; Ross J. S. Hoffman, *Edmund Burke: New York Agent* (Philadelphia: American Philosophical Society, 1956), 15, 195–198, 200–203 (quotes at 201), 209–211, 212–217, 222–223, 231–233; Richard Bourke, *Empire and Revolution: The Political Life of Edmund Burke* (Princeton, NJ: Princeton University Press, 2015), 235–236, 310, 312, 316, 321–322.

2. Gage quoted in Edwin G. Burrows and Mike Wallace, *Gotham: A History of New York City to 1898* (New York: Oxford University Press, 1999; hereafter, *Gotham*), 213; *Historical Memoirs of William Smith*, ed. William H. W. Sabine, 3 vols. (New York: New York Times, 1969; hereafter, Smith, *Memoirs*), 1:117. For Dunmore's and Tryon's correspondence, see CO 5/1102–1104, National Archives of the United Kingdom (hereafter, UK-KeNA).

3. Michael D. Hattem, *Past and Prologue: Politics and Memory in the American Revolution* (New Haven, CT: Yale University Press, 2020); Jonathan Eacott, *Selling Empire: India and the Making of Britain and America, 1600–1830* (Chapel Hill: University of North Carolina Press, 2016), 194; Taylor, *American Revolutions*, 112.

4. Benjamin W. Labaree, *The Boston Tea Party, 1773: Catalyst for Revolution* (New York: Oxford University Press, 1968, 88–89); James M. Vaughn, *The Politics of Empire at the Accession of George III: The East India Company and the Crisis and Transformation of Britain's Imperial State* (New Haven, CT: Yale University Press, 2019), 214–215; Justin du Rivage, *Revolution against Empire: Taxes, Politics, and the Origins of American Independence* (New Haven, CT: Yale University Press, 2017), 167–168; Benjamin L. Carp, "Did Dutch Smugglers Provoke the Boston Tea Party?" *EAS* 10 (2012): 340, 344, https://doi.org/10.1353/eam.2012.0014; Jill Lepore, *These Truths: A History of the United States* (New York: W. W. Norton, 2018), 88–89; Cathy Matson, *Merchants & Empire: Trading in Colonial New York* (Baltimore: Johns Hopkins University Press, 2003), 305; Raymond A. Mohl, "Poverty in Early America, A Reappraisal: The Case of Eighteenth-Century New York City," *New York History* 50 (1969): 12, 15, https://www.jstor.org/stable/23169029; Gary B. Nash, "Urban Wealth and Poverty in Pre-Revolutionary America," *Journal of Interdisciplinary History* 6 (1974): 560, https://doi.org/10.2307/202532; Mike Rapport, *The Unruly City: Paris, London, and New York in the Age of Revolution* (New York: Basic, 2017), 24–25; Joseph S. Tiedemann, *Reluctant Revolutionaries: New York City and the Road to Independence, 1763–1776* (Ithaca, NY: Cornell University Press, 1997), 179.

5. John Gilbert McCurdy, *Quarters: The Accommodation of the British Army and the Coming of the American Revolution* (Ithaca, NY: Cornell University Press, 2019), 219; Taylor, *American Revolutions*, 112–113 (North quoted at 113); Andrew Jackson O'Shaughnessy, *The Men Who Lost America: British Leadership, the American Revolution, and the Fate of the Empire* (New Haven, CT: Yale University Press, 2013), 52; Leslie Stephen and Sidney Lee, eds., *The Dictionary of National Biography,* 21 vols. plus supplements (New York and London, 1885–1901; repr. Oxford: Oxford University Press, 1959–1960; rev. ed., www.oxforddnb.com; hereafter, *DNB*). For printings of the act, see *New-York Gazette; and the Weekly Mercury* (hereafter, *NYGM*), 6 September 1773; *Rivington's New-York Gazetteer* (hereafter, *Rivington's*), 9 September 1773.

6. Smith, *Memoirs*, 1:156.

7. Michael D. Hattem, "'As Serves our Interest best': Political Economy and the Logic of Resistance in New York City, 1765–1775," *New York History* 98 (2017): 62, https://doi.org/10.1353/nyh.2017.0037; Pigou & Booth to James & Drinker, 4 October 1773, Henry S. Drinker Papers, Pennsylvania Historical Society (hereafter, PHi); Benjamin Booth to James and Drinker, 4 August 1773, Henry S. Drinker Papers, PHi.

8. *New-York Journal; or, the General Advertiser* (hereafter, *NYJ*), 21 October 1773; *Rivington's*, 21 October 1773; *NYGM*, 25 October 1773; "SCÆVOLA," *To the COMMISSIONERS appointed by the EAST-INDIA COMPANY* . . . (New York, 1773), Charles Evans and others,

American Bibliography: A Chronological Dictionary of All Books, Pamphlets and Periodical Publications Printed in the United States of America [1639–1800], 14 vols. (Chicago and Worcester, MA, 1903–1959; rev. ed., www.readex.com; hereafter, Evans), Nos. 12999, 42521.

9. A TRADESMAN, *To the Free-Holders and Free-Men, Of the City, and Province of New-York* (New York, 1773), Evans, No. 13040; *Gotham*, 213–214.

10. Tryon to Dartmouth, 3 November 1773, CO 5/1104, f. 458, UK-KeNA; Dartmouth to Tryon, 8 January 1774, CO 5/1105, f. 1–2, UK-KeNA; Haldimand to Dartmouth, 5 January 1774, Haldimand Papers, Add. MS 21,695, f. 1–3, British Library (hereafter, Uk).

11. John Maunsell to John Folner, 20 December 1773, AO 13/105, UK-KeNA; POPLICOLA [Vardill], *To the Worthy Inhabitants of New-York* (New York, 1773), Evans, No. 12956; ISAAC VAN POMPKIN, *To the Agents Of their High Mightiness the Dutch East-India Company* (New York, 1773), Evans, No. 13037. Vardill wrote other articles under the same pseudonym. See *Rivington's*, 18 November, 2, 23 December 1773; Evans, No. 12955, 12957. For other contributions to the debate, see "JOHN BEETES VAN CATCH MONEY," *TRANSLATION of a LETTER Found on board the Sloop ILLICIT, Captain PERJURY, wrecked at OYSTER BAY* (New York, 1773), Evans, No. 12381. Vardill also corresponded with George Washington around this time; see Vardill to Washington, 20 September 1773, in *The Papers of George Washington: Colonial Series*, ed. W. W. Abbott and Dorothy Twohig, 10 vols. (Charlottesville: University of Virginia Press, 1983–1995; hereafter, Washington, *Papers, Colonial Series*), 9:326–327; Washington to Vardill, 15 December 1773, in Washington, *Papers, Colonial Series*, 9:407–408. For more on Vardill, see also Steven Graham Wigley, "John Vardill: A Loyalist's Progress" (MA diss., University of British Columbia, 1975).

12. Du Rivage, *Revolution against Empire*, 188; DeLancey to Burke, 7 April, 7 July 1773, Hoffman, *Edmund Burke*, 123; DeLancey to Rockingham, 4 February 1769, 26 October 1773, Wentworth Woodhouse Muniments, Sheffield City Archives and Local Studies Library.

13. HAMPDEN [McDougall], *The ALARM. Number I.* (New York: [John Holt?], 1773), Evans, No. 12799; this was also published in *NYJ*, 14 October 1773; HAMPDEN [McDougall], *The Alarm. Number II.* (New York: [John Holt?], 1773), Evans, No. 12800; this was also published in *NYJ*, 21 October 1773; HAMPDEN [McDougall], *The Alarm. Number V.* (New York: [John Holt?], 1773), Evans, No. 12803; this was also published in *NYJ*, 11 November 1773. For the other issues, see *The Alarm. Number III.* (New York: [John Holt?], 1773), Evans, No. 12801; *The Alarm. Number Iv* (New York: [John Holt?], 1773), Evans, No. 12802; *NYJ*, 28 October, 4 November 1773. See also A TRADESMAN, *To the Free-Holders and Free-Men, Of the City, and Province of New-York*, Evans, No. 13040.

14. Leopold S. Launitz-Schürer Jr., *Loyal Whigs and Revolutionaries: The Making of an American Revolution in New York, 1765–1776* (New York: New York University Press, 1980), 101–102; *Rivington's*, 11 November 1773; Tryon to Dartmouth, 3 November 1774, CO 5/1104, f. 458–460, UK-KeNA; CASSIUS, *To the FRIENDS of LIBERTY, and COMMERCE* (New York, 1773), Houghton Library, Harvard University; *NYJ*, 21 October, 11, 18 November 1773; *NYGM*, 15 November 1773.

15. *The ASSOCIATION of The Sons of Liberty, of NEW-YORK* (New York, 1773), Evans, No. 12652; *PROCEEDINGS at a numerous Meeting of the CITIZENS of NEW-YORK* (New York, 1773), Evans, No. 12894.

16. Some have alleged that the figure "K—y" is John Kearsley Jr., of Philadelphia, but given the strong New York focus, as well as the context in which "K—y" appears, it is more probable that it is Kelly.

17. *Rivington's*, 2 December, 1773; Tiedemann, *Reluctant Revolutionaries*, 177; Smith, *Memoirs*, 1:157–158, 162; SCÆVOLA, *To the Commissioners Appointed . . .* (New York, 1773), Evans, No. 1299; Petition of Henry White, Benjamin Booth, and Abraham Lott, 1 December 1773, CO 5/ 1105, f. 7, UK-KeNA; Roger J. Champagne, *Alexander McDougall and the American Revolution* (Schenectady, NY: New York State American Revolution Bicentennial Commission/Union College Press, 1975), 45–46; letter from [Henry] White and other agents in Smith Jr.'s hand to Captain of Tea Ship, 29 December 1773, William Smith Jr. Papers, Manuscripts and Archives Division, New York Public Library (hereafter, NN).

18. Mark Peterson, *The City-State of Boston: The Rise and Fall of an Atlantic Power, 1630–1865* (Princeton, NJ: Princeton University Press, 2019), 322; Taylor, *American Revolutions*, 113; Lepore, *These Truths*, 89; du Rivage, *Revolution against Empire*, 193; Lawrence Glickman, *Buying Power: A History of Consumer Activism in America* (Chicago: University of Chicago Press, 2009), 323n24.

19. Tiedemann, *Reluctant Revolutionaries*, 182; Smith, *Memoirs*, 1:163; Thurman to Amos Heyton, 26 December 1773, John Thurman Jr. Papers, box 2, New York State Library; Bourke, *Empire and Revolution*, 324–326; Rockingham to Burke, 30 January 1774, in *The Correspondence of Edmund Burke*, ed. Thomas W. Copeland, Lucy S. Sutherland, and others, 10 vols. (Chicago: University of Chicago Press, 1958–1978), 2:516; *Gotham*, 214–215 (George III quote at 215); du Rivage, *Revolution against Empire*, 170–171; O'Shaughnessy, *Men Who Lost America*, 22, 23, 52–53 (North quotation at 53).

20. Vaughn, *Politics of Empire*, 215; Tiedemann, *Reluctant Revolutionaries*, 182; DNB; Mary Lou Lustig, *Privilege and Prerogative: New York's Provincial Elite, 1710–1776* (Madison, NJ: Fairleigh Dickinson University Press, 1995), 168.

21. Smith, *Memoirs*, 1:180–181; *NYJ*, 21 April 1774; *NYGM*, 25 April 1774; *Gotham*, 215; Jane T. Merritt, *The Trouble with Tea: The Politics of Consumption in Eighteenth-Century Global Economy* (Baltimore: Johns Hopkins University Press, 2017), 107; Cruger to Burke, 4 May 1774, Hoffman, *Edmund Burke*, 527.

22. *NYGM*, 25 April 1774; Barbara Clark Smith, *The Freedoms We Lost: Consent and Resistance in Revolutionary America* (New York: New Press, 2010), 95.

23. *NYJ*, 12 May 1774; *NYGM*, 16 May 1774.

24. Alexander McDougall, "Political Memorandums," McDougall Papers, New-York Historical Society (hereafter, NHi); du Rivage, *Revolution against Empire*, 46, 47, 49–51, 59, 179.

25. *Rivington's*, 13 January 1774; McDougall, "Political Memorandums," 12, 13 May 1774.

26. Tiedemann, *Reluctant Revolutionaries*, 186–187.

27. McDougall, "Political Memorandums," 13, 16 May 1774; Hattem, "'As Serves our Interest best,'" 63; Tiedemann, *Reluctant Revolutionaries*, 187; Haldimand to Dartmouth, 5 January 1774, 15 May 1774, Haldimand Papers, Add. Mss. 21695, f. 1–3, 102–103, Uk.

28. Du Rivage, *Revolution against Empire*, 162, 177; McDougall, "Political Memorandums," 16 May 1774; Smith, *Memoirs*, 1:186; Tiedemann, *Reluctant Revolutionaries*, 187; Carl Bridenbaugh, *Cities in Revolt: Urban Life in America, 1743–1776* (New York: Knopf, 1955), 22; *Gotham*, 175–176.

29. Smith, *Memoirs*, 1:186; *Biographical Directory of the United States Congress, 1774–2005* (Washington, DC, 2005; rev. ed., bioguide.congress.gov; hereafter, *Biog. Dir. Cong.*); John Austin Stevens Jr., *Colonial New York. Sketches Biographical and Historical 1768–1784* (New York: John F. Trow and Co., 1867), 72; Maya Jasanoff, *Liberty's Exiles: American Loyalists in the Revolutionary World* (New York: Knopf, 2011), 28, 33; Tiedemann, *Reluctant Revolutionaries*, 187–188.

30. McDougall, "Political Memorandums," 16 May 1774; Steven Pincus, "The Rise and Fall of Empires: An Essay in Economic and Political Liberty," *Journal of Policy History* 29 (2017): 312, doi:10.1017/S0898030617000070; Philip Ranlet, *The New York Loyalists* (Knoxville: University of Tennessee Press, 1986), 42. Historians and editors have generally argued that McDougall and his associates wanted a smaller committee because it would be more "efficient." See *The Selected Papers of John Jay*, ed. Elizabeth M. Nuxoll and others, 7 vols. (Charlottesville: University of Virginia Press, 2010–2021; hereafter, Jay, *Selected Papers*), 1:84; Tiedemann, *Reluctant Revolutionaries*, 187–188.

31. McDougall, "Political Memorandums," 16, 19 May 1774; *NYJ*, 19 May 1774; *Rivington's*, 19 May 1774; *To the Public* (New York: 1774), Evans, No. 13669; Roger J. Champagne, "New York and the Intolerable Acts," New-York Historical Society, *Quarterly* 45 (1961): 202–203; Smith, *Memoirs*, 1:186, 187; *Biog. Dir. Cong.*

32. *Rivington's*, 26 May 1774; *NYGM*, 23 May 1774; Haldimand to Dartmouth, 1 June 1774, Haldimand Papers, Add. Mss. 21695, f. 106–107, British Library; Colden to Dartmouth, 1 June 1774, CO 5/1105, f. 326–327, UK-KeNA; Colden to Dartmouth, 6 July 1774, CO 5/1105, f. 335–336, UK-KeNA.

33. The DeLanceys in the Committee of Fifty-One who became loyalists were John Alsop, Theophylact Bache, Gerardus W. Beekman, Benjamin Booth, John DeLancey, Elias Desbrosses, Abraham Duryee, Peter Goelet, James Jauncey, David Johnson, Edward Laight, Leonard Lispenard, Abraham P. Lott, Isaac Low, Gabriel G. Ludlow, Thomas Marston, William McAdam, Charles McEvers, John Moore, Thomas Pearsall, Miles Sherbrooke, Peter Van Schaack, Richard Sharpe, Charles Shaw, John Thurman Jr., Alexander Wallace, Abraham Walton, William Walton, Richard Yates, and Hamilton Young.

The McDougallites who became revolutionaries were Abraham Brasher, John Broom, George Bowne, Joseph Bull, Peter T. Curtenius, Joseph Hallet, Nicholas Hoffman, Francis Lewis, Peter Van Brugh Livingston, Alexander McDougall, Thomas Randall, Henry Remsen, Isaac Sears, David van Horne, and Jacobus Van Zandt. See *At a Meeting at the Exchange . . .* (New York, 1773), Evans, No. 13125; Colden to Dartmouth, 5 October 1774, CO 5/1105, f. 356–358, UK-KeNA; Records of the New York Revolutionary Committee of Correspondence, 30 May 1774, New York City Misc. Mss., box 10, NHi (hereafter, New York Revolutionary Committee); Richard Alan Ryerson, *The Revolution is Now Begun: The Radical Committees of Philadelphia, 1765–1776* (Philadelphia: University of Pennsylvania Press, 1978) 42.

34. Staughton Lynd, "The Mechanics in New York Politics, 1774–1788," *Labor History* 5 (1965): 226–227, https://doi.org/10.1080/00236566408583948; Gouverneur Morris to [Thomas] Penn, 20 May 1773, Peter Force, *American Archives: Consisting of a Collection of Authentick Records, State Papers, Debates, and Letters and Other Notices of Publick Affairs*, 6 series, 9 vols. (Washington, DC: Published under authority of an act of Congress, 1837–1853), 4th ser., 1:342–343.

35. Lynd, "Mechanics in New York Politics," 225; Hattem, "'As Serves our Interest best,'" 63–64; Taylor, *American Revolutions*, 355, 356.

36. Records of the New York Revolutionary Committee, 23 May 1774; McDougall, "Political Memorandums," 23 May 1774.

37. Hoffman, *Edmund Burke*, 136, 138, 139; Force, *American Archives*, 4th ser., 1:307.

38. Hoffman, *Edmund Burke*, 136; Records of the Revolutionary Committee, 6, 7 June 1774; Launitz-Schürer, *Loyal Whigs*, 114–115.

39. Records of the Revolutionary Committee, 11 June 1774; Force, *American Archives*, 4th ser., 1:306–307; C. A. Weslager, *The Stamp Act Congress* (Newark: University of Delaware Press, 1976), 234–239; Lepore, *These Truths*, 91.

40. Champagne, *Alexander McDougall*, 58–59; Records of the Revolutionary Committee, 29 June 1774.

41. Records of the Revolutionary Committee, 29 June 1774; Smith, *Memoirs*, 1:188.

42. Records of the Revolutionary Committee, 4 July 1774; Champagne, *Alexander McDougall*, 60; *Biog. Dir. Cong.*; Launitz-Schürer, *Loyal Whigs*, 115.

43. Tiedemann, *Reluctant Revolutionaries*, 193–194; Jay, *Selected Papers*, 1:90–92; *Advertisement* (New York, 1774), Evans, No. 13095; *NYJ*, 7 July 1774; *NYGM*, 11 July 1774; *Rivington's*, 14 July 1774.

44. Smith to Philip Schuyler, 9 July 1774, Schuyler Papers, NN.

45. Records of the Revolutionary Committee, 7 July 1774; Smith to Philip Schuyler, 9 July 1774, Schuyler Papers, NN; Launitz-Schürer, *Loyal Whigs*, 117; *Rivington's*, 14 July 1774.

46. William Sidney to William Samuel Johnson, 28 July 1774, William Samuel Johnson Papers, Connecticut Historical Society; Records of the Revolutionary Committee, 13 July 1774; *Rivington's*, 14 July 1774; Jay, *Selected Papers*, 1:90–92.

47. Pincus, "Rise and Fall of Empires," 312; Steve Pincus, "Addison's Empire: Whig Conceptions of Empire in the Early 18th Century," *Parliamentary History* 31 (2012): 105, https://doi.org/10.1111/j.1750-0206.2011.00280.x.

48. *Proceedings of the Committee . . .* (New York: 1774), Evans, No. 13477; *Committee Chamber* (New York: 1774), Evans, No. 13478; *NYJ*, 21 July 1774; Jay to Scott, [20 July 1774], in Jay, *Selected Papers*, 1:92–93; Jay, *Selected Papers*, 1:90–92; Edmund Burke, "To the Electors of Bristol," 3 November 1774, *The Works of the Honourable Edmund Burke*, 8 vols. (London: Henry G. Bohn, 1854–56), 1:446–449.

49. Tiedemann, *Reluctant Revolutionaries*, 195–196; *NYGM*, 25 July 1774; *To the Inhabitants of the City and County of New-York* (New York: 1774), Evans, No. 13662; *NYJ*, 28 July 1774.

50. Records of the Revolutionary Committee, 25 July 1774; Jay, *Selected Papers*, 1:93; Colden to Dartmouth, 2 August 1774, CO 5/1105, f. 364, UK-KeNA.

7. Unite or Die

1. Robert G. Parkinson, *The Common Cause: Creating Race and Nation in the American Revolution* (Chapel Hill: University of North Carolina Press, 2016), 675; Joseph M. Adelman, *Revolutionary Networks: The Business and Politics of Printing the News, 1763–1789* (Baltimore: Johns Hopkins University Press, 2019), 5; John A. Garraty, Mark C. Carnes, and

Paul Betz, eds., *American National Biography*, 24 vols. plus supplement (New York: Oxford University Press, 1999–2002; rev. ed., www.anb.org).

2. Adelman, *Revolutionary Networks*, 114–115; Lester C. Olson, *Emblems of American Community in the Revolutionary Era* (Washington, DC: Smithsonian Institution Press, 1991), 34.

3. Benjamin Irvin, *Clothed in Robes of Sovereignty: The Continental Congress and the People Out of Doors* (New York: Oxford University Press, 2011), 19; Benjamin E. Park, *American Nationalisms: Imagining Union in the Age of Revolutions, 1783–1833* (New York: Cambridge University Press, 2018), 32–33; Albert Matthews, "The Snake Devices, 1754–1776," *Proceedings of the Colonial Society of Massachusetts* 11 (1907): 409–453.

4. Parkinson, *Common Cause*, 683; *Rivington's New-York Gazetteer* (hereafter, *Rivington's*), 11, 25 August 1774; Olson, *Emblems*, 34–35.

5. *The Price of Loyalty: Tory Writings from the Revolutionary Era*, ed. Catherine S. Crary (New York: McGraw-Hill, 1973), 328.

6. Rhinelander to John Vardill, 5 January 1775, AO 13/105, National Archives of the United Kingdom (hereafter, UK-KeNA). See "true blue" in *Oxford English Dictionary*, 2nd ed., 20 vols. (Oxford: Oxford University Press, 1989; www.oed.com) where the *Gentleman's Magazine* reference is also located.

7. *The Diaries of George Washington*, ed. Donald Jackson and Dorothy Twohig, 6 vols. (Charlottesville: University of Virginia Press, 1976–1979), 3:275; Jill Lepore, *These Truths: A History of the United States* (New York: W. W. Norton, 2018), 90–91; Alan Taylor, *American Revolutions: A Continental History, 1750–1804* (New York: W. W. Norton, 2016), 124.

8. *Diary and Autobiography of John Adams*, ed. L. H. Butterfield and others, 4 vols. (Cambridge, MA: Harvard University Press, 1961; hereafter, JA, *D&A*), 2:102; John Adams to Abigail Adams, 28 August 1774, *Adams Family Correspondence*, ed. L. H. Butterfield, Marc Friedlaender, Richard Alan Ryerson, Margaret A. Hogan, Sara Martin, Hobson Woodward, and others, 15 vols. published to date (Cambridge, MA: Harvard University Press, 1963–), 1:145–146; Leif Jerram, "Space: A Useless Category for Historical Analysis?" *History and Theory* 52 (2013): 400–419, https://www.jstor.org/stable/24542993; Barney Warf and Santa Arias, "Introduction: The Reinsertion of Space into the Social Sciences and Humanities," in *The Spatial Turn: Interdisciplinary Perspectives*, ed. Warf and Arias (London: Routledge, 2009), 1. See also John Gilbert McCurdy, "From Fort George to the Fields: The Public Space and the Military Geography of Revolutionary New York City," *Journal of Urban History* 44 (2018): 625–644, https://doi.org/10.1177%2F0096144218759028.

9. JA, *D&A*, 2:102; W. Harrison Bayles, *Old Taverns of New York* (New York: Frank Allaben Genealogical Co., 1915), 142–143, 205, 246, 255–256; *Historical Memoirs of William Smith*, ed. William H. W. Sabine, 3 vols. (New York: New York Times, 1969; hereafter, Smith, *Memoirs*, 1:208); John Austin Stevens Jr., "Old New York Taverns," *Harper's New Monthly Magazine* 80 (1890), 842–864, esp. 863–864.

10. JA, *D&A*, 2:102–104.

11. JA, *D&A*, 2:105–106; Richard M. Ketchum, *Divided Loyalties: How the American Revolution came to New York* (New York: Henry Holt, 2002), 281.

12. Silas Deane to Elizabeth Deane, [August 1774], *Collections of the Connecticut Historical Society*, 31 vols. (Hartford, CT: Published for the Society, 1860–1967), 2:143–147,

esp. 144; Roger J. Champagne, *Alexander McDougall and the American Revolution* (Schenectady, NY: New York State American Revolution Bicentennial Commission/Union College Press, 1975), 67.

13. *New-York Gazette; and the Weekly Mercury* (hereafter, NYGM), 22 August 1774; *New-York Journal; or, the General Advertiser* (hereafter, NYJ), 25 August 1774; *Rivington's*, 25 August 1774; JA, *D&A*, 2:109.

14. NYGM, 5 September 1774; NYJ, 8 September 1774; Irvin, *Clothed in Robes of Sovereignty*, 25–27. John Jay quietly departed for Philadelphia on 29 August 1774.

15. Cynthia A. Kierner, *Traders and Gentlefolk: The Livingstons of New York, 1675–1790* (Ithaca, NY: Cornell University Press, 1992), 206; Carl L. Becker, *The History of Political Parties in the Province of New York, 1760–1776* (Madison, WI: [s.n.], 1909), 143–144; JA, *D&A*, 2:126; Taylor, *American Revolutions*, 123; Lepore, *These Truths*, 91; Jerrilyn Greene Marston, *King and Congress: The Transfer of Political Legitimacy, 1775–1776* (Princeton, NJ: Princeton University Press, 1987), 80–81; Champagne, *Alexander McDougall*, 68–69; JA, *D&A*, 2:106.

16. Champagne, *Alexander McDougall*, 69–70; Irvin, *Clothed in Robes of Sovereignty*, 28–44; Taylor, *American Revolutions*, 126; Smith to Tryon, 10 December 1774, D(W)1778/II/1008, Staffordshire Record Office.

17. Taylor, *American Revolutions*, 126–127; Irvin, *Clothed in Robes of Sovereignty*, 44–45; Justin du Rivage, *Revolution against Empire: Taxes, Politics, and the Origins of American Independence* (New Haven, CT: Yale University Press, 2017), 8; Smith to Philip Schuyler, 22 November 1774, Philip Schuyler Papers, Manuscripts and Archives Division, New York Public Library (hereafter, NN).

18. Barbara Clark Smith, *The Freedoms We Lost: Consent and Resistance in Revolutionary America* (New York: New Press, 2010), 123–124, 127; Barbara Clark Smith, "Social Visions of the American Resistance Movement," in *The Transforming Hand of Revolution: Reconsidering the American Revolution as a Social Movement*, ed. Ronald Hoffman and Peter J. Albert (Charlottesville: University Press of Virginia, 1995), 38–49; Leopold S. Launitz-Schürer Jr., *Loyal Whigs and Revolutionaries: The Making of an American Revolution in New York, 1765–1776* (New York: New York University Press, 1980), 121–122; Michael D. Hattem, "'As Serves our Interest best': Political Economy and the Logic of Resistance in New York City, 1765–1775," *New York History* (hereafter, NYH) 98 (2017): 66, https://doi.org/10.1353/nyh.2017.0037.

19. Colden to Dartmouth, 7 December 1774, CO 5/1106, f. 1–2, UK-KeNA; Scott to Richard Varick, 15 November 1775, Gilder Lehrman Coll., on deposit at New-York Historical Society (hereafter, NHi).

20. Rhinelander to William Elery, 5 April 1775, Frederick and Philip Rhinelander Letter—and Order-book, Rhinelander Family Papers, NHi; NYJ, 15 December 1774; Cathy Matson, *Merchants & Empire: Trading in Colonial New York* (Baltimore: Johns Hopkins University Press, 2003), 306–308.

21. *The Following Persons . . .* (New York, 1774), Charles Evans and others, *American Bibliography: A Chronological Dictionary of All Books, Pamphlets and Periodical Publications Printed in the United States of America* [1639–1800], 14 vols. (Chicago and Worcester, MA, 1903–1959; rev. ed., www.readex.com; hereafter, Evans), No. 13485; Daniel Dunscomb, *The Mechanics . . .* (New York, 1774), Evans, No. 42653; NYJ, 17, 24 November 1774; NYGM, 28 November 1774; Smith to Schuyler 22 November 1774, Philip Schuyler Papers, NN; Champagne, *Alexander McDougall*, 70.

22. Hughes to Lamb, November 1774, John Lamb Papers, reel 1, NHi; Haldimand to Dartmouth, 7 September 1774, Haldimand Papers, Add. MS 21,695, f. 112–113, British Library.

Those in *italics* were DeLanceyites but their allegiance in the Revolution could not be determined; those in **bold italics** were DeLanceyites who became loyalists; those in <u>*underlined italics*</u> were DeLanceyites who became Patriots; those in **bold** were McDougallites but their allegiance in the Revolution could not be determined; those in <u>**underlined bold**</u> were McDougallites who became Patriots; those in <u>UNDERLINED ALL-CAPS</u> were McDougallites who became loyalists; those whose partisanship is unknown but became loyalists are in <u>UNDERLINED SMALL CAPS</u>; those whose partisanship is unknown who became Patriots are in *ITALICIZED ALL-CAPS*; and those whose partisanship or allegiance could not be identified have been left unformatted.

Those colonists who kept their places were **John Alsop**, **Abraham Brasher**, <u>*John Broome*</u>, *Joseph Bull*, **Peter T. Curtenius**, John **DeLancey**, <u>*James Duane*</u>, Abraham Duryee, **Joseph Hallet**, Nicholas Hoffman, <u>*John Jay*</u>, *David Johnson*, *Edward Laight*, **Francis Lewis**, *Leonard Lispenard*, **Philip Livingston**, **Peter Van Brugh Livingston**, *Abraham P. Lott*, *Isaac Low*, *Gabriel H. Ludlow*, **Alexander McDougall**, *Charles Nicoll*, **Thomas Randall**, **Henry Remsen**, **Isaac Sears**, *Charles Shaw*, *Peter Van Schaack*, *Abraham Walton*, and *William Walton*.

Those who lost their places were *Theophylact Bache*, <u>WILLIAM BAYARD</u>, *Gerard W. Beekman*, *Benjamin Booth*, **George Bowne**, *Elias Desbrosses*, *Gerardus Duycchink*, *Peter Goelet*, *James Jauncey*, *William McAdam*, *Charles McEvers*, *Thomas Marston*, John Moore, *Thomas Pearsall*, *Richard Sharpe*, *Miles Sherbrooke*, *John Thurman Jr.*, <u>**David Van Horne**</u>, <u>*Jacobus Van Zandt*</u>, *Alexander Wallace*, *Richard Yates*, and *Hamilton Young*.

The new additions were *JOHN ANTHONY*, Theophilus Anthony, Francis Bassett, Robert Benson, John Berrien, Victor Bicker, Lancaster Burling, *WILLIAM DENNING*, Lawrence Embree, Edward Fleming, William W. Gilbert, William Gosorth, Thomas Ivers, George Janeway, *FREDERICK JAY*, <u>SAMUEL JONES</u>, *JOHN LASHER*, **William W. Ludlow**, **John B. Moore**, **Hercules Mulligan**, <u>LINDLEY MURRAY</u>, *JEREMIAH PLATT*, <u>RUDOLPHUS RITZEMA</u>, *John Roome*, **Isaac Roosevelt**, *NICHOLAS ROOSEVELT*, *COMFORT SANDS*, *Joseph Totten*, **William Ustick**, Jacob Van Voorhees, and John White. Data has been extracted from *NYJ*, 24 November 1774; *At a Meeting at the Exchange . . .* (New York, 1773), Evans, No. 13125.

23. Colden to Dartmouth, 7 December 1774, CO 5/1106, f. 1–4, UK-KeNA.

24. Smith to Tryon, 10 December 1774, D(W)1778/II/1008, Staffordshire Record Office. Smith felt compelled to be a bystander at this moment, telling Tryon, "I have pondered much upon this Subject, perceiving personal Danger in resisting, and public Distress in humouring the Vulgar Opinions." He did, however, note that he would try to persuade members of the Royal Council ("the Politicians") to "adopt Clauses in their Address to the King, declarative of some Sobriety of Sentiment, that a Door may be opened for Negotiations, upon <u>decent Terms</u>, and friendly to the union of the different ranches of the Empire."

25. William B. Sprague, *Annals of the American Pulpit*, 9 vols. (New York: Robert Carter & Brothers, 1857–1869), 5:462–465; Patricia U. Bonomi, *A Factious People: Politics and Society in Colonial New York* (New York: Columbia University Press, 1971), 310, 311; *Biographical Directory of the United States Congress, 1774–2005*, Washington, DC, 2005; rev. ed.,

bioguide.congress.gov; hereafter, *Biog. Dir. Cong.*); *Rivington's New-York Gazetteer*, 28 November 1774; *Diaries of Gouverneur Morris*, ed. Melanie Randolph Miller and Hendrina Krol, 2 vols. (Charlottesville: University of Virginia Press, 2011–2018), 2:884–889; Isaac Wilkins, *Short Advice to the Counties of New-York / by a Country Gentleman* (New York: James Rivington, 1774), 7, Evans, No. 13722; Peter Force, *American Archives: Consisting of a Collection of Authentick Records, State Papers, Debates, and Letters and Other Notices of Publick Affairs*, 6 series, 9 vols. (Washington, DC: Published under authority of an act of Congress, 1837–1853), 4th ser., 1:1293–1297; [Seabury], *A View of the Controversy . . .* (New York: James Rivington, 1774), Evans, No. 13603; Philip Gould, "Wit and Politics in Revolutionary British America: The Case of Samuel Seabury and Alexander Hamilton," *Eighteenth-Century Studies* 41 (2008): 383, 384, https://www.jstor.org/stable/30053556.

26. Hamilton to McDougall, [1774–1776], in *The Papers of Alexander Hamilton*, ed. Harold C. Syrett, Jacob E. Cooke, and others, 27 vols. (New York: Columbia University Press, 1961–1987), 26:353–354; McDougall to Unknown, 14 April 1775, in *Papers of John Adams*, ed. Robert J. Taylor, Gregg L. Lint, Sara Georgini, and others, 21 vols. published to date (Cambridge, MA: Harvard University Press, 1977–   ; hereafter, JA, *Papers*), 2:414–415; Adams to McDougall, 5 June 1775, in JA, *Papers*, 3:14.

27. Rhinelander to John Vardill, 5 January 1775, AO 13/105, UK-KeNA; I. N. Phelps Stokes, *The Iconography of Manhattan Island, 1498–1909*, 6 vols. (New York: R. H. Dodd, 1915–1928), 4:870.

28. Rhinelander to John Vardill, 5 January 1775, AO 13/105, UK-KeNA; Amicable Society Members, New York City Misc. Coll., box 14, f. 17, NN; Smith, *Memoirs*, 1:102–103; *The Papers of George Washington: Revolutionary War Series*, ed. Philander D. Chase, Frank E. Grizzard Jr., Edward G. Lengel, David R. Hoth, and others, 30 vols. published to date (Charlottesville: University of Virginia Press, 1985–   ; hereafter, Washington, *Papers, Rev. War Series*), 5:672, 18:74; *The Papers of General Nathanael Greene*, ed. Richard K. Showman, Dennis Conrad, Roger N. Parks, and others, 13 vols. (Chapel Hill: University of North Carolina Press, 1976–2005), 1:240–241.

29. Oliver DeLancey Sr. to Oliver DeLancey Jr., 4 January 1775, D(W)1778/II/1090, Staffordshire Record Office.

30. Champagne, *Alexander McDougall*, 74; Launitz-Schürer, *Loyal Whigs*, 129–130; Burke to DeLancey, 14 March 1775, in Ross J. S. Hoffman, *Edmund Burke: New York Agent* (Philadelphia: American Philosophical Society, 1956), 262–263; Smith, *Memoirs*, 1:206–207.

31. *Journal of the Votes and Proceedings of the General Assembly of the Colony of New-York* (hereafter, *Assembly Journal*), 1, Evans, No. 14291; Colden to Dartmouth, 3 January 1775, CO 5/1106, f. 14, UK-KeNA; Colden to Dartmouth, 4 January 1775, CO 5/1106, f. 16–17, UK-KeNA.

32. *Assembly Journal*, 1, Evans, No. 14291.

33. Smith, *Memoirs*, 1:207, 209.

34. Burke to DeLancey, 14 March 1775, in Hoffman, *Edmund Burke*, 262; *Assembly Journal*, 14, Evans, No. 14291.

35. Washington, *Papers, Rev. War Series*, 5:292; *Colonial Albany Social History Project*, http://exhibitions.nysm.nysed.gov//albany/welcome.html; Bonomi, *Factious People*, 277, 308–309; John P. Kaminski, *George Clinton: Yeoman Politician of the New Republic* (Mad-

ison, WI: Madison House, 1993), 15; Champagne, *Alexander McDougall*, 75; *Assembly Journal*, 23, Evans, No. 14291.

36. Rhinelander to Vardill, 5 January 1775, AO 13/105, UK-KeNA; McDougall to Samuel Adams, 29 January 1775, McDougall Papers, reel 1, NHi.

37. Eran Shalev, *Rome Reborn on Western Shores: Historical Imagination and the Creation of the American Republic* (Charlottesville: University of Virginia Press, 2009), 5–6, 24, 30–31, 38, 116–117; McDougall to Samuel Adams, 29 January 1775, McDougall Papers, reel 1, NHi.

38. *Assembly Journal*, 28, 42, 43, 45, 50, Evans, No. 14291.

39. Force, *American Archives*, 4th ser., 1:1291, 1296; *To the King's Most Excellent Majesty . . .* (New York, 1775), 1, 2, 5, 6, 10–11, Evans, No. 14295; Burke to DeLancey, 14 March 1775, in Hoffman, *Edmund Burke*, 262–263.

40. D. A. Story, *The deLanceys: A Romance of a Great Family* ([Toronto]: T. Nelson & Sons, 1931), 19; Burke to the Assembly Committee of Correspondence, 7 June 1775, Hoffman, *Edmund Burke*, 268–269; Launitz-Schürer, *Loyal Whigs*, 136; du Rivage, *Revolution against Empire*, 6, 162; McDougall to William Cooper, 9 February 1775, McDougall Papers, box 1, NHi; Champagne, *Alexander McDougall*, 78–79; Roger J. Champagne, "New York Politics and Independence, 1776," New-York Historical Society, *Quarterly* 46 (1962): 281–282.

41. Burke to the Assembly Committee of Correspondence, 7 June 1775, in Hoffman, *Edmund Burke*, 268–271.

42. *Assembly Journal*, 120, Evans, No. 14291; *NYJ*, 2 March 1775; Smith, *Memoirs*, 1:221; *To the Freemen and Freeholders of the City and County of New-York* (New York, 1775), Evans, No. 14500; Kenneth Owen, *Political Community in Revolutionary Pennsylvania* (New York: Oxford University Press, 2018), 1–2, 8–9; Douglas Bradburn, *The Citizenship Revolution: Politics and the Creation of the American Union, 1774–1804* (Charlottesville: University of Virginia Press, 2009), 20.

43. Champagne, *Alexander McDougall*, 79; *NYJ*, 9 March 1775.

44. *NYJ*, 9 March 1775; David L. Ammerman, *In the Common Cause: American Response to the Coercive Acts of 1774* (Charlottesville: University Press of Virginia, 1974), 150–151; Joseph S. Tiedemann, *Reluctant Revolutionaries: New York City and the Road to Independence, 1763–1776* (Ithaca, NY: Cornell University Press, 1997), 217; Eric Nelson, *The Royalist Revolution: Monarchy and the American Founding* (Cambridge, MA: Harvard University Pres, 2014), 2; Ruma Chopra, *Unnatural Rebellion: Loyalists in New York City during the Revolution* (Charlottesville: University of Virginia Press, 2011), 33.

45. Smith, *Memoirs*, 1:211; *Colonial Panorama, 1775: Dr. Robert Honyman's Journal for March and April*, ed. Philip Padelford (San Marino, CA: Huntington Library, 1939), 28; Force, *American Archives*, 4th ser., 2:137–138.

46. Force, *American Archives*, 4th ser., 2:139; Carl Abbott, "The Neighborhoods of New York City, 1760–1775," *NYH* 55 (1974): 39, 40, 46, 47–51; Tiedemann, *Reluctant Revolutionaries*, 27; Herbert S. Klein and Edmund P. Willis, "The Distribution of Wealth in Late Eighteenth-Century New York City," *Histoire sociale / Social History* 38 (1985): 260; Kathryn Lasdow, "Theophylact Bache's Water Lots: How Merchants Turned the East River into Exclusive Land," SHEAR Annual Conference, 19 July 2019, Cambridge, MA; Lepore, *New York Burning*, 21–22, 243; Edwin G. Burrows and Mike Wallace, *Gotham: A*

History of New York City to 1898 (New York: Oxford University Press, 1999), 187–190; Thelma Willis Foote, *Black and White Manhattan: The History of Racial Formation in Colonial New York City* (New York: Oxford University Press, 2004), 82; Jason M. Barr, *Building the Skyline: The Birth and Growth of Manhattan's Skyscrapers* (New York: Oxford University Press, 2016), 89–91.

47. Smith, *Memoirs*, 1:211; Force, *American Archives*, 4th ser., 2:139; Staughton Lynd, "Who Should Rule at Home? Dutchess County, New York, in the American Revolution," *William and Mary Quarterly* 18 (1961): 330–331, https://doi.org/10.2307/1921169; *NYJ*, 16 March 1775; McDougall to Quincy, 2 March 1775, McDougall Papers, reel 1, NHi. The other delegates were Philip Livingston, John Jay, James Duane, John Alsop, Isaac Low, Francis Lewis, Abraham Walton, Abraham Brasher, Leonard Lispenard, and Isaac Roosevelt.

48. Laight to Vardill, 29 March 1775, AO 13/105, UK-KeNA; Ellison to Thomas Ellison Sr., 27 January 1775, in *Magazine of American History with Notes and Queries*, vol. 8 (New York: A. S. Barnes and Co., 1882), 281; Smith, *Memoirs*, 1:211.

49. Rhinelander to Elery, 5 April 1775, Frederick and Philip Rhinelander Letter—and Order-book, Rhinelander Family Papers, NHi; Rhinelander to Hodgson and Donaldson, 4 October 1775, Frederick and Philip Rhinelander Letter—and Order-book, Rhinelander Family Papers, NHi.

50. *NYJ*, 16, 23 March 1775.

8. The Din of War

1. Philip Ranlet and Richard B. Morris, "Richard B. Morris's James DeLancey: Portrait in Loyalism," *New York History* 80 (1999): 185–210, https://www.jstor.org/stable/23182484 200–202; DeLancey to Rockingham, 4 February 1769, Wentworth Woodhouse Muniments, Sheffield City Archives and Local Studies Library; D. A. Story, *The deLanceys: A Romance of a Great Family* ([Toronto]: T. Nelson & Sons, 1931), 19.

2. Philip Ranlet, *The New York Loyalists* (Knoxville: University of Tennessee Press, 1986), 114, 117; Joseph S. Tiedemann, *Reluctant Revolutionaries: New York City and the Road to Independence, 1763–1776* (Ithaca, NY: Cornell University Press, 1997), 215; *Historical Memoirs of William Smith*, ed. William H. W. Sabine, 3 vols. (New York: New York Times, 1969; hereafter, Smith, *Memoirs*), 1:269; Morris, "Portrait in Loyalism," 201–202.

3. John W. Tyler, "Thomas Hutchinson's Enemies List: Unmasking Conspiracy and Wickedness in the Patriot Cause," *New England Quarterly* 93, no. 4 (2020): 555, https://doi.org/10.1162/tneq_a_00862; Bernard Bailyn, *The Ordeal of Thomas Hutchinson* (Cambridge, Mass.: Harvard University Press, 1976), 274–330 (quotes at 278, 305); Liam Riordan, "A Loyalist Who Loved His Country too Much: Thomas Hutchinson, Historian of Colonial Massachusetts," *New England Quarterly* 90, no. 3 (2017), 344–384, esp. 379–381, https://doi.org/10.1162/tneq_a_00624; *The Diary and Letters of His Excellency Thomas Hutchinson*, ed. Peter Orlando Hutchinson, 2 vols. (Boston: Houghton, Mifflin & Co., 1884–1886), 1:487, 506, 542, 543, 545, 569–570, 572, 574, 587; 2:4, 19, 26, 31, 34, 35, 45–46, 95, 110, 121–122, 132, 221, 223, 246, 257, 337. For more on loyalists in London, see Mary Beth Norton, *The British-Americans: The Loyalist Exiles in England, 1774–1789* (Boston: Little, Brown, 1972), 45–46.

4. James DeLancey Claim, AO 12/19, f. 179, 202, 217, National Archives of the United Kingdom (hereafter, UK-KeNA).

5. Kenneth Cohen, *They Will Have Their Game: Sporting Culture and the Making of the Early American Republic* (Ithaca, NY: Cornell University Press, 2017), 33–34; Robert Black, *The Jockey Club and Its Founders* (London: Smith, Elder, and Co., 1891), 11–13, 18–22, 138–139, 152–153, 158; https://www.thejockeyclub.co.uk/the-racing/our-heritage/ (accessed 22 October 2019); Morris, "Portrait in Loyalism," 204. Anne Warren, who was the eldest daughter of Susannah DeLancey Warren and Adm. Sir Peter Warren and James DeLancey Jr.'s cousin, married Augustus's younger brother, Charles FitzRoy, first Baron Southampton, in 1758. See Story, *deLanceys*, 16, 67; Leslie Stephen and Sidney Lee, eds., *The Dictionary of National Biography*, 21 vols. plus supplements (New York and London, 1885–1901; repr. Oxford: Oxford University Press, 1959–1960; rev. ed., www.oxforddnb.com; hereafter, *DNB*), entry on FitzRoy, Charles. See also *Middlesex Journal*, 30 January–1 February 1770,

6. *Middlesex Journal*, 8–11 July 1775; Smith, *Memoirs*, 1:269; Norton, *British-Americans*, 45.

7. *Diary and Autobiography of John Adams*, ed. L. H. Butterfield and others, 4 vols. (Cambridge, MA: Harvard University Press, 1961; hereafter, JA, *D&A*), 2:106–107; Cynthia A. Kierner, *Traders and Gentlefolk: The Livingstons of New York, 1675–1790* (Ithaca, NY: Cornell University Press, 1992), 206–208; Laight to John Vardill, 27 March 1775, AO 13/105, UK-KeNA.

8. Robert Livingston Sr. to Robert R. Livingston, 5 May 1775, quoted in George Dangerfield, *Chancellor Robert R. Livingston of New York 1746–1813* (New York: Harcourt, Brace, 1960), 55; Maya Jasanoff, *Liberty's Exiles: American Loyalists in the Revolutionary World* (New York: Knopf, 2011), 24; Justin du Rivage, *Revolution against Empire: Taxes, Politics, and the Origins of American Independence* (New Haven, CT: Yale University Press, 2017), 9.

9. Tiedemann, *Reluctant Revolutionaries*, 219; MSS. New-York Conventions, 1775–1778, Jared Sparks Coll., Houghton Library, Harvard University (hereafter, MH-H); Richard Bourke, *Empire and Revolution: The Political Life of Edmund Burke* (Princeton, NJ: Princeton University Press, 2015), xviii; Steve Pincus, *The Heart of the Declaration: The Founders' Case for an Activist Government* (New Haven, CT: Yale University Press, 2016), 93–94; Chatham to Rockingham, 31 January 1775, in George Thomas, *Memoirs of the Marquis of Rockingham and his Contemporaries*, 2 vols. (London: Richard Bentley, 1852), 2:269; du Rivage, *Revolution against Empire*, 173–175; Andrew Jackson O'Shaughnessy, *The Men Who Lost America: British Leadership, the American Revolution, and the Fate of the Empire* (New Haven, CT: Yale University Press, 2013), 54, 55–57; Ross J. S. Hoffman, *Edmund Burke: New York Agent* (Philadelphia: American Philosophical Society, 1956), 173–175.

10. Rick J. Ashton, "The Loyalist Congressmen of New York," New-York Historical Society, *Quarterly* (hereafter, NYHS, *Quart.*) 60 (1976): 100; Peter Force, *American Archives: Consisting of a Collection of Authentick Records, State Papers, Debates, and Letters and Other Notices of Publick Affairs*, 6 series, 9 vols. (Washington, DC: Published under authority of an act of Congress, 1837–1853), 4th ser., 2:351–357; New-York Conventions, Jared Sparks Coll., MH-H; Rhinelander to William Elery, 5 April 1775, Frederick and Philip Rhinelander Letter—and Order-book, Rhinelander Family Papers, New-York Historical Society

(hereafter, NHi); *New-York Gazette; and the Weekly Mercury* (hereafter, *NYGM*), 17 April 1775; *Rivington's New-York Gazetteer* (hereafter, *Rivington's*), 20 April 1775.

11. Force, *American Archives*, 4th ser., 2:351–357; Laight to Vardill, 29 March 1775, AO 13/105, UK-KeNA.

12. *Rivington's*, 27 April 1775; *NYGM*, 23 April 1775.

13. Jill Lepore, *These Truths: A History of the United States* (New York: W. W. Norton, 2018), 92–93; O'Shaughnessy, *Men Who Lost America*, 84–85; *DNB*; Alan Taylor, *American Revolutions: A Continental History, 1750–1804* (New York: W. W. Norton, 2016), 132; Jane Kamensky, *A Revolution in Color: The World of John Singleton Copley* (New York: W. W. Norton, 2016), 184–185; John Richard Alden, *General Gage in America: Being Principally A History of His Role in the American Revolution* (Baton Rouge: Louisiana State University Press, 1948), 65–69; David Hackett Fischer, *Paul Revere's Ride* (New York: Oxford University Press, 1994), 95–97, 316–317, 320–321.

14. Fischer, *Revere's Ride*, 270–271, 324–325; [McDougall's notes on Lexington], 23 April 1775, McDougall Papers, reel 1, NHi; *Hartford Courant*, 23 July 1916.

15. O'Shaughnessy, *Men Who Lost America*, 51, 59; Gage to Dartmouth, 23 April 1775, Dartmouth MSS, Staffordshire County Record Office.

16. Smith, *Memoirs*, 1:221, 222.

17. Roger J. Champagne, *Alexander McDougall and the American Revolution* (Schenectady, NY: New York State American Revolution Bicentennial Commission/Union College Press, 1975), 82–83; *A Narrative of the Military Actions of Colonel Marinus Willett*, ed. William M. Willett (New York: G. & C. & H. Carvill, 1831), 27–28; New Yorkers that received firearms, 23 April 1774, Muster Rolls Coll., NHi; NYHS, *Quart.* 23 (1939): 29–31, 60–62, 109–110, 138–142; Robert R. Livingston to Mary Stevens Livingston, 27 April 1775, Livingston Family Papers, Manuscripts and Archives Division, New York Public Library (hereafter, NN); same to same, 3 May 1775, Livingston Family Papers, NN.

18. Appraisement of Sundry Arms taken from non-associators by the Gen. committee, New York City Misc. Mss. box 12, no. 15, NHi; Inglis, "Breif [*sic*] Notes," 13 May 1776, Charles Inglis Journals and Letterbooks, Loyalist Coll., Harriet Irving Library, University of New Brunswick (hereafter, NBFU); Roome Claim, AO 12/30, f. 182–190, UK-KeNA; John Milner to Myles Cooper, 3 December 1775, in *The Cause of Loyalty: The Revolutionary War Correspondence of Myles Cooper*, ed. Christopher F. Minty and Peter W. Walker (forthcoming); I. N. Phelps Stokes, *The Iconography of Manhattan Island, 1498–1909*, 6 vols. (New York: R. H. Dodd, 1915–1928), 4:885–886; *Papers of John Adams*, ed. Robert J. Taylor, Gregg L. Lint, Sara Georgini, and others, 21 vols. published to date (Cambridge, MA: Harvard University Press, 1977–   ; hereafter, JA, *Papers*), 3:205–208.

19. Inglis to Vardill, 2 May 1775, Egerton MS, 2135, British Library (hereafter, Uk); Laight to John Vardill, 27 March 1775, AO 13/105, UK-KeNA.

20. Colden to Dartmouth, 3 May 1775, in *Documents Relative to the Colonial History of the State of New-York*, ed. E. B. O'Callaghan and Berthold Fernow, 15 vols. (Albany, NY: Weed, Parsons and Co., 1853–1887; hereafter, *N.Y. Col. Docs.*), 8:571–572; Cruger to Burke, 4 May 1775, D(W)1778/II/1257, Staffordshire Record Office.

21. Burke to Charles O'Hara, May 1775, in Hoffman, *Edmund Burke*, 182; Bourke, *Empire and Revolution*, 450; O'Shaughnessy, *Men Who Lost America*, 23–24, 54–55, 59, 167–168, 173–174, 175 (George III quote at 24); Brendan Simms, *Three Victories and a Defeat: The Rise and Fall of the First British Empire, 1714–1783* (New York: Basic, 2007), 590, 593,

595; James M. Vaughn, *The Politics of Empire at the Accession of George III: The East India Company and the Crisis and Transformation of Britain's Imperial State* (New Haven, CT: Yale University Press, 2019), 213; Pincus, *Heart*, 93; Julie M. Flavell, "Government Interception of Letters from America and the Quest for Colonial Opinion in 1775," *William and Mary Quarterly* (hereafter, *WMQ*) 58 (2001), 408–415 (New Yorkers' quotes at 411), https://doi .org/10.2307/2674191; Stephen Conway, "From Fellow-Nationals to Foreigners: British Perceptions of the Americans, circa 1739–1783," *WMQ* 59 (2002): 89, https://doi.org/10 .2307/3491638.

22. *New-York, Committee-Chamber . . .* (New York: [John Holt], 1775), Charles Evans and others, *American Bibliography: A Chronological Dictionary of All Books, Pamphlets and Periodical Publications Printed in the United States of America* [1639–1800], 14 vols. (Chicago and Worcester, MA, 1903–1959; rev. ed., www.readex.com; hereafter, Evans), No. 14322; Champagne, *Alexander McDougall*, 83–84; Leopold S. Launitz-Schürer Jr., *Loyal Whigs and Revolutionaries: The Making of an American Revolution in New York, 1765–1776* (New York: New York University Press, 1980), 157–158; *A General Association . . .* (New York: [John Holt], 1775), Evans, No. 14339; *Resolved, That Copies of the Association . . .* (New York: [John Holt], 1775), Evans, No. 14329; *Committee-Chamber . . .* (New York: [John Holt], 1775), Evans, No. 14323.

23. Patricia U. Bonomi, *A Factious People: Politics and Society in Colonial New York* (New York: Columbia University Press, 1971), 310; Stokes, *Iconography*, 4:885; *The Following Persons . . .* (New York: [John Holt], 1775), Evans, No. 14033; *General Committee . . .* (New York: [John Holt], 1775), Evans, No. 14325; *Committee-Chamber . . .* (New York: [John Holt], 1775), Evans, No. 14324; Carl L. Becker, *The History of Political Parties in the Province of New York, 1760–1776* (Madison, WI: [s.n.], 1909), 197–200.

24. Champagne, *Alexander McDougall*, 84; Smith, *Memoirs*, 222–223; *Pennsylvania Journal*, 29 April 1775; *Extracts from Bradford's Journal . . .* (New York: [1775], John Holt), Evans, No. 14028; White, *To the Public . . .* (New York, 1775), Evans, No. 14624.

25. *NYG*, 8 May 1775; Ketchum, *Divided Loyalties*, 339–340; Smith, *Memoirs*, 1:223; Wilkins Claim, T 79/70, f. 21–26, UK-KeNA; Wilkins Claim, T 79/71, f. 10, UK-KeNA.

26. *DNB*; Ron Chernow, *Alexander Hamilton* (New York: Penguin, 2004), 51, 52, 56, 63–64; Clarence H. Vance, *Myles Cooper* (New York: Columbia University Press, 1930), 278. 279; Thomas Jones, *History of New York during the Revolutionary War*, 2 vols. (New York: Printed for the New-York Historical Society, 1879), 1:55; *Gentleman's Magazine*, vol. 46 (London: Printed for D. Henry, 1777), 326–327; Stokes, *Iconography*, 4:886, 888; *Catalogue of Columbia College* (New York: Printed for Columbia, 1844), 24.

27. Deas Claim, AO 12/24, f. 397–403, UK-KeNA; Benson Memorial, Frederick Mackenzie Papers, box 1, f. 2, William L. Clements Library, University of Michigan (hereafter, MiU-C); Benson Claim, AO 13/12, f. 255, UK-KeNA; JA, *Papers*, 3:1–2; *Adams Family Correspondence*, ed. L. H. Butterfield, Marc Friedlaender, Richard Alan Ryerson, Margaret A. Hogan, Sara Martin, Hobson Woodward, and others, 15 vols. published to date (Cambridge, MA: Harvard University Press, 1963–), 1:191.

28. Colden to Dartmouth, 7 June 1775, in *N.Y. Col. Docs.*, 8:579–581, 582–583; Dartmouth to Tryon, 1 July 1775, in *N.Y. Col. Docs.*, 8:587–588.

29. Paul David Nelson, *William Tryon and the Course of Empire: A Life in British Imperial Service* (Chapel Hill: University of North Carolina Press, 1990), 128–129; Tiedemann,

Reluctant Revolutionaries, 2–3; Lepore, *These Truths*, 93; Taylor, *American Revolutions*, 141–142.

30. *The Papers of George Washington: Revolutionary War Series*, ed. Philander D. Chase, Frank E. Grizzard Jr., Edward G. Lengel, David R. Hoth, and others, 30 vols. published to date (Charlottesville: University of Virginia Press, 1985–   ; hereafter, Washington, *Papers, Rev. War Series*), 1:27–28, 32–34; Taylor, *American Revolutions*, 142; Tiedemann, *Reluctant Revolutionaries*, 3; *NYG*, 26 June 1775; Stokes, *Iconography*, 4:837, 894; *The Diaries of George Washington*, ed. Donald Jackson and Dorothy Twohig, 6 vols. (Charlottesville: University of Virginia Press, 1976–1979), 3:180, 181, 182; Smith, *Memoirs*, 1:228c–228d; Tryon to Gage, 26 June 1775, Gage Papers, MiU-C; Tryon to Dartmouth, 4 July 1775, in *N.Y. Col. Docs.*, 8:589–590. See also Joseph Jackson, "Washington in Philadelphia," *Pennsylvania Magazine of History and Biography* 56, no. 2 (1932), facing 118, https://www.jstor.org/stable/20086796.

31. McDougall to JA, 5 June 1775, in JA, *Papers*, 3:14–16; Washington, *Papers, Rev. War Series*, 1:34–36; Taylor, *American Revolutions*, 133–135; Smith, *Memoirs*, 1:232, 242; Tryon to Dartmouth, 4 July 1775, in *N.Y. Col. Docs.*, 8:589; same to same, 7 July 1775, in *N.Y. Col. Docs.*, 8:592; John Pownall to Tryon, 6 September 1775, in *N.Y. Col. Docs.*, 8:635; Tryon to Dartmouth, 11 November 1775, in *N.Y. Col. Docs.*, 8:643–644; Ruma Chopra, *Unnatural Rebellion: Loyalists in New York City during the Revolution* (Charlottesville: University of Virginia Press, 2011), 172.

32. Thompson Claim, AO 12/30, f. 290–292, UK-KeNA; Kempe to Myles Cooper, 7 November 1775, in Minty and Walker, *Cause of Loyalty*; Sears to Roger Sherman, Eliphalet Dyer, and Silas Deane, 28 November 1775, Sol Feinstone Coll., #1254, David Library of the American Revolution (now at American Philosophical Society); Holger Hoock, *Scars of Independence: America's Violent Birth* (New York: Crown, 2017), 38–39.

33. George Washington to Philip Schuyler, 20 August 1775, in Washington, *Papers, Rev. War Series*, 1:331; Aaron Sullivan, *The Disaffected: Britain's Occupation of Philadelphia during the American Revolution* (Philadelphia: University of Pennsylvania Press, 2019), 4–6, 10; Hoock, *Scars of Independence*, 18; T. H. Breen, *The Will of the People: The Revolutionary Birth of America* (Cambridge, MA: Harvard University Press, 2019), 88–89, 97; Donald F. Johnson, "Forgiving and Forgetting in Postrevolutionary America," in *Experiencing Empire: Power, People, and Revolution in Early America*, ed. Patrick Griffin (Charlottesville: University of Virginia Press, 2017), 171–173; Jill Lepore, *This America: The Case for the Nation* (New York: Knopf, 2019), 18; Johann N. Neem, "A Nation of Nations Must Still Be a Nation: On Nationalism, Globalization, and Writing History," *Los Angeles Review of Books*, 30 August 2019, https://lareviewofbooks.org/article/a-nation-of-nations -must-still-be-a-nation-on-nationalism-globalization-and-writing-history/ (accessed 12 September 2019).

34. Joyce D. Goodfriend, *Who Should Rule at Home? Confronting the Elite in British New York City* (Ithaca, NY: Cornell University Press, 2017), 237–238; New Yorkers that Received Firearms, 25 April 1775, Muster Rolls Coll., NHi; Bonomi, *Factious People*, 277; Lorenzo Sabine, *Biographical Sketches of Loyalists of the American Revolution*, 2 vols. (Boston: Little, Brown and Co., 1847–1864), 2:210; Force, *American Archives*, 4th ser., 2:513; *St. James's Chronicle*, 3–5 October 1776; Judith L. Van Buskirk, *Generous Enemies: Patriots and Loyalists in Revolutionary New York* (Philadelphia: University of Pennsylvania Press, 2002), 157–159, 191–192.

35. *The Selected Papers of John Jay*, ed. Elizabeth M. Nuxoll and others, 7 vols. (Charlottesville: University of Virginia Press, 2010–2021; hereafter, Jay, *Selected Papers*), 1:207, 208–210; Inglis, "Breif Notes," 4, 20 February 1776, NBFU; Phillip Papas, *Renegade Revolutionary: The Life of General Charles Lee* (New York: New York University Press, 2014), 143–145; Mike Rapport, *The Unruly City: Paris, London, and New York in the Age of Revolution* (New York: Basic, 2017), 80; Lee to Sears, 6 March 1776, in New-York Historical Society, *Collections for 1871* (New York: Printed for the Society, 1872), 345–346; Sears to Lee, 17 March 1776, in New-York Historical Society, *Collections for 1871*, 359.

36. Jay, *Selected Papers*, 1:208–210; Papas, *Renegade Revolutionary*, 144–145; T. Cole Jones, *Captives of Liberty: Prisoners of War and the Politics of Vengeance in the American Revolution* (Philadelphia: University of Pennsylvania Press, 2020), 114–115; Robert Seaman to William Tryon, 19 December 1777, CO 5/1109, f. 33–34, UK-KeNA; Tryon to Dartmouth, 3 January 1776, CO 5/1107, f. 57, UK-KeNA.

37. Rhinelander to Robinson and Chorley, 28 December 1776, Frederick and Philip Rhinelander Letter—and Order-Book, Rhinelander Family Papers, NHi; Adrian Coulter Leiby, *The Revolutionary War in the Hackensack Valley: The Jersey Dutch and the Neutral Ground, 1775–1783*, rev. ed. (New Brunswick, NJ: Rutgers University Press, 1992), 43; Washington to Samuel Tucker, 7 August 1776, in Washington, *Papers, Rev. War Series*, 5:616–618.

38. Lepore, *This America*, 26, 28; Chopra, *Unnatural Rebellion*, 46; Van Buskirk, *Generous Enemies*, 12–13; Norton, *British-Americans*, 32–33; Evarts B. Greene and Virginia D. Harrington, *American Population before the Federal Census of 1790* (New York: Columbia University Press, 1932), 102–104; Smith, *Memoirs*, 1:281; Tryon to Dartmouth, 5 September 1775, in *N.Y. Col. Docs.*, 8:632; *NYG*, 18 December 1775; John Austin Stevens Jr., *Colonial Records of the New York Chamber of Commerce, 1768–1784* (New York: John F. Trow and Co., 1867), 41, 47–49; Bache Claim, T 79/70, f. 207–210, UK-KeNA; Heron Claim, AO 12/14, f. 203–207, UK-KeNA; Heron to Myles Cooper, 31 December 1775, in Minty and Walker, *Cause of Loyalty*; UK-KeNA; Allicocke Claim, AO 12/14, f. 355–360, UK-KeNA; Allicocke Claim AO 13/63, f. 51, 62, 62a–62b, UK-KeNA; Ewald Gustav Schaukirk, "Occupation of New York City by the British," *Pennsylvania Magazine of History and Biography* 10 (1887): 420, https://www.jstor.org/stable/20083166. See also Philip Papas, *That Ever Loyal Island: Staten Island and the American Revolution* (New York: New York University Press, 2007).

39. Charles Inglis to Richard Hind, 31 October 1776, in *The Life and Letters of Charles Inglis*, ed. John Wolfe Lydekker (London: Published for the Church Historical Society, 1936), 156–172; Inglis to Cooper, 2 January 1776, in Minty and Walker, *Cause of Loyalty*; Inglis, "Breif Notes," 4, 11 February 1776, NBFU; Milner to Cooper, 10 August 1775, in Minty and Walker, *Cause of Loyalty*.

40. Force, *American Archives*, 4th ser., 3:1052–1054; Tryon to Hicks, 14 October 1775, New York City Misc. Mss., box 11, nos. 6–10, NHi; same to same, 19 October 1775, New York City Misc. Mss., box 11, nos. 6–10, NHi; Hicks to Tryon, 18 October 1775, New York City Misc. Mss., box 11, nos. 6–10, NHi.

41. Edmund Fanning Claim, T 79/70, f. 26–37, UK-KeNA; Rachel Wetmore Claim, AO 12/25, f. 190–198, UK-KeNA; John Tabor Kempe to Myles Cooper, 7 November 1775, in Minty and Walker, *Cause of Loyalty*; Washington, *Papers, Rev. War Series*, 5:145–147; Kempe Claim, AO 12/30, f. 22–165, UK-KeNA; Catherine Snell Crary, "The

American Dream: John Tabor Kempe's Rise from Poverty to Riches," *WMQ* 14 (1957): 176, 179, https://doi.org/10.2307/1922109; Inglis to Cooper, 29 December 1775, in Minty and Walker, *Cause of Loyalty*; Seabury to Cooper and Wilkins, 4 September 1775, in Minty and Walker, *Cause of Loyalty*; Frances Hutcheson to Frederick Haldimand, 10 July 1776, Haldimand Papers, Add. MS 21680, f. 121–126, British Library (hereafter, Uk); same to same, 14 August 1776, Haldimand Papers, Add. MS 21680, f. 141–143, Uk; Ebenezer Huntington to Jabez Huntington, 23 June 1776, Huntington Family File, box 1, Huntington Library (hereafter, CSmH); Orderly Book of Col. David Waterbury's Regiment, CSmH.

42. Thomas Lyttelton, 2d Baron Lyttleton, quoted in Simms, *Three Victories and a Defeat*, 603; Washington, *Papers, Rev. War Series*, 5:245–247.

43. Stokes, *Iconography*, 4:818, 5:922–993; *Pennsylvania Journal*, 17 July 1776; *New-York Times*, 9 July 2004, 22 October 2016; Taylor, *American Revolutions*, 161; Inglis, "Breif Notes," 9 July 1776, NBFU. DeLanceyites also invested in other civic areas. For instance, Jacob Walton and James Jauncey helped repair the battery and made carriages and guns available therein, amounting to over £100. See Stokes, *Iconography*, 4:834, 835.

44. Arthur S. Marks, "The Statue of King George III in New York and the Iconology of Regicide," *American Art Journal* 13 (1981): 65–66, https://doi.org/10.2307/1594285; Stokes, *Iconography*, 5:992–993; "The Statues of King George III and the Honorable William Pitt Erected in New York City 1770," NYHS, *Quart.* 4 (1920): 49, 50, 52; Michael Kammen, *Colonial New York: A History* (New York: Charles Scribner's Sons, 1975), 370–371; David Armitage, *Civil Wars: A History in Ideas* (New Haven, CT: Yale University Press, 2017), 136–137; *Journals of the Provincial Congress, Provincial Convention, Committee of Safety and Council of Safety of the State of New-York*, 2 vols. (Albany, NY: Thurlow Weed, 1842), 1:518; Jay, *Selected Papers*, 1:266–267.

45. Michael Kammen, "The American Revolution as a *Crise de Conscience*: The Case of New York," in *Society, Freedom, and Conscience: The American Revolution in Virginia, Massachusetts, and New York*, ed. Jack P. Greene, Richard L. Bushman, and Kammen (New York: W. W. Norton, 1976), 138–142; Milner to Cooper, 1 September 1775, in Minty and Walker, *Cause of Loyalty*; Inglis, "Breif Notes," 20 February 1776, NBFU.

46. Papas, *That Ever Loyal Island*, 45, 48, 53, 54–55; McDougall to Jay, 20 March 1776, in Jay, *Selected Papers*, 1:212.

47. O'Shaughnessy, *Men Who Lost America*, 82, 86, 88–91; *DNB*. Richard Howe was created first Baron and first Earl Howe in 1788; see *DNB*.

48. *DNB*; O'Shaughnessy, *Men Who Lost America*, 92; Simms, *Three Victories and a Defeat*, 510, 518–519, 556.

49. Richard Howe to Washington, 13 July 1776, in Washington, *Papers, Rev. War Series*, 5:296–297; William Howe to Washington, 16 July 1776, in Washington, *Papers, Rev. War Series*, 5:341–342; same to same, 1 August 1776, in Washington, *Papers, Rev. War Series*, 5:537–538; Richard Howe to Washington, 19 August 1776, in Washington, *Papers, Rev. War Series*, 6:76; William Howe to Washington, 21 September 1776, in Washington, *Papers, Rev. War Series*, 6:360–363; *DNB*; Ira D. Gruber, *The Howe Brothers and the American Revolution* (Chapel Hill: University of North Carolina Press, 1972), 94–95.

50. O'Shaughnessy, *Men Who Lost America*, 92; Chopra, *Unnatural Rebellion*, 51; Grant quoted in John A. Tilley, *The British Navy and the American Revolution* (Columbia: University of South Carolina Press, 1987), 122; *The American Journal of Ambrose Serle*, ed. Ed-

ward H. Tatum (San Marino, CA: Huntington Library, 1940), 54; Denbigh to the Earl of Loudoun, 7 July 1776, Loudoun Papers, box 134, CSmH; Clinton to Gage, 7 August 1775, Henry Clinton Papers, vol. 10, f. 32, MiU-C.

51. JA, D&A, 419–423; Washington to Lund Washington, 19 August 1776, in Washington, *Papers, Rev. War Series*, 6:82–87; Richard Howe to Franklin, 16 August 1776, in *The Papers of Benjamin Franklin*, ed. Leonard W. Labaree, William B. Willcox, Claude A. Lopez, Barbara B. Oberg, Ellen R. Cohn, and others, 43 vols. published to date (New Haven, CT: Yale University Press, 1959–), 22:565–566; *Journals of the Continental Congress, 1774–1789*, ed. Worthington Chauncey Ford, Gaillard Hunt, John C. Fitzpatrick, Roscoe R. Hill, and others, 34 vols. (Washington, DC, 1904–1937), 5:766; *The Works of John Adams, Second President of the United States: with a Life of the Author*, ed. Charles Francis Adams, 10 vols. (Boston, 1850–1856), 3:75–81; Tatum, *American Journal of Ambrose Serle*, 100–101.

52. Robert G. Parkinson, *The Common Cause: Creating Race and Nation in the American Revolution* (Chapel Hill: University of North Carolina Press, 2016), 75; Tatum, *American Journal of Ambrose Serle*, 154–155.

53. Inglis to Cooper, 1 December 1776, in Minty and Walker, *Cause of Loyalty*; Jason K. Duncan, *Citizens or Papists? The Politics of Anti-Catholicism in New York, 1685–1821* (New York: Fordham University Press, 2005), 35; Jay, *Selected Papers*, 1:364–365. The identity of "Lott the hero" has not been identified.

54. Inglis to Cooper, 1 December 1776, in Minty and Walker, *Cause of Loyalty*; Milner to Cooper, 9 December 1776, in Minty and Walker, *Cause of Loyalty*; Milner to Cooper, 26 December 1776, in Minty and Walker, *Cause of Loyalty*; Papas, *That Ever Loyal Island*, 4.

55. Boucher to Germain, 27 November 1775, Germain Papers, vol. 4, MiU-C.

56. [First Declaration of Dependence], 16 October 1776, Y1776, NHi; [Second Declaration of Dependence], 28 November 1776, Y1776, NHi; Inglis to Cooper, 28 October 1776, in Minty and Walker, *Cause of Loyalty*; Jasanoff, *Liberty's Exiles*, 33.

57. Jasanoff, *Liberty's Exiles*, 32–33; David Armitage, "The Declaration of Independence and International Law," WMQ 59 (2002): 39–64, https://doi.org/10.2307/3491637; R. W. G. Vail, "The Loyalist Declaration of Dependence of November 28, 1776, NYHS, Quart. 31 (1947): 68–71; *New-York Journal; or, the General Advertiser*, 7 December 1775; NYG, 18 December 1775; Pauline Maier, *American Scripture: Making the Declaration of Independence* (New York: Knopf, 1988), xvii–xviii.

58. Tryon to Germain, 28 March 1777, CO 5/1108, f. 137, oaths at f. 141–201, UK-KeNA.

59. Chopra, *Unnatural Rebellion*, 76–77; Tryon to Germain, 24 December 1776, CO 5/1108, f. 19–20, UK-KeNA; Donald F. Johnson, *Occupied America: British Military Rule and the Everyday Experience Revolution* (Philadelphia: University of Pennsylvania Press, 2020), 147.

60. Jay, *Selected Papers*, 1:387; Inglis to Myles Cooper, 22 January 1777, Minty and Walker, *Cause of Loyalty*; Wetherhead to Cooper, 23 January 1777, Minty and Walker, *Cause of Loyalty*; John Milner to Cooper, 3 February 1777, Minty and Walker, *Cause of Loyalty*; Edward G. Gray, "Liberty's Losers," WMQ 70 (2013): 188–189, https://doi.org/10.5309/willmaryquar.70.1.0184; Gary B. Nash, "Review: *Essays on the American Revolution*, edited by Stephen G. Kurtz and James H. Hutson," WMQ 31 (1974): 314, https://doi.org/10.2307/1920916.

61. Rhinelander to Messrs. Rowlinsons & Chorley, 7 June 1777, Frederick and Philip Rhinelander Letter—and Order-book, Rhinelander Family Papers, NHi; Rhinelander to Stephen Smith, Son & Russell, 7 November 1776, 10 June 1777, Frederick and Philip Rhinelander Letter—and Order-book, Rhinelander Family Papers, NHi; Rhinelander to Messrs. Ranlinsons & Chorley, 28 December 1776, Frederick and Philip Rhinelander Letter—and Order-book, Rhinelander Family Papers, NHi.

62. Eric Nelson, *The Royalist Revolution: Monarchy and the American Founding* (Cambridge, MA: Harvard University Press, 2014), 31; James Murray to Charles Steuart, 18 September 1774, quoted in Mary Beth Norton, *1774: The Long Year of Revolution* (New York: Knopf, 2020), 348; *Parliamentary History of England*, ed. Thomas C. Hansard, 36 vols. (London, 1806–1820), 18:771; Michael D. Hattem, *Past and Prologue: Politics and Memory in the American Revolution* (New Haven, CT: Yale University Press, 2020); *The Autobiography of Benjamin Rush: His "Travels Through Life" together with his Commonplace Book for 1789–1813*, ed. George W. Corner (Princeton, NJ: Princeton University Press, 1948), 117–118. In December 2020, Serena R. Zabin wrote: "The claim that 'we assume all Americans must be classified as either "'Patriots'" or "'Loyalists'" . . . has been untenable for at least half a century now." See Zabin, "Not Your Grandpa's Military History," *Reviews in American History* 48, no. 4 (2020): 508, https://doi.org/10.1353/rah .2020.0074. See also Sung Bok Kim, "The Limits of Politicization in the American Revolution: The Experience of Westchester County, New York," *Journal of American History* 80, no. 3 (1993): 868–889, https://doi.org/10.2307/2080407.

63. Hattem, *Past and Prologue*; Jack P. Greene, *The Constitutional Origins of the American Revolution* (New York: Cambridge University Press, 2010), 117–121, 134–139; Brendan McConville, *The King's Three Faces: The Rise & Fall of Royal America, 1688–1776* (Chapel Hill: University of North Carolina Press, 2006), 192–219; Gordon S. Wood, "Revolutionary Royalism: A New Paradigm?" *American Political Thought* 5 (2016): 132–146, esp. 138–139, https://doi.org/10.1086/684561; Simms, *Three Victories and a Defeat*, 538. See also Eric Nelson, "Flipping His Whigs: A Response to Gordon S. Wood," Scholars at Harvard, https://scholar.harvard.edu/files/ericnelson/files/nelson_response_to _gordon_s_wood_.pdf (accessed 26 August 2019).

Epilogue

1. Adams to Washington, 6 January 1776, in *The Papers of John Adams*, ed. Robert J. Taylor, Gregg L. Lint, Sara Georgini, and others, 21 vols. published to date (Cambridge, MA: Harvard University Press, 1977–   ), 3:395.

2. Philip Ranlet and Richard B. Morris., "Richard B. Morris's James DeLancey: Portrait in Loyalism," *New York History* (hereafter, *NYH*) 80, no. 2 (1999): 196, https://www .jstor.org/stable/23182484; Bryant Lillywhite, *London Coffee Houses* (London: George Allen and Unwin, 1963), 407, 408–409; Mary Beth Norton, *The British-Americans: The Loyalist Exiles in England, 1774–1789* (Boston: Little, Brown, 1972), 67–68; Julie Flavell, *When London was the Capital of America* (New Haven, CT: Yale University Press, 2010), 125; *The Diary and Letters of His Excellency Thomas Hutchinson*, ed. Peter Orlando Hutchinson, 2 vols. (Boston: Houghton, Mifflin & Co., 1884–1886), 1:506; Ross J. S. Hoffman, *Edmund Burke: New York Agent* (Philadelphia: American Philosophical Society, 1956), 184; Jane Kamensky, *A Revolution in Color: The World of John Singleton Copley* (New

York: W. W. Norton, 2016), 278; *Laws of the State of New-York, comprising the Constitution, and the Acts of the Legislature, since the Revolution, from the First to the Fifteenth Session, inclusive*, 3 vols. (New York: Thomas Greenleaf, 1792–1797), 1:26–38, esp. 26–27, Charles Evans and others, *American Bibliography: A Chronological Dictionary of All Books, Pamphlets and Periodical Publications Printed in the United States of America* [1639–1800], 14 vols. (Chicago and Worcester, MA, 1903–1959; rev. ed., www.readex.com), Nos. 24602, 32555.

3. Maya Jasanoff, *Liberty's Exiles: American Loyalists in the Revolutionary World*(New York: Knopf, 2011), 123–127; Norton, *British-Americans*, 66; Stefan Bielinski, *An American Loyalist: The Ordeal of Frederick Philipse III* (Albany, NY: New York State Museum, 1976), 31; Hutchinson, *Diary*, passim; McDonald Papers, vol. 4, 546, Westchester County Historical Society. I am grateful to Kieran O'Keefe for pointing me toward the McDonald Papers and providing an unverified transcription. Frederick Philipse III died two years after arriving in Britain.

4. Bayard to Cooper, 4 February 1779, *The Cause of Loyalty: The Revolutionary War Correspondence of Myles Cooper*, ed. Christopher F. Minty and Peter W. Walker (forthcoming); Norton, *British-Americans*, 216; Jasanoff, *Liberty's Exiles*, 125, 127; Wallace Brown, *The King's Friends: The Composition and Motives of the American Loyalist Claimants* (Providence, RI: Brown University Press, 1965), 78; Morris, "Portrait in Loyalism," 203, 205; Leslie Stephen and Sidney Lee, eds., *Dictionary of National Biography*, 21 vols. plus supplements (New York and London, 1885–1901; repr.; Oxford: Oxford University Press, 1959–1960; www.oxforddnb.com); DeLancey will, James DeLancey Papers, box 2, f. 5, New-York Historical Society. Few New York loyalists socialized with Thomas Hutchinson, for instance. In his *Diary*, the likes of Myles Cooper, Thomas Bradbury Chandler, Isaac Wilkins, and John Vardill appear, but the likes of James DeLancey do not. The same can be said for Chandler. See Hutchinson, *Diary and Letters*, passim; Thomas Bradbury Chandler, "Memorandums," Keller Library, General Theological Seminary.

5. Jasanoff, *Liberty's Exiles*, 147–152.

6. D. A. Story, *The deLanceys: A Romance of a Great Family* ([Toronto]: T. Nelson & Sons, 1931), 19, 21; *Twelfth Annual Report of the American Scenic and Historic Preservation Society* (Albany, NY: J. B. Lyon Co., 1907), 182.

7. Jasanoff, *Liberty's Exiles*, 125, 137–138; Low to Nicholas Low, 15 August, 7 September 1786, Nicholas Low Papers, box 1, Library of Congress; Wetherhead quoted in Robert Ernst, "Isaac Low and the American Revolution," *NYH* 74 (1993): 146, https://www.jstor.org/stable/23181863.

8. Ruma Chopra, *Unnatural Rebellion: Loyalists in New York City during the Revolution* (Charlottesville: University of Virginia Press, 2011), 220–221.

9. Elizabeth M. Smith-Pryor, *Property Rites: The Rhinelander Trial, Passing, and the Protection of Whiteness* (Chapel Hill: University of North Carolina Press, 2009), 13, 258n5; Harry Yoshpe, "The DeLancey Estate: Did the Revolution Democratize Land-Holding in New York?," *NYH* 17 (1936): 172, https://www.jstor.org/stable/23134588; Valerie H. McKito, *From Loyalists to Loyal Citizens: The DePeyster Family of New York* (Albany, NY: SUNY Press, 2015), passim, esp. 85; Aaron Nathan Coleman, "Justice and Moderation? The Reintegration of the American Loyalists as an Episode of Transitional Justice," in *Consequences of Loyalism*, 185–186; *Commercial Advertiser*, 7 January 1805; *New-York Gazette*, 7 January 1805; *Mercantile Advertiser*, 8 January 1805; *Republican Watch-Tower*, 9 January 1805. https://registers.trinitywallstreet.org/files/history/registers/registry.php;

Edward Pessen, "Political Democracy and the Distribution of Power in Antebellum New York City," in *Essays in the History of New York City: A Memorial to Sidney Pomerantz*, ed. Irwin Yellowitz (Port Washington, NY: Kennikat Press, 1978), 24, 26, 36; *The Papers of George Washington: Revolutionary War Series*, ed. Philander D. Chase, Frank E. Grizzard Jr., Edward G. Lengel, David R. Hoth, and others, 30 vols. to date (Charlottesville: University of Virginia Press, 1985–   ), 25:570–571; *Biographical Directory of the United States Congress, 1774–2005* (Washington, DC, 2005; rev. ed., bioguide.congress.gov).

10. Edwin G. Burrows and Mike Wallace, *Gotham: A History of New York City to 1898* (New York: Oxford University Press, 1999), 273–274, 277–283; James Hardie, *Description of the City of New-York* (New York: Samuel Marks, 1827), 111; *The Law Practice of Alexander Hamilton*, ed. Julius Goebel Jr. et al, 5 vols. (New York: Columbia University Press, 1964–1981), 1:419–543; *The Papers of Alexander Hamilton*, ed. Harold C. Syrett, Jacob E. Cooke, and others, 27 vols. (New York: Columbia University Press, 1961–1987), 3:512; Livingston to Charles DeWitt, 9 May 1784, quoted in *Political Correspondence and Public Papers of Aaron Burr*, ed. Mary-Jo Kline and Joanne Wood Ryan, 2 vols. (Princeton, NJ: Princeton University Press, 1983), 1:4; *Independent Gazette*, 20 December 1783; Edward Countryman, *A People in Revolution: The American Revolution and Political Society in New York, 1760–1790* (Baltimore: Johns Hopkins University Press, 1981), 175.

11. See *The Papers of Benjamin Franklin*, ed. Leonard W. Labaree, William B. Willcox, Claude A. Lopez, Barbara B. Oberg, Ellen R. Cohn, and others, 43 vols. published to date (New Haven, CT: Yale University Press, 1959–   ), 4:53–63; Peter Kalm, *Travels into North America*, transl. John Reinhold Forster, 3 vols. (London: William Eyres, 1770–1771), 1:247–267; DeLancey to Rockingham, 4 February 1769, Wentworth Woodhouse Muniments, Sheffield City Archives and Local Studies Library.

Appendix

1. Lorenzo Sabine, *Biographical Sketches of Loyalists of the American Revolution*, 2 vols. (Boston: Little, Brown and Co., 1847–1864). For Adams's statements, see Thomas McKean to Adams, January 1814, in *The Works of John Adams, Second President of the United States: with a Life of the Author*, ed. Charles Francis Adams, 10 vols. (Boston, 1850–1856; hereafter, JA, *Works*), 10:187; Adams to Jedidiah Morse, 22 December 1815, in JA, *Works*, 10:193; Adams to Thomas Jefferson, 12 November 1813, in JA, *Works*, 10:79.

2. Useful reference works include Henry J. Young Coll., William L. Clements Library, University of Michigan; Sabine, *Biographical Sketches*; Peter Coldham, *American Loyalist Claims* (Baltimore: National Genealogical Society, 1980); Esther Clark Wright, *The Loyalists of New Brunswick* (Fredericton, NB: E. C. Wright, 1955), 255–345; Kenneth Scott and James A. Owre, *Genealogical Data from Inventories of New York Estates* (New York: New York Genealogical and Biographical Society, 1970).

3. *New-York Gazette; and the Weekly Mercury*, 3 November 1777, 17 August 1778.

4. Brown's Claim, AO 12/24, f. 176–181, National Archives of the United Kingdom; Markham Scrapbook Coll., Provincial Archives of New Brunswick.

5. See Colin Nicolson, "The Friends of Government: Loyalism, Ideology and Politics in Revolutionary Massachusetts," 2 vols. (PhD diss., University of Edinburgh, 1988).

6. Probated Wills, 1665–1815, JS0038–82, JS0038–92, New York State Archives (hereafter, N-Ar); Record of Wills and Probates, JS0043–92, N-Ar.

7. For a useful online source, see "An American Family Grows in Brooklyn: The Lefferts Family Papers at the Brooklyn Historical Society," available at https://lefferts.brooklynhistory.org/ (accessed 25 December 2019).

8. For the issues of identifying children as loyalists, see Philip Ranlet, "How Many Loyalists Left the United States?" *The Historian* 76 (2014): 295–296, https://doi.org/10.1111/hisn.12034.

9. Nicolson, "Friends of Government," 2:368–369.

10. See also David C. Humphrey, *From King's College to Columbia, 1746–1800* (New York: Columbia University Press, 1976), 143–144.

11. Wallace Brown, *The King's Friends: The Composition and Motives of the American Loyalist Claimants* (Providence, RI: Brown University Press, 1965), 9–10, 98–101; Philip Ranlet, *The New York Loyalists* (Knoxville: University of Tennessee Press, 1986), 173; Harrington, *New York Merchant*, 231–232. See also Carl L. Becker, *The History of Political Parties in the Province of New York, 1760–1776* (Madison, WI: [s.n.], 1909), 158–164; Ruma Chopra, *Unnatural Rebellion: Loyalists in New York City during the Revolution* (Charlottesville: University of Virginia Press, 2011), 47–48; Joseph S. Tiedemann, *Reluctant Revolutionaries: New York City and the Road to Independence, 1763–1776* (Ithaca, NY: Cornell University Press, 1997), 208; Leopold S. Launitz-Schürer Jr., *Loyal Whigs and Revolutionaries: The Making of an American Revolution in New York, 1765–1776* (New York: New York University Press, 1980), 178–179; Alexander C. Flick, *Loyalism in New York during the American Revolution* (New York: Columbia University Press, 1901), 9–10; John C. Miller, *Origins of the American Revolution* (Boston: Little, Brown & Co., 1943), 186; James Bell, *A War of Religion: Dissenters, Anglicans, and the American Revolution* (Basingstoke: Palgrave, 2008), 211–221; J. C. D. Clark, *The Language of Liberty 1660–1832: Political Discourse and Social Dynamics in the Anglo-American World* (New York: Cambridge University Press, 1994), 297–381; John A. Ragosta, *Wellspring of Liberty: How Virginia's Religious Dissenters Helped Win the American Revolution and Secured Religious Liberty* (New York: Oxford University Press, 2010), 89–90; Thomas E. Buckley, *Establishing Religious Freedom: Jefferson's Statute in Virginia* (Charlottesville: University of Virginia Press, 2013), 69, 71–72; Joseph S. Tiedemann, "Presbyterianism and the American Revolution in the Middle Colonies," *Church History* 74 (2005): 316–319, https://doi.org/10.1017/S000964070011025X.

12. Maya Jasanoff, *Liberty's Exiles: American Loyalists in the Revolutionary World* (New York: Knopf, 2011), 8, 118, 172–175; Chopra, *Unnatural Rebellion*, 13; Edward Countryman, *A People in Revolution: The American Revolution and Political Society in New York, 1760–1790* (Baltimore: Johns Hopkins University Press, 1981), 104–108; Tiedemann, *Reluctant Revolutionaries*, 208–209.

13. Holly Brewer, "Subjects by Allegiance to the King? Debating Status and Power for Subjects—and Slaves—through the Religious Debates of the Early British Atlantic," in *State and Citizen: British America and the Early United States*, ed. Peter S. Onuf and Peter Thompson (Charlottesville: University of Virginia Press, 2013), 29–35.

14. Tiedemann, *Reluctant Revolutionaries*, 24–25; Joyce D. Goodfriend, "The Social Dimensions of Congregational Life in Colonial New York City," *William and Mary Quarterly* 46 (1989): 283, https://doi.org/10.2307/1920254; Sydney V. James, *A People among Peoples: Quaker Benevolence in Eighteenth-Century America* (Cambridge, MA: Harvard University Press, 1963), 142, 145; Arthur J. Mekeel, *The Quakers and the American Revolution* (York, UK: Sessions Book Trust, 1996), 282–300. This point is also made in Jessica Choppin

Roney, "'First Movers in Every Useful Undertaking': Formal Voluntary Associations in Philadelphia, 1725–1775" (PhD diss., Johns Hopkins University, 2008), 316–330; quotes taken from Arthur J. Mekeel, "New York Quakers in the American Revolution," *Bulletin of Friends' Historical Association* 29 (1940): 50, 51.

15. Thomas Jones, *History of New York during the Revolutionary War*, 2 vols. (New York: Printed for the New-York Historical Society, 1879), 1:2. See also Joyce D. Goodfriend, "Archibald Laidlie and the Transformation of the Dutch Reformed Church in Eighteenth-Century New York City," *Journal of Presbyterian History* 81 (2003): 149–162, https://www.jstor.org/stable/23337616; Tiedemann, *Reluctant Revolutionaries*, 23–24.

16. Adele Hast, *Loyalism in Revolutionary Virginia: The Norfolk Area and the Eastern Shore* (Ann Arbor: UMI Research Press, 1982), 175; Bell, *A War of Religion*, 205–206; Ragosta, *Wellspring of Liberty*, 188; Nicolson, "Friends of Government," 2:370–371.

17. Robert Michael Dructor, "The New York Commercial Community: The Revolutionary Experience" (PhD diss., University of Pittsburgh, 1975), 44, 45, 46, 47, 49, 50, 63, 66–67.

INDEX